For Labor, Race, and Liberty

For Labor, Race, and Liberty

George Edwin Taylor,

His Historic Run for the White House, and

the Making of Independent Black Politics

Bruce L. Mouser

The University of Wisconsin Press

Publication of this volume has been made possible, in part,
through support from
the ANONYMOUS FUND OF THE COLLEGE OF LETTERS AND SCIENCE
at the University of Wisconsin–Madison.

The University of Wisconsin Press
1930 Monroe Street, 3rd Floor
Madison, Wisconsin 53711–2059
uwpress.wisc.edu

3 Henrietta Street
London WC2E 8LU, England
eurospanbookstore.com

1   3   5   4   2

Printed in the United States of America

Library of Congress Cataloging-in-Publication Data
Mouser, Bruce L.
For labor, race, and liberty: George Edwin Taylor, his historic run for
the White House, and the making of independent black politics / Bruce L. Mouser.
       p.   cm.
Includes bibliographical references and index.
ISBN 978-0-299-24914-4 (pbk.: alk. paper)
ISBN 978-0-299-24913-7 (e-book)
1. African American presidential candidates—Biography.
2. African American politicians—19th century—Biography.
3. African American politicians—20th century—Biography.
I. Title.
E185.97.T39M68   2011
324.2092—dc22
[B]
2010011577

Contents

List of Illustrations   vii
Preface   ix
Acknowledgments   xix
List of Abbreviations   xxiii

Introduction   3

1   From Orphaned Black to Printer's Devil: Taylor's
Early Years in "God's Country"   14

2   Labor Agitator, Newspaper Editor, and Political Novice:
Schools of Hard Knocks   28

3   Emergence of a Black Activist: Succeeding in
the African American World   57

4   Taylor as the National Democrat: Black and Equal   86

5   Taylor's Campaign to Become President: A Duty to
Himself and His Race   107

6   Escape to a Warm Place: Retreat and Reconstruct   135

Conclusion   146

Appendix A: Taylor's Interview with the Sun after
the 1904 Election   155
Appendix B: Election Data for Nine Political Parties and
Candidates in the 1904 Election   159
Appendix C: Chart of George Edwin Taylor's Life   161
Notes   167
Bibliography   219
Index   241

Illustrations

Bird's-eye view of La Crosse, Wisconsin, 1887   9

Nathan Smith   17

Marcus "Brick" Pomeroy   20

"Buffalo Bill" Cody and "White Beaver" Powell   26

John Q. Adams   61

T. Thomas Fortune   65

William Calvin Chase   69

Hon. Frederick Douglass   72

Booker T. Washington   79

William T. Scott   97

George Edwin Taylor, 1904   121

George Edwin Taylor, 1904 presidential poster   126

W. E. B. Du Bois   133

Preface

Frequently when I was introduced as one of the Presidential candidates, I saw people pass the wink around. They didn't think I saw it, but I want to tell you the colored man is beginning to see a lot of things that the white folks do not give him credit for seeing. He's beginning to see that he has got to take care of his own interests, and what's more, that he has the power to do it.

George Edwin Taylor,
interview given to the *Sun* (New York City),
20 November 1904

In 1904 an African American who was a longtime resident of Wisconsin and Iowa ran for president of the United States. How this came to be is the subject of the present work. George Edwin Taylor's birth in the slaveholding state of Arkansas in 1857 occurred only five years after the publication of Harriet Beecher Stowe's *Uncle Tom's Cabin*, which rallied the nation against an oppressive and dehumanizing slaveholding system and propelled the nation toward a civil war that liberated and enfranchised the slaves. Taylor's political career ended forty-eight years later, in grim contrast, between the publication of Thomas Dixon's provocative *The Leopard's Spots* (1902) and *The Clansman* (1905), both of which portrayed African Americans as belonging to a physically aggressive and biologically inferior branch of the human race. These novels profoundly shaped America's attitudes about race and the character of African Americans, and Taylor's life and interactions with white Americans were influenced greatly by them as well. During that half century of change America's black slave population traveled from a time of bondage to one in which the federal government guaranteed equal voting rights and a degree of integration, then to a phase of stagnation, slippage, and the reemergence of white dominance in America's South, and finally—in full circle—to a time of disenfranchisement and Jim Crow–inspired racial and physical separation.

Coming of age in La Crosse, Wisconsin, as a journalist and political activist in the 1880s, Taylor encountered phenomenal success for a person of his race and station within a small and confined space, followed by crushing defeat when he confronted dismissive government- and Ivy League–educated black competitors who were vying for influence at the national level at the turn of the century. His story reveals much about maturing as an African American in a predominantly white working-class setting and succeeding through sheer skill and energy. It speaks to the experience of editors of black-owned newspapers at a time when it was possible to publish a paper with little capital investment, compete with the established white press for customers and advertisers, and still engage with other black editors for relevance within the nation's black community. It addresses the difficulty of bridging principles of empowerment, self-reliance, and political action of the late nineteenth century with those of litigation and courtroom maneuvers of the early twentieth. Taylor's political life extended the time of grassroots black political activism of the nineteenth century and nearly collides with a new vanguard-led movement in the twentieth that resulted eventually in the formation of the National Association for the Advancement of Colored People. His African American world was profoundly influenced by Frederick Douglass, who provided leadership to the newly liberated black community following the Civil War, Booker T. Washington, who advocated self-help and accommodation in the 1880s and 1890s, and finally W. E. B. Du Bois, who believed that sufficient progress would only come from the efforts of a "talented tenth" that would serve as a spearhead of the black community. And Taylor shared the stage with all these men.

At the same time, Taylor was unique for his time and place. He was a Democrat attached to a radical and rural Populist tradition when most of his northern black colleagues were Republicans and were concerned mainly with urban issues, except when discussing living conditions and civil rights in the South. He championed the laboring masses and a grassroots organizational style, while leaders in emerging and educated urban black communities were advocating a top-down leadership model. An avid joiner, he was a founder and high office-holder of numerous state and national organizations, regardless of whether they advanced economic or political agendas or facilitated fraternal ties. He supported an eight-hour workday, equal pay for equal work, safe working conditions, a graduated income tax, public ownership of railroads, cheap money, free trade, voting rights for the District of Columbia, and pensions for impoverished and landless ex-slaves who had received no wages in slavery times—all issues that fundamentally separated him from those championed by his urban colleagues. He encouraged the development of economic cooperatives to provide investment capital for small borrowers. He called for an increase in the number of black officers in the military and proportionate patronage in government service. He opposed imperialism in all its forms. He believed that blacks could be power brokers in national politics, and he was convinced that it was possible to use voting numbers as leverage to protect civil rights and force changes in the platforms of established parties and the actions of politicians.

Above all, Taylor was a visionary and a reformer in a gilded age, and he was willing to pay a price for pressing an aggressive reformist agenda. That price was high. Once he came to believe that his had become an isolated voice among many and that he was being left behind by an emergent leadership class with other objectives, Taylor retreated from his obsessions and retired to a satisfying but ordinary life in Florida. Taylor was far ahead of his time with respect to political issues. Others told him that his time was not yet come and that African Americans should wait before engaging in separate political action. Taylor refused to accept that answer in 1904 and sacrificed his political career in the process. He was among the last and the first of his class.

My first encounter with George Edwin Taylor came in the mid-1970s. I remember it well. I was then engaged in a research effort to collect as much information as possible from old city records regarding black settlement patterns in La Crosse, Wisconsin. I found a single reference to a former black newspaper owner and editor from La Crosse who in 1904 had made an unsuccessful bid for the office of president of the United States. President? Black? It was perhaps understandable that histories of La Crosse had ignored black settlers in a time when historians tended to focus on standard topics. But how could a former candidate for president, of whatever color, have escaped the attention of all of La Crosse's historians? My immediate response was to search available encyclopedias and biographies to learn more about him. Surely he would be mentioned elsewhere. To my surprise, his name appeared nowhere. I checked the shelves where monographs on black political history were located and found him mentioned here and there in a sentence or two but little more. A real mystery, our man Taylor.

Teaching and other research interests kept me from pursuing the elusive Taylor, at least until the early 1980s, when, entirely by chance, I decided to search for the newspaper he owned and edited in La Crosse, the *Wisconsin Labor Advocate*. Neither the university nor the local public library had copies of the paper, nor did the State Historical Society of Wisconsin. Yet as a youngster I had found great pleasure in rummaging through old newspapers kept in a room behind the furnace of a Carnegie library located directly across the street from my grandmother's house, so I knew that occasionally it was possible to find treasures. (At least I thought they were treasures.) I do not recall how I ended up in the La Crosse Public Library's storage area, but it was there that I found a full run of Taylor's paper, still in the original mailing wrappers. That discovery renewed my interest in black La Crosse and in Taylor.

But, once again, teaching responsibilities and other research topics interrupted my search for Taylor. With the exception of his newspaper, there was little else immediately available to tell me much about him. He left no letters or diaries, and he vanished from my La Crosse–based scope once he left Wisconsin for Iowa. Rather than focus my efforts upon Taylor's activities as a newspaper editor and politician, I continued to collect bits and pieces about black settlement patterns and presented lectures on settlement topics in local libraries where I had conducted research.

When I retired from teaching in 1996 and became able to conduct research and write without the inconvenience of having to earn a living, I reconsidered Taylor's life and the black experience in La Crosse. It was obvious to me that no one in the area or in the region was interested in continuing my research about La Crosse's black settlers and bringing that research to publication. Simply to clear my desk and my mind of old things, I decided either to write something in quick order or to burn files that had accumulated over nearly thirty years. I was more than willing to surrender it all to someone else because my primary research topic was the African slave trade and commercial transition along the African coast before the period of European colonialism. I gave myself a year to finish a single article out of several cabinets of unfinished research projects; otherwise, I would dispose of the lot. At the end of 1997 I met with Richard W. Brown, executive director of the La Crosse County Historical Society, and we discussed the possibility of serializing a history of black settlement in that society's bimonthly magazine. At that moment my purpose was more to rid my den and mind of incomplete research than to commence a project that would consume a year or two of my attention. The society published five articles: three in 1998, and another two in 1999.

There remained, however, the unresolved question of what to do about Taylor and what should be done with the rest of the collected data. To carry Taylor's story beyond Wisconsin would require a significant commitment, with the likelihood that what I found would require considerable effort to find a publisher. Should I bury all the information I had collected over the years in the society's basement, where it would gather dust amidst an antiquarian's dream of old furniture and period clothing, or should I assemble it into a form that others might use? Brown and I agreed that it was possible to print the whole of my findings as an "occasional paper" of the society. That was completed in 2002 as *Black La Crosse, Wisconsin, 1850–1906: Settlers, Entrepreneurs, & Exodusers.* With joy in my heart, I buried my files within the society's collection in 2003 and returned to African topics.

The phenomenal ascendancy of Barack Obama on the national scene after 2004 and the possibility that he might actually become a viable contestant for the Democratic Party's nomination in 2008 revived my interest in Taylor, but only to the extent that my unfinished research respecting him reappeared on my worktable as a potential area of added attention. When Obama actually won the Democratic Party's contest in midsummer of 2008, however, Taylor's file acquired new importance, and it made its way to the top of my "active" pile and remained there.

At first glance it seemed that the parallels between Taylor's life and Obama's were uncanny. Born in 1857, Taylor was forty-seven years old when he was a candidate for the presidency, as was Obama. Both were raised by single parents, Obama by a mother whose husband had left her and Taylor by a single mother. Both ultimately were cared for during their formative years by surrogate parents, Obama by his grandparents in Hawaii and Taylor by foster parents in West Salem, Wisconsin. Both attended private academies paid for with extraordinary sacrifice and expense by those in charge of their education. Both were recognized as exceptionally gifted in language and with a unique ability to speak before and move large crowds. Both were community organizers, Obama on Chicago's South Side and Taylor in Wisconsin's labor movement and Iowa's nonpartisan associations. Both rose from relative obscurity to national prominence within the span of a decade and a half. And both were ambitious—not solely for themselves but also for a cause and for the benefit of America's working class.

But there also was a profound difference. Obama achieved his success within a predominantly white political party in a time when third-party movements simply were not taken seriously. And Obama was living in an age when blacks were represented at all levels of government and business and when it was possible for a "person of color" to dream of high political office and expect that it might be achievable. The notion that a separate African American party might capture the support and imagination of a majority of the nation's voters in Obama's time was unrealistic. Taylor, in contrast, was part of a far different era and tradition. At the end of the nineteenth century and beginning of the twentieth, third-party politics in the United States was viable and occasionally successful, although seldom at the national level. In fact, only the Republican Party had emerged from humble beginnings and as a regional party to gain control of the federal government. Still, third-party movements and ethnic-specific alliances could exert significant influence by attracting voters from established parties and thus force parties to modify platforms in ways that maintained their attractiveness to a plurality of voters. Taylor's 1904 election attempt within a race-specific party, however, was doomed from the start. None expected him to win the election; a modest showing in states that contained large numbers of African American "workingmen" voters was all that was anticipated.

This biographical sketch of George Edwin Taylor could not have been written ten years ago. To be sure, I had spent nearly thirty years collecting and analyzing local data and making sense of the regional context. Still, research methodologies and the availability of old and new sources have changed so drastically over the past five years as to make it possible to search for data in bits and pieces as never before imagined. As a practical matter, search engines available on the Internet have opened an incredible volume of data for the researcher, but along with that has remained the manual energy and time required to bring meaning to these ever-larger piles of bits and pieces. Databases and data servers available in most standard university libraries can now put tens of thousands of articles available online and covering centuries of publication at one's fingertips. That one is able to search for names and phrases in thousands of old newspapers and official records is astounding. Newspapers served in this project as a major source of date-specific material for the reconstruction of a timeline, a circumstance that I would have easily dismissed as unattainable and unreliable a decade ago. The searchability of digitized monographs and dissertations has simplified and amplified access and immediacy. None of these tools were readily available thirty years ago or even a decade ago. In fact, I am astounded by the volume of new data being added almost daily.

The searchability of data online created another dilemma that became apparent only when I was far into the project. Search engines are only machines, and how they retrieve data depends entirely upon the accuracy, ability, and imagination of the questioner. Late in the research, for example, I discovered at least forty combinations of searchable word phrases for the National Colored Men's Protective Association by substituting the word "colored" with "Negro," "Afro-American," "African-American," and "black" and the word "association" with "league"; by reversing the order of "National" and "Colored" in all of those combinations; or by deleting the word "Men's." I found that many names of organizations for that period were equally imprecise, for newspaper editors relied upon uncertain sources, substituted for sensitive words that might have offended readers, or simply invented names that they believed more accurately described groups. But the sample of forty combinations for one association was sufficient to convince me that it might be impossible to conduct an exhaustive study of any of these groups and that a more inventive questioner would certainly find combinations I had not even considered.

The volume of data also raises logically the degree to which such a study should or might be documented. For nearly fifteen of my thirty years of teaching I was often responsible for classes in historiography and methods. If some scholars preferred documentation with in-text notations, I instead tilted to the opposite extreme. I envision that a historian—and especially a biographer—must be a good storyteller and that his or her task is to present an interesting and meaningful tale that has been constructed by following the truth wherever it might lead. He should adhere to scholarly rules of data collection and be able to document his material to specific sources. At the same time, a historian should be more than a chronicler; his task is also to interpret and add value to the tale. Seldom should the source of information enter the narrative, unless he is party to it. Occasionally, empty holes appear in the data. A chronicler can simply report the hole and move on; that luxury does not exist for the historian. Nor may an historian avoid new approaches in research and presentation. The latter obligation requires him to present his writing to a variety of writing styles and approaches and to accommodate himself to those new demands when possible.

In Taylor's case I also confronted the issue of whether to summarize his writings or to quote them extensively because of their contents and contexts or because his writings ably demonstrated his style, command of language, use of satire, and knowledge of circumstances within the black community that were changing profoundly before his eyes. In some cases, especially when those instances were fundamental for explaining his actions, I chose to use long quotations. Nothing was repeated, however, unless it illustrated an attitude, an emotion, or a deeply held principle. And since Taylor left no diaries, journals, or letters, his only voice was found in his editorials. His words, taken over time and in sequence, revealed an evolution of thinking and became the evidence for shifting approaches to challenges facing the black community in a time of great change and adversity. I am aware that some will read long quotes, while others will not. With that in mind, I made a conscious effort to keep the quotes as brief and as focused as possible. But I also know that many documents used in this reconstruction are extremely hard to find and that some readers will be disappointed if I fail to provide them in the volume. That choice was made simpler when it became possible to place a number of relevant documents on a permanent Internet site established for such a purpose by Murphy Library,

University of Wisconsin–La Crosse, at http://murphylibrary.uwlax.edu/digital/TaylorGeorge/.

My preferred method for documentation is the use of endnotes. Endnotes serve two purposes, with both being useful and necessary for different types of readers. As a reader, I often am as fascinated by the documented search as I am by the narrative. As a writer, I face the issue of what to do with all those additional resources that I should provide the reader, especially those who are as fascinated by the search as I am. In my case I decided to use the endnote as a place to indicate the primary and secondary sources and to provide the reader with resources that shed additional light upon the subject. Often sources differed, for that is the nature of first-, second-, and often thirdhand reports, especially in newspapers that clip, abbreviate, or expand on stories to suit particular readerships. Rather than choose from many solutions, I chose to use the endnote for optional choices. In some cases an endnote contains more words than the narrative to which it refers.

Usually every author has regrets. The foremost in this instance was my lack of foresight in finding funding sources to pay for travel to Iowa, Florida, and elsewhere where additional sources might be found. That was overcome to a degree by the fact that Oskaloosa, Ottumwa, and Albia in Iowa are but a five-hour drive from La Crosse. I was able to spend sufficient time in Iowa researching archives and newspapers found only locally, but more time there would have been helpful. Fortunately, I found willing people in Iowa who were interested in this topic, and I was able to rely upon them to search for new data once I had visited and left the field. Because Taylor's period in Florida was after he had abandoned his national interests, I depended upon published sources for data from Florida, with the exception that several persons in Tampa, St. Augustine, and Jacksonville helped me clarify questions regarding his activities there. Had I had financial resources sufficient to visit Florida-based archives, I am reasonably certain that more about Taylor's life in Florida could have been added to this narrative.

Another regret relates to research that could have been conducted in St. Paul, Chicago, and Des Moines. These were the largest cities to affect African American attitudes in the upper Midwest. I am belatedly convinced that Taylor spent part of his three-year hiatus from 1887 to 1891 in one or all of these cities. But I also know that conducting research in one or all would consume a significant amount of time, effort, and expense, with a distinct possibility that little additional information might be learned to clarify Taylor's life history. Still, those areas should be researched for information about Taylor's activities, his interactions with local black leaders, and the black communities that existed there during important periods in Taylor's life.

The issue of personal papers can be daunting. Taylor left nothing behind except a complete newspaper run of *Wisconsin Labor Advocate* from 20 August 1886 to 6 August 1887 and a few clippings from his *Negro Solicitor*. His campaign literature likely came from his pen. But that is all. Others who lived in his time and place and who interacted with him either once, occasionally, or often may have left records, recollections, or pamphlets that mention Taylor and the objectives of associations that he began, led, or supported. I have not attempted to find those; that I leave to others who—I trust—will be encouraged to search those sources.

And finally, I am certain that had I scheduled my time and effort more carefully, I would have read through more black-edited newspapers that survive from Taylor's period in history. My observations from reading several, however, indicate to me that Taylor was a minor figure in the national black community and that nearly all papers of the time were allied in some way with the Republican or Democratic parties or were independents that were representing other agendas. None championed the associations or party that Taylor represented. It was as if he were ignored, deliberately or otherwise, and his agenda failed in part because few people were aware of his or their existences. Nearly all reports of his activities were found instead in white-edited papers, and while some were sympathetic to his cause, most reported his activities as newspaper filler and as the odd bit of information that might interest readers who were bored with the regular news.

To be sure, there are always regrets, but there is also the satisfaction of having completed a task and moving to the next project. I am especially appreciative that so many still-working scholars were willing to lend me time to review chapters or parts of chapters that contained interpretations of their own works or periods in the African American experience about which they have special knowledge.

Acknowledgments

Research and writing of this sort cannot be accomplished without significant assistance. Luckily, the general framework of Taylor's life course had taken form over thirty years of data collection and writing. Over time, however, certain persons have been instrumental in providing guidance and helping to produce that timeline. Edwin Hill, Special Collections Librarian and Director of the Area Research Center at the University of Wisconsin–La Crosse, is a dedicated conservator of western Wisconsin's past and a champion for anyone who wishes to research the history of the La Crosse region. Linda Sondreal, Assistant at the Area Research Center, knows the collection with the intimacy of having worked within it for more than twenty years, and often she anticipated my needs even before I thought of them. Without that surviving record and the assistance of Hill and Sondreal, much of this narrative as it relates to Taylor's years in La Crosse would have been difficult to construct.

I also am indebted to other local repositories and those employed there who provided me valuable assistance. The La Crosse Public Library's Archives & Local History Room served as the city's only archive before the university built its research center, and LPL collected state and national census records, city directories, guides to cemeteries and obituaries, genealogical records, photographs, personal papers, and newspapers. It also maintained numerous biographical files for noteworthy persons in the community. For the last thirty years many persons have served me at that site, but the most valuable for the present research has been its current director, Anita Taylor Doering. The La Crosse County Historical Society has collected personal papers of La Crosse citizens and a large photo and postcard collection, and it opened its entire resources for my use. The city and county of La Crosse also have maintained excellent records, all of which have been available without reservation for my search.

Murphy Library at the University of Wisconsin–La Crosse has been immensely accommodating in permitting me to continue my research after retirement and allowing it to be conducted in a convenient setting. With the exception of items held in rare book or pamphlet collections, the University of Wisconsin System has opened its statewide library holdings to authorized users anywhere within the system, thereby reducing costs associated with research travel. The interlibrary loan office at the University of Wisconsin–La Crosse has always honored my requests, no matter how obscure. Two persons in that office, Lavonia McCarty and Mary Baldwin, have exercised great patience, searching dubious references and locating many that turned out to be important for Taylor's narrative.

Once the research subject and environment changed from Wisconsin to Iowa, sources and resources there became invaluable in permitting me to use time and effort efficiently. Hal Chase and John Zeller in Des Moines were helpful, pointing me in profitable directions and sharing data collected over many years. Dorothy Schwieder of Ames was encouraging, suggesting sources that I otherwise would have missed. At the State Historical Society of Iowa in Des Moines, Jerome Thompson alerted me to a scrapbook kept by George Woodson of Buxton, Iowa, that contains the only surviving clippings from the newspaper published by Taylor in Oskaloosa. Sharon Avery, archivist at the society, was exceptionally obliging in researching family links within Iowa and Florida. In Oskaloosa, Pam Howard of the Mahaska County Genealogical Society informed me of sources that only someone familiar with the local scene would have known. That was also the case with Dee Hall, Mary Ford, and Ricki King of Ottumwa. In Florida I was assisted in Tampa by Gary Mormino of the University of South Florida; in Jacksonville by Maryann Sterzel (Library Director of the *Florida Times-Union*), Patricia Morrison (Jacksonville Public Library), and Eileen D. Brady (Eartha M. M. White Collection at the University of North Florida Library); in Orlando by Valada Flewellyn; in St. Augustine by Patricia Griffin of Florida State University in Tallahassee; and by Daniel Schafer and James Crooks, both of the University of North Florida and published historians of Jacksonville topics. Great appreciation is extended to Christopher Reed of Roosevelt University in Chicago, who searched through area newspapers for accounts of meetings held in Chicago that were important to this study.

I am particularly indebted to those who read portions or all of the manuscript. Two of my earliest critics were Nancy Fox Mouser and Victoria Bomba Coifman (Afro-American and African Studies Department, University of Minnesota), both of whom are demanding and unforgiving. Those readers with special knowledge of La Crosse's history were Richard W. Brown, Charles Haas, and Anita Doering. Among my former colleagues in the history department at the University of Wisconsin–La Crosse, Martin Zanger, James Parker, and William Pemberton read early drafts and were exceptionally helpful. Others who read all or sections of the manuscript and who made valuable comments were Shawn Alexander of the University of Kansas, Omar Ali of Vanderbilt University, John Betton of the University of Wisconsin–La Crosse, Robert Busby of Liverpool Hope University (U.K.), Hal Chase of Des Moines Area Community College–Urban Campus, James Crooks of the University of North Florida, Melinda Elder of the Open University (U.K.), Audrey Mouser Elegbede of the University of Wisconsin–La Crosse, Patricia Griffin of Florida State University in Tallahassee, David Henige of the University of Wisconsin–Madison, Deborah Hoskins of the University of Wisconsin–La Crosse, John McKerley of the University of Maryland, David Peavler of Towson University, Christopher Reed of Roosevelt University, Ramon Sarró of the University of Lisbon (Portugal), Daniel Schafer of the University of North Florida, Leslie Schwalm of the University of Iowa, Dorothy Schwieder of Iowa State University, Nikki Taylor of the University of Cincinnati, Hanes Walton, Jr., of the University of Michigan, and Joan Yeatman of the University of Wisconsin–La Crosse. Each brought special expertise and perspective to the task, and to each I extend my lasting gratitude. Of course, all errors are mine.

Of these, however, the most crucial for permitting me leeway to spend time on this project has been my wife, Nancy Fox Mouser. Nancy has always supported my research by providing me a comfortable world in which to live. I could not have completed this project without her indulgence.

Abbreviations

AACI	Afro-American Council of Iowa
AALI	Afro-American League of Iowa
AAPAI	Afro-American Protective Association of Iowa
CPNPA	Colored People's National Protective Association
NAAC	National Afro-American Council
NAAL	National Afro-American League
NACW	National Association of Colored Women
NCDL	National Colored Democratic League
NCMPA	National Colored Men's Protective Association
NNDL	National Negro Democratic League

For Labor, Race, and Liberty

Introduction

I firmly believe that one of the greatest obstacles to the progress of the Negro is his over estimation of the advancement he has made already. He has done much, but he shouldn't be content to rest with that. He should press on until he has reached the top of the ladder and then reach up to see if there isn't another ladder on top of that one. We are in danger of thinking too much of ourselves.

George Edwin Taylor,
speech given in Keokuk, Iowa,
1898

One of Taylor's most enduring traits was his ability to stand above the fray, almost like an outsider looking in. Perhaps this "other" status, whether in white society or in black, was sufficient to permit him to pause, reassess, and then reconstruct in ways that others who were integral to a circumstance could not. The speech that he delivered to an Emancipation Day audience in Keokuk, Iowa, on 10 August 1898 is a case in point.[1] His audience was composed of celebrants, for this day in August was the black midsummer equivalent to the Fourth of July and had been observed as a special day since Britain freed its slaves in the West Indies on 1 August 1834. Up and down the Mississippi River it was a time for singing, dancing, eating, marching, and matchmaking. But it also was a patriotic time of remembrance and of speeches of uplift and promise. Taylor could have delivered a message of encouragement and assurance (and perhaps he did), but what caught a newspaper reporter's attention and his pen was that part of Taylor's speech in which he delivered words of criticism not against a person or a policy but against a whole people. How Taylor could say such things repeatedly and still be invited to address groups time after time says much about his personality and his ability to assess and describe in a pragmatic, inoffensive, and lively way the circumstances of the day. That is no small feat, for people tend to react negatively to those who bring criticism.

George Edwin Taylor's journey to prominence in the closing decade of the nineteenth century and the beginning of the twentieth is unlike that generally reported in African American scholarship. Born to a slave father and a free black mother in Arkansas in 1857, Taylor lived his formative years in or near La Crosse, Wisconsin, before moving to Iowa, where he remained until 1910. It was while he lived in Iowa that the National Negro Liberty Party selected him as its standard-bearer and candidate for the office of president of the United States in the 1904 election campaign. Taylor lost that election.

Taylor championed a worldview and a constituency that differed significantly from those of the eastern black establishment or graduates of government-organized Freedmen's Bureau schools or institutions sponsored by northern churches or philanthropists. Taylor's world was more akin to that of displaced war refugees who found themselves surrounded by dissimilar people or the world of those who moved in small groups out of the South to form colonies or fill occupational niches in the upper Midwest as farmers, miners, barbers, whitewashers, domestic workers, cooks, and general day laborers.[2] He was not the beneficiary of any of the educational opportunities that the federal government initiated during Reconstruction through the Freedmen's Bureau to create a black leadership class. His lifelong struggle was not in cities of the East Coast or boardrooms of newspapers, halls of academe, or courtrooms at either the state or the federal level. Nor were most of Taylor's companions well educated and well bred. Class membership was not an issue for Taylor early in his life, but class identification was as relevant within America's black community in the late nineteenth century as it is in that of the twenty-first. Nor was Taylor a true member of the rural and black masses, but he changed into a working-class labor agitator and late-emergent black activist and veteran orator who happened also to be exceptionally articulate, energetic, and certain of his course. He could never gain membership among the churchmen, educators, editors, and politicians whom he may have admired because he lacked their credentials.

Taylor's time was one of enormous change, some good, but also much that was not. The Civil War years had promised emancipation and equality, and to a degree they had been obtained through passage of the Thirteenth (1865), Fourteenth (1868), and Fifteenth (1870) amendments to the nation's Constitution and as a consequence of federal legislation that disenfranchised those who had oppressed and enslaved African Americans before the war. Laws passed during Reconstruction to improve educational and economic opportunities brought further change in the South, but always remaining was a pervasive and foundational land- and race-specific economic system that confined 90 percent of black Americans to subservient and servile stations, with little prospect of measurable improvement.[3] The Civil Rights Act of 1875, which marked the peak of civil rights legislation, guaranteed equal access to transportation, restaurants, hotels, theaters, and amusement centers and required equal consideration in jury selection and duty, but it did little to remove the endemic separateness that continued to exist throughout the nation.[4] In the South, even by 1875, Reconstruction was in the process of ending. The Hayes-Tilden compromise of 1877, which resulted in Rutherford B. Hayes becoming president of the United States, relaxed federal vigilance in the South, and whites increasingly reasserted control over their states and citizens.

In the North circumstances for black Americans were not as debilitating as in the South, but changes in laws to empower blacks came slowly, partly because a palpable "color line" in occupational choices, residential placement, the use of common facilities, and political participation existed there as well both before the war and continuing after its end.[5] Laws put in place to impose changes in the South and applied only to the South during the period of occupied Reconstruction were not enforceable in the North, following the accepted maxim that member states in good standing retained the right to make laws that regulated their own citizens. That maxim was matched by a foundational "doctrine of white supremacy" and an acceptance that blacks were "biologically inferior," as were all who were not a part of the white race.[6] Fundamentally, most northerners who had fought against southern secession had not gone to war to give blacks equal voting rights, equal treatment and admission, or equal employment opportunity in their own hometowns. By 1877 they were no longer interested in reoccupying the South to force compliance with federal laws or to protect legal rights gained by African Americans in the 1860s and 1870s. Many black Yankees, those who had never known slavery and had lived their lives in the North, believed that whites had favored blacks by rescuing them from an oppressive African existence and had led them to a more civilized world.[7]

In the year after Taylor's arrival in Wisconsin, the legal struggle for voting rights for blacks there was decided. Wisconsin's voters had defeated suffrage referenda in 1846, 1849, 1857, and again in 1865, but following the last referendum, the Wisconsin Supreme Court ruled in *Gillespie v. Palmer et al.* (1866) that the vote count for the 1849 referendum had been incorrectly interpreted and that blacks actually had obtained equal voting rights in 1849, seventeen years earlier and twelve years before the beginning of the Civil War.[8] That ruling effectively ended debate that periodically consumed discussion within the state legislature and ushered in a period of gradual civil rights legislation that brought general compliance with the federal laws that were being applied in the occupied South.

Although the voting question was thus decided, the problem of black equality and integration into society remained a delicate issue, for a color line existed in La Crosse and throughout the upper Midwest. Part of that dated from the pre–Civil War period, when there was endemic belief among midwestern whites of all classes that blacks were inferior: while blacks could improve through education and individual effort, they were not expected to reach a level of acceptance or privilege equal to that held by whites.[9] Once the war commenced, however, many in Wisconsin supported black recruitment to the Union cause. Employers attached to the river's commerce generally encouraged migration of black laborers up the Mississippi River to work as cooks, stewards, and cargo handlers, while white workingmen opposed them because large numbers competed for jobs.[10] There also was widespread fear that black emancipation would bring a sudden flood of newly freed workers northward to complicate difficult working conditions and drive down wages, despite a determined campaign by employers to convince workers otherwise—that northern blacks would instead migrate southward to take advantage of opportunities opening there at the war's end.[11] The Northwest Union Packet Company of La Crosse hired "several hundred" black workers in 1866, for example, and for the next several years violent clashes occurred in La Crosse between black and white workers.[12] Local newspapers did little to stem the growth of such violence, and some, especially the *La Crosse Democrat*, edited by Marcus "Brick" Pomeroy, even encouraged it with vitriolic editorials against "scores of lousy, ragged, filthy, half-starved" blacks who roamed La Crosse's streets and clogged its courts.[13] But there also was a sentiment, especially among many workers and Democrats, that blacks were the innocent pawns of ill-considered Republican and capital-driven policies at the national level following the war and that neither the whites nor the blacks were at fault for their unequal treatment in La Crosse.[14] None of those attitudes changed with the arrival of new immigrants from Europe who carried with them their own negative sentiments toward race and ethnic differences.

The color line in La Crosse took other forms at the personal level. Blacks, for instance, complained that they were not welcome in certain churches, and other facilities were not open to them on a regular basis.[15] Transient blacks were required to stay in black-operated boardinghouses, often little more than spare rooms within black households. There were no black-owned business enterprises in La Crosse other than those operated by barbers, and even barbers would not openly cut the hair of a black man for fear of offending white customers. Restaurants also were restricted not by law but by custom. Single blacks ate in boardinghouses or in their own homes if married. Those who could invest found that certain areas of the city became the sections where black-owned houses were to be located. Schools were open to all races, and in fact the First Ward School was geographically near a major black housing district, with the result that blacks were overrepresented in the city's schools during the 1870s and 1880s. Railroad travel and entertainment might be segregated, depending more on the whim of the ticket taker than on the law. Intermarriage occurred and was legally sanctioned by La Crosse law and practice, but in most registered instances those marriages were of single black males marrying divorced or widowed white single mothers.[16] Generally, there was an attitude of separateness sufficient to require most blacks in La Crosse to segregate themselves into like-race groups for services and interactions, whether those involved housing or a railroad car. In a larger sense, however, that was the case for nearly all La Crosse residents, whether that segregation was based on class, region of origin, language, business type, immigration status and nationality, race, or profession, with the exception that whites could meld more easily into the larger population.

Taylor was born of uncertain status in the slaveholding state of Arkansas, but he spent his formative years in the upper Midwest and in a distinct physical and cultural setting that influenced his character and his responses to life's challenges. La Crosse in 1865 was a frontier boomtown that believed itself a gateway city to the West. Located on an important bend in the upper Mississippi River and blessed with great physical beauty (locals referred to it as God's Country) and lush forests of pine trees, La Crosse enjoyed a period of significant economic development and population growth during and after the Civil War. It quickly became a major port for ship building and ship repair upon the river, and its massive lumber-milling industry supplied the booming river commerce with unending supplies of scrap firewood for the huge appetites of paddle wheelers connecting St. Paul, Minnesota, to cities on the lower Mississippi. La Crosse's Yankee-bred investors were convinced that La Crosse would become an important railroad hub for commerce and a necessary transportation terminus and jumping-off location for migration northward from Chicago. At its peak La Crosse was the headquarters for eight companies operating paddle wheelers on the river, ten saw mills that processed nearly 250 million board feet of lumber per year, and a major repair location for three railroad lines joining Chicago and St. Paul. Until 1885 La Crosse was Wisconsin's second largest city.[17]

The La Crosse that Taylor knew best was that of the late 1870s and mid- to late 1880s. Pre–Civil War settlers had come prominently from three regions of the country: the South by way of the Mississippi River, the Ohio Valley along the river highways used extensively in midcentury, and New England, whose residents saw the upper Midwest as a frontier where fortunes could be built. By 1865, when Taylor arrived in Wisconsin, migration patterns were changing, so that 42 percent of La Crosse County's population by 1870 was foreign born. That percentage remained consistent for the remainder of the century. La Crosse was the largest town in La Crosse County, and it would remain that county's population center. After the Civil War, Germans and Norwegians made up nearly two-thirds of its foreign-born population, with German and Norwegian spoken openly on the streets and in the workplace. German and Norwegian newspapers, singing societies, and ethnic-specific churches also flourished.[18] That also was true in housing and work patterns, with certain occupations being staffed by particular ethnic groups and boardinghouses catering to special segments of the population and to those with particular culinary tastes.[19] Wood-carvers in the furniture industry, for example, tended to be from Bohemia, with the result that some of La Crosse's remaining buildings from that period show elaborate woodworking and designs that link them to particular trade groups. By 1880 there was a definite northern European flavor to La Crosse, and that characteristic could easily be seen, heard, and sensed when visiting the city's center.[20]

The town infrastructure was advanced for the time. By 1885 nearly all wooden structures in the city center had been destroyed by fires and replaced with iron and brick structures, and La Crosse gave the appearance of a bustling and growing town. It was contained on the west by the Mississippi River, but bluffs to the east were nearly five miles away, which meant that La Crosse had ample room for residential growth. It was a well-planned city, carefully platted and designed, with numbered streets counting from the river to the eastern bluffs and named streets running perpendicular from east to west. Downtown streets were brick paved and wide. The town itself was divided into north and south sections that were separated by the La Crosse River and a marsh that turned into a lake whenever the rivers flooded.

The city's economic life was vibrant and expansive by 1885. The downtown merchant and professional area was large by frontier standards. It also was densely populated with tenants who crowded the third stories of nearly all buildings located in that sector of the city. Three other industries were prominent in the city's success. The timber and woodcarving industry would peak in 1895, but until that time it or its derivative industries would employ nearly half

Bird's-eye view of La Crosse, WI, 1887. Murphy Library, University of Wisconsin–La Crosse.

of those workers who lived within La Crosse. The river commerce was linked indirectly to the timber industry, but in addition it supplied visitors who came by riverboat, thus generating income for hotels and restaurants. The railroads were the third industry that was prominent in the city's success. In 1885 the city's manufactures also produced horse-drawn buggies, farm plows and iron works, shoes, cigars, flour, saddlery, and numerous industries necessary on the frontier, where items often needed to be made for local consumption. La Crosse became and remained a major brewery center in the upper Midwest.[21]

Those traits attracted adventurous high-risk-taking investors and also helped to create particular approaches to capital and perceptions of self-worth, especially in La Crosse's early period, when many of its attitudes took form. That personality characteristic might be best described as "boomtown," a tendency to look for easy and immediate solutions for problems, quick turnaround of investments, and lack of connectedness to places and people while at the same time encouraging the growth of artificial attachments and a need to become involved intensively in associations or cooperative ventures, even if one were required to invent them when they were absent. Long-term and deliberate planning was restricted to those who intended La Crosse to be the final destination of migration. A significant number of La Crosse's residents, however, were transient, working at the mills and moving as the tree line retreated. Others treated La Crosse as a temporary way station, stopping for a year or two and moving on when investments failed or opportunity appeared elsewhere or just when the need to move surfaced. Such a boomtown was especially attractive for the flimflam man, the snake oil salesman, and the flamboyant character who flitted from one wife and one thing to another and involved himself in any organization that would attract a crowd. The role model and mentor in such a town, with the exception of those attempting to join the moneyed class, was he who was loudest, richest, and most extravagant in manner, accommodation, and dress. Such was La Crosse for those with mobile skills and few family or professional attachments in the 1870s and 1880s.

Black migration into western Wisconsin came in two forms before and during the Civil War. The first of these followed the migration trails and railroad lines overland, and this one was commonly used by slaves fleeing the South or by black Yankees who had never experienced slavery but were looking westward for land and economic opportunities. Although racial prejudice existed in the upper Midwest before the Civil War, it was compensated for to a degree by the availability of new land or recently partitioned and inexpensive land. Interestingly, many of western Wisconsin's earliest black settlers came as extended free family units that had been encouraged to leave North Carolina, and these groups came with moderate capital and purchased farmland near the towns of Pleasant Hill and Hillsboro. These were free-born farmers, and they came with some education, agriculture-based objectives, and close-knit family values.[22] Other groups came via the Mississippi River, and they were very different. Many of those from Missouri settled in the southwestern part of the state, in Grant County and near Lancaster and Platteville, and were groups of freedmen brought northward in the late 1840s and early 1850s to farm and develop land. Nearly 150 were living in Grant County in 1863, and it was anticipated that many of them would return to the South once the war ended.[23]

Blacks who came during the war came under very different circumstances and generally along a different path. Some were brought northward by soldiers who had met them while in the South, and many were children, servants, or small family units. Some represented desperate tales of hardship and confusion that accompanied war, and many were called "contraband negroes."[24] But there also were larger groups that came as refugees, brought by church groups that answered appeals from leaders to provide support for freed slaves collecting in captured towns along the lower Mississippi River and its branches.[25] The arrival in 1862 and 1863 of groups of 50 to Beaver Dam, 75 to Fond du Lac, and 150 to Racine generated local concern that they would be followed by even larger numbers and that wages for local workers would be reduced accordingly.[26] Such fears created resentment among a population that already was apprehensive of a flood of freed blacks moving northward either during or at the war's end.

The black settlers who came to La Crosse County were of three types. The skilled tradesmen tended to be black Yankees, and they came from free families in New York State, Virginia, and Pennsylvania and from towns along the Ohio River that bordered both slaveholding and nonslaveholding states. Some of these came as early as the mid-1850s, when La Crosse was growing rapidly. Many were unmarried males who found spouses in La Crosse, some of whom were white. Their principal conveyance westward was riverboats on the Ohio and Mississippi rivers. Only a few were farmers, and the latter tended to come as refugees from the South during the Civil War or soon thereafter.[27] A third group were blacks from the South who were recruited to fill vacancies created during the Civil War, when many of Wisconsin's single workers were drafted into military service. When the war ended and these draftees returned to their towns, a degree of resentment spread through certain industries, such as river commerce and grain and timber milling industries during the war and lumbering and factories after it. Blacks also were brought in as strike breakers in the late 1860s and early 1870s, a circumstance that produced friction within western Wisconsin's working class.[28]

While La Crosse received occasional strike-breaking infusions of temporary black labor, the majority of black arrivals who intended to remain in La Crosse from 1856 onward were black Yankees who brought urban attitudes and professional skills, at least to the degree that they could easily move from one town to another and carry their skill in a suitcase or a moving trunk. They were better educated than were rural blacks, and they belonged to a higher commercial class. They often brought capital with them, for they perceived the frontier to be a place where a careful and prudent man could invest small money and receive a guaranteed and sizeable profit in short order. La Crosse attracted barbers in significant numbers at a time when barbering was considered almost a monopoly for black skilled professionals.[29] Demand for barbers and beard trimmers was high in 1875, for the river trade, the railroads, and passenger traffic on both had made La Crosse a popular port of call, with large hotels dotting the riverbank and near railroad depots. Hotels required the service of black cooks, maids, and doormen. The demand for black service trades (barbers, maids, domestics, coachmen, household staff, horse tenders, waiters, doormen, stewards) continued high and undisturbed until white Yankee settlers were overtaken numerically by new European immigrants who flooded into the city in the 1870s and 1880s. That transformation occurred during the peak of Taylor's professional career in La Crosse.

Whether black or white, La Crosse's residents between 1850 and 1880 were aware of class differences. Old-moneyed Yankees married within their group and tended to speculate in land, property development, railroad construction, flour milling, factory development, timber milling, and riverboat commerce. The vast majority of whites were not so fortunate; they were workers who made those ventures operate smoothly and were poor with little personal capital other than muscle, or they were lower-middle-class entrepreneurs and merchandisers. Black residents (125 persons, or 1.6 percent of the total population in the city of 7,785 in 1870) divided about equally between those with special skills (barbers, household staff, steamboat stewards, horse tenders attached to the "swells," or moneyed class) and day laborers (whitewashers, fishermen, cooks, and maids).[30] Within the skilled category, some owned and operated service-related businesses, with the more successful accumulating sizeable assets, investing in land and property development, and joining biracial clubs and churches that catered to the merchant class. Of these, the barbers belonged to the highest status group and were known for maintaining family connections along the river systems and providing apprenticeships for younger arrivals attached in some way to the extended family lineage. In a sense, while family mattered most to barbers, this group was self-focused and cared most for its own members, with little obligation felt to those at the bottom of the class or to the black community at large.

That characteristic similarly was visible among whites but perhaps obvious to a lesser degree because the white population was significantly larger (a ratio of 50:1 in 1880), and those at the bottom of the social and economic order participated within a culture that protected them through fraternal memberships and workingmen's groups. They had more options. Among whites, moreover, there was a middle class of businessmen that belonged neither to the Yankee-based upper class nor to day workers who labored long hours in the mills or factories. This middle class tended to have small capital for speculation and to chase easy money and a quick investment turnover. Respectable marriageable women were scarce in a boomtown, with the consequence that—like the working class—this group tended either not to marry at all or to marry often. The ideals of personal commitment and loyalty were similarly scarce. Most invested wildly and often, perhaps believing that something would bring reward but not knowing what might work; success that came from meager investment today surely would be replicated tomorrow by someone else who would spoil the idea through saturation. Role models for those seeking success tended to be flamboyant, loud, risk taking, and willing to change course quickly when either opportunity or adversity surfaced. No one trusted government or anyone in command. Attachments were shallow and brief. That was La Crosse.

For Taylor, arriving as an orphan with no attachments to people or location, La Crosse was a welcoming place, but it possessed challenges that were daunting for someone unsure of his identity either as a person or as a member of a larger group. Taylor lived in or nearby La Crosse from ages seven through thirty-three, years during which his personality and responses to life's challenges took form.

1

From Orphaned Black to Printer's Devil

Taylor's Early Years in "God's Country"

[Taylor's classmate Bertha Kinney] reported that he was a good student and also took part in local school debates. . . . In later years, [he] ran an Iowa newspaper and made political speeches in support of the Republican Party. Reports have it that he was supported for the presidency by fellow blacks.

Hazel Rahn Heider,
Along the Waterloo Road

George Edwin Taylor was born of dubious status in Little Rock, Arkansas, on 4 August 1857 to Amanda Hines (a free black) and Bryant (Nathan) Taylor (a slave).[1] In antebellum Arkansas, a slaveholding state of the "new South," marriages between slaves were illegal, although some owners permitted slaves to signal unions through the practice of "jumping the broomstick."[2] When both partners were slaves, children always belonged to the mother's owner. A relationship between slaves and nonslaves or free blacks was not sanctioned or recognized in any form, but when it did occur, the status of children was problematic. It generally followed the circumstances of the father—if he were known—according to the common law practice of *partus sequitur patrem*. At the time of Taylor's birth, Arkansas had approximately seven hundred free blacks and was preparing to force their removal from the state on the pretense that their presence among slaves "tended to cause unrest" and that they were not really American citizens at all, basing the latter argument on the ruling handed down by the U.S. Supreme Court decision in *Scott v. Sandford* (1857, the Dred Scott decision).[3]

14

On 12 February 1859 Arkansas's Free Negro Expulsion Act was signed into law. It ordered all free blacks to leave the state by 1 January 1860 or be seized and "hired out for a year"; if they refused to leave after that, they would be "sold into slavery."[4] Children under the age of seven were required to leave with their parents, but those between the ages of seven and twenty-one would be hired out until they reached twenty-one, at which time they would be required to leave the state or be sold into slavery.[5] Amanda Hines fled with infant George to Alton, Illinois, where she was befriended by Owen or Joseph Lovejoy, both abolitionists and "conductors" of an "underground railroad" that meandered northward parallel to the Mississippi River and away from the slaveholding South.[6] Hines died of tuberculosis in Alton in 1861 or 1862 when George was only four or five years of age.[7] Orphaned and soon without a sponsor, George found himself a "waif" and essentially abandoned at the peak of the Civil War. He wandered about the city of Alton for several years, during which time he "slept in dry goods boxes" and fended for himself, although it is difficult to imagine that no one assumed a degree of responsibility for his welfare during that period.[8] That unsettled and traumatic existence ended in the spring of 1865, when, at age seven, he boarded a side paddle wheeler, the *Hawkeye State*, then active on the Mississippi River between St. Louis, Missouri, and St. Paul, Minnesota, and disembarked at La Crosse, Wisconsin, on 8 May 1865.[9]

La Crosse in 1865 had a small but active resident black community (eighteen households of sixty-seven persons), and several of these (six households) were engaged in the Mississippi River commerce between St. Louis and St. Paul. Among the latter were Albert and Elizabeth Burt; he was a cook and steward aboard a paddle wheeler, and she operated a boardinghouse for single black workers in La Crosse. Another was Joseph Grisson and his wife, Isabella; he worked as a steamboat porter. Others included commercial fisherman Matthew Schooley and his wife, Anna, and Henry and Agnes (white) Southall; Henry was a steamboat cook.[10] Of these families, the Southalls likely cared for Taylor while he remained in La Crosse, for the names of two boys later identified as George Taylor and George Southall in La Crosse records often became confused, with contemporaries of Taylor often describing George Southall and not George Taylor as the person who ran for president in 1904.[11] It is likely that Southall or others who were similarly engaged in the river commerce had found Taylor at Alton and had brought him onboard the *Hawkeye State* and to La Crosse. The fact that the Southalls left La Crosse for places unknown in 1868 suggests that George Taylor at age ten chose not to go with them, that he found another household that agreed to provide him care over the long term, or that he was "bound out" or apprenticed by the county court to someone who would give him guidance.[12] Taylor attended school in La Crosse for a year or more before moving to a farm near West Salem, about fifteen miles east of La Crosse.[13] There he joined the household of a black farmer named Nathan Smith, who became Taylor's foster parent until he reached the age of twenty.[14] That Taylor suffered no lasting debilitating effects from his early years in Alton—unless the health issues that appeared later in his life can be traced back to his youth—is a testament to the care he received from his new parents.

During the next decade, Taylor lived on the Smith property, a farm that required labor and daily attention, since cows needed milking on a regular basis. The Smith household also cared for other orphans and court-assigned persons from the La Crosse area.[15] Others who lived near the Smith farm remembered Taylor attending District 5 School (Kinney Road School on the William Gray farm) near West Salem. School generally was conducted in two terms, one of four months in the winter and one of two to three months in the summer, when many hands were required for farmwork. A neighbor of the Smiths who attended one of these schools wrote that Taylor was known locally as an excellent debater of political issues.[16]

Nathan Smith, Taylor's foster father, was born in 1820 in Tennessee and had been a slave in his youth. His wife, Sarah (Sally), was born in 1835, also a slave.[17] They had two daughters while in the South, but they had left them with friends before moving northward and away from the battlefields of the Civil War. They arrived in La Crosse prior to 1864 and for several years lived in La Crosse before moving to a farm near West Salem.[18] This move coincided with the Smiths also becoming responsible for the care of several white, African American, and mixed-race children from La Crosse. The frontier was, after all, an unforgiving place where people died young, where mothers frequently died during or soon after childbirth, and where extended families did not exist among persons who were transient or participating in the great American expansion westward immediately following the Civil War. Nathan and Sarah Smith were perhaps also not that uncommon, taking in orphaned or abandoned children when those children filled economic (farming) and emotional (parenting) needs.

The Smiths sent one of their foster boys (Kelly Vaughn) to Gale University at Galesville, Wisconsin, and one to Wayland University/Academy at Beaver Dam, Wisconsin.[19] Neither of these schools was truly a university or even a college in the modern sense, but both were the closest to higher schools that many rural Wisconsin communities had to offer in the mid-nineteenth century. At the same time, both were far better than the schools available in most upper midwestern towns, alone a testament to Smith's progressive expectation of his foster children. Gale University had been formed in 1858. Its colleges included

Nathan Smith. Murphy Library, University of Wisconsin–La Crosse.

schools of letters, agriculture, law, and theology and a preparatory school lead-ing to the freshman class. For a time it even positioned itself to become western Wisconsin's medical school. Gale University continued until 1939, although it never achieved the prominence its founders envisioned.[20]

Wayland University, however, was of a very different sort, and Wayland was the school that Taylor attended. Located at Beaver Dam, Wisconsin, Wayland was named after Dr. Francis Wayland, president of Brown University in Provi-dence, Rhode Island, who had written modestly for its inaugural in 1855: "It is my earnest wish that their dream of making Wayland a 'Brown University of the Middlewest' will be crowned with success." Wayland expected to rival both the University of Chicago and Kalamazoo College as a center of Baptist teach-ing. Wayland struggled financially for survival until 1869, when it affiliated of-ficially with the rapidly expanding University of Chicago. Boys who graduated from Wayland transferred to the University of Chicago for advanced collegiate training, especially in the law curriculum. That arrangement continued until 1875, although Wayland suffered from poor administration and a lack of fund-ing. In 1877 Wayland was reorganized to more closely resemble an "Eastern-styled" residential preparatory academy, which it remained for the remainder of the century.[21] Restructuring of Wayland likely occurred at the same time as the beginning of Taylor's enrollment.

More is known, however, about the school and how it operated between 1877 and 1879, years in which Taylor attended. Elmer Ferris, who graduated from Wayland in 1881, wrote a novel that described Wayland as expensive by local standards. Wayland had ninety-five students in 1877, with sixty-eight of them "working their way through" with odd jobs.[22] The school was coeduca-tional, with boys' and girls' dormitories. Each dorm room was spartanly fur-nished with a stove, two cots, tables, bureaus, and chairs, and each housed two students. New students ate a formal dinner and an informal breakfast in the dining hall, providing the semblance of an eastern residential school. The year was divided into three terms, the first of fifteen weeks and the second and third of twelve weeks each. Tuition was $10 for the first term and $8 for the rest. Weekly room rent was 25¢ to 30¢, and incidentals were estimated at 25¢ to 30¢ per week. Cost for board was considered the greatest expense, projected at $2.50 per week.[23] Ferris estimated that it cost a student $150 per year to attend Way-land, a significant sum for country boys and their sponsors.[24] Ferris suggested that once students learned school ways, however, they could move off campus in the second year, reducing housing and board costs by half and finding oppor-tunities for local work at the same time.[25] The school's curriculum divided into two tracks, classical (which included preparatory and collegiate) and English.[26]

The curriculum, however, emphasized oratory and language for all students. All enrolled in the classical course studied Latin and Greek, and those in the English course could study German and French. Taylor attended Wayland for two years (1877–79) and took the classical course.[27] Taylor left Wayland before finishing its three-year curriculum because of "ill-health" and financial difficulty.[28] It is intriguing that all of Taylor's records at Wayland identify him as George Edward Taylor. Clearly, by 1877 he had adopted the surname of Taylor but had not yet settled on the middle name of Edwin.

After leaving Wayland in 1879, Taylor obtained employment with Mark "Brick" Pomeroy of La Crosse, who had acquired considerable fame as a newspaperman and who became for Taylor the model of what a journalist and a successful man should be. Pomeroy had served his newspaper apprenticeship in New York State and Pennsylvania and had worked in Milwaukee before moving in 1860 to La Crosse, where he became owner and editor of the *La Crosse Democrat*. Pomeroy became infamous during the Civil War for opposing the Republican Party, for labeling President Lincoln "the Widow Maker," and for calling for his assassination. After his *Democrat* achieved a huge national circulation, Pomeroy moved his center of publication to New York City in 1868, mainly at the invitation of William "Boss" Tweed.[29] There he continued his tirades against Republicans, capital, tight money, and big business, and he remained there for nearly a decade, until he ran afoul of Tweed.

Pomeroy's pen never mellowed. Called a "curmudgeon," Pomeroy practiced his trade with flare and delighted in offending those with whom he disagreed. He supported a graduated income tax, an eight-hour workday, women's right to vote, and "paper currency," which he believed would ease credit to farmers and workingmen. In 1876 Pomeroy was instrumental in founding the pre-Populist Greenback Party, which sent twenty-one members to the U.S. Congress in 1878.[30] Greenbackers were persons who supported the printing of paper money (known in the United States as "greenbacks") whose value was not based on either gold or silver. When Pomeroy returned to La Crosse in May 1879 and resumed publication of the *La Crosse Daily Democrat* (also called the *Democrat* and *Pomeroy's Democrat*), he certainly sought to bring with him the enthusiasm of Greenbacker successes of 1878.[31] From his reestablished midwestern base Pomeroy established himself as a prominent voice within the Wisconsin Union Greenback Labor Party and organized and encouraged Greenback Clubs nationwide in an attempt to advance his own recognition as the party's leader and make it a national party with national objectives. A National Greenback Party convention had been scheduled to convene in St. Louis in June 1880, and he intended to have his name placed in nomination as the party's

Marcus "Brick" Pomeroy, editor of the *La Crosse Democrat*. Murphy Library, University of Wisconsin–La Crosse.

standard-bearer for the office of president of the United States. That attempt failed, however, and Pomeroy left for Denver, Colorado, where he remained a publisher.[32]

Taylor claimed that he had worked for Pomeroy as a printer's apprentice, a "devil," after his return from Wayland and before becoming city editor of the *La Crosse Daily Democrat*. At that time the city editor was a relatively new position in the newspaper business. That person was responsible for the hometown news page and for keeping track of reporters who were working on local stories. It is also likely that Taylor had worked for Pomeroy during summer school breaks and perhaps for the *Democrat*'s successor, the *Daily News*, in which Pomeroy maintained partial ownership after he left for Denver.[33] In any case, a year's work under Pomeroy's supervision would have given Taylor a significant mentoring experience and heightened his status among those who distrusted established parties, an acceptance that would enhance his opportunities later in life.

At the same time, Pomeroy was not the ideal model or tutor that Taylor should have followed. While Pomeroy was exciting and controversial and was certainly well known within the nation's journalistic community, he also embodied many of those attributes of the "boomtown" man who had few attachments and who either thoughtlessly or calculatingly leaped from one goal and place to another. His first wife, Anna, for instance, refused to live with him and divorced him in a public spectacle, during which time he had an equally public affair with his future wife, Louise. For Pomeroy, newspapers came and went as effortlessly as did his changes in editorial opinions, and he made geographical moves with similar ease. He was an eternal optimist and was constantly reinventing himself. His ambitions were boundless and occasionally unrealistic and unrealized. He was flamboyant in dress, and so were his language and demeanor.[34] And yet he used his pen to champion the working class and fight against capital interests, tariffs, and hard money.[35] While Pomeroy had opposed the Civil War and Republican Party on the premise that the war did little to support the working class, his attitude toward blacks, while openly and highly offensive in print, was apparently ambiguous or perhaps even positive in private. He employed several blacks in his workplace as typesetters and even took one from La Crosse to New York when he moved his printing business there in 1868.[36]

But Pomeroy also represented a person who had perhaps endured a life history that Taylor could understand. Pomeroy's mother had died when he was not yet two years old, and he was raised by an uncle and aunt (childless at the time) and on a farm where he shared chores with a younger stepbrother.

Another of his paternal uncles instilled in him a high value for education; Pomeroy attended a small school and could read the Bible by the age of ten. He worked as a "poor dirty-fingered type-setter" during his apprenticeships with several newspapers. He purchased his first printing press and began his own printing business when he was merely twenty years old. He was known for his wit and satire and became identified early as a "wide-awake, live, and kicking editor." Ridicule was his favorite weapon, and his readers "enjoyed [it] most." He was considered a prankster and a "dandy, always dressing in the height of fashion and in faultless taste." He was a self-proclaimed "ladies man" and "free-lover" and even claimed publicly to have fathered an illegitimate child. In 1876 he married for the third time to Emma, twenty years his junior and a brilliant writer and typesetter, and during a period of frustration he retreated to a small farm in Illinois to raise chickens. But there is little doubt that he was loyal to his employees and savage to his enemies. He encouraged workingmen to band together "for a common purpose in a war of labor against capital— poverty against wealth."[37] Still, Pomeroy was not a good role model for a young black man in his early twenties. Pomeroy's motto was *No one wounds me with impunity.*"[38]

Taylor returned to La Crosse from Wayland in 1879 and entered his chosen profession of journalism while Pomeroy still lived in La Crosse and at an important time in workers' struggles in Wisconsin. The battles for black legal equality were already past in Wisconsin, although Taylor's foster father, Nathan Smith, who was known to be active in politics in both West Salem and La Crosse, surely would have participated in that movement and shared that experience with his foster son.[39] Taylor also could easily see that a color line existed in La Crosse, for black boarders were restricted by local custom to certain providers, and other restrictions on black full participation in La Crosse's society still remained. Taylor certainly knew of La Crosse's lumbermen's strike in 1873 that had been called to reduce the workday from eleven hours to ten and of the animosity the mill owners caused by importing black strikebreakers.[40] That strike occurred at precisely the time that the nation was entering a recession that lasted from 1873 until 1879. The strike failed, and all strike organizers were dismissed from city mills and blacklisted. When conditions changed with the return of "better times" and by the time of Taylor's appearance in La Crosse, however, the issue of black workers in the mills had been resolved (all of them were gone), and workers were prepared again to press their old and many new demands. Indeed, a new wave of union sentiment swept through Wisconsin's lumber and manufacturing trades. Steelworkers struck in Milwaukee in 1881 and won wage increases. That victory rekindled interest among cigar makers, printers, railroad workers, coal heavers, tanners, brewery workers, flour barrel coopers, and others, with most of the newly re-formed Knights of Labor assemblies championing the eight-hour workday, which Pomeroy also had promoted.[41]

But it was perhaps the 1881 lumbermen's strike in Eau Claire, Wisconsin, that most influenced Taylor's thinking. Laborers there were working a twelve-hour day, and they were trapped in a system in which the company paid them in cash only at the end of the logging season. In the meantime, lumber workers purchased goods on credit at the company-owned store, an arrangement that benefited the company by capturing both the labor and the actual spending power of its workers.[42] In Eau Claire, workers in 1881 had demanded that they be given periodic cash payments, which could be spent elsewhere, as well as a reduction of the workday. The strike began peacefully with a full week of work stoppage. The mayor of Eau Claire, however, closed all the taverns, which had become rallying locations for strike supporters, and he asked Governor William Smith (Republican, 1878–82) to send troops to maintain order. When 376 troops arrived with bayonets fixed, town officials arrested the strike leaders, despite the rally of nearly three thousand workers that had gathered to support them. While the strike failed to obtain the strikers' demands, its major significance was that this was the first use of troops in Wisconsin to suppress a strike, an important turning point in that state's labor history.[43] La Crosse's Democratic *Morning Chronicle* in an editorial of 29 July 1881 condemned the use of a state militia in this case:

> The alacrity with which the soldier boys responded to the governor's invitation to a free ride and picnic at the expense of the state was creditable to the boys, but the call was unnecessary and discreditable to the state administration. The foreign population may stand it to be ordered around with a bayonet at their backs, on pain of being punched by order of the governor if they hesitate. They have been brought up that way. . . . The people of Wisconsin have not yet arrived at the condition of servility which bows cringingly and gracefully to centralized power backed by bayonets. The laws must be enforced against high and low, rich and poor, but there should be some clearly defined breach of the peace and at least an effort on the part of civil authorities to enforce authority, neither of which clearly appears in the case in question, before military power of the state is invoked.[44]

It is possible that Taylor authored the above editorial, for he contributed to La Crosse's mainstream newspapers, including its *Daily Republican and Leader* and the *Morning Chronicle*, as well as Chicago's *Inter Ocean*, a Republican publication known for its sophistication, the loyalty of its readers, its appeal to the middle class, and its popularity among Chicago's black merchant and upper classes.[45]

Despite the decisive action taken to end the Eau Claire strike, sentiment for easing the money supply and for improving working conditions for workers remained popular throughout the state. Many among the working class continuing to support an eight-hour workday and to oppose the gold and silver standards, the power of railroads, and the perceived overwhelming influence of money interests in the state's and nation's capitals.[46] This was a time when most members of organized labor regarded the Republican and Democratic parties and their newspaper allies as governed by personal ambitions and under the control of capital interests having little regard for issues of importance for workingmen and farmers. There was little doubt that workers in La Crosse naively considered La Crosse to be a major manufacturing center and a center of labor organization in Wisconsin, viewing it as second or third only to the Oshkosh and Milwaukee areas in manufacturing jobs. This was a time of labor organizing, with Terence Powderly's Knights of Labor seeking and obtaining support in manufacturing centers throughout the state.[47]

But workers as a collective group within Wisconsin in 1881 were anything but united in their searches for solutions. In La Crosse increasing numbers of workingmen, if not most, supported the objectives of the Knights of Labor and opposed both the Democrats and the Republicans. They accused the established parties of conspiring to fuse their tickets for crucial offices and form a united front against labor's influence. Indeed, both parties did oppose workers' and farmers' organizations, which they considered as destructive of existing patterns, describing those who supported such groups as dynamiters and anarchists who sought only to spread confusion and socialistic and communistic ideas. While outwardly opposing "organized labor," both parties (and especially the Democrats) portrayed themselves as the only genuine advocates of workingmen's interest, a heavy sell in La Crosse during this period.

Pomeroy and his popularity in La Crosse as a nonconformist, a cynic, and a defender of workingmen's issues in the Greenback era and the growth of labor sentiment statewide in the early to mid-1880s set the stage for Taylor's own rebellion and mistrust of established parties and for his support for alternatives. As a regional center of communications, La Crosse had easy access to many fringe-party publications, stretching from Democratic Socialist, to labor, Prohibition, Christian, Silver Republican, Greenback, Granger, People's, and so forth. Only a few newspapers in the upper Midwest were published for a specifically black audience, and nearly all of them were urban focused because of the composition of their readership. They were unfriendly to Populism, farmer alliances, and Democratic issues.[48] In 1881, moreover, Taylor was attracted to problems that were Wisconsin and labor based and to that group of farmers and workers who still suffered from the lingering effects of the economic downturn that had begun in 1873.[49] Nearly all laborers and farmers in the La Crosse area were dissatisfied with the status quo and wanted change in one form or another, and Taylor found himself increasingly in their camps.

Into this La Crosse landscape of 1881 entered a charismatic, admired, and ostentatious free thinker named Dr. Frank "White Beaver" Powell, and Taylor attached himself to Powell's coattails and his immediate popularity. Powell was born in 1847 in Kentucky into a family in which it was expected that Frank and his two younger brothers would become physicians like their father. Powell graduated from Louisville Medical College and Kentucky School of Medicine, after which he volunteered in the frontier army in Nebraska as a scout (1873 – 74) and as a surgeon in Wyoming (1875 –77). It was during that period that Powell became closely associated with William Cody ("Buffalo Bill"), who also was Brick Pomeroy's friend. He acquired his honorific title of "White Beaver" after treating Winnebago Indians who were experiencing a smallpox epidemic. After leaving the army, Powell worked for brief periods for pharmacists in Illinois and Nebraska and eventually opened a pharmacy and practiced medicine in Lanesboro, Minnesota (1877 –81), only sixty miles west of La Crosse. During this time Powell also traveled extensively with Buffalo Bill's Wild West Show, becoming famous for his shooting skills with a pistol. He wore outlandish buckskin garb and sported a magnificent handlebar mustache. In 1881 Powell moved from Lanesboro to La Crosse, where he was to operate a medical college until 1900, assisted by his physician brothers George ("Night Hawk") and William ("Bronco Bill").[50] He had married in 1879, but by the time he arrived in La Crosse he was divorced, and he remained unmarried throughout his residence in La Crosse.[51]

Powell was a master of self-promotion. Like many frontier doctors, he added "Indian" homeopathic and herbalist assumptions to his medical practice; concocted numerous potions, nostrums, and salves of dubious value; and advertised his products widely in regional and national newspapers for magical cures, which he promised would treat nearly all known ailments.[52] He thereby gained the enmity of nearly all physicians in the upper Midwest; they called him a "quack" or the "Cough Cream man." Like Buffalo Bill, Powell wrote several popular dime novels about life on the frontier, and he even became the subject of three written by William Cody.[53]

In La Crosse, Powell was courted by the Democratic "gang," which was attracted by his pledge to provide free care for Native Americans and his goal of

"Buffalo Bill" Cody and "White Beaver" Powell. Murphy Library, University of Wisconsin–La Crosse.

establishing a medical college in the city. For a time, Ellis Usher, owner and editor of the *Morning Chronicle* and an important voice in the statewide Democratic Party, believed that Powell would champion the Democrats and be useful in popularizing that party's message among the working class and farmers, many of whom had joined the Granger movement.[54] That was true for a time, but Powell soon also became captivated by the enthusiasm among laborers and farmers who sought either to challenge the party's leadership or to create an entirely new party—a Workingmen's and/or a Farmers' Party—that would better represent their interests.

For Taylor between 1880 and 1885, La Crosse provided significant opportunity for professional training and acceptance in a small space. His role models were professional journalists, all of whom were extravagant in manner and temperament. If there were positive African American role models with successful families, they would have included John Birney, Zacharias Moss, George Williams, John Vinegar, and Charles Wilkins, all of whom were self-employed barbers. But of this group only Birney had achieved prominence as a savvy investor, and, for all practical purposes, Birney belonged to a special protected class in white American society.[55] James Poage and his wife were attached to the house of one of La Crosse's wealthiest entrepreneurs, with wife Anna directing the household staff. But both James and his model family would scarcely have noticed the presence of Taylor, for they were upper class by virtue of proximity to La Crosse's white elites. Taylor had no black role models—there was no one his age, except for single men engaged in apprenticeships or transient to greener pastures elsewhere or those beyond his class and grade. In effect, Taylor's models were either his foster father or white editors and business leaders who were premier examples of boomtown obsessions.

Labor Agitator, Newspaper Editor, and Political Novice

Schools of Hard Knocks

> George Taylor is remembered as an excellent newspaper man, a tireless worker and once a really bright politician. His color was not more than skin deep, as in all his activities he displayed the attributes of the white man, designing in his politics, eager for gain in his business, revengeful in his journalism.
>
> *La Crosse Tribune,*
> 19 April 1907

In 1880 Taylor was a young and perhaps unhealthy man of twenty-three with a classical education that had emphasized eloquence and oratory, and yet likely, as a consequence of maturing in rural La Crosse County, he was still a farmer at heart, with farming values. He quickly acclimated to urban life in La Crosse, however, and discovered his niche in journalism. Having worked first for Brick Pomeroy as a printer's apprentice, or "devil," then for both the mainstream *Morning Chronicle* (Democratic) and the *Republican and Leader,* Taylor found himself, like White Beaver Powell, increasingly attracted to the causes of laborers and farmers, perhaps in Taylor's case because of the long-term influence of Nathan Smith, his foster father.[1] During this period three small newspapers in La Crosse were linked to labor causes. George M. Read owned and edited the *Sunday News* (later called the *News* and *La Crosse News*), which began in 1882. In February 1886 Read declared that paper the official journal of the Knights of Labor assemblies being established in La Crosse.[2] Two other papers, the *La Crosse Free Press* and the *La Crosse Evening Star*, existed about the same time, and both also claimed to represent the laboring classes.

The years 1884 and 1885 were significant ones for Taylor, with three events of sufficient importance to have influenced his life course. One concerned a public lynching in La Crosse in October 1884 of the murderer of one of the city's leading citizens, Frank Burton, who also was a close friend of Smith. In that incident both Powell and Smith had been leaders of the lynch mob, although legal enquiries later failed to identify any person by name or color who had been involved. While lynching might have been indefensible, it was a type of frontier justice that substituted for a corrupt or sluggish justice system and an option that appealed to the working class, which generally mistrusted government and the party machines that dominated city halls and their courts. In this case La Crosse's white population chose to protect everyone who had participated in the lynching, including Nathan Smith. This event may have emboldened Taylor to believe that La Crosse's population was different from that of other regions in the nation where whites were increasingly challenging equal protections for black citizens.[3]

The second event was an unexpected announcement by La Crosse's mayor, William Roosevelt, on 21 March 1885 that he would not seek reelection in the balloting that was scheduled to occur two weeks later, on 7 April. Roosevelt's message caught both the Democrats and the Republicans by surprise, and Powell took advantage of the momentary confusion to declare his candidacy for that office as an independent.[4] At that time Taylor was working for the *Evening Star*, whose principal investor was Frank Powell. Powell's decision to enter politics effectively transformed the *Evening Star* into his campaign newspaper, with Taylor, now hired as the paper's editor and Powell's campaign director, expected to carry the campaign through his editorial and writing skills.[5] This elevated Taylor and set him on a path of political action far different from that of simple laborer and journalist.

The third event was Taylor's marriage to Mary Hall of Prairie du Chien on 15 October 1885.[6] For whatever reasons, Mary's name does not appear in La Crosse records, perhaps indicating that she never moved to La Crosse. No known children were born to this marriage. Taylor later claimed in 1894 that he had never been married, perhaps an indication of his disregard for her or his inability to establish and maintain a family unit. His 1894 claim alone would not have been unusual on a frontier when it was possible, although illegal, to abandon a marriage simply by moving to another city and conveniently forgetting that marriage vows had been spoken or papers filed in a distant place. But it is equally possible that Taylor's marriage to Mary was short-lived or ended in divorce or in something tragic.[7]

The more advantageous of these events for Taylor's immediate advancement in La Crosse, however, was Powell's campaign for mayor and his victory when ballots were counted on 7 April 1885. George Read's *La Crosse News* also had supported Powell's run for office, partly because Powell was a Mason and partly because Read tended to support anyone who opposed anyone in control of city hall. Even the *Morning Chronicle*, a Democratic paper, had deserted the party to support Powell's candidacy.[8] With the *Chronicle* and the *La Crosse News* in his corner and with controlling financial interest in the *Evening Star*, Powell exploited antiestablishment sentiments and declared himself in support of laborers.[9]

The explosion of Populist and labor sentiments in Wisconsin and throughout the Midwest in 1885–86 was keenly experienced in La Crosse. The White Beaver Assembly of the Knights of Labor formed on 8 January 1886, and a second assembly was created the next night.[10] By the end of January, Powell had declared himself a candidate as an independent for reelection as mayor (terms were then for one year) and recommended that La Crosse laborers form a separate party to advance their own interests. He also advised them to select a full ticket for all city and county offices, partly because he was the lone independent in city government at that time, and he needed allies to move his agenda forward. On 24 February seven hundred workingmen and farmers met and formed a loosely structured committee, formulated a viable labor-focused ticket for the upcoming April election, and endorsed Powell to lead that ticket. Read in the *La Crosse News* declared: "La Crosse is today the pivotal point of politics in Wisconsin"—certainly an exaggeration, but one that reflected the high degree of labor enthusiasm then sweeping the city.[11] But the 24 February meeting was important for other reasons as well. A formal platform of principles was printed in the *La Crosse News* in addition to a list of ward committeemen from which members of a central committee had been selected. George Taylor was listed as a committeeman from the Second Ward, and he was chosen to serve on the group's governing committee, which was led by Read. At the 24 February meeting both Taylor and Read addressed the assembly of workers, which later (according to Read) was described by the *Chronicle*'s editor as led by "hoodlums, tramps and dynamiters."[12]

During the 1886 election campaign Taylor played an increasingly prominent role as the "brains of the *Star*" and as Powell's campaign manager.[13] Powell linked his own future to labor sentiment, paper money, and the eight-hour workday movement, and through his newspaper and Read's *La Crosse News* he encouraged development of a separate political party—Workingmen. That name, however, changed nearly weekly during the campaign period.[14] When the election results were counted on 6 April 1886, the labor ticket had won every position in city government except for two, an alderman and a constable, both representing farming districts within the county.[15] Read declared proudly that "the ship and cargo's ours," an ominous message delivered to the established parties.[16] In the *Evening Star* of 7 April, Taylor wrote the first essay that can with some certainty be attributed to him:

> The working element of the city of La Crosse have reason to be proud of the grandest victories ever won at the polls. Although a personal warfare was waged on the candidate of labor on the workingmen's ticket with all the venom that inspired malice at their command it proved to no avail. . . . Both the old parties owe a large portion of their defeat to the tools they made use of in the election and the thanks of the men elected on the workingmen's ticket are due to the *Nord Stern, Leader, Chronicle* and the so-called *Free Press* for their scurrilous abuse of the labor ticket, abuse which the working men, have nobly resented with their ballots.[17] There is a lesson to be learned from this election, and if the old parties are not too self-sufficient they will benefit by it. That is it never pays to wage a warfare on a man when he represents a popular principle. Dr. Powell was the candidate of the masses and they have endorsed him in spite of all the dirt that has been heaped upon him. It is a matter beyond question that if it had not been for the fire the majority of the labor ticket would have been much larger (probably double) than it now is."[18]

Meanwhile, Powell consolidated his popularity within Wisconsin, while Taylor successfully attached himself to Powell's growing status for his own purposes and for those of workingmen. Physicians and newspaper editors in Minneapolis, St. Paul, and Chicago when reporting his victory regularly characterized Powell as being little more than the "Cough Cream man" and challenged his medical practices. Powell either ignored them or challenged them in court, all to the delight of La Crosse's and Wisconsin's newspaper readers. Even "newly arrived immigrants, Indians, blacks, and other disenfranchised individuals . . . rallied behind Powell" because of his delivery of medical attention at small cost.[19] After his 1885 election, Powell continued his travels with Buffalo Bill and largely ignored his affairs in La Crosse, which were mainly ceremonial in any case, leaving those necessary tasks undone or in the hands of his brothers (George "Night Hawk" and William "Bronco Bill") and those who had been influential in his election, among whom was George Taylor. For all practical purposes, condemnation of Powell for his lackadaisical style of governance seemed only to enhance his stature in La Crosse and within Wisconsin.[20]

Perhaps the most dramatic statewide event in 1886 for the immediate courses of both Taylor and Powell, however, was the strike of Milwaukee's workers, many of whom were Polish workers newly recruited to the Knights of Labor. Labor historian Robert Ozanne described it as "the Eight-Hour Day Explosion of 1886," but it involved more than that.[21] It had begun in Milwaukee with the formation of an Eight-Hour League, which agitated successfully to convince that city's common council in March to extend the eight-hour workday to its nearly three thousand employees. Powell had attempted to implement the same policy in La Crosse during his first term, but the La Crosse city council, then controlled by Republicans and Democrats who believed that Powell's election had shut them out of expected patronage, refused to accept that recommendation.

This victory in Milwaukee's common council, however, led to massive recruitment of new league members. In April cigar manufacturers granted workers an eight-hour workday, followed by the E. P. Allis Works, although Allis reduced wages accordingly. By the end of that month, twenty-one major manufacturers had followed suit, but nearly two hundred had refused, with the result that a series of work stoppages and boycotts spread throughout Milwaukee, with nearly seven thousand workers on strike at one point. In a massive parade on 2 May 1886, nearly fifteen thousand workers marched, with many carrying red flags of the socialist movement and tricolor flags of the Eight-Hour League.[22] Similar marches were occurring in Chicago, and the mainstream press reported that these demonstrations were coordinated and instigated by anarchists, socialists, and communists. Rumors circulated that there might be violence. Consequently, Wisconsin's governor, Jeremiah Rusk, a Republican, sent a state militia of four companies of infantry and artillery (which included the all-Polish Kosciusko Guards) to Milwaukee to oppose what newspapers were describing as the "Polish" revolt. For the next three days, laborers marched throughout the city, closing factories and enticing workers to join their ranks. At the gates of the Bay View Rolling Mills on 5 May, Governor Rusk authorized the state militia to "fire on them," and "at least eight" laborers were killed and an equal number were wounded. Rusk certainly was reacting to similar problems in Chicago, where a bomb had been thrown into a group of policemen, who returned fire, killing an undetermined number of workers; that event became known around the world as the Massacre at Haymarket Square. Rusk's order to end the strike with military force brought a temporary halt to labor advance in Milwaukee and a reversal of many concessions granted workers by employers in the previous months. The goal of an eight-hour workday ended suddenly and forcefully. Many employers reimposed the ten-hour workday and reversed other concessions already given to workers.[23]

Powell and other labor advocates were outraged by Rusk's actions and labor's retreat in Milwaukee, and they announced that they would oppose Rush in the next election. In Milwaukee, Robert Schilling, editor of the German-language *Volksblatt* who had been instrumental in the early formation of the Knights of Labor and had been one of the founders of the Greenback Party, was charged with "incitement to riot," but the grand jury failed to bring him to trial.[24] That he was charged at all increased his popularity, clearly projecting him as a candidate for high office in Wisconsin, if he chose to run. Before moving in 1881 to Milwaukee, where he had become the state organizer for the Knights of Labor, Schilling had been president of Coopers' International and had been state chairman of the Ohio Greenback Party. By 1886 Schilling was well schooled in labor agitation and well prepared to use his talents in the advance of labor interests.

At Powell's and Taylor's instigation, workers in the La Crosse area rallied to the possibility of an alternative statewide political party, one that would support and be led by workers and that might be known either as the Working-men's Party, Union Labor, or the People's Party. None of these labels was new, and there were perhaps a half-dozen smaller parties or groups that might have become rallying points for this discontent. At Milwaukee and other large towns in the state, similar changes were contemplated. Powell, however, perceived confusion at the state level and, as before in La Crosse, declared himself as an independent candidate for governor of the state of Wisconsin. He indicated that he would join with any party that truly advanced workingmen's interests and that would endorse his candidacy.[25] In late May the La Crosse central committee of its locally formed Workingmen's Party preemptively issued a statewide convention call for a meeting that would take place in La Crosse on 13 July 1886 for the purposes of forming a new political party to support those interests and to select a statewide ticket.[26]

The speed with which these events of May and June occurred, however, produced the first split among La Crosse's labor supporters. Read, who had always championed the Knights of Labor and its principles and who had served as the first chairman of La Crosse's Workingmen's Party, found himself at odds with Powell's opportunism and his lack of credentials as a laborer even in the Knights' loose definition of the term. In his *News* Read publicly resigned his role as party chairman, declared himself and his newspaper independent of the new party, and wrote: "There is no such thing today as a Powell Labor movement; there is a Labor cause, but D. F. Powell is daily proving himself unfit to be mentioned at all in connection therewith."[27] Read accused both Powell and Taylor of abandoning the objectives of the Knights of Labor, of attempting to fabricate a "Powell boomlet" for governor, and of planning to rig any convention to be held in La Crosse in favor of Powell—which of course was true. Perhaps equally problematic for Read was an addition of the word "Farmers" to the La Crosse party's name, which was thenceforward to be known as the Workingmen and Farmers Party, a turn that was out of touch with activism at the time, which came mainly from factory workers rather than from farmers. In any case, it is clear that Read had severed his relationship with Powell and with Taylor. To carry his displeasure even further, Read traveled early in July to Milwaukee, where he was reported to be "branding the doctor as an enemy to the labor cause."[28]

The 13 July statewide meeting did occur in La Crosse, but perhaps with consequences unexpected by either Taylor or Powell. Of the 114 delegates attending the convention, 68 came by train from the Milwaukee area (approximate population, 150,000), with only 14 representing La Crosse (approximate population, 20,000, but still the second largest urban manufacturing center in Wisconsin).[29] Milwaukee's and Chippewa County's delegates had been instructed by their own local conventions not to select a state ticket while at La Crosse, thereby postponing the issue of Powell's self-nominated candidacy.[30] Schilling from Milwaukee dominated the La Crosse meeting while claiming that the convention was "an invalid and unauthorized affair."[31] In turn, La Crosse's delegates accused the Milwaukee delegation of having received funds from the state Democratic Party to attend and sabotage the La Crosse convention. In frustration, Powell announced that he would not be the candidate of this particular convention, but he warned that he would run as an independent if this or any convention endorsed the Democratic Party ticket.[32] The convention then ended only after selecting committees for permanent organization and for resolutions. Taylor was chosen one of four members of the latter committee, which produced thirteen resolutions, likely from Taylor's hand:

Resolved, . . .
1. The re-organization of our state bureau of labor and industrial statistics and a placing of a man at the head of it who will see that the laws for its government are properly executed.
2. That the public lands be reserved for actual settlers, and that all lands now held for speculative purposes be taxed at their full value, and the forfeiture of all lands now held by grant where the contract has not been faithfully fulfilled.

3. The repeal of all laws that do not bear equally upon capital and labor, and the removal of unjust technicalities, delays and discrimination in the administration of justice.

4. The enactment of laws to compel corporations to pay their employees weekly, in lawful money, for the labor of the preceding week, and giving mechanics and laborers a first lien upon the product of their labor, to the extent of their full wages.

5. The abolition of the contract system on national, state and municipal works.

6. The enactment of laws providing for arbitration between employees and employed, and to enforce the decision of the arbitrators.

7. The prohibition by law of the employment of children under fifteen years of age in workshops, mines and factories.

8. To prohibit the hiring out of convict labor.

9. The enactment of a law for the levy of a graduated income tax.

10. The enactment of a law which will confer equal privileges upon all worthy persons who desire to exercise the rights of citizenship.

11. The establishment of a national monetary system, and annulment of the so-called national banking charters.

12. The enforcement of the law against the importation of foreign labor under contract.

Resolved, [13.] That we favor law and order and condemn all officials, anarchists and communists who seek to advance their interests or theories in violation of the rights of man to life, liberty, and pursuit of happiness.[33]

This set of resolutions—assuming that Taylor was either the author or a major participant in its production—reflects a significant grasp of issues that confronted the labor movement and the "toiling masses" in 1886. It also demonstrated a thoughtful talent for explaining those issues in language easily understood by its intended readers and using the language of labor. It was tightly written, and it in quick order indicated what the party proposed and a plan for implementation. That plan called for direct legislation. In only one case, number 10, did this set of resolutions address the question of "equal rights," and that only dealt with newly arrived immigrants who were in line to become citizens of the United States.

More importantly from Taylor's perspective, however, the La Crosse convention selected a temporary state central committee to which Taylor gained membership. He was selected as that committee's secretary, always a crucial position for someone interested in participating in crucial decision making, for in organizational structures of that day the position of secretary also was interpreted generally as only one step away from that of leader. The convention adjourned, a ploy to postpone further action and move the meeting away from western Wisconsin and from Powell and to the more centrally located town of Neenah, Wisconsin. There it would reconvene on 16 September 1886 to select a statewide ticket and formalize an organizational structure for the new party following rules of representation established at the La Crosse meeting.[34]

Taylor interpreted the La Crosse conference and his selection as secretary of the new and as-yet-unformed statewide party as an opportunity to launch a new newspaper in La Crosse, one that he would own and edit (with Powell's considerable financial support as an advertiser and sponsor) and that would enhance his and Powell's political agendas statewide. The *Evening Star* vanished within a few months, likely because Powell withdrew his support from that newspaper in favor of Taylor's *Wisconsin Labor Advocate*. In its first issue, dated 20 August 1886, and in a series of editorials, all of which were certainly from his pen, Taylor announced clearly and eloquently that this publication would represent workingmen and whatever newly established statewide party that might emerge from the upcoming Neenah conference:

> The signs of the times indicate that many of the citizens of the United States are becoming firmly convinced that the government, in its various departments and functions, has been largely controlled and administered in the interests of a favored few to the injury of many less favored, though composing the most numerous and equally deserving class; that the old political parties, the Democratic and Republican, have become the tools of designing men and combinations of men; that political corruption prevails in our legislative bodies; that consolidated wealth exercises a demoralizing influence over legislation, both State and National; that monopolies are flourishing, and the people are suffering under the weight of unequal and unjust burdens, the result of official dishonesty in his [*sic*] places; that labor is made subservient to the will and greed of capital, and that workingmen are being reduced to a condition but little better than slavery.[35]
>
> The only hope for improvement in the condition of the working and producing class is in the success of a reform party, whose principles and motives shall be to destroy the old corrupt parties and defeat dishonest politicians, who have so long and absolutely controlled those parties.
>
> The Republican and Democratic parties owe their long continued success and power to the aid they have received from the press, more than to all other sources of assistance. The Reform party cannot hope for success in the contest with so powerful opponents unless it is similarly equipped to meet the enemy on the political battlefield.
>
> The *Advocate* proposed to be an effective weapon of political warfare, always aimed at the enemy, and ever ready to face the foe when danger threatens the right. Whatever influence and ability it may possess or can command will be devoted to the advancement of the cause of reform.

Trusting we shall merit and receive the approval and encouragement of all true friends of political reform, we issue the first number of *THE WISCONSIN LABOR ADVOCATE.*

THE LABOR PARTY.

The labor party is gradually gaining strength throughout the state, and it will continue so to do as long as it is managed as it now is, in the interest of the producing classes. Farmers and workingmen generally are fully aware of the fact, that they can never expect any mercy shown them by and through monopolies, and they are also sensible of the fact, that both of the old political parties are neither more nor less than the acknowledged machines of monopolistic owners of the land. Now then, farmers and workingmen, the question presents itself to you, and it is for you to answer this fall by your action in the convention of the state, to be held at Neenah, on the 16th of September, and your vote to be cast at the state election this fall, are you satisfied that the promotion of the best interest of the producing classes of the land are ignored by both the Democratic and Republican parties? Do you not know that it is a fact, that the interests of corporations and monopolies are fostered to the detriment of those whose labor produces all the wealth of the country, namely: the farmers and laboring men, by both the old parties? Reader, are you not positively certain that these two old political parties are as rotten, as a rotten egg upon which a six-year-old hen has set for nine weeks without hatching? Don't every intelligent man upon reflection know that all that any professional politician, or political schemer cares for is the filling of his own pocket with money, even though to do so he has to virtually rob the credulous public, who willingly accept his smooth tongued explanation? If we know all this, and we do, we ask in the name of justice to ourselves, and for the protection of this grand government and our posterity, is it not time to place a check upon this ruinous state of affairs? It certainly is, and the most available way of effecting this end is by every farmer, laboring man and all who believe in having a government for the people, uniting our power to assist the labor party in defeating old parties in the coming election, from the state officers down to the county. Send a man who represents the labor party, to the legislature, the state senate, the house of representatives and eventually to the United States senate, and name your next governor and the entire state ticket, for you have the power if you will only exercise it. When this is done, and not till then, will we see a government for the people.

The people have started the ball and now keep it rolling until it has traversed the entire land.[36]

This first issue of the *Advocate* demonstrates that by 1886 Taylor had grasped the language of labor and was able to articulate it clearly. Effective use of language of that sort comes slowly, often after years of study and reading. Labor-focused newspapers had multiplied during this period, and surely Taylor had read some of them. It was customary for small newspapers to "exchange" with other papers, which meant that a variety of newspapers would be found in an editor's office. The language of protest appears here in its mature state, suggesting that Taylor was philosophically ready to assume that role when workingmen began to organize in La Crosse.

What is more interesting, however, is his neglect of topics that perhaps might have been expected of a black journalist of his day. There were the obligatory amusing and space-filler notices, such as the shocking revelation that Mrs. Evenden of Hannibal, Missouri, had drowned while in a tub with other naked women and two men who presumably were not the women's spouses. But there were consequential items, which included reports that Susan B. Anthony had announced the beginning of the Women's National Association, the Prohibition Party of Wisconsin had nominated Charles Alexander of Eau Claire as governor of the state, and Milwaukee brewers who had given wage increases to workers in May had rescinded them, and their workers had asked for a boycott of their products. Conspicuously absent were mentions of race relations within the state or elsewhere in the nation. But the black press in America, while of longevity already by 1886, tended to restrict itself to an urban-based readership. A new black-edited newspaper in St. Paul, Minnesota, had debuted in 1885, but it, like the majority of such papers, "equated race progress with the Republican Party" and with its agenda, which happened to oppose most workingmen's interests.[37] While that was about to change in the late 1880s and early 1890s, perhaps it was not unusual for Taylor to have little contact with or much interest in issues that confronted blacks elsewhere, especially in the southern states.[38] From 1880 to 1886 race apparently was not yet an important issue for him. It is equally likely that Taylor had focused his attention in the first issue of the *Advocate* only upon crucial questions then confronting workers in La Crosse and Wisconsin.

Taylor's avoidance of black problems cannot be easily dismissed, however. In the *Advocate*'s issue of 27 August 1886 Taylor gave front-page billing to a story relating to an illness attributed to voodoo witchcraft, with the unambiguous indication that charms and fetishes occupied no place in Taylor's civilized world.[39] Taylor also included a brief account of a black maid who had applied for a position with a white lady in Austin, Texas, but the minstrel-like dialogue in that account was filled with demeaning comments and a clear impression that the maid had been too demanding in her terms and that her character had been less than honorable. Both of those effectively identified him as reflecting northern-based prejudices that had little positive to say about the southern black experience, except that it was backward and often not very admirable.

Taylor's principal interests remained labor and the growing estrangement between what he perceived as the labor movement's agency in the political arena and its complacency with regard to the established political parties:

> The Knights of Labor are beginning to get the idea through their heads that all laws, good and bad, are the outgrowth of and have their basis in politics. This is a truth all honest labor agitators must accept, if they desire their resolves, platforms, promulgations, etc., to be ought but glittering "generalities." The press will cheerfully allow workingmen to preach, pray, exhort, and sing about their wrongs, but the moment they whisper politics the capitalistic press exclaims, "don't" and we hear the distant echo "communists," "socialists," "anarchists," etc. One vote in the right direction will accomplish more than a thousand talks in the same direction.[40]

Taylor's sense of race did appear early, however, when he responded aggressively and personally after officials of the Knights of Labor in Milwaukee questioned the composition of La Crosse's delegation that had been selected to attend the upcoming Neenah convention:

> While in Milwaukee last Monday, the [*La Crosse*] *News* man [George Read] was asked how many negro voters resided in La Crosse county. He replied, "Fifteen or twenty, probably; why?" "Because," said his interrogator, "the county Labor convention, I notice, elected two [blacks—George Taylor and his foster father, Nathan Smith] as delegates to the convention at Neenah. We supposed, down here, that you had at least 500 of that class [blacks], and could account for such action only in that way. I am glad you have no more."
>
> Well Mr. *News* man, suppose you think you've got a horse [horselaugh] on the two negroes this time. To your Milwaukee interrogator (If Milwaukee is cursed with such a personage) we can only say this, it speaks well for the two negroes under the circumstances, don't it?
>
> As for you, *newsy* [George Read], suppose you informed the interrogator that you were thrown out of a smaller kettle than the county convention, by this same Labor party here in La Crosse, while the negro still lives? If you had only had the presence of mind to extend your finger so that your quizzer could see under your finger nails, he would have undoubtedly remarked that judging from present appearance, "Mr. *News*man" you are blacker than either of those negroes above mentioned.[41]

But in this same issue of the *Advocate* Taylor also returned to his predominant theme, one that he retained consistently through the election cycle:

> The Labor party is fast gaining strength, nearly every county in the state has already taken steps to send a delegation to the state convention which meets at

Neenah, the 16th of September. While there are three or four men who have been mentioned as probable candidates, still there is but one who seems to meet the wishes of the Labor party. . . .

The earnestly engaged representatives of the party are working for a better end than that of selling out the party, and the conclusion is to fuse with no party, but to place in the field a straight Labor ticket. It is generally conceded in nearly every strong-hold of the state that Dr. Frank Powell of this city stands alone to-day as the candidate before the Neenah convention. That the doctor is eminently able, and earnestly interested, in the great cause of labor reform no one who knows him can deny. The only great opposition that he will meet with will be from those who are deeply interested in the success of one of the old parties. They will bitterly oppose his nomination because they realize that he is the strongest man that the Labor party could possibly settle upon. If Powell is the nominee, the entire western and northern portion of the state will roll up a surprisingly large majority for him, Milwaukee and the southern part of the state will not be far behind.[42]

In his *Advocate* for 3 September 1886 Taylor continued his attack:

Workingmen have been slow to learn the deceptions that have heretofore been practiced upon them, but they have learned by experience that they can hope for no improvement in their condition by entrusting their interests to the keeping of the old parties; therefore they will place in the field a ticket of their own selection and fight the battle as principals in the contest instead of allies to one of the old parties, well knowing that they can secure right and justice only by the defeat of both the old parties.

The answer to the question, "How will workingmen vote?" is, They will vote for the candidates whom they will place in nomination, not for candidates nominated by another party which they have abandoned, because it is controlled by those who have proven themselves unworthy [of] the confidence of the people. . . . [43]

The People's Man:

As we have many times said before, there is no man in the state whom the democrats or republicans fear as much as they do Mayor Powell. They call him a demagogue, a quack, a long-haired Indian and a designing politician. No name is too mean to apply to him.

What can be the occasion for all this abuse? Should the Doctor deem it necessary he could produce newspaper compliments without number, both in praise of his wonderful medical skill and his brilliant capabilities. The sheerest argument of all is, that the Doctor is only interested in this Labor movement for personal gain. This point may be well taken in Oshkosh or Milwaukee, but here, or wherever the Doctor is known, the accusation is at once branded as an unreasonable falsehood. Does it stand to reason that a man whose business is worth over $30,000 [approximately $700,000 in 2008 dollars] a year, would be liable to sacrifice his business to enter upon an uncertain campaign, and that, when to be victorious would only bring about one-sixth of the money that his present business is worth? Does it appear reasonable to even suppose that any man would be so entirely insensible of the very first law of nature, as to be willing to subject himself to the vile criticisms of politicians, give up his all, and dive into the fearful abyss of political life, only to achieve the honor of being governor of the state of Wisconsin? What particular honor is there in being governor of a state? We have seen many an honored governor, and we have also seen many a dishonored one. The office does no honor to the man, but man may do great honor to the office.

Kind reader, to draw to a close, the fact is simply this: both of the old parties are convinced that Powell is the only man that can defeat them, hence their only object is to divide the ranks of the Labor party, they care not so much whether we endorse one of their men or not, so that we leave out Powell. Shall we surrender our powerful forces to the political war cry of the minority, without ever claiming what we already have? The answer of the producing classes is, never!

We know that Powell is the man who the laboring classes want, and we also know that he is the thorn in the flesh of the old politicians. In politics, there is no more true saying than this: "just what our enemies don't want, is what we most need."[44]

In the intervening week Taylor's views, his spirited and articulate rhetoric, his flair for asking the question "Why?" followed by an answer, and his support for Powell received statewide attention. At the same time, however, Taylor came gradually to appreciate that La Crosse and a few smaller allied delegations could scarcely expect to carry the Neenah convention for Powell or avoid endorsing the candidate of the Democratic Party for the office of governor if that were the sense of the convention. First, he reprinted an article from the *Milwaukee Sentinel* that had minimized Powell's candidacy and had advocated joining the Democratic ticket, and he then answered it with a feisty rejoinder in his editorial of 10 September:

> It seems to be taken for granted that the Milwaukee delegation have the power to control the state convention to be held at Neenah next Thursday. True, Milwaukee is strong, and many of the delegates are known to us to be true men, working in the interest of Labor reform, while from the above and other instances, we are forced to believe that a number of them are not so earnestly inclined. While other papers and men have long since proclaimed this fact, we have endeavored to explain it away, because we hate to acknowledge that the

good people of Milwaukee would allow themselves to be used as tools, with which to make traps to inveigle the earnest, illtreated sons of toil. To the delegates from Milwaukee we would say measure your steps before you advance, you know the past, now look to the future. This Labor party is here to stay and nothing you can do will destroy it while you may do much to foster it. Should you by any means whatever, manipulate matters, so as to lend your assistance to the side of Democracy, remember that you will be forever branded as the worst enemy the Laborers of Wisconsin have to contend with.

You say: "anything to defeat Rusk."

We say: "any honorable way to defeat both the old parties. You propose to have a war with men, we propose to battle for principles." What is gained by defeating Rusk and electing a man every way worse. We want no Bouck, no Jonas, and no Stowell to beat Rusk. We want a man, who is willing to represent the Labor party, give us Dr. Powell, a farmer or some good business man. Do not judge the people of the state by Milwaukee any more than you would by La Crosse.

Milwaukee will send 68 delegates perhaps for fusion, while 15 counties that we know will send delegates to protest against fusion of any kind. As we have stated before, never in the history of these United States has a political party sprung into existence with the chances of immediate success that the Labor party has. Will we submit to fusion with the rotten old Democratic party under the circumstances? Never. Whether it pleases Milwaukee or displeases her, better to "bust" the party, and give up in despair, than sell out, or buy in. Workingmen of Wisconsin, stand firm, and be true to yourselves, put up a full slate ticket, work with all your might, make good selections and nominate no man who wants the Labor party to be second to any political party, and if we stand up for ourselves and work earnestly for the success of our cause, we have good reason to believe that we will succeed even this fall.

Near at hand.

Only a few days more and the Labor party of this state will have an opportunity to lay out the road that will lead to the ultimate success of the party, or seal its doom for years to come, and thus consign the destiny of the producing classes to the ignominy of serving the greedy and unscrupulous politicians of the state. . . .

Workingmen, stand by your principles, do not allow the welfare of the producers of this great state be covered up by saying "anything to beat Rusk." Be true to yourselves, and remember that there are other years to come. Do not lose sight of the fact that *all things have a beginning*, why not have the beginning of the State Labor party date for the campaign soon to open?

We speak of demagogues, traitors, tricksters, wire-pullers and the like, but the veriest one of them all, is he who figures to sell out his party to the enemy.[45] *What? Unite with the Democrats? No sir, never! never!*

> When you get to the state convention next Thursday workingmen, do not allow yourselves to be bought by the eloquence of Schillings or Dollars or any other inducement, but *stand boldly for the principles of the party, labor earnestly to nominate a respectable and genuine state ticket and if it become necessary, bravely die the death of political defeat on election day, to be resurrected three years hence, rather than suffer yourselves to be made tools of to construct the Democratic ship. Oppose the Republican party, and also oppose the Democratic party, but be bold in defense of the Labor party, and success will perch upon our banner in the end.*[46]

Despite Taylor's lively writing and Powell's drive to obtain the gubernatorial selection as standard-bearer of the newly designated Wisconsin People's Party, the Neenah convention, which occurred on 16 September, turned out to be a disappointment, at least to a degree. As expected, Schilling and Knights of Labor leaders from Milwaukee controlled the convention, but Powell and Schilling reached an early understanding, in part because Schilling wanted to create a party that represented a broad spectrum of farmers and laborers within the state, thereby encouraging a successful statewide ticket. It was apparent that the delegates were about evenly divided, with some in Milwaukee still supporting fusion with the Democratic Party on the gubernatorial ballot, while western Wisconsin tended to support Powell and a complete party ticket. A Mrs. Severance, a suffragist from Milwaukee, however, surprised the delegates by preemptively nominating Greenbacker John Cochrane of Dodge County to lead the party's ticket for governor and Powell for lieutenant governor even before the nomination process was to have begun, which brought Taylor's immediate objection. Taylor, even though recognized as "one of Powell's right-hand men," apparently had not been informed of the arrangement.[47] Taylor insisted upon placing Powell's name in nomination, and an "informal vote" was called, with Cochrane winning by a two-to-one margin. Powell asked for a unanimous vote for Cochrane, which carried the convention. Schilling then offered Powell second billing as lieutenant governor, which the delegates passed by voice vote. Powell declined, leaving him still available for selection as the county party's candidate for the Wisconsin Senate.[48] Perhaps even more importantly for Taylor, the convention voted to participate in an industrial and labor conference that was to convene in Cincinnati, Ohio, in February 1887 for the purpose of organizing the National People's Party from the many third parties, which had lacked a national organization to give them cohesion. Severance, Powell, Taylor, and Schilling were selected to be four of nine delegates representing the Wisconsin People's Party at that convention. More importantly, Taylor was chosen for membership on the Wisconsin People's Party's central committee and was elected its secretary, elevating him to a high statewide office and transforming his *Advocate* into an official voice of the new party.[49] The party's platform outlined its goals, which included many of the objectives of workingmen's groups in Wisconsin:

PLATFORM.

1. The use of violence in any form to settle disputes is utterly unjustifiable in a civilized community, whether advocated by fanatical anarchists, or practiced by corrupt politicians in our state and none but those who have not developed out of barbarism, would result in its use.

2. Land, money, the means of communication and all public improvements, like the post office, should be owned or controlled by the people, represented in a just government.

3. Bureaus of labor statistics should be conducted in the interests of the whole people, and not serve to furnish sinecures to political hacks.

4. All laws should be simplified, so that there is but one subject, and that worded in plain language, which will enable the people to understand the law, without paying enormous fees to lawyers.

5. Arbitration should be generally introduced to take the place of strikes and other injurious means of settling labor disputes, child labor be prohibited in factories, mines and workshops; no more contractors be permitted to prevent the reformation of convicts or undersell honest manufacturers by contracting for the labor of prisoners; proper measures be provided for the safety of people working in mines, manufactures or buildings; regular weekly cash payments secured for the employees of corporations; the contract system be abolished on public work, and other measures be provided to protect those who are unable to protect themselves under a system that enables the few to luxuriate on the proceeds of the labor of the many.

6. The one man power has no place in a republic, hence all public officials, as far as practicable, should be elected by a direct vote of the people, and the votes be allowed to recall all unfaithful inefficient and dishonest officials.

7. The right to vote is inherit in all mankind, and should not be abridged, except in cases of minors, idiots, insane, and criminals.

8. A graduated income tax is the only equitable system of taxation, placing the burden of government on those who can best afford to pay, instead of laying it on the farmers and producers, and exempting millionaire bondholders and corporations.

9. To relieve the tax-burdened and mortgage-ridden people of the extortions of monopolists, the government should loan money directly to the people, at a rate of interest not to exceed 3 per cent., and should establish postal savings banks.

10. That congress be instructed to furnish money that shall be increased in volume in proportion as the industries and population of this nation increases, and shall be full legal tender for all debts, personal and national.

11. The extraordinary increase in the intervention of labor-saving machinery, requires a material reduction in the hours of labor. When the machinery does the work, some of it should be lifted from the shoulders of man. But owing to the growth of monopoly, farmers and workingmen have received no benefit from labor-saving machinery. It has cheapened production only to benefit the monopolists.

12. A revision of the patent laws giving inventors a premium for their inventions, and then giving its free use to all the people, will prevent the system of monopoly now existing and stop the robbery of both inventors and the people by heartless and greedy capitalists.

13. All land grants should be declared forfeited, and land restored to the people from whom it was practically stolen, and all alien ownership of land prohibited.

14. The importation of foreign labor under contract, practiced by capitalists and corporations who pretend to be in favor of protecting American labor against the pauper labor of Europe, is gross in consistency, and the law against this evil should be rigidly enforced.

15. We denounce the practice of the Republican and Democratic politicians in conducting campaigns on issues that should have been buried as they were settled a score of years ago, and declare that the time has come when all progressive and honest citizens should leave these parties, both of which have long ago outlived their days of usefulness and become the subservient tools of the corporate and other aggregated wealth of the country, and aid us in building up a party of the whole people, not of a class, or a clique, and we hereby constitute ourselves such a party, under the name of The People's Party of Wisconsin.[50]

In subsequent issues of the *Advocate* Taylor demonstrated his dedication to labor and the People's Party ticket and platform, reporting county conventions around the state and the lists of the party's nominees for local and state offices. But Taylor also included news regarding nonpartisan Knights of Labor conventions and positions as well as those of other Populist movements around the country, with an increasing attention given to the campaign being waged by the People's Party of New York City, led by Henry George. Without question, Taylor had access to wire news services and was exchanging with newspapers from midwestern and eastern states.

The *Advocate*'s issue of 15 October 1886 contained Taylor's first extensive article on successful "Colored" residents of Washington, D.C., including biographical sketches of Frederick Douglass, Congressman John R. Lynch of Mississippi (1873–77), Senator Blanche Bruce of Mississippi (1875–81), and Congressman Robert Smalls of South Carolina (1875–79).[51] But it is unclear whether Taylor was engaged in a process of personal discovery or simply expanding the newspaper's coverage. It is doubtful, however, that any article about success-ful black citizens would have been of major interest to his readers, who were primarily white workers and farmers in Wisconsin. Still, in an article published on 29 October, Taylor turned to a new theme that increasingly drew his attention and pen—that of the plight of black workers and voters in the South and comparisons of those conditions to those among workers of all races in the North. This is a portion of a speech given by Henry George and reprinted in the *Advocate*:

> Now that slavery has been abolished, the planters of the south find that they have sustained no loss. Their ownership of the land upon which the freedmen must live gives them practically as much command of labor as before, while they are relieved of a responsibility, sometimes very expensive. The negroes as yet have the alternative of emigrating [to Africa and elsewhere], and a great movement of that kind seems now about commencing, but as the population increases and the land becomes dear, the planters will get a greater proportionate share of the earning of their laborers than they did under the system of chattel slavery, and the laborers a less share—for under the system of chattel slavery the slaves always got at least enough to keep them in good physical health, but in such countries as England, there are large classes of laborers who did not get that.[52]

Despite Taylor's and Powell's best efforts in 1886, the People's Party's statewide ticket failed in the November election because labor organizations across the state did not support the ticket enthusiastically and some county committees failed to organize sufficiently to nominate candidates and place their names on local ballots. Without adequate grassroots support and lacking newspaper affiliates to circulate the party's message, workingmen and farmers split their ballots to vote Democratic in some cases and People's Party in others, thus dividing their votes in many instances. This resulted in Republican victories in nearly every region, with the exception of Milwaukee, where the People's Party won almost all offices and even sent Theo Fritz to the Wisconsin Senate, where he was to be its lone non-Republican and non-Democratic member. Milwaukee's workers also sent Henry Smith, Jr., to Congress, where he served one term, from 1887 to 1889.[53]

Powell seemed willing to retreat to his task as mayor and enjoy a temporary respite from the limelight once his candidacy for the Wisconsin Senate failed, but such an option was neither an interesting nor a viable one for Taylor. In-stead, he explained to his readers the reasons for the defeat of the People's Party at the polls and in the meantime retained his role as secretary of the new statewide party. Taylor seemed determined to continue with his pledge to advance labor's agenda. And he vigorously defended the state party's decision to participate in the upcoming industrial and labor conference to be held in Cincinnati. That conference was being roundly criticized by the national Knights of Labor and by George Read of the *La Crosse News*, who accused both Powell and Taylor of lacking sufficient credentials to represent workingmen's interests at that conference. Taylor responded to this criticism by ill-advisedly announcing "Boys! Boys! the K. of L. is not a political organization. Don't you remember?" But he even more recklessly added: "He who thinks that the Knights of Labor ought not to be interested in the Cincinnati Convention is worse than a lunatic, no matter if his name be T. V. Powderly," who happened to be the founder of the Knights, and "if the Labor Reform Political Movement is against the interests of the Knights, then, the sooner it is known that the *ADVOCATE* is against the Knights, the better we shall feel."[54]

Between 22 and 24 February 1887 only Taylor and Powell from La Crosse and Schilling from Milwaukee represented Wisconsin's party at the conference of industrial labor held in Cincinnati.[55] Twenty-five states sent delegates, and Henry George, who had failed to win the mayoralty of New York City in the previous election, delivered the convention's main address.[56] This conference, which included eight hundred representatives from the Knights of Labor, Agricultural Wheelers, Corn-Growers, Farmers' Alliances, antimonopolists, "Colored men," woman suffragists, Greenbackers, and Grangers, established a new national party called Union Labor.[57] Schilling created heated debate by suggesting that the Greenback Party be dissolved and that its members be folded into the new party.[58] The new party developed a progressive platform that represented issues held by convention participants and parties subsumed under the new party's cooperative umbrella. Taylor was one of four speakers to address the ratification meeting that met at the end of the convention.[59]

While Taylor returned from Cincinnati rejuvenated and committed to labor's causes, events in La Crosse soon turned disadvantageous for his continued success. Even with his parting shot against the Knights of Labor still fresh in the minds of his La Crosse readers, Taylor sought to transform the local party. One of his first actions was to convene a meeting at which the name of the local party was changed to Union Labor and affiliated with the new party, which described itself as a "political confederation rather than a political party."[60] The renamed local party adopted the reform platform of Union Labor and announced its intention to develop a full ticket for the next local election.[61] In the *Advocate* Taylor rhetorically asked his readers: "Why wait longer and fill up the rear of the two old political parties? Study for yourselves and see what has been done during the past ten years by either the republican or democratic parties. Look at what they are now doing, then conclude whether or not it is better for you to stand by them, or cast your lot with the new Union Labor party."[62] But Taylor's advocacy for Union Labor was not without opposition. Read, editor of the *La Crosse News*, repeated a demeaning description of the new party as "Taylor-Powell-Northwestern-Labor-Reform," clearly implying that Taylor had advanced his own interests ahead of those held by most workingmen and members of the Knights of Labor and had placed himself personally at the head of the state labor and reform-focused movement.[63] Beginning in March 1887, Taylor's editorials became more strident in tone, with Henry George's slogan "Landlords must go!" appearing repeatedly and with Taylor increasingly labeling those workingmen who had voted against the party as "traitors."[64]

When Powell declined to run for mayor for a third time in 1887 (indicating that he might travel instead with Buffalo Bill's Wild West Show to London), Taylor turned to Powell's brother George "Night Hawk" Powell and thus inadvertently entered into an arena of sibling rivalry that further tarnished Taylor's reputation and success in La Crosse.[65] George Powell was not a novice at the political game. He had been a Republican, but he also had helped to lead the city during those periods when White Beaver was on the entertainment circuit with Buffalo Bill and when he was engaged in politics outside La Crosse. George had assisted Taylor in the *Evening Star* and the weekly operation of the *Advocate*, even writing articles and "poems" for the paper when Taylor was absent from the city.[66]

A near-fatal blow to Taylor and his paper came in consequence of his alignment with George Powell, which had the result of producing a significant estrangement with his financial benefactor and most important advertiser. The two Powell brothers had never been close allies, and Frank's decision to follow a different path in 1887 led to serious arguments between the two brothers, enough so that the local nonlabor press liberally reported their disagreements. When the Union Labor Party met in convention on 29 March to endorse George Powell's candidacy as mayor, Taylor noticeably was not confirmed as a member of the local party's central committee, a demotion of significant proportions.[67] Indeed, Taylor seemed increasingly willing to attack: "If the members of the [Union] Labor Party of La Crosse don't want to deal fairly with the *people* then *The Advocate* is positively against the members of the Labor party."[68] Frank Powell could clearly notice that Taylor—through his editorial changes—was becoming a liability and that politicians who hoped to make their base in La Crosse could not evolve successfully in that direction. But

Taylor was anything but contrite in his criticisms of White Beaver. In the 8 April 1887 issue of the *Advocate*, Taylor delivered a stinging broadside:

> Intelligence has repeatedly come to this office that the present mayor of this city [Frank Powell] is busily engaging himself in doing all with his power (but that's but little) to injure the chances for the election of the labor ticket this spring. How ungrateful; how inopportune; how ridiculous. . . . Twice have we made him mayor of this growing city. . . . But how does he repay their efforts? . . . It is only a very few days since we were told by the mayor himself that he would openly fight the Labor party, and do all in his power to defeat the ticket. . . . Every workingman who so earnestly supported the mayor in the two former city campaigns should now turn their backs upon him. He should be looked upon as a common deserter. . . . If White Beaver was the only one that was commendable in the Labor party of La Crosse then it were better that there never had been such a party.[69]

In a parting and devastating shot against his brother George and certainly against Taylor, Frank Powell had published in the *Morning Chronicle* (Democrat) an editorial on the morning of the 19 April 1887 election in which he criticized his brother and his political ambitions and challenged voters to reconsider a vote for Union Labor:

> Weak, indeed, must be the course of a man who, with nothing to gain (but contempt) by such a course, should even think it necessary for his own aggrandizement to assail one in who the same mother's blood flows, knowing, if he knows anything, that his actions would subject him to the scorn of the very ones whose suffrages he demands. Was he willing to barter his reputation for fair dealing and integrity for such petty revenge upon his own kin? It seems so. Poor, shortsighted mortal, let us hope that his counselors, the intellectual "detective," Marsh, the journalist Taylor, and others of like caliber, advised him badly. Of Reed [Read], another adviser, I will not speak harshly, for, God knows, his humiliation must be great enough to being forced to play an accompaniment to George Taylor's organ: and really Reed is not a bad fellow at heart, for he is full of the material with which the abode of Satan is said to be paved, viz: "good intentions." Would it, I repeat, be honorable in you to vote for a man who fain would stand upon his own brother's political grave while reaching for ambition's bauble?[70]

La Crosse's voters basically followed White Beaver's advice, and "George Powell and his entire ticket went down in flames."[71]

Taylor's future and that of his newspaper and printing businesses were now in doubt. Taylor answered his critics with two notices on 22 April:

The evening luminary [the *Republican and Leader*] is shedding its precious tears over the "lamented future" of Taylor, the *ADVOCATE* man. Borrow no uneasiness on account of Taylor, friend Finch, for the future will find him just where the past has, poor, but fighting for the cause of labor and the prosperity of our glorious institutions. The Labor party still lives and so does Taylor. . . .

Mayor Frank Powell displayed the black hand all through the campaign that ended last Tuesday. For his trouble in so doing, the working classes will remember him in the future, and the common talk of the business men of the city is, that he played anything but a manly part in the campaign. The "dusky man" of the ADVOCATE, was good enough to save him (Frank Powell) from a severe attack of political paralysis in the state convention that was held in this city on the 13th of July last, and also in the Neenah convention, but because we were honest enough to stand by the true colors of the Union Labor party this spring, and support George Powell, his esteemed brother, for mayor, against the wishes of the "noted Beaver," we were branded by him as the "dusky man."[72] With pride, we own our color; but the color is on the surface, and not buried beneath a shroud of transparent whiteness, that displays a heavy coat of diabolical blackness in the background, as does the right honorable mayor of La Crosse, Frank Powell. All good citizens agree that he has clearly shown the "black hand."[73]

After the stinging defeat of the Union Labor ticket and no longer having the financial support of White Beaver, which had compensated for advertisers and subscribers to guarantee his newspaper's success, Taylor changed the focus of his newspaper coverage to national news, probably to compete more effectively with established papers. But that coverage also gave more attention to African American problems in the South and in cities. Even when addressing nationwide labor issues, those issues assumed a decidedly African American tenor. Labor successes in Iowa, for example, tended to emphasize areas settled by African Americans and coal-mining areas. More attention was given to events occurring in Minnesota, Kansas, Iowa, and Vermont than to those in Wisconsin. And the editorial tone of the *Wisconsin Labor Advocate* also became decidedly defensive and argumentative. Taylor openly accused owners of capital in La Crosse of firing employees whom they suspected of having voted for People's Party candidates in the 1886 statewide election. This, he said, made it difficult for workingmen and advertisers to show any public support for newspapers such as his. Taylor was convinced that there was an anti-Taylor conspiracy afoot in La Crosse. In that regard he was most likely correct. Both the "establishment" presses and the *La Crosse News* were upset by Taylor's shifting purpose, and all were unrestrained in attacks against his ideas and—additionally—against his race.[74] Taylor, now self-described as the "dusky" or "severely tanned" editor of the *Advocate*, complained often about hecklers, who made it difficult for him to sleep at night, and about the reluctance of the police to respond to his requests for assistance.[75]

Nor was Taylor yet finished with those workingmen who had voted the "fusion" ticket. And he seemed intent only upon digging himself deeper into the hole in which he now found himself:

> We advised the workingman to vote the Labor ticket, claiming that it was for his best interest to do so. . . . But it appears that the majority did not agree with us, if we are to consider that the election returns decide the will of the majority. Be it as it may, we all know this much now, . . . the election of the fusion ticket has already toughened the backbone of the capitalists. And what have they done to prove it? not very much; oh, no; in less than 15 days from the day of election they increased the hours of labor in some of the saw-mills from ten, to twelve hours a day. That's all. . . .
>
> Workingmen, can you see the point now? Do you need any more convincing argument than the above mentioned comparison? . . . It occurs to us that a blind man could see the point in this case, and still you allowed yourselves to be blinded by the smoothe election day arguments of the nabob corps, and in consequence voted their ticket. This action on the part of the workingmen of La Crosse, who voted the fusion ticket this spring, reminds us of the farmer who planted a beautiful apple orchard, believing that all of his trees were of the early varieties. . . . His trees grew and thrived exceedingly well. He eagerly watched them and carefully cultivated them for five or six years. Bye and Bye his trees began to bloom and show of fruit bearing. This filled the old farmer with delight, and he would every day, take a walk around the orchard from tree to tree and examine the blossoms to see if he could tell the variety of apple he had. A few weeks elapsed and the blossoms blew away, leaving a little, tiny, green ball, to represent the faded flowers. No picket guard was ever more vigilant, than was this farmer in watching his fruit forest. A month later and it was time for his summer apples to ripen, but there was not a sign of a ripe apple in his orchard. On examination he soon satisfied himself that he had made a mistake and that his trees were all late varieties. In a rage of disappointment and disgust, he caused every tree in his orchard to be cut down, notwithstanding they are loaded with half-ripe fruit that only requires a few weeks more to mature. After he cooled down and came to himself, and viewed the situation as it actually was, he could only exclaim: what a fool I am, only a few weeks more and I would have had a magnificent crop of apples, but now I only have a crop of dry leaves and a lot of trash on my land that must be cleared away besides.
>
> We say the workingmen who voted the fusion ticket in preference to the Labor ticket this spring, reminded us vividly of this impulsive rash-minded

farmer. He has destroyed a promising crop, and besides strewn a heap of brush all over his field that he must remove with his own hands, though it may take him two years to learn how to remove them.[76]

While clever and somewhat folksy, such comments did little to endear him to the constituency of readers that he needed, and they increased his marginal identification within a community where the successful black entrepreneur usually sought only to meld into society and avoid identification as African American. Jacob Tenney, editor of the *Commercial Advertiser & Record*, for example, called Taylor "a descendant of the cannibal race." Taylor clearly was surprised by the slur, which he said he might have expected "in the South," but he could not resist the temptation to respond, with subsequent consequences:

> We have but three causes for regrets, not that the color of our skin is black, not that we do not receive a liberal patronage from the people of La Crosse and vicinity, and not that the *Commercial Advertiser* will hurt our business, but because the editorial fraternity of Wisconsin is scourged by the "it" that writes the *Commercial Advertiser*, because the businessmen of La Crosse will be humbugged to some extent by this "it" and because this same "it," is a disgrace, not only to the editorial fraternity, but also to the noble race he represents. Though you are only an "it" Jacob, you have our regrets, and when you want to write on cannibalism again, come over and borrow our encyclopedia so that you can get your article charged with a little common sense. You are externally white, but God only knows the color of your heart, while our surface is black the inside can be no worse.[77]

On 2 July 1887 Taylor's house and then his office were burglarized, and he claimed that his lists of subscribers were taken.[78] It probably would have been wiser for him to have ignored the incident or at least not to have reported it so openly in the *Advocate*. If employers were punishing those who advocated labor's causes, the theft of his subscription lists would have been a blow to Taylor's continued success, for it would have revealed names of those who continued to sustain him. The last surviving issue of the *Wisconsin Labor Advocate* was printed on 6 August 1887, at which time Taylor praised the newspaper's success over the preceding year. He also announced that the *Advocate* was revising its mailing list, which certainly removed the Young Men's Library Association of La Crosse as a regular recipient, with the unforeseen consequence that no later issues of Taylor's newspaper have survived.[79]

Taylor's activities between August 1887 and December 1889 are largely untraceable; neither his name nor his activities nor even references to his newspaper have been found in rival newspapers or in city directories. The exact date for the termination of the *Labor Advocate* is unknown. The last known long-term activity for Taylor in La Crosse involved a printing company that he owned and operated, but after August 1887 no advertisement for that firm appeared in local newspapers. But it is certain that Taylor had obtained a degree of distinction within Wisconsin and while at Cincinnati, with the consequence that he traveled often to give lectures, even while conducting his newspaper business in La Crosse.[80] Such lectures provided him a small income, broadened his worldview, and introduced him to issues of national importance to labor and to persons of color.

It is equally certain, however, that by August 1887 Taylor had grown beyond his La Crosse base, at least in the sense that he no longer believed himself to be welcome there. And once he turned against the Knights of Labor fraternity, he effectively had separated himself from his labor base as well. His readers tired of his feuds with Read's *La Crosse News* and others who questioned his motives. Taylor even openly criticized the chairman of the state Union Labor Party, describing him as "exceedingly dull, for while nearly every other state chairman is doing something, he is apparently doing nothing."[81] It is equally possible, however, that Taylor simply had retreated from La Crosse, perhaps to his foster father's farm near West Salem, where he had spent more than a decade of his young life. Nathan and Sarah Smith throughout his La Crosse years had been his foundation and support and the only functioning family that he had experienced. But Taylor, if he intended to remain a journalist and political activist, could scarcely use Nathan as a mentor for success in either of those endeavors. Perhaps Taylor had grasped too high and too quickly and was in a process of re-evaluation and transition onto a stage far different from one that contained him within a city or a state.

But there is a tantalizing reference from the *Iowa State Bystander* in 1898 that Taylor had traveled "West" after leaving La Crosse and before his appearance in Iowa in 1891.[82] In La Crosse's history the direction "westward" generally referred to two paths followed in migration: the river and the railroad. The Mississippi River connected directly between St. Paul and New Orleans, and commercial shipping used that lane once the river's winter ice had broken. La Crosse was a major port city and source for wheat, corn, and fuel (firewood). La Crosse also was connected to St. Paul by three major railroad lines, which served the cities daily. It is certainly possible, if not likely, that Taylor spent the period between 1887 and 1890 in the "West" at St. Paul or at destinations even farther along the path of the railroad.[83]

There also is a possibility, however, that Taylor traveled westward to Denver, Colorado, where Brick Pomeroy had moved his newspaper business in 1880.

Several times Taylor claimed that he became the city editor of *Pomeroy's Democrat* when he left Wayland University. Upon his arrival in Denver in 1880, Pomeroy purchased the *Great West*, which within a year became known as *Pomeroy's Democrat*. That paper continued to be issued until 1891. Perhaps Taylor rekindled his friendship and working relationship with Pomeroy. Taylor often wrote that Pomeroy was his role model.[84]

To a degree, Taylor's experiences in La Crosse carried him through four types of marginal status. As an orphan, reaching La Crosse at an age when he would have understood that status, Taylor was without biological ties and adrift in a world without relatives or kin who might have provided him identity and groundedness. Taylor adjusted well to that status, for nowhere is there mention of a rift between him and those surrogates who chose to care for him. As a black child in a largely white community (the 1870 census listed only the Smith household in Campbell Township as black), Taylor was marginal, but he was attached to a household that was protected and to a degree highly respected by the larger population. Whether in La Crosse, West Salem, or Beaver Dam, Taylor was unique—well spoken, articulate, well educated for the region, highly regarded, and energetic. Those characteristics served him well in La Crosse, a bustling boomtown with high ambitions and remarkable growth potential. The decade of the 1880s alone had brought an increase of 79 percent to La Crosse's population, which totaled more than 25,000 by 1890. But even with those small numbers La Crosse was still the second largest city in Wisconsin.[85]

At another level, marginality can be an acquired status, one delivered by others or earned through one's own actions. During his early work career in La Crosse from 1880 to 1887, Taylor conformed closely to norms expected from persons new in professions, and he wrote for newspapers of all political types. When he attached himself in 1885 to the political fortune of Frank Powell and Powell's newspapers and to the boomlet of labor, however, Taylor became identified with controversial issues and marginalized by a portion of the population. The difference in this instance was the combinations of marginality that could be applied to his identity. He was controversial, and he was black. He was outspoken, and he was willing to identify his enemies and those who opposed his causes, even if these persons normally would have been his supporters. He had moved from newspaper to newspaper, perhaps normal enough on the frontier and following the pattern of others who had preceded him. When meeting adversity, Taylor believed himself to be the victim rather than contributing to his problem, someone who was being arbitrarily and maliciously marginalized by others. And finally, Taylor added to that marginality by willingly feeding his enemies with additional ammunition with which to carry their attacks upon his character.

In the latter sense of marginalization, perhaps Taylor's final period in the La Crosse area was a time for reflection, identity reconstruction, and reinvention. From 1880 to the time of his involvement with Powell, Taylor had improved his standing and degree of acceptance. But his sudden rise in public exposure during Powell's ascendancy also had its disadvantages and drew attention to his color. Taylor needed to come to terms with that new reality. To be sure, Taylor knew that he was black, but he apparently had not reconciled that circumstance to his level of acceptance. His skill, wit, and command of language had served him well, but that changed in 1887, either through a process of self-discovery or by excesses in his pen that allowed others to notice his difference. La Crosse was a major communications center on the Mississippi River and railroad line, and surely he would have had contact with neighboring black-edited newspapers. If he traveled widely during the three-year hiatus following the collapse of his newspaper, whether to the "West" or elsewhere, he would have become aware of issues confronting America's black population in both the North and the South. He would have encountered ideas of racial pride, solidarity, and separation as well as those of accommodation, self-help, and assimilation.[86] And he would have recognized a predominant Republican political bias within that same population. Taylor was not naive.

But by 1890 Taylor also was sufficiently able to have noticed that participation in third-party alliances as a black person carried special hazards. While in La Crosse, Taylor had missed in time the Greenback phase of pre-Populism, but he had expended considerable energy in the building of common objectives for farmers and workingmen both before and after the 1886 La Crosse and Neenah conventions, and he had been one of the founders of Wisconsin's People's Party. His newspaper was one of that party's official organs, and he had acted as the party's secretary in its first year. He had played a prominent role at the 1887 Cincinnati Convention of Industrial Workers, which created the Union Labor Party and fielded candidates for the presidency and vice presidency in 1888. But Taylor knew from experience that such cooperative political ventures included organizations and people who were unfriendly to blacks and who believed that while blacks might participate as members, they always were to be considered as lesser partners who might improve with time but who could never aspire to positions of effective leadership. Taylor surely knew as well that such organizations were fragile with respect to member loyalty. That had been the case in La Crosse County and in much of Wisconsin outside of Milwaukee in 1886. Only in Milwaukee had workers remained faithful to the party, an indication that labor would likely lead whatever third-party movement eventually succeeded in Wisconsin or would play a prominent role in established parties that chose to adopt a part of labor's platform.

To what degree Taylor was aware of farmer-labor cooperation in the South and of the extent to which blacks were involved as members of either biracial groups or separate farmer-labor organizations is unknown. Perhaps the closest that Taylor had come to Union Labor issues as they related to conditions in the South was through his activities at the Cincinnati convention in 1887. Unfortunately, the record of his activities between 1887 and 1890 is absent. That which survives from the early part of that period indicates that Taylor was fundamentally preoccupied with defending his motives against those who had identified him as a problem. For Taylor, his political choices were apparent. He could continue down a path of third-party and labor-led activism that had been only moderately successful nationwide in 1886 and dismally ineffective in 1888, or he could defend his ideals within one of the established parties where likelihood of change seemed at least conceivable. Taylor's world, after all, was still quite small in 1890.

3

Emergence of
a Black Activist

Succeeding in
the African American World

I have had an original idea, the only one I ever had, and it is this: Don't
go down to Alabama to solve the Negro problem. Begin right here on
this platform. Convince your Caucasian neighbor that you are his equal
man to man. Don't go away south to do it. Begin here and then show
Illinois and Missouri the record of Iowa and spread it all over the union.
Booker T. Washington in the greatest speech he ever made, said the same
thing. His text was "Put down thy bucket here."

George Edwin Taylor,

speech given in Keokuk, Iowa,

1898

Taylor never explicitly explained why he left La Crosse or the "West."[1] In
January 1891 he found, however, a place where he could give free rein to
his talents within the black world: Oskaloosa, Iowa.[2] Perhaps Taylor was recruited by the editor of the *Iowa District News* of Oskaloosa, a black-owned
and black-edited newspaper that lasted for only one year (1890–91).[3] There
were other Oskaloosa papers of that time that might have sought him for his
writing skills: the *Oskaloosa Messenger*, *Farmer and Miner*, *Public Opinion*,
Oskaloosa Herald (a Republican paper), and *Saturday Globe*.[4] Iowa also had
been a destination of black settlement prior to, during, and following the Civil
War, mainly in Iowa's heavily black-populated southeastern coal-mining
counties and, late in the century, meat-processing plants being established
along railroad lines that crossed the same area.[5] Iowa's Mahaska County, of

which Oskaloosa was the county seat, had a black population of nearly 1,600, virtually three times that of Milwaukee in 1890, and the neighboring towns of Mount Pleasant, Ottumwa, and Albia also had sizeable black populations. Oskaloosa's black community itself supported two churches and sustained a black-edited newspaper.[6] Seventy black students were enrolled in Oskaloosa's schools.[7] The town also was the site of Oskaloosa College and William Penn College, the latter founded by Quakers, who maintained a policy of enrollment without regard to race.[8] Or Taylor may have moved to Oskaloosa because there was a strong Union Labor sentiment there, especially among farmers and miners, who had well represented the state of Iowa at the Union Labor Party's convention in Cincinnati in 1887. They kept third-party options available to Iowa voters in the years that followed, although, curiously, there is no evidence that Taylor participated in any Union Labor activism once he arrived in Iowa, despite his role in the national party's foundation.[9] Or perhaps he had visited the area before and simply intended to use his organizational and political skills in that section of Iowa with the largest number of black voters.[10]

One cannot discount the possibility, however distant, that Taylor was attracted to the region because of the presence of health spas in nearby Ottumwa, Iowa, where doctors claimed miraculous cures for nearly all known diseases. One of these spas, the Mineral Springs Infirmary, advertised itself as the "Carlsbad of the West," with a spring that contained "wonderful curative powers" and "the strongest alkaline-saline waters ever discovered."[11] With homeopathic friends in La Crosse who made extravagant assertions for their own medicinal potions and nostrums, Taylor surely knew of these Iowa-based claims, especially if he were subject to any ailments for which the Ottumwa-based doctors promised relief.

Nor can one dismiss the possibility that Taylor moved to Iowa to establish and lead an Iowa-based association to protect civil rights and privileges. While Taylor had been an active participant in the inaugural development of biracial proto-Populism and the fusion of workingmen's and farmers' interests in Wisconsin, and while those interests remained integral to his thinking, by the time he reached Iowa in 1891 Taylor had narrowed his focus from biracial cooperation to self-help issues important only within the black community. If the status of civil rights, opportunity for patronage appointments, and advancement within the nation's black community in 1887 were undergoing accelerating decline instead of steady progress, then the dilemma for Taylor was to find a path that would lead to personal satisfaction as well as progress for the race. The world Taylor entered in Iowa was very different from the one he left behind in La Crosse, although subsequent events suggest that he was fully engaged in learning about that world and accommodating to it before he arrived in Oskaloosa in 1891.

For most black political activists, protecting and defending civil rights had become the most important objective of the nation's black community by 1891. In its ruling in *Civil Rights Cases* (1883) the U.S. Supreme Court had struck down the Civil Rights Act of 1875, but it had done so using language that had encouraged southern states to end "special favorite" privilege and to dismantle much of the progress in civil rights mandated and enforced by the federal government between 1865 and 1883. In addition, the court decision had generated a doubt that rights gained generally for blacks in the North were actually enforceable by law. In its majority opinion Justice Joseph Bradley had launched the debate with a single sentence: "When a man has emerged from slavery, and by the aid of beneficent legislation has shaken off the inseparable concomitants of that state, there must be some stage in the progress of his elevation when he takes the rank of a mere citizen, and ceases to be *the special favorite of the laws*, and when his rights as a citizen, or a man, are to be protected in the ordinary modes by which other men's rights are protected."[12] Such reasoning effectively ended the likelihood of new protections from a federal source and made it possible for southern states to pass laws that, while remaining within boundaries set by the Fourteenth and Fifteenth Amendments, removed blacks from state voting rolls by requiring special requirements for voting privilege.[13] National Republican administrations increasingly ignored those maneuvers, partly because of fatigue with the issue of civil rights and racial equality and partly because national leaders were leery of enforcing federal laws and committing to what could amount to new federal occupation of the South. Meanwhile, Republican regimes in the South that had depended upon black voters to keep them in power were overwhelmed by newly empowered Democratic voters, who seized control of state after state.

During this dismantling of Reconstruction, nearly all black political activists in the North, whether they remained within the Republican Party as traditionalists or activists or had abandoned it for Democracy or socialism or Populism, believed by 1890 that negative change in the South had accelerated, and they knew not what course would stop it or even slow it down. Loyalty to the Republicans was no longer working, and, in consequence, much of their allegiance to that party was governed by little more than blind trust. Nor could they depend on the U.S. Supreme Court to champion their cause, as demonstrated by its majority opinion in *Civil Rights Cases*. It was as though the nation had come to believe that it was time for blacks to assume responsibility for themselves without specially tailored protection or any guarantees of outcomes.[14]

Nor could those black activists who had converted to "Democracy" expect a great migration of voters to follow them into the Democratic Party, for that party at the national level seemed intent upon excusing the excesses of its southern-affiliated parties. In effect, increasing numbers of blacks believed that they had been abandoned by both parties, that they were on their own, and that they needed to find among themselves a degree of nonpartisan consensus on particular issues affecting the entire black community—or at least discuss them to identify areas where they could cooperate for racial betterment. This, then, was the black world that Taylor encountered when he was most distant from his La Crosse base.

Indeed, those three years, when Taylor disappeared from the data, were important for explaining Taylor's full transformation from labor supporter to black political activist by the time he arrived in Oskaloosa in 1891. During those years several changes or events occurring in the upper Midwest most likely influenced the timing and thoroughness of his transition. Among the less partisan changes was the appearance of an influential newspaper in St. Paul, located only 140 miles northwest of La Crosse and probably the "West" to which Taylor had traveled in 1887. St. Paul's *Western Appeal* had commenced publication in 1885, when Taylor was just beginning his political career in La Crosse. It described itself initially as a nonpartisan and progressive newspaper, but it soon declared itself Republican when it became obvious that political alliances and subsidies were important if black newspapers hoped to thrive.[15] In 1888 it published editions in Chicago and Louisville, Kentucky, and in 1889 printed additional versions in St. Louis and Dallas, Texas. The *Appeal* called itself a "people's paper," and it unambiguously condemned America's inconsistent racial policy, disenfranchisement efforts gaining ground in the South, lynching, and discrimination of all types.[16] The *Appeal*'s editor, John Quincy Adams (not related to President John Quincy Adams), believed in "persistent protest and agitation, stating that 'no wrongs are ever righted except by protest.'"[17]

What annoyed Adams most was a perception that civil rights in the North, and especially those in Minnesota, were being undermined at the local level by an emergent "color line" that discriminated against blacks in housing, public accommodations, and employment. He believed that the trend had been encouraged by the Supreme Court's decision in *Civil Rights Cases*. And he argued that if such legal violations continued, Minnesota's white population, which by 1885 was losing its Yankee and Civil War–experienced majority, would be encouraged to breach other civil rights as well. In 1887 the *Appeal* sponsored a lawsuit against the Clarendon Hotel of St. Paul, which had refused accommodation to a black customer. While the Second Judicial District Court in St. Paul

John Q. Adams, editor of the *St. Paul Appeal*. Penn, *Afro-American Press*.

ruled in favor of the plaintiff in that suit, it awarded him only $25 in damages, leaving the impression that laws protecting blacks could be violated as long as offenders were willing to pay a fine.[18]

This case and the court's response to it led Adams, along with Fredrick L. McGhee, a newly arrived and still-Republican lawyer who had moved to Minnesota from Chicago, to call for a nonpartisan state convention of black leaders to devise a strategy to "protect" black civil rights. That convention met in 1887 and organized the Protective and Industrial League, which planned to advance "the material interest of the race as well as to protect them in their political rights."[19] The league also established committees to promote business opportunities, social interactions, inexpensive housing, homeownership, and material assistance to members. It even discussed the possibility of recruiting blacks from the South who might establish "colonies" of farmers within Minnesota.[20] Taylor surely would have known of these events in Minnesota and of the league's objectives, which were progressive and would have appealed to Taylor's workingmen's values.

Similar responses to discrimination occurred in Taylor's home state of Wisconsin. In 1889 in Milwaukee, which then had the state's largest black population (about 500 of a total of 204,000), two blacks were refused drinks in a local tavern. This was not a rare occurrence, but, as in Minnesota, an apparent color line had been crossed. Milwaukee black activists brought a lawsuit against the tavern and the bartender. In *Howell v. Litt*, the court ruled in favor of the plaintiff and essentially rejected the argument given in *Civil Rights Cases*, stating that there could be no exceptions to the general rule that blacks should be guaranteed equal treatment in public venues.[21] Had Taylor remained in Wisconsin during his three-year hiatus, he certainly would have known of this case and its implications for civil rights.

Other events in the Midwest also would have been known to Taylor and would have illustrated the power of voting blocs in the American political process. The 1880s and especially the 1890s was a time when third-party movements—similar to Taylor's Wisconsin-based People's Party—were challenging state-based Democratic and Republican parties and occasionally winning elections, especially at the city, county, and state levels. Nearly all of these third parties were composed of farmers and workers who still suffered from economic adjustments that came with the recession of 1873 and that continued to punish producers for the rest of the century. When third parties obtained even limited success at state levels, however, national parties, which essentially were collections of state parties, found it more difficult if not impossible to maintain control of a coalition of state parties. Mainstream national parties, then, tended to listen carefully when issue-oriented groups threatened to enter statewide contests and tempt voters to support single-issue politics. That had been the case with the Greenbackers, Union Labor advocates, and Grangers in the North and Midwest and Farmers' Alliancers, Readjusters, and Agricultural Wheelers in the South.[22] Major parties accordingly modified their platforms by including the issues important to the protesting groups or at least fused or combined their tickets by supporting the same candidates on the ballot or offering them offices and patronage at the state level. This type of "fusion politics" was clearly the case in several midwestern and southern states where Populist and People's parties flourished into the 1890s and in nearby Kansas, where blacks and farmers joined forces to form a highly competitive party.[23]

Among black voters, however, there were many who believed that neither the Republicans nor the Democrats, whether at the state or the national level, were concerned about black issues or blacks as voters. Even T. Thomas Fortune, editor of the *Freeman* of New York, believed that "none of them [parties] cares a fig for the Afro-American further than he can use them. . . . It is now time for parties to serve us, if they desire our support."[24] Meanwhile, the Republican Party continued to "wave the bloody shirt" to remind blacks that Republicans had fought for their emancipation, while Democrats espoused causes that, at least on the surface, supported farmers' and workingmen's interests and opposed big capital.[25] In effect, the political opportunities open to Taylor during his crucial hiatus of 1887–90 were wide-ranging, and they no longer restricted him to either party.

For a time, especially with the emergence of lily-white Republicans in the South, it appeared that blacks might even abandon the Republican Party, which had been their home since the Civil War, and lend support to agrarian-based third parties or Democratic candidates in an era of resurgent Democratic rule while accepting "a seat or so" in legislatures or patronage positions as consolation prizes.[26] The changes made by Democrats to the Mississippi Constitution in 1890 that effectively removed black voting in that state, however, and the rapid spread of similar attempts throughout the South were viewed by all black intellectuals and editors of black newspapers with alarm and were roundly criticized in the mainstream black press.[27]

With the late 1880s also came a phenomenal production of political pamphlets and public announcements that addressed issues that were particular to that community. While most of them decried the growing incidences of lynching and disenfranchisement efforts gaining ground in the South, some addressed the possibility of political choice, of voting for another political party. The election of Grover Cleveland in 1884 as the first Democrat to control the executive branch since the beginning of the Civil War, for example, had created new patronage opportunities for blacks and options for young activists in his party. It also had encouraged many young Republicans, who were sympathetic to workingmen's causes and who were Republicans only because the party contained 90 percent of black voters, to stage a minirebellion against black elders who had controlled federal patronage appointments for so long. That surge of mutiny was particularly evident in the midwestern states of Illinois, Indiana, Ohio, Pennsylvania, and Kansas. It was also evident in eastern states where powerful Democratic machines dominated city politics and local patronage appointments.[28]

But the late 1880s also were a time of general uncertainty, of reinvention, and of opportunity, and even those who were politically committed to a specific party and agenda sought forums where black issues could be discussed in a nonconfrontational manner and without a dominant white presence. "Calls" for issue-specific (mainly antilynching) inaugural conventions were issued, with some resultant organizations surviving, although most did not. These convention calls, most for meetings to be held in Chicago or nearby midwestern cities, likely had more impact upon Taylor's transition from labor agitator to black activist than did the successes of labor and agrarian Populist movements then gaining momentum in the Midwest and the South. One of the more promising of the non-party-affiliated forums that resulted from these calls was a reconstituted National Afro-American League (NAAL). T. Thomas Fortune of the *Freeman* had founded the original NAAL in 1887, but that league had failed for several complicated reasons.[29] Fortune, a Democrat who others identified as a "full-fledged social and economic critic," was born a slave in Florida in 1856, and he had followed his father into politics in the Jacksonville area after the Civil War.[30] Fortune left Florida in 1874 and for two years attended classes at Howard and Harvard universities, after which he taught school briefly in Florida. Then, at age twenty-four, Fortune cofounded the New York *Globe* (1880–84), which eventually became the *Freeman* (1884–87) and then the *Age* in 1887. His influence on black journalism and black political awareness for nearly three decades was profound.[31]

Fortune had come to believe by 1884 that the country and the nation's black community were both gripped in an unending struggle between capital and labor, that the Civil War had ended involuntary servitude only to replace it with industrial slavery, and that both races were heading toward a "spirit of rebellion."[32] In his *Black and White: Land, Labor, and Politics in the South* (1884), Fortune had broadcast his adherence to economic ideas then being advanced by Henry George, and he blamed the Republican Party for abandoning the

T. Thomas Fortune, editor of the New York *Age*. Penn, *Afro-American Press*.

principles of Lincoln and Sumner.[33] In his *The Negro in Politics* (1885), Fortune had argued that blacks would obtain power only through independent yet collective thinking and had asked his readers to consider voting as a bloc and for their own economic interests.[34] Fortune believed that education was a special obligation of the federal government, which had sanctioned slavery in the first place, and he believed it possible for progress to be made, but only if governmental commitment to education were to continue and expand. But Fortune also believed that economic issues were paramount: "Two assumptions were foremost: that capital is the product of labor, pure and simple; and that land is universal, God-given common property, like air and water."[35]

Fortune's early nonpartisan and exclusively black NAAL had faltered in its early years, but he refused to accept complete defeat.[36] Building on the successful model of New York's Afro-American League, Fortune issued a new convention call in 1889 for all groups interested in a nonconfrontational forum to convene in Chicago on 15 January 1890 to establish a new organization and dispel critics who believed his original league to have been little more than a front for Democratic activism.[37] In Minnesota, Fortune's call resulted in the formation of the nonpartisan Afro-American League of St. Paul; its first purpose was to choose delegates to the upcoming Chicago meeting. Both McGhee and Adams of the *Appeal* represented the league at the Chicago meeting, and both were selected to serve on the redesigned league's executive committee.[38] In Wisconsin, Milwaukee's blacks formed a similar league and began immediately to press for passage of a civil rights bill. They introduced the bill into Wisconsin's legislature in 1889, when Democrats were in the majority in both houses. Democrats stripped the bill of most of the equal access venues listed in it, but, even in that diminished form, the bill still failed to pass in the Wisconsin Senate.[39]

Fortune wanted a new organization or a reconstituted nonpartisan NAAL to focus on issues of disenfranchisement, mob rule, unequal distribution of school funds, use of chain gang labor (the convict-lease system), Jim Crow laws only then being written in the South, and District of Columbia voting rights, all of which were nonpartisan and specific to the black community. Fortune recommended a top-down organizational model, with state branches established by the national league. This was a different structure that placed the initiating authority within the national league rather than at the state level. He suggested creating national "departments" to promote an Afro-American Bank, emigration of blacks out of the South, legislative assistance for state branches, technical education, and cooperative industry in which people would invest for common goods and manufactures.[40] Above all, the league was to have exclusive and closed black-only membership and was to provide a forum where black Democrats and black Republicans could openly discuss and debate issues important only to the black community. Because it was to be nonpartisan, patronage appointments would not be part of its mission or its discussions. This league also would act as a bridge between two groups then emerging: those who advocated industrial education, self-help, and gradual improvement (southern or Tuskegee school) and those who championed agitation, political action, and litigation (northern school), whether they occurred in a courtroom or a newspaper editing room or through the development of optional voting choices.[41] All of these would have interested George Taylor and his background in "cooperative" labor activism.

At about the same time and before Taylor moved to Iowa, at least four other national discussion groups formed nationwide with goals similar to those of the NAAL but with more activist flavors.[42] Three of these were centered in the Midwest, while one was based in the Northeast. The National Colored (or Negro) Men's Protective Association (NCMPA) declared itself to be nonpartisan, but from its beginning many of its members were self-identified Democrats.[43] Its first conference was held in 1888, corresponding in time with Grover Cleveland's campaign to retain the presidency for a second term and with the appearance of the Union Labor Party on a general election ballot for the first time.[44] Like the NAAL, the NCMPA opposed lynching, holding of persons in virtual servitude through oppressive land-use policies, and disenfranchisement efforts then spreading rapidly in the South.[45] Women were welcome within this group, despite its name.

Another, eventually known as the National Negro Democratic League (NNDL, sometimes also Negro National Democratic League), was "called" by a group of black Democrats who met in Indianapolis when the Republicans nominated Benjamin Harrison to lead that party's ticket in 1888 and when it appeared possible that Grover Cleveland might lead the Democratic ticket to victory for yet a second term.[46] The NNDL's purpose was to establish a forum for state-based Democratic leagues and clubs that, until then, had not coordinated their efforts at the national level. Many of these state-based groups had existed for the sole purpose of producing lists of persons eligible for patronage when and if Democratic Party candidates won city or state elections. In contrast to those state-based leagues, the NNDL intended to focus all lists it would generate on only "high-level [patronage] positions."[47] Herbert A. Clark of Mississippi, J. Milton Turner of St. Louis, and Charles H. J. Taylor from Kansas City, Kansas, were this group's principal organizers.[48] While in St. Louis they distributed a call for a general conference (the National Convention of Independent Voters) to convene in Indianapolis, where they would formalize the new league.

That conference in September 1888 became famously known for its disorder, "punctuated by several fistfights," with weapons being drawn when rival Republicans interrupted its session.[49] It also was ridiculed by the mainstream black press, especially that edited by George Knox of the *Indianapolis Freeman*, then a black Democrat paper, who accused its organizers of being interested only in patronage.[50] Much of the black Republican press interpreted the existence of such a group ominously as "the handwriting on the wall, foretelling for sure the dissolution of the Republican Party," which already was losing support among some black thinkers.[51] Peter H. Clark of Ohio (socialist and educator in Cincinnati) served as the league's first president from 1888 to 1890, followed by William T. Scott of Illinois (Democrat and editor of the *Cairo Gazette*) from 1890 to 1892, Charles H. J. Taylor of Kansas (Democrat and editor of the *Public Educator*) from 1892 to 1896, A. E. Manning of Indiana (Democrat and editor of the *World* of Indianapolis) from 1896 to 1898, and Edward E. Lee (chairman of the United Colored Democracy of New York) from 1898 to 1900.[52]

Internal dissension marked the NNDL from its beginning. During its first years it failed to generate interest or support, primarily because Republican victory in the 1888 election left its members with little to debate or any political spoils to divide. By 1892, however, the possibility of victory for the Democratic ticket enlivened the league and led to the first open battle between the "old-Democratic faction headed by C. H. J. Taylor" and the "new-Democratic faction headed by Thomas Fortune," especially regarding political patronage, for black Democrats were preparing in 1892 literally to "beat a path to Cleveland's door" if he were elected.[53] When Cleveland returned to office and failed to appoint the expected number of black Democrats to patronage positions, Charles H. J. Taylor of Kansas and H. C. C. Astwood of Louisiana struggled for control of the league and seriously damaged its reputation among many black Democrats.[54] Charles Taylor and Calvin Chase, editor of the *Washington Bee*, engaged in such a heated debate in 1894 that Taylor sued Chase, and Chase spent three months in jail.[55]

NNDL certainly was interested in securing patronage appointments for its members.[56] Charles Taylor argued that an old guard of Republican blacks held the most sought after appointments, and as long as the old guard survived, no opportunities for young black politicians would be available in that party.[57] This group also sought a grassroots, bottom-up organizational style that recognized the prior existence and local importance of state clubs and recommended a loosely structured system that would meet in biennial sessions and during national conferences of the Democratic Party.[58] In that way the NNDL differed significantly from the top-down model envisioned by Fortune for the NAAL, whose meeting schedule would not be linked to the election cycle.

The NNDL was not alone in appealing to black Democrats, however. A rival National Democratic Association of Colored Men (aka the National Association of Democratic Clubs) was led by James A. Ross of Buffalo, New York, where he was editor of the *Globe* in 1892. Ross had grown up in Cairo, Illinois, and was a lawyer and dedicated Democrat. It is uncertain when the National Democratic Association of Colored Men had its origin, but it was fully functioning by the

William Calvin Chase, editor of the *Washington Bee*. Penn, *Afro-American Press*.

1892 election.[59] Ross and H. C. C. Astwood, chair of the NNDL executive committee, attempted unsuccessfully in 1892 to merge the two groups, and a second attempt was made in 1895.[60] The likely reason for failure to fuse was the fact that Ross's association consisted of northeastern state- and city-based organizations, and it had few national objectives other than patronage opportunities and attachment to the national party as a separate Negro Bureau. Equally likely, however, black Democrats—then as now—tended to lack unity or singleness of purpose. By 1898 the National Democratic Association of Colored Men had disappeared, and Ross, its principal advocate, had become a member of the NNDL executive committee and would become that league's president in 1904.[61]

A final group with relative longevity was the Negro Lincoln League, a group of Republicans headquartered in Minneapolis. This group was the forum for black Republicans who wanted change within that party's platform to reflect issues that directly influenced the lives of common folk. This group supported the free coinage of silver at a time when the parent party supported the gold standard. It championed proposals then circulating in Washington, D.C., for pensions for ex-slaves who had received no wages during slavery times. And it opposed imperialism late in the century. In 1904 a small group from this league fielded candidates for the office of president and vice president on the National Negro Lincoln Party ticket.[62] Essentially, this league was a home for disaffected black Republicans who simply could not vote for a Democrat, no matter that the Republican Party platform failed repeatedly to meet their expectations.

This was the black world when George Taylor entered it in 1887, at the point when he was alienated from his La Crosse audience and readership and coming to terms with his black identity. Essentially, black political activists had wide choices of party affiliation. Most were Republican, but many voted their own personal interests, depending on where they were located and the issues that were prevalent in their region. Yet, despite these political choices, by the time Taylor arrived in Iowa on 1 January 1891 he had declared himself a Republican, if for no better reason than it was the home of a larger number of black voters and the place where his talents might be more rewarded. He was, after all, a pragmatic man. Others who identified themselves as independent Republicans, known by others as "Negrowumps," were as interested in workingmen and farming issues as was he, and they moved as events changed in the nation and as patronage opportunities opened and closed.[63] Taylor knew that where he fit generally in the spectrum of black Republican thinking mattered little and that his skills as an organizer, a labor agitator, an enthusiastic speaker, and an editor marked him and gave him group acceptance wherever he might declare his allegiance. Although he could not match the stature or financial support of a Calvin Chase, a Charles Taylor, or a T. Thomas Fortune, he was as well read as a midwestern journalist would need to be. While it is uncertain precisely where Taylor spent his three-year hiatus, he had already reinvented himself by 1891, having transitioned from labor agitator to black political activist. He may have attended any or all of the conferences held in Chicago, only three hundred miles and six hours by train south of La Crosse, as one of scores whose names were not listed because they were not registered delegates or were unknown or insignificant to the leadership. But of these groups it is certain that he was amply involved in the NCMPA even before his arrival in Iowa; otherwise, he surely would not have been elected its president in June 1892.[64] In 1892 Taylor was thirty-four years of age.

Once in Iowa, Taylor in quick order became sufficiently known to be selected as one of Iowa's five at-large delegates to the Republican National Convention, which was scheduled to meet in Minneapolis from 7 to 10 June 1892.[65] Approximately 13 percent of delegates attending the Minneapolis meeting were African Americans.[66] There, representing the "liberal element" among Iowa's Republicans and Iowa's only black delegate, he joined with activist blacks in a caucus that advocated an aggressive and protective black agenda within the national party. Taylor's abilities as a writer and witty orator and his election as president of the NCMPA a few days earlier likely were enough to give him name recognition within the caucus and earn him a degree of respect.[67] Taylor also joined many black Republicans who had criticized President Harrison for his inaction regarding disenfranchisement actions taking place in the South and for his acquiescence when blacks were removed from federal patronage positions in the South.[68]

At the Minneapolis Convention, Taylor was chosen, along with Frederick Douglass and Charles Ferguson, both elder statesmen in the civil rights struggle, to carry the caucus's recommendations to the party's platform committee.[69] That committee received their petition, which included a demand for a "new force bill," but the national committee incorporated none of the caucus's requests into the party's platform. That objective failed, as did, ultimately, Taylor's candidate as the party's nominee, Governor William McKinley of Ohio.[70] Severely disappointed, Taylor "bolted" the party even before the convention had adjourned, and he wrote a scathing broadside that publicly "flayed the Republican attitude."[71] Douglass, meanwhile, remained loyal to the Republican Party and "condemned blacks who [openly] supported Democracy," although even Douglass was dismayed when all of the caucus's suggestions were so easily dismissed.[72]

Taylor's "National Appeal" of 1892 was addressed to blacks and to those whites who claimed to support black rights and guarantees. It declared his firm break with the Republican Party, and it demonstrated a significant transformation in his thinking, his careful and clever play on words such as "protection," his transition from the language of labor to that of politics, and both his intemperance and his ability to change course quickly—useful but dangerous

Hon. Frederick Douglass. Penn, *Afro-American Press.*

strategies learned while in La Crosse. His gift of using the rhetorical question to guide his reader to his answer was striking. Easily discernible was his threat of individual and group agency to achieve change if necessary. "Wait" was no longer an acceptable reply. His appeal also demonstrated a significant grasp of the issues then confronting the national African American community in both the North and the South and a determination to bring change and reform within the democratic process but to do it within one of the major parties, if possible.

A NATIONAL APPEAL

Addressed to the American Negro and the Friends of Human Liberty. May we be Permitted to Peacefully Live as Common Citizens of the Country that is as Dear to us as Life, or Must We Submit to the Cruel, Merciless Judgment of Judge Lynch, the Faggot, and the Enemy's Bullet?[73]

The world beyond the boundaries of the United States will doubtless look upon this appeal with great astonishment, when it is recognized as coming from a class of American citizens whose *claims* upon *America* are anteceded only by the original American (the Indian). We, the American Negroes, have been grafted into the fibres of the American government so firmly, that we have lost every vestige of our African ancestry, save the *color* of our skin, which hangs on as a barrier to our progress and happiness. Three centuries more will suffice to erase this impediment, and, strange, as it may seem, many of our alleged friends (white) say, *wait!* But can we afford to wait three centuries longer as time of grace for the states and territories of the United States to learn that we are human beings—American citizens?

LOYALTY TO THE UNION:

When we were slaves we were at the mercy of our masters. They were, then, our only protection. But when the voice of God, by the hand of Abraham Lincoln, proclaimed us to be free people, and the subsequent order from the same sacred power placed the immortal flag of the Union in our hands, and the musket on our shoulders and napsack on our backs, and commanded us to fight for the preservation of *our* Union and the maintenance of human liberty, then we presumed that we had gained the favor of a new master (the Federal government), and had *earned* the right to claim his protection in the simple discharge of our rights and duties as common citizens.

REPUBLICAN PARTY UNTRUE:

What has been our experience? Twenty-seven years have come and gone since we were clothed with the rights of citizenship, by law, and endowed with all the privileges incident thereto, and yet, during this period, 10,091 Negroes have been shot down like dogs; skinned alive; hung to trees; or burned to stakes, without the interference of the federal government only in one instance. But we are told to be patient, to wait! Yes, wait! wait until the majority of our race are murdered, and possibly by that time public sentiment will be awakened sufficiently to force us to waft our way Bishop-Turner-ward, across the sea, or, more likely, into the middle of some *black sea.*[74]

But we must not talk thus plainly else we lay ourselves liable to the charge of indulging in fanaticism. We must not tell the whole *truth*, or we give license to our friends (?) to charge us with disloyalty to the party-politic that nobly championed our cause thirty, twenty-seven, twenty-four and twenty years ago. But, my fellow-negroes and fellow lovers of liberty, it is not what was nor what has been that we are now contending for. The past will never more return. The present and future demand our attention.

OUR CONDITION GROWS WORSE:

Were it not true that our condition in many of the states has grown alarmingly worse within the last three years, and especially within the last and present years, we might not be warranted in taking the steps we are now taking. But when we look over the records of the recent state legislative acts of Texas, Tennessee, Kentucky, Alabama, Arkansas, and other southern states, and see the legalized discriminations against us in direct violation of the federal constitution, and observe that not even the slightest emotion is aroused on the part of the present administration or the federal congress we are forced to convene ourselves together from time to time and swing high and far the tocsin of our ignoble, inhuman, Un-American treatment.[75] Within the last twelve months there have been more Negroes murdered single-handed, three to one, than in any previous year since 1872, even including the four years under Democratic rule. More states have passed discriminating laws against us during the last year than during all the years that have intervened since the reconstruction period. One state, within the last year, has practically disfranchised the negro. What does all this mean? Is it purely incidental, only accident; or does it prove that it is time for us to wake up and open our eyes, and view the situation as it is and not as we would it were?

THE MOST IMPORTANT ISSUE:

General J. S. Clarkson has said the most potent question before the American body politic to day, is the Negro problem, but the administration evidently differs from him and so does his party, according to the Minneapolis convention.[76]

We submit that protection to American industries is much needed, and we suggest that to protect the lives of American citizens upon American soil is equally needful. Observation and experience have taught us that a platform that declares for a free ballot and a fair count is as naked in accomplishments as a wired skeleton. It suggests to us the lesson of "Bricks without Straw."

DEMAND PROTECTION:

Protect the lives of the citizen, be he black or white, and the ballot will be cast with no uncertainty, and the count will be rendered accordingly. If the party that was once sacred to our race when led by [Abraham] Lincoln, [Ulysses S.] Grant, [Charles] Sumner, [Salmon] Chase, [William] Seward, [William] Garrison and [Wendell] Phillips is still sincere, why don't it stand by the cardinal principles of the original party founders, who advocated human equality before the law, who condemned "*State Rights*," and demanded protection for all of the citizens of the Union in all parts of the Union?

OUR OWN BLAME:

I am satisfied that our silence, as a race, and our blind political action have, to some extent, augmented our present deplorable condition in the south.

I wish to call the attention of every Negro and lover of liberty in the land to the excited interest of the federal congress, at this time manifested, on account of the recent conflict between the Carnegie strikers and Pinkerton men, which resulted in the killing of seventeen persons. No one deplores this situation worse than me, and I yield to no one in my contempt for the Pinkerton system, but it awakens new thoughts of surprise within us to note that congress is more concerned in the shooting of these seventeen people than in the killing of the whole 10,091 Negroes during the past 27 years, or the killing and burning at the stake of the 17 Negroes for alleged crime during the past nine months.

GOING TO LIBERIA:

Hundreds of Negroes are to day enroute to Liberia, many of whom are penniless and half naked, but they prefer a foreign home without money or raiment, if they may only [be] permitted to breathe the *pure* air of *liberty*, to their native American home, without protection to their lives. We appeal to the conscience of the world to pass judgment upon this situation.

TO EXTERMINATE THE NEGRO:

In the State of Alabama is found an organization known as the "Knights of the White Shield." The advertised object of this organization is to exterminate the Negro. Are we not forced then to organize for our own protection?

It is not the purpose of this organization to injure or aid any political party, for the writer has never cast a ballot only for Republican candidates, except twice in local elections, when my judgment led me to vote the People's Party ticket, of which I am neither ashamed nor sorry.

The time has come when the condition of our race in the south demands that every Negro in the north stand up to be counted with the race. We must strike at the root of the evil which threatens our existence and menaces our progress. We must hew to the line, let the chips fall where they may. Let us realize the fact that the welfare of our race and the lives of American citizens are paramount to the success of any political party. An enemy is an enemy and a friend is a friend, no matter what may be his political affiliation.

We denounce state rights and adhere to the supremacy of the Federal government. We heartily endorse the Federal constitution, and are forever ready to offer our lives for its defense. Under it we claim the rights of citizenship and demand protection to our lives. We appeal to the lovers of liberty everywhere and the American people especially, in whom we still have faith, to assist us in peacefully securing what the law of the land, as well as the divine law of God already accord us: *Equality before the law; protection to our lives.*

The National Colored Men's Protective Association of America will meet in national convention in the city of Indianapolis, Ind., September 22d, 1892, for the purpose of furthering these ends.

All friends of human liberty who sympathize with us in this effort for the protection of human life will be welcomed to our convention.

Respectfully submitted to the public.
GEO. E. TAYLOR,
Pres. National Colored Men's Protective Ass'n of America.
Oskaloosa, Iowa, July 14, 1892.[77]

At its annual meeting held in Indianapolis on 22 and 23 September 1892 the National Colored Men's Protective Association's members affirmed Taylor's position as president and endorsed his appeal, which included opposition to tariffs among other distinctly non-Republican issues.[78] "An Iowa delegate [C. C. Curtis] offered a resolution endorsing Grover Cleveland [Democratic presidential candidate], but that was rejected."[79] It was apparent at that meeting, however, that there remained significant divisions among those attending the conference, especially from Indiana's delegates, who were closely allied to the Republican Party and who believed the association to be taking a decidedly activist turn. Yet delegates from twenty state organizations were represented at the Indianapolis meeting, and they decided to expand the national association's activities by establishing committees and branches in each of the remaining states, envisioning the NCMPA as an alternative to the newly reconstituted National Afro-American League.[80] Effectively, however, the association had taken significant steps to shift its focus from discussion to political and social action upon supporting Taylor's appeal. Moreover, it had expanded its purpose to include issues important to southern blacks, thus entering an arena of activity far different from that experienced by most northern black activists.

It was at the eight-day Congress of Negroes (Congress of African Ethnology, Congress on Africa, or National Convention of Colored Men), which met in Chicago on 26 and 27 June 1893 as a part of the World's Columbian Exposition, however, where the National Colored Men's Protective Association made its full transformation and obtained its greatest national acceptance. The NCMPA's officers had originally planned to meet in St. Louis, but they changed the venue to Chicago, where the meeting would attract greater participation, especially from those visiting the Columbian Exposition, which had generated enormous national interest and controversy and which would attract blacks who otherwise might not have attended the conference.[81] There it acquired a formal constitution and received its official recognition within the community of black organizations, of which there were then several contending for memberships.[82] Forty states sent more than three hundred delegates, but nearly six hundred attended sessions. How these delegates were selected remains unclear, unless the call for the convention had been sent to all leagues or associations, of which there were many state-based groups at the time that contained the word "protective" in their titles. By that date, moreover, Fortune's reconstituted NAAL was no longer functioning as a viable forum at the national level, with even the *Indianapolis Freeman* asking whether it had died.[83] To the old leadership this new association represented an innovative forum led by a new voice, articulate and unencumbered by the scars of former battles among black activists. Refreshingly, Taylor was not one of them.

One of the convention's first resolutions, which defined the overly ambitious and non-party-specific objectives of the association's leaders, asked that "all the leagues, both state and national and every associations [*sic*] in this country to meet [with] the National Colored People's Protective Association of America and unite with them in the next annual session."[84] In effect, the association was following an inclusive organizational model put in place by the Union Labor Party at its Cincinnati conference in 1887. On the second day, Douglass made his appearance and addressed the convention, essentially giving his personal endorsement to this new forum and recognizing Taylor as an emerging voice within the nation's black community, despite Taylor's public exit from the Republican Party a year earlier and his spirited attack on that party in his "National Appeal."[85] Douglass's presence and brief speech alone were significant, for, even in his waning years, Douglass remained the titular head of America's black society, and he was still able to command respect and expect deference for his opinions.[86]

At this meeting, Taylor received his formal appointment as the association's president and interacted, likely for the first and perhaps the only time, with upper- and middle-class black intellectuals from the United States and England, all a precursor to his involvement with anti-imperialist sentiments then circulating in Africa and Europe.[87] The list of the NCMPA's newly elected officers included T. T. Allan of Louisiana, J. E. Knox of Arkansas, Ida B. Wells of New York, William H. Sinclair of South Carolina, and M. M. McCloud of Mississippi as vice presidents.[88] Indeed, southerners held six of the eleven association offices reported in the press. In his convention address President Taylor indicated his support for a plan of "negro colonization" inside the United States, a scheme he described as "perhaps the most feasible plan for bettering the condition of the colored people."[89] The conference passed resolutions condemning lynching and disenfranchisement efforts approved in southern states and the "'jim crow' car system," and it even debated the issue of Hawaiian annexation.[90] That meeting was a crucial platform for launching Taylor upon the national scene, for consolidating his reputation as a witty and gifted speaker and a contender for high office in a number of "colored" associations, and for confirming the association's credentials among a growing number of groups with similar objectives.[91]

Yet against that enthusiastic and impressive beginning the association apparently failed to deliver on its grand promises. No documented record of annual national conference proceedings or even of conference calls has been found, suggesting that the time was not yet right for such an organization to thrive at a national level. Nothing positive apparently resulted from a trip Taylor made through the South in 1894, a time when southern black Populists were reaching their peaks in influence through fusion with Republican state parties, but also when they were entering their most difficult period.[92] As a national forum for discussion, the association remained active until 1900, but it had changed its formal name to Colored People's National Protective Association (CPNPA) sometime between 1894 and 1896.[93] Perhaps it was simply too midwestern and too all-encompassing to be taken seriously.

These also were the years of the second Grover Cleveland administration (Democrat, 1893–97), a time when black Republicans who had obtained patronage positions during the Harrison administration (Republican, 1889–93) struggled to retain those posts, and a pause between the collapse of the reconstituted NAAL and its resurrection as the National Afro-American Council (NAAC) in 1898. During that interim, women formed both the National League of Colored Women and the National Federation of Afro-American Women, which soon merged to form the National Association of Colored Women (NACW), partly because of their voiced perception that black men had been unable and unwilling to provide the NAAL with effective leadership.[94] In 1895 the National Federation of Colored Men was organized to fill the vacuum following the collapse of the NAAL. It initially sought to address the question of black workers in trade unions. Within a year, however, that federation had shifted its emphasis to the persistent problem of lynching and, while professing nonpartisanship, sought to bring changes in the Republican Party's platform that would protect black citizens from mob violence.

These also were years when Booker T. Washington, principal of Tuskegee Normal and Industrial Institute in Alabama, captured the imagination of blacks who were witnessing violence in the South and accelerating attacks on

Booker T. Washington, principal of the Tuskegee Institute. Penn, *Afro-American Press.*

civil rights and were searching for solutions. Frederick Douglass had died in February 1895, and no national leader had emerged to take his place. Washington believed that much of white rage against blacks in the South had been caused by the surge in "radical" black Populism and a belief by many whites that Populist success in the South of whatever color would result inevitably in a second Reconstruction.[95] Even Charles Taylor, who was president of the

National Negro Democratic League in 1894, warned Alabama's black voters that the collapse of the Republican Party in that state had "left the colored voter with the option of either assimilating with the more conservative element of the Democratic Party or with the untrustworthy and dangerous Populist Party."[96] In a September 1895 speech at the Atlanta Exposition Washington asked blacks to set aside the nation's pledge of integration and social and economic equality temporarily and to focus instead upon self-improvement and do so through industrial education. Washington's speech essentially incorporated Taylor's midwestern values of bootstraps uplift but without the political agitation that Taylor brought from the workingmen's movement and that had become such a crucial part of southern black Populism. It also avoided the focus on education of a leadership class still promoted by most northeastern black activists. And it became enormously popular among white philanthropists who sought a black leader who would promise gradual improvement while accepting the status quo. Through their generous financial support Washington was able to build a crucial newspaper base from which to promote his vision of racial progress.

From mid-1896, and with the collapse of southern Populism and a major victory for the Republican Party at the national level later in that year, there were increasing indications that the NAAL might be revived, for most black intellectuals were not participants in these new groups. None called for joining the Colored People's National Protective Association, perhaps an indication that, although it survived as late as 1900, it and its leadership model were not acceptable.[97] Calvin Chase of the *Washington Bee* was the first to insist that either the NAAL be revived or that an entirely new forum be devised. Fortune eventually agreed, but only after repeated pleas from scores of powerful black voices.[98] Had the CPNPA/NCMPA survived during this period as a viable alternative forum, some discussion of its potential use and Taylor's role in it would have occurred in the eastern black press; that it wasn't mentioned suggests that it no longer operated as a functioning option at the national level. Or it may have remained active only at the regional level, primarily in the Midwest. Perhaps it was what the *Colored American* in 1898 had classified as one of the "popgun movements" or "flashes in the pan" and nothing worth discussing.[99]

But there also was uncertainty that Taylor's NCMPA even existed after 1896, despite Taylor's announcement in 1899 through the press that he was still its president. The confusion surrounds the formation of the Negro National Protective Association in Washington, D.C., in May 1897. In his biography of George Washington Murray, John Marszalek describes a vacuum of leadership between the collapse of the NAAL in 1892 and the formation of the NAAC in

1898. Taylor's association would have filled that vacuum, but apparently that had not happened. Marszalek characterized the new Washington-based association as a "shadowy organization" whose leadership list held powerful names. T. Thomas Fortune of New York and John Mitchell, Jr., of Richmond "promulgated its philosophy," and Calvin Chase was "favorable."[100] A constitution was adopted for the National Racial Protective Association in late 1898, but by the end of 1899 that organization also had vanished.[101]

At the state level Taylor's association achieved notable success. Within Iowa, where Taylor was most focused and most active, the Afro-American League of Iowa (AALI) had already been formed in Keokuk in 1890, but that league was as ineffective as the NAAL, which it was designed to represent at the state level, and by 1893 it had basically disappeared.[102] And in March 1893, even before the NCMPA convened in Chicago during the Columbian Exposition, 111 delegates representing local "protective" groups had met in Des Moines to form the Afro-American Protective Association of Iowa (AAPAI), with a "new [but short-lived] black newspaper, the *Weekly Avalanche*" of Des Moines, designated as one of its official organs. The AAPAI elected T. L. Smith of Keokuk as its first president; Smith also happened to have been the founder of the AALI.[103] By the time of its second meeting in Ottumwa in July 1894, protective association units had been formed in most towns with black residents. At the 1894 meeting, which was essentially the first for a fully constituted state body, the association decided that persons should not hold similar offices at both the state and national levels, that the newly established *Iowa State Bystander* would be invited to become "one of the official organs" of the association, and that the association would endorse the "work of Ida B. Wells" with respect to antilynching proposals. But the association went further. It endorsed the nonpartisan and "protective" principles of the NCMPA as well as "actions of the [Iowa] colored miners" and "[law]suits brought by R. N. Hyde of Des Moines, under the civil rights law."[104] Taylor participated actively in this second meeting and delivered a detailed report on Iowa's black population in which he outlined his own philosophy regarding black workers. Taylor suggested that black youths should avoid the unskilled labor of domestic, hotel, and restaurant service and instead should complete high school education and attend college if possible. He emphasized that agriculture was a promising sector of black economic advancement in Iowa. Taylor was reelected as the association's "statistician," the only listed officer charged to deal with foundational issues affecting the group.[105] Within a few days Charles Ruff, then editor of the *Iowa State Bystander*, accepted the association's invitation and designated his newspaper as an official organ of the association.

The friendly interaction between Taylor and Ruff, the latter a Republican and outspoken and caustic editor, was short-lived. Taylor was a Democrat, and he was as eager to espouse Democratic principles in a weekly newspaper, the *Negro Solicitor* of Oskaloosa, which he started to publish in February 1893, as was Ruff to champion Republican ones in the *Bystander*.[106] Taylor made four missteps in 1894 and 1895 that infuriated Ruff and led to a series of articles in the *Bystander* that damaged Taylor's reputation as a nonpartisan and reasoned leader at both the state and national levels. Unfortunately, only one side of these debates survives, and that was through the editorials written by Ruff in the *Bystander*; no issues of the *Negro Solicitor* have survived. The first was Taylor's accusation that Republicans were "buying up the Negro churches, body and soul," certainly an unwise choice of words to describe the reality that the black church was a center of social and political action at the local level and that most black ministers supported the Republican Party. Ruff asked Taylor to provide proof for his charge and accused Taylor of being paid by the Democrats to attack the black church. Taylor accepted Ruff's challenge and replied, but Ruff refused to publish Taylor's letter, describing it as written in "the language and manners of a blackguard [scoundrel] and a street gamin [street urchin]," and he invited "newspaper men in and out of the state, Democratic and Republican," to distance themselves from Taylor's "empty" and offensive rhetoric.[107] Taylor in turn described Ruff as the "vile, untutored individual who furnishes the editorial reading matter" for the *Bystander*.[108]

Once having entered a period of editorial warfare, and Taylor now being coined the "'Mitey' Mahaska Editor" and the *Negro Solicitor* the "moribund Oskaloosa sheet," editorials took a turn for the worse. At one point Taylor apparently had described Ida Wells as a "young Afro-American adventuress" and "insinuated" that her efforts to stop lynching in the South had been "fruitless," both of which were true but perhaps again an unfortunate choice of words. Ruff demanded a retraction, stating bluntly: "There is not a paper in the entire north that has not treated Miss Wells with respect and serious consideration, with the exception of the Oskaloosa sheet." He suggested that Taylor "pray three times a day for a restoration of conscience."[109]

A third issue of contention was Taylor's editorial endorsements of white candidates over black ones, especially if the latter were Republicans. Ruff believed that black papers should support black candidates regardless of party affiliation, but nearly all black candidates happened to be Republicans, which made that choice much easier in Ruff's case. In March 1895 Taylor ran for the office of city clerk in Oskaloosa, and he did not endorse the candidacy of blacks in Iowa's Mahaska County who were seeking other offices on the Republican ticket. Ruff's attack was withering: "He is for Taylor first and last and all the time, and Taylor only."[110] And he continued, accusing Taylor of sponsoring a "Sunday [train] excursion" to Burlington, Iowa, having supplied participants with "fifty cases of beer" and a "red-hot 'crap' game in one of the cars." Ruff concluded: "It is indeed sad to think of the hosts of friends who have wished for many a day that George would get a better paying situation."[111] Obviously, sarcasm was a popular tool of editors in those days.

Still, Ruff continued to publish announcements and reports about the AAPAI's activities, perhaps only because he was president of the association's Des Moines branch and gave that group significant press exposure. Nearly two full newspaper pages covered the state association's July 1895 convention in Des Moines. Taylor played a prominent role in that meeting, demonstrating clearly that he had used his office as statistician to provide direction to the association and its deliberations. Ruff, however, demonstrated the influence of his own pen and newspaper by noting that there were "many in the convention who opposed everything Taylor presented on the simple ground of origin and not because it was wrong. To a few delegates a motion or resolution by Taylor was a red flag."[112] But at the same time Ruff praised Taylor as an excellent organizer and expediter. Fortunately for Taylor and his own future in nonpartisan efforts, Ruff sold the *Bystander* in July 1896, and the newspaper's new editor, John Cay Thompson, was interested in transforming the *Bystander* into a more temperate voice for change, even though he and the *Bystander* remained rigidly Republican.[113]

If those activities were not sufficient to occupy Taylor's attention, he also was a highly sought-after and entertaining speaker at Emancipation Day celebrations throughout the state and was active within Iowa's Prince Hall (Colored) United Grand Lodge (AF&AM), obtained the status of a thirty-third-degree Mason, and in late December 1900 represented the Iowa United Grand Lodge at the national Masonic convention held in Jacksonville, Florida.[114] He also was deeply involved with the Knights of Pythias (Colored), and he served as Iowa's state grand chancellor between 1895 and 1900.[115] In August 1897 he chaired the Supreme Lodge of the Knights of Pythias in Columbus, Ohio, and in October 1899 that of the Supreme Lodge held in Richmond, Virginia. In Richmond he became known to John Mitchell, Jr., editor of the *Richmond Planet*, for his elaborate wardrobe.[116]

Black fraternal organizations such as the Masons and the Knights of Pythias generally served more functions than did their white equivalents, and their hierarchies were considerably more complicated. In the Midwest, Prince Hall Masonry was the more exclusive of the two, while the Knights of Pythias was open to nearly any person who could afford its fees and dues.[117] Both provided benefits to their members. These might include protections "against poverty and other misfortunes"; death, illness, and burial benefits; a communal and group structure; political representations; and respectability, social capital, self-worth, and racial pride.[118] But perhaps more importantly, fraternal organizations were significant venues for creating friendships, engaging in social and political networks, and grooming leadership skills. These associations also championed manhood, group membership, racial identity, and self-esteem, all items in short supply for black males during this period.[119] But even Taylor's agency within Iowa's fraternal organization was not without controversy. In 1897 he was accused of usurping the role of Iowa's "organizer" within the Knights, which meant that he had collected dues or fees and had not shared them with Rev. J. W. King, who claimed that he should have received income from dues.[120]

Taylor also involved himself in an alternative business venture in 1897 when he and George H. Woodson, a lawyer and Republican activist from Muchakinock near Oskaloosa and president of Iowa's Afro-American Council after 1898, incorporated the American Negro Industrial and Commercial Incorporation, which would be centered at Oskaloosa and was expected to raise $125,000 in capital stock from shares sold at $25 each. This cooperative enterprise intended to provide working capital for blacks through loans and joint investments, and it was to be governed by a committee composed of Woodson, Taylor, L. A. Wills, and F. P. Davis, all of Oskaloosa.[121] In effect, this business venture incorporated the best of self-help and uplift advocated by the Tuskegee Machine and satisfied the objectives of both the NAAL/NAAC and the NCMPA/CPNPA. This was the only known example of Taylor's extension into investment enterprises. Yet even this was one that expected to expand opportunities within the black community by extending credit.

Most of Taylor's activity within Iowa's African American community was nonpartisan, at least as it related to interactions within Iowa's Afro-American League and Council and the state branch of the Afro-American Protective Association. By 1897 these included advocacy of issues relating to equal access to credit; proportionate black representation in jury pools; school integration and increasing calls within both the white and black communities for schools specifically established for blacks; equal protection at the worksite; and opportunities for governmental appointments at local, state, and federal levels based on the percentage of blacks within local and national populations. These associations also advocated equal treatment and equal pay in the workplace, an issue then being addressed only by women's groups.[122] But overwhelmingly, the issue of protection of civil voting rights and acts of violence against blacks in the South and increasingly in border and northern states became a major focus for these nonpartisan groups.

Similarly, the major question was the matter of which national party best would listen to black concerns and act positively upon them and whether blacks should assume an activist course to accomplish those aims. At both the state and national levels the Afro-American League and its successor, the Afro-American Council, as well as its state affiliates had sought after 1898 to provide black Americans with that single focus. Increasingly, however, confusion arose from competing agendas within the national council, and that group turned into little more than a dysfunctional debating society. Its members advocated either accommodation and firm attachment to the Republican Party or aggressive action to support civil and economic rights with a willingness to accept alternative political affiliations if necessary.[123] In the latter instance all parties were worth considering, although the Republican Party remained the choice of a vast majority of black voters based on voting patterns and on Frederick Douglass's earlier observation that the "Republican party is the deck; all else is the sea."[124]

4

Taylor as
the National Democrat

Black and Equal

Mr. Taylor is the coming Fred Douglass of America, but with very different political attachments, and Iowa democracy is proud of him.

Taylor County Democrat,
27 July 1893

While Taylor had abandoned the Republican Party in 1892, it is less clear at what precise point he moved completely to the Democratic camp, although a later account reported that he campaigned vigorously for the Grover Cleveland/Adlai Stevenson ticket within the states of Illinois, Indiana, Ohio, and Iowa during the 1892 election.[1] Taylor also had participated in a camp rally in Ottumwa in August 1892, at which time he reportedly told his audience that "if Jeff Davis were alive, he, Taylor, would rather vote for him for the office of president than for Benjamin Harrison," the Republican candidate for president.[2] Taylor's firm conversion to Democracy, however, likely had come after he issued his "National Appeal" late in 1892 and certainly before he began publication of the *Negro Solicitor* in February 1893, for his first issue's header had proclaimed it a Democratic weekly. Frederick Douglass, Bishop Alexander Walters, and Bishop Henry McNeal Turner had already indicated serious dissatisfaction with the Republicans by that date, and others similarly frustrated with Republican inaction were moving in the same direction, although Douglass never formally ended his affiliation with the party.[3] Taylor's shifts from Workingmen and Farmer to People's to Union Labor and then to Republican by the time he moved from Wisconsin had represented significant and speedy changes of thinking, but his spirited attacks on Democrats in Wisconsin had been based on his belief in 1887 that the Wisconsin party was unrepresentative of workers' interests and that actions taken there by certain Democratic officials in 1889 and 1890 had made it impossible for him to support that state's Democratic Party.

Taylor's affiliation with the national Democratic Party was reasonable, since Democrats in much of the North tended to champion issues important to workers and farmers more than did Republicans. Stated simply, his dilemma in 1893 was the fact that most black intellectuals and black voters were Republicans, and many black leaders advocated caution and gradualism with respect to progress. Most black leaders opposed organizations that aggressively promoted black political action or third-party involvement, especially at a time when southern white Democrats (and some southern Republicans) were insistently advancing "lily-white" programs to limit black voting and civil rights within their states—with the actual possibility that similar sentiments might creep northward.[4] In 1892 and 1893 Taylor apparently considered that those issues could be addressed best from inside the Democratic Party rather than through separate organizations that might challenge Democrats at the polls. Many believed, however, that if black voters were less linked to the Republican Party, both parties would become more interested in issues important to black voters and blacks might be recognized for the "balance of power"—leverage—they were capable of delivering.[5] But there also were those who believed that the 1890s represented a decade of serious and possible reform that might only be obtained through victory of a third party.[6]

After 1890 Taylor detached himself from Populist alliances and labor currents sweeping the Midwest and South and after 1892 allied himself enthusiastically to the Democratic Party, which was making a particular effort to attract black voters in the North while doing little to oppose disenfranchisement efforts in the South.[7] At the state level he became sufficiently active within the party to be chosen an unofficial Iowa delegate to the 1896 Chicago national party convention, although Taylor's involvement at that convention could not be confirmed in any official party document.[8] By that date, his newspaper, as the only black-edited Democratic paper in the state, had improved his name recognition, as had his early leadership role in Iowa's branch of the AAPAI (Iowa's branch of the Colored People's National Protective Association). His activities in Iowa's Knights of Pythias (Colored) identified him as prominent and influential within Iowa's "colored" fraternal circles, an important consideration in the upper Midwest at the time. Taylor also was an entertaining lecturer and traveled widely and often within the state. At the national level, by 1896 he also had become a prominent voice in the National Negro Democratic League (NNDL).[9]

Taylor's role in the NNDL before 1896 is unclear. Assuming, however, that reports of his attending the national party's 1896 convention in Chicago as an unlisted delegate are correct and that he was active there in promoting the league's agenda once among the delegates, his presence and activities would have improved his stature within associations affiliated with the party. Perhaps his campaigning for Cleveland after leaving the Republican Party in 1892 had demonstrated his commitment to "Democracy" and amplified his potential role within the league. In 1896, moreover, while Iowa's listed delegates had followed the time-honored practice of placing in nomination the name of Iowa's Democratic ex-governor, Horace Boies, who indeed was a viable candidate for that office, Taylor had championed the candidacy of William Jennings Bryan of Kansas instead. It is doubtful, as was later claimed, that Taylor seconded Bryan's nomination, especially if that were to imply a speech on the convention's floor.[10] Whatever the circumstances of that convention, Taylor by 1896 had reached a new level of accomplishment in his political career. To a degree Taylor had replicated the success and national recognition that he had gained in 1887 at the Union Labor convention in Cincinnati when he had shared the stage with Henry George.

Taylor campaigned vigorously for Bryan in black communities in eastern and midwestern states and produced a celebrated and provocative broadside on what would become his favorite topic for the next decade. It asked the rhetorical question: Why should blacks trust Republicans to support their interests? It answered the question by suggesting that blacks consider supporting another ticket, in this case led by William Jennings Bryan, who personally championed issues that were better for blacks' immediate economic needs. In his 1896 "National Appeal," Taylor criticized both parties for abandoning civil rights protection and "OUR CAUSE," but he asked his readers to lose their dependency on one or both parties and act independently by voting their own selfish interests and stated bluntly that the days of "my father Abraham [Lincoln]" were long past, if not forgotten. For Taylor, the primary issues in 1896 were economic. In language similar to that used by Henry George and T. Thomas Fortune, Taylor returned directly to his labor and Populist rhetoric, appealing to "my fellow working man, or my farmer friend" and "coal miner," to "sweat" and the unending struggle of "Capital vs. Labor," and finally to basic necessities of food and clothing. He challenged his readers to "Boldly stand up" and vote for issues that supported their own needs, no matter the cost or party. And rhetorically Taylor asked how either gold or silver, or protective tariffs, or labor lockouts could possibly help African Americans improve their own lives. He promised blacks that they could exercise leverage and obtain influence only through votes, but he also cautioned that rewards would be small if those votes were lost to Bryan's opponent. Inherent in his broadside was the serious proposition that blacks could lose their dependency only by acting pragmatically and selfishly, and, if necessary, either independently or as a separate group. And he asked them to reconsider their obligations to the past.

NATIONAL APPEAL TO THE AMERICAN NEGRO: "Why we should favor the Chicago Platform."

By Geo. E. Taylor,
Oskaloosa, Iowa.

In addressing this appeal to the Negroes of the Country, I do not wish to establish the conclusion that the argument herein, is not equally applicable to all races, whose conditions of servitude and position in the industrial and commercial realms are similar to ours; but I address myself thus, that my fellow Negro, may realize and appreciate, that the political, economic, financial, industrial and commercial questions of the hour, appeal to his considerate study and demand his most reasonable calculations; not from the standpoint of Negro—Partisan—Political logic, but upon the broad gauged scale of our common American citizenship; of our national interest in the mighty questions political, which enter into the life or death, the prosperity or stagnation of the commercial and industrial fabric of this, our common country.

It were well, perhaps, if the suggestions here made, were placed before the millions of other men, who, like the Negro, must toil for food and raiment.

For the first time in the history of our citizenship, fellow Negroes, are we confronted in a National campaign with issues that cannot be construed, as purely, strictly, partisan.

For the first time in the history of our citizenship, do we find the democratic platform declaring for measures which point more directly in the line of advantage to our race, than does that of the republican party.

Without consuming time to discuss this point, I simply direct you to a careful study of both platforms, for the proof of my propositions.

NEGROES TURNED DOWN.

Surely, you will bear out the truth of this remark: The experience of the Negro delegates to the St. Louis [Republican National] convention (I do not refer to the hotel catastrophe) who were among contested delegations, the wholesale turning down of Negro National Committeemen, and the absolute disregard for all of the great men of the race, such as the honorables: Jno. R. Lynch, B. K. Bruce, J. M. Langston, P. B. S. Pinchback, N. W. Cuney, Wm. Pledger, Perry Carson, and a hundred others of almost equal prominence, in itself, argue to you and to me, that a new era has dawned upon the once "grand old party" and that the "first born," (the Negro) is nearly, if not altogether forgotten.[11]

Indeed my fellow Negro, it is as clear to me as the evening star upon a bright moon-light winters night, that, the day has already passed into history, never more to return, when any political party shall especially espouse OUR CAUSE.

WE, MUST BE MEN.

And, I am satisfied, that it is thus. It is but the sequel to our progress, our development, and our prosperity. For we shall soon (if not already) find ourselves compelled to burst the traditional bands of partisanship and make a common survey of the political forest, using the same stakes, the same chains and the same blue pencils that the dominant races have used since the establishment of the government. . . .

CAPITAL VS. LABOR.

The sceptre of the king and the muscle of the common folk, have usually been discernible in party platforms, but the gildings, the trimmings, the silver edges and the gold linings, have generally been so deftly and artistically blended, that you nor I, could adequately comprehend the real meaning of the platforms, until the manipulators placed such constructions upon them as suited their own exalted end.

Since the days of Abraham Lincoln, and before, the great political issue (though adroitly covered up) in this country has been "Capital vs. Labor."

Today we have the same issue, in an intensified, magnified sense. Is it hard for you to decide, my fellow Negro, or my fellow workingman, or my farmer friend, upon which side of this controversy rests your interests.

The glittering hand of the gold King (the capitalist) has for thirty years fanned the frying brow of the laborer of the land and wiped away the streams of sweat with the kerchief of "promise," or the napkin of fancied "hope," until at last; perseverance and patience have reluctantly weakened and the climax is now upon us.

Hence, we find the millionaire, the capitalist, the bond holder, the banker, the money gambler, the stock exchange broker, with a few conscientious, exceptions, all arrayed in battle, attire, and stationed upon the highland of international recognition,(?) proclaiming their unswerving allegiance to the present single gold standard.

They swear by the St. Louis platform. Why? Because they had that platform made to order;—made to their order, not made to the order of the republican party hosts, but made to the order of the manipulators, the gold barons of the land, who either import royal dukes or princes to marry their daughters, or export their sons and daughters to Europe that they may marry into the royalty and thus perpetuate their golden heirloom. . . .

A Tribute to Lincoln.

Since you and I were made free men by the voice of God, transmitted by father Abraham, to what period are we compelled to go back, to reckon the beginning of panics, industrial discord, financial convulsions, strikes, lockouts, boycotts, etc. History compels you to answer, "1873." What occurred about that period? The demonetization of silver. What followed? Armies of tramps, destitution, starvation upon the one hand, and millionaires upon the other.

Is it not true that the same has been the role, with occasional variations, until the present day? There is but one answer: "Yes."

Can you, my fellow Negro, reason out any objections that you should make to the remonetization, or the liberation of silver?

Can you answer to your own satisfaction, "Why should gold be king and silver slave?" Are you afraid that silver will drive from your pocket book the gold that you now posses[s]?

I urge you to candidly discuss, study, investigate and search out these propositions, which are the meat, the bread, the water and the clothes of the present campaign. Take them home with you and I am satisfied that you will conclude, that the Chicago [Democratic Party] platform declarations are the sentiments of the masses, the common people, in which case there is but one thing to do; support the platform and candidates who represent your principles.

Boldly stand up for liberty and freedom, free coinage of silver and gold, and prosperity. I am enthusiastically constrained, to urge the support of Bryan and Sewall for president and vice-president, believing that they come nearer representing the ideas of the people on the great issues of the day than do the other candidates. . . .

Lincoln's Principles Forgotten.

For the first time since the death of Abraham Lincoln do we find the republican national platform as silent as an untouched dumb-bell on the Negro question.

Does not this silence disturb you to some degree, my fellow Negro?

Is it not clear to you that by leaving you out, a strong appeal is made to that element who have always ignored and despised you?

Because of this silence are not the southern gold bug sugar planter, cotton raiser, and capitalist found flocking in great armies to the support of this platform and McKinley?

Can you refrain from noticing the unusual effort on the part of the republican managers to capture the votes of the southerners?

To fully comprehend the attitude of the republicans at this time toward us it is only necessary to read the platform and study the McKinley speech of acceptance. Read, and read between the lines. . . .

Negroes Don't Share Protection.

We are not so dumb or so poorly advised but that we know that nearly every factory or work-shop in which protected articles are manufactured keeps a padlock on their doors against the entrance of Negro labor. Then where is the benefit to the Negro resulting from this protective tariff policy? . . .

Work Out Our Own Salvation.

Every man is an artist and is destined to hew out his own course in life.

We must learn the lesson of true manliness, which cannot be construed to rest upon "dependence."

Would we reach the highest mark in life as men and citizens we must do our own reading, our own thinking, our own acting.

The education of our fathers will not serve us. The clothes our fathers wore will not fit us now. The reputations our fathers bore for truth and veracity will not serve as our recommendation.

The huts in which our fathers lived and reared large families we find to be too small for the accommodation of our families.

The obligations of our fathers are not our obligations.

The contracts we are making our fathers will not be called upon to fill, and the political contracts of our fathers were all fully kept by them.

If we are in fact free men then let us exercise that freedom as our minds may dictate without feeling in any wise obligated by the history of thirty years ago.

It is impossible for us to succeed in carrying out the program of Lincoln and Sumner when there is no party today that adopts such a program. . . .

We now have the new man, the new woman, the new political methods, the new republicanism, the new Democracy.

We are under special obligations to *none*. Our main political duty, our whole duty, our only (political) duty is to strive to serve our country's highest and best interest and promote the welfare of the sovereign people by our political actions, to the best of our ability, as "God gives us to see the right."

By so doing we will serve well our individual interests and prove our worthiness to the title, "American Citizen." . . .

I am, Very respectfully, Geo. E. Taylor. Oskaloosa, Ia., Sept. 21, 1896.[12]

Taylor's was a new and refreshing voice in the party, and it spoke to the "common folk" in terms they understood. This broadside is significant in another sense, however. In it Taylor demonstrated a unique ability to connect working-class issues with those confronting the vast majority of black voters. It demonstrated a unique and unusual ability to mix the rhetoric of labor and Populism with that of Washingtonian "uplift" and individual responsibility. Taylor was not afraid to suggest that a literacy test might be useful for all citizens and, in effect, nearly endorsed some laws being passed in the South. This broadside also confirmed that Taylor had acquired useful skills in avoiding troublesome topics and turning an argument to serve his purposes. While his 1892 "National Appeal," which came after the Republican Party had rejected his recommendations, had attacked the Republican Party directly for advocating patience—"Wait!"—and trust in the party and its platform, his 1896 "National Appeal" suggested positive steps for reaching independence and separate action. While "alleged friends (white)" had suggested "wait" as answers to questions in 1892, Taylor by 1896 was no longer willing to delay for either party.

A decade had seen Taylor shifting thoughtfully from Union Labor to Republican and then Democratic, with a bit of Populism in the middle. His rhetoric also shifted from a personal stand in which race was a minor part of the problem to one in which race was the sole problem. He had moved from labor agitator to veteran black activist. He had shifted from "protection" as a defense against the excesses of owners of capital, to a position in which "protection" had gradually become an agency in safeguarding civil rights, and by 1896 to advocacy of economic interests in the form of voting for personal and group rewards. And Taylor may have understood that numbers of votes alone would not compensate for the fact that the white-dominated labor movement almost universally had a low opinion of black workers and of federal efforts to give blacks "special favorite" treatment and that they easily might fuse to oppose blacks in good times as well as bad. Others within the black community had a historical memory that indicated that another and potentially more effective method for securing protections involved litigation in the courts, where civil rights needed to be defended against those who sought to change definitions and degrees of application of laws. That approach was working throughout the upper Midwest by the mid-1890s. Taylor, like his mentor, Pomeroy, was willing to reconsider with changing conditions and adjust his language and message as necessary, but, also like Pomeroy, he tended to rely too tightly and too long upon a narrow path. By 1896 Taylor's motto had become "An enemy is an enemy and a friend is a friend," only slightly different from Pomeroy's "No one wounds me with impunity."[13]

Bryan's defeat in November 1896 was a disappointment, but that loss did not stop Taylor from remaining involved in nationwide and regional black intellectual and political communities, especially regarding economic issues. For some black activists, 1896 was the nadir of black influence in America's political history, and as the old guard vanished or retired, new leadership emerged from a direction far different from what had been followed before. If anything, however, Taylor's "National Appeal" of 1896 and his new-found name recognition only fueled his ambition and dedication to "OUR CAUSE," which to Taylor was economic, "the paramount problem of the age."[14] This was a period of enormous retreat for blacks in the South, but it also was one of increasing clarity regarding the national platforms and economic agendas of both established parties. Indeed, by the end of 1896 Taylor had become vice president of a newly organized group known as the Negro National Free Silver League of America, whose purpose was to expand the nation's money supply during a period of economic recession. That league advanced the position that he and many black Democrats held, especially those with Greenback, labor, and Populist backgrounds. In Taylor's case that meant returning to the approach of his mentor, Pomeroy of La Crosse, who had been a one-time leader of the Greenback Party, and to Schilling of Milwaukee, who had been an active Greenbacker before converting to full-time labor activist. To them, easy money was good for farmers and workers, and poor blacks shared that condition. To Taylor, all poor blacks were working class. Taylor was to become the free silver league's president in August 1897.[15]

Taylor's activities supporting the minting of coins in both gold and silver and opposing the exclusive gold standard were extensive from 1896 to 1900 as well. From 27 to 29 July 1897 a conference of prominent black bimetallists from the midwestern states of Illinois, Missouri, Kansas, Nebraska, and Iowa met in Oskaloosa, planning to establish an organization that would circulate information in an interstate region and include all northern midwestern states. Indications were strong that support would be forthcoming from Minnesota, Wisconsin, Michigan, Ohio, and Indiana. Taylor received letters of endorsement from William T. Scott of Cairo, then president of the Negro Silver League of Illinois; Harry Graham, president of the Missouri Negro Free Silver League; Fredrick McGhee of St. Paul, who had left the Republican Party in 1893; and William Jennings Bryan, former candidate for president.[16] This organization, to be known as the Negro Inter-State Free Silver League, planned its inaugural conference to be held in Quincy, Illinois, for 25 and 26 August, at which time formal articles of organization would be adopted and proclamations would be distributed to explain the league's purposes and reasons why blacks should not blindly follow the Republican Party. Taylor as acting president issued a call for the first regional conference.[17]

That meeting occurred as scheduled and was well reported in Quincy's newspapers.[18] The *Quincy Morning Whig* sarcastically tagged Taylor as the "Oskaloosa free silver Moses" who intended to lead blacks to a Promised Land and away from the Republican Party.[19] Taylor envisioned this association as having two primary purposes. Its short-term objective was to provide a forum for discussion among leaders within the midwestern region. A single constitution would be established, and all state-based groups would use the same constitution or articles of operation; Taylor was an excellent organizer. Clearly, the plan was to have branches in all midwestern states before the 1900 campaign season, and all of these branches would engage in education to inform blacks of economic issues confronting them. Taylor suggested that the league faced two battles in the interim: "One is with the white republicans, who consider that all negro votes belong to them. The other is with the white democrats, who doubt the sincerity of the negro who would break away from the republican ranks."[20] Taylor's answer to this dilemma was to "organize and maintain our organization among ourselves," effectively declaring its independence from all parties.[21] For Taylor the basic issue in 1897 was economic in nature, and only blacks could be expected to protect black interests. Taylor was convinced that free silver would open a vast money supply and ease the burden on the working class: "We don't need any but actual workingmen to fight this workingmen's cause." But Taylor also acknowledged in 1897 that "the word 'democrat' is a hateful word to the negro, just as the word 'republican' is a blissful one to him."[22] Still, he believed it possible to educate America's blacks to accept the Democratic Party as a friend and ally. At the end of the conference, officers were elected to supervise organizational work in various midwestern states, and Oskaloosa was designated as the regional league's headquarters.[23]

In that and the next year, Taylor also consolidated his positions as the president of what remained of the Colored People's National Protective Association and as secretary (1898–1900) and then president (1900–1904) of the National Negro Democratic League.[24] Between 1896 and 1900, moreover, the National Negro Democratic League received nominal recognition within the Democratic Party and became, without fanfare, the Negro Bureau within its national party structure, even though the national party did nothing to oppose acts of violence against blacks in southern states or to control its southern-affiliated parties. James A. Ross's rival Democratic league meanwhile had fused with the NNDL. Federal officials and court decisions emanating from Washington seemed only to codify attempts to separate the races through the common-law maxim of "states' rights," which enabled states to develop statutes to protect "public safety" and, as long as facilities for whites and blacks were considered to be equal, provisions of the Fourteenth Amendment had not been violated. This policy essentially established the doctrine of "separate but equal," whether that pertained to a streetcar, a drinking fountain, a lunch counter, a school, or a park bench.[25]

During that same period, numerous bipartisan but predominantly Democratic anti-imperialist leagues developed nationwide, and many black leaders who opposed territorial expansion either joined these groups or affiliated with them through separate race-specific bodies. These organizations opposed American imperialism during the Spanish-American War of 1898 and became even more agitated when it became evident that America's enthusiasm for liberating "colored brothers" or "colored Filipino cousins" in Cuba, Puerto Rico, or the Philippines was rooted in a paternalistic attitude that denied those being liberated the right or even the ability to govern.[26] Many African American intellectuals interpreted such notions as little different from those held by most white southerners, and they rejected that attitude outright, for to do otherwise would challenge fundamentals guaranteed to America's black citizens in amendments to the Constitution. In July 1899 a group met in Chicago to form the bipartisan Colored National Anti-Imperialist League, but that group floundered until it joined forces with Col. William T. Scott, who had moved from Cairo to East St. Louis, Illinois, and Louisiana ex–state senator T. B. Stamps to form a nonpartisan (but largely Democratic) National Negro Anti-Expansion, Anti-Imperialist, Anti-Trust, and Anti-Lynching League.[27] Scott was elected president of this redesigned league, and Taylor was one of twenty-two members of its executive committee.[28]

How Taylor was able to play an energetic role in these national bodies, travel long distances to participate in political campaigns, and recruit memberships that were important if such societies were to survive and grow is difficult to comprehend, especially when he also maintained an active social, commercial, and political life within Iowa. This was not a time when one could travel easily to a destination, deliver a speech, and return to one's base in a matter of days, unless one's base was located near major lines of transportation. Associations tended to meet often, which meant that Taylor spent considerable time traveling and arranging meetings, especially while he maintained a leadership role in so many. Fortunately, Oskaloosa and nearby Ottumwa and Albia in Iowa were located alongside railroad lines that led northward to St. Paul and eastward directly to Chicago, the latter the major hub of railroad travel in the Midwest.[29]

Taylor returned often to Oskaloosa, nevertheless, at least enough to have left a significant mark there as well. He married Cora E. Cooper Buckner on 25 August 1894.[30] Cora was fifteen years younger than Taylor, "well educated and . . . handsome," and had been married before, and she brought a child to her marriage with Taylor.[31] She also was a gifted typist, a skill that was only then gaining popularity. She worked actively as coeditor of the *Negro Solicitor*, wrote editorials (only one of which survives), and gave Taylor's newspaper continuity during his frequent absences on the lecture circuit or when he was involved in organizational or political work outside Oskaloosa.[32] But Taylor also was a resident of Oskaloosa. The *Waterloo Daily Courier*, for example, reported in

William T. Scott, editor of the *Cairo Gazette*. Penn, *Afro-American Press*.

August 1896 that Taylor "fell from the top of his office building while repairing a skylight" and "was severely injured."[33] The articles and editorials he and his wife published in the *Negro Solicitor* were reprinted in other papers.[34] Taylor's editorial, republished by the weekly Democratic *Broad Ax* of Salt Lake City in April 1898, demonstrates a writing style and a tenor that served him well and that helped to sustain his attraction broadly within the black community:

STATE DISFRANCHISEMENT.

The negro has for some years been boiling with anger and spitting flames of vituperation because of the legislative action of Mississippi, Georgia and some other states that have amended their state constitutions so as to actually disfranchise a large percentage of negroes and a respectable percentage of whites. The constitutional amendment referred to is based upon a property or intellectual qualification, very similar to that which has existed in some of the New England states for nearly a century.

It is unfortunate for the Negro that he is incompetent to pass the required examination requisite to claim the rights of franchise in those states, but he may as well make the best of the situation and proceed to qualify himself, for such is the ultimate standard of American citizenship that sooner or later will be adopted by every state in the Union.

As a principle or proper measure we most emphatically endorse it, but as a direct means of overcoming the political influence of the negro, or any particular class or race, we object. Ignorance is the father of crime, in fact, ignorance itself is crime. Unfortunately the largest percentage of illiteracy in the United States is found in the southern states and in those very states that have adopted the "property and intelligence" qualification.

The great lesson taught by the acts of those state legislatures that have disfranchised so many by the exactions referred to is "get property," or "become frugal and industrious; learn to read and write," or are you too old to learn, encourage, and assist others of the race who are not too old.

After all, we can see in the distant future, a profit to the negro, in the very acts of those southern states which directly strikes at the apparent vitals of negro citizenship. If you desire consolation look to the east for a parallel law, in states too that stood foremost in the crusade against human slavery. The facts are that a "property and intelligence qualification" for voters is by no means a democratic and southern idea.

Every citizen of the United States ought to be a contributor toward the support of the government as well as competent to at least understand the principles of true American government.— *The Negro Solicitor*, [April 1898,] Oskaloosa, Iowa.[35]

What seems most remarkable is Taylor's support for the "Booker T. Washingtonian" notion that all voting citizens—whether black or white—should be expected to read and write and have a competent stake in America's dream. Perhaps Taylor had taken, at least in this editorial, a moderate and conciliatory position, if only to make it palatable to middle- and upper-class blacks in the North and Northeast, many of whom were inclined to blame southern rural blacks for their own deplorable and worsening conditions.[36] It is equally certain, however, that by 1898 Taylor literally had shared the stage with Washington on several occasions and had read his "Atlanta Compromise" of 1895, in which Washington had stated that "it is important and right that all privileges of the law be ours, but it is vastly more important that we be prepared for the exercise of these privileges."[37] In effect, Washington had been willing to close temporarily the ballot box if that concurrently would open schools, a compromise that Frederick Douglass, who died earlier in the year that Washington delivered his compromise, would not have tolerated.[38] There are other elements in the editorial that deserve more attention, however. Taylor almost justified southern attempts to impose qualifications for voting, suggesting that they were neither Democratic nor southern ideas alone. He also appeared to repeat a Populist sentiment that poor whites and poor blacks throughout the nation were equally the victims of the established parties to reduce voting power and influence through competency testing. In that regard Taylor demonstrated his agrarian and upper midwestern roots, believing that both blacks and whites in the long term would profit from these new regulations and, once empowered through "industrial education," could forge an alliance to obtain power as a voting bloc and a "balance of power" within the political process.[39]

Taylor was voicing an outlook then being advanced in Virginia by a biracial Populist movement composed of the remnants of the People's Party, the Colored Farmers' Alliance, the Readjusters, the Reform Party (Knights of Labor), and the Populists.[40] That movement struggled with the problem of attracting black and white voters to a new political party without giving the appearance to poor whites that they were allying themselves with former slaves and thereby raising the question of race. Indeed, a propaganda campaign launched by southern Democrats and lily-white Republicans claimed that a Populist victory in any region of the South would surely result in a second Reconstruction, a prospect unacceptable to white southerners.[41] The Virginia Populists of the middle to late 1890s sought only to detach voters from established parties and to empower a party that would champion the interests of underrepresented persons whose issues were being ignored at the state level.[42] Unfortunately, that attempt resulted in failure, with most discarding the ideal of "interracial cooperation" and moving toward "racially separate political spheres" and "white solidarity."[43] But that generally also was the track record of most splinter parties that sought to organize and campaign outside the two major established parties.

While Taylor's advocacy of change was similar to that of the Virginia Populists, his approach was more moderate, and perhaps that was sufficient to insure that his reputation within northern- and midwestern-dominated black associations remained as strong and flourished as long as it did. The *Broad Ax* of Salt Lake City, for instance, characterized Taylor in 1898 as "one of the greatest leaders of the negro race in this country" and described his *Negro Solicitor* then as circulating "throughout the states of Iowa, Illinois, Indiana, Missouri, Kansas, Nebraska, Minnesota, Michigan, Virginia, Georgia, Alabama, South

Carolina, Florida and Arkansas," an indication that his appeal was more than simply midwestern based.[44] The claim that the *Solicitor* was so widely circulated could not be substantiated through other sources, however, despite the fact that he reported in 1898 that the paper had 1,640 subscribers.[45] Even the *Iowa State Bystander*, a Republican paper, which incidentally reported in 1898 that it had only 450 subscribers and that otherwise opposed Taylor's political views, described him as "entitled to a station among the leading men of the race."[46]

In August 1898 Taylor ceased publication of the *Negro Solicitor* for practical and perhaps for personal and political reasons. His major rival in Iowa for readership, the *Iowa State Bystander*, had updated its format and appearance in April of that year and had expanded its coverage with improved news, notes, "brieflets," items, and "doings" for nearly all small black communities within Iowa, thereby attracting many new customers in coal-mining and meat-processing towns located close to Oskaloosa and Taylor's base of readers and advertisers.[47] The *Bystander* also covered international news, items of interest to women, churches and their conventions, and Republican politics at the state and national levels. Its network of local reporters and sales and advertising agents was extensive. Taylor surely found his redesigned competition to be formidable as long as he was restricted to an Iowa readership, and he lacked sufficient financial resources and time to remodel his own product. The degree to which subscriptions to the *Solicitor* had fallen in consequence of Populist setbacks in the South is unknown but may have been considerable. Taylor failed to retain his readers in part because he often was absent from Oskaloosa on official association business, and during those absences he occasionally suspended his newspaper's publication. That alone would have confused readers and upset advertisers. But Taylor also aggressively espoused liberal policies and was a known Democrat, attempting to retain the loyal readership of local persons who mainly were Republicans. By that date those blacks in the South who had put their faith in the Colored Farmers' Alliance had suffered significant election defeats and were perhaps less interested in his message of resistance. Those issues collectively kept him from maintaining a loyal base of black readers and lost his advertisers, who shifted their support to the *Bystander* if they intended to continue advertising within a black press in a time of increasing segregation.[48] Unfortunately, no issues of the *Negro Solicitor* have survived to provide insight regarding its general content, its approach, or the character of its advertisers.[49]

There is, however, a single and undated editorial from the *Negro Solicitor* of approximately the same time that suggests another reason for the newspaper's suspension. Taylor was angry. The chairman of Mahaska County's Democratic Committee had compared African Americans to monkeys, and Taylor had been offended enough to write an editorial and to permit his fury to manifest itself—once again—through his pen. It was during the 1898 election season, and Taylor was deeply engaged in his political role as leader of Mahaska County's black Democratic voters and as the person who would champion their cause through the columns of the *Negro Solicitor*. Unfortunately, only a fragment of that dispute is known, and Taylor repeated none of "the insults hurled at the Negro of this county by their [party's] chairman" in his editorial.[50] Taylor reminded the local Democratic faithful that it was "hard" for blacks to vote for the Democratic ticket in times when Democrats nationally were acting badly and that those who had left the Republican Party in 1892 "do not now propose to submit to indignant slavery at the hands of the party of our adoption." Taylor admitted openly that this particular dispute was a local one and that it was between him and the party's chairman, whom he described unflatteringly as "an awkward, ungainly, half-tamed, poorly civilized, three hundred pound, would-like-to-be-considered-democratic-leader." Taylor demanded that those Democrats on the county ticket distance themselves verbally from their chairman's words or forfeit his "feeble support" for their candidacies. And Taylor warned the party that his threat was "not thrown out as a 'feeler,' nor for sympathy, but as the plain expressions of one who worships manhood and scorns a would-be pirate."

Taylor acknowledged that his intemperate words would result in charges that "Taylor never was a democrat and now he's got money from the other side and he's ready to flog."[51] The attack upon him was personal. It was more serious than an issue of party loyalty. His own humanity had been challenged, and he had responded in a way reminiscent of circumstances in La Crosse in 1887. There he had attacked and burned bridges, enough so that he believed himself no longer able to play a meaningful role at the local level. That also may have happened in Oskaloosa. In La Crosse he reassessed and changed course.

From August to late September 1898 Taylor was fully engaged in political and organizational speech making in "the East."[52] Upon his return to Oskaloosa in September, Taylor did not resume his newspaper's publication but instead contributed "weekly and monthly articles for many leading dailies and magazines among which is the *Sunday Des Moines Leader*." He informed John Lay Thompson, editor of the *Bystander*, that he was preparing to "enter the lecture field in the near future."[53] Early in 1899, however, he obtained employment with the firm of A. B. Little of Coalfield in Iowa's Monroe County, serving as superintendent of its mining operation at the Black Diamond Mine site, which was "worked almost entirely by negroes."[54] The *Daily Iowa Capital* reported that Taylor was "the first negro to occupy such a position in the state."[55] Although Taylor remained with A. B. Little for only one year, he did not in the meantime divorce himself fully from publishing efforts. In August 1900 the *Broad Ax*, which had moved from Salt Lake City to Chicago, noted that Taylor had "composed a [Democratic] campaign song book" that was available for purchase by writing directly to him at his Oskaloosa address.[56] And even more interestingly, Taylor was listed in Oskaloosa's 1900–1901 city directory as an insurance agent.[57]

The year 1900 was a pivotal and difficult one for Taylor. His move from Oskaloosa to the coalfields was made without the company of his wife, Cora, who continued to live at the Oskaloosa residence, although she had accompanied him to the Kansas City Convention in July 1900.[58] His Colored People's National Protective Association remained active, but no mention of it appeared in newspapers after 1899. And he maintained a leadership position as secretary of the National Negro Democratic League. The latter role, however, was complicated. By 1900 the NNDL constitution specified that offices were only of two-year duration, yet the league's president, Edward E. Lee, refused to announce a convention call to select new officers. Citing the constitutional requirement, Taylor announced that the league would convene in Kansas City at the same time as the Democratic National Convention.[59] By 1900 it was expected that the league's presidency would remain in the hands of the incumbent or would fall to the person who had served as secretary. In that year, however, dissension once again characterized the league's leadership ranks, with a contest developing between A. E. Manning, who represented the old guard, and George Taylor with his new allies. Manning, who had been president of the league from 1896 to 1898, championed the candidacy of Fredrick McGhee, the politically savvy lawyer from St. Paul who was increasingly active within the newly formed Minnesota Equal Rights Association.[60] McGhee had left the Republican Party in 1893 "and never looked back," and he had campaigned vigorously for Bryan during the 1896 presidential campaign. Much like Taylor, he was comfortable in describing himself as "a poor darkey."[61] He also, like Taylor the labor advocate, advised his listeners: "We [the working class] have made this country and we can make it over again, if we want to."[62] McGhee was a member of the National Negro Anti-Imperialist League, a prominent legal activist within the Legal Bureau of the National Afro-American Council (NAAC), and an alternate delegate to the Democratic National Convention in 1900.[63] He also was an active participant in the Negro Inter-State Free Silver League.

Perhaps McGhee and Manning wanted in 1900 only to lift the National Negro Democratic League beyond its Populist and bottom-up roots and create an alternative to the National Afro-American Council, which even the *Iowa State Bystander* was describing in 1899 as fragmented between those who reasoned for direct political action and political options and those who supported patience and self-improvement, effectively leaving the group argumentative and unable to reach consensus for addressing problems facing the black community.[64] Or perhaps they believed it was still possible for the league to play a positive role in bringing change within the Democratic Party, even if that only pertained to the northern part of it. Or they may have hoped that blacks might have leverage in elections and that blacks might vote for their own economic interests rather than remain loyal to the party of Lincoln. "After a stirring contest," however, Taylor was elected president of the league, a term that would run from 1900 to 1902. Perhaps in frustration at his failure to lead the league in another direction, McGhee asked the league's executive committee, chaired by his benefactor, Manning, to prepare a public announcement that explained why African Americans should "no longer blindly follow the Republican Party."[65] In a separate memorandum Taylor wrote directly to the Democratic national party headquarters, encouraging it to champion equal black participation within the party and through its Negro Bureau.[66] And a committee of four chaired by McGhee wrote a lackluster appeal to black voters to enumerate reasons why Negroes should vote the Democratic ticket.[67]

Soon after the convention ended, however, the *Dallas Morning News* reported that a "serious split" among "colored Democrats" continued, with three factions contending for recognition by the national party and for those benefits attached to the party's newly instituted Negro Bureau.[68] Bishop Henry McNeal Turner of Atlanta, head of the African Methodist Episcopal Church, was one of those contestants, although by 1900 Turner's attention was focused mainly on immigration to Liberia and removing as many blacks as possible from the South. Taylor, as the duly elected president of the NNDL, believed that the party's Negro Bureau was to be controlled by whomever NNDL had elected as its president. The third faction consisted of those dissatisfied with Taylor's victory over McGhee. J. Milton Turner (1840–1915) of St. Louis led this group, which included McGhee; William A. Crosthwaite of Nashville; J. A. Sweeney, William Miller, and A. E. Manning of Indianapolis; Harvey A. Thompson of New York; A. T. Watkins of Chicago; and Senator J. K. Jones of Illinois.[69] Indeed, this represented a major division of Democrats, for those who supported McGhee and opposed Taylor were powerful and honorable voices in the black community. Until that time, Taylor and McGhee had campaigned vigorously for Democratic candidates and had cooperated on free silver issues. Both clearly were dedicated Democrats. But to what degree they enjoyed each other's company is unknown, although they differed significantly on expectations they had for black action. Certainly, many would have taken exception to an odd and argumentative message that Taylor gave to his readers, suggesting that the "Negro needs more nerve, business nerve, a less disposition to be desultory; more stern stability in industrial and business matters; more patience and push; he must talk less about his own business affairs and think more; calculate more and dream less; be more religious and less sentimental; learn to measure the distance between men and monkeys; cultivate more pride and less vanity; give more attention to home and family and less to society: think less of titles and more of merit."[70]

This "split" became public within a few days after Taylor's election, when Turner maneuvered to be introduced at the Democratic National Convention as the league's president, much to the discomfort of the league's newly elected officers. After the convention concluded its business, Turner—clearly demonstrating his disregard for Taylor and for his election as president of the league—continued to claim in the national press that he was "the only Negro sufficiently qualified to conduct the Campaign in behalf of Democracy among the colored voters," plainly challenging Taylor to respond.[71] Once Taylor received assurance that the party's Negro Bureau would be controlled by the NNDL, he acted promptly and hand-carried an ultimatum to Senator Jones, who had become the spokesman for the group, with the consequence that Turner returned empty-handed to his home base in St. Louis.[72] But this "split" had ended neither smoothly nor quietly. For several months black-owned newspapers carried reports that described the dispute in detail, suggesting that black Democrats were irreconcilably divided. Taylor and McGhee never reconciled.

As if that were insufficient to make 1900 an interesting year, Taylor also had attended the National Anti-Imperialist League meeting in Indianapolis on 16 August, at which meeting (attended by three to four hundred persons) "many members of [the] National [Civil] Liberty Party were present."[73] At that meeting there was a lively discussion of the advantages of organizing an entirely new political party, one that would oppose all variations of imperialism and that would contest both established parties in 1904. Still, the greatest applause during the speech of the meeting's chairman came with Taylor's suggestion that "many of the sympathizers in the movement were disposed to give their support to William J. Bryan," who, incidentally, was the candidate of the Democratic Party.[74]

Bryan's defeat in 1900, for a second time, was again a disappointment for Taylor and all northern black Democrats who could conclude that legal changes promoted by Democrats in the South were altering the dynamic of national politics and that blacks increasingly were being ignored and deserted by both parties.[75] The 1900 election demonstrated that the nation was splitting into two distinct sections and that consensus was no longer possible, unless of course it was to the detriment of black civil rights. But that alone may not account for Taylor's near silence during the next four years. Black Democrats remained divided into at least two increasingly antagonistic camps, and that was manifest in the near paralysis of the National Negro Democratic League during those years. While Taylor was president of three national associations—he also had become president of the Negro Knights of Pythias of America in 1900—and on the executive committees of several others, he spent much of his time in Iowa or giving lectures in the Midwest.[76] Although no notices appeared in the press, he also still may have been president of both the Negro National Free Silver League of America and the regional Negro Inter-State Free Silver League. By his own account, he left his employment with the firm of A. B. Little in 1900 and served two terms as a justice of the peace (an elected and not insignificant office that included the title of "judge") in the small Iowa farming and coal-mining community of Hilton in Monroe County (Albia).[77] He then purchased a 290-acre farm between the towns of Hilton and Foster and "engaged in farming and stock raising" for approximately three years.[78] His wife, Cora, did not follow him to Hilton and his farm refuge.

During that period Taylor became known for giving lectures and writing articles.[79] He also maintained active friendships with George H. Woodson, with whom he had been a business partner (the American Negro Industrial and Commercial Incorporation in 1897), and with Samuel Joseph Brown, a young black lawyer and Woodson's legal partner in nearby Albia.[80] Early in 1904 Taylor moved for medical treatment to nearby Ottumwa and was reported to be "practicing law."[81] The latter description is likely an exaggeration, unless it meant that he was involved in the field of law enforcement as a justice of the peace in neighboring Monroe County. The *Ottumwa Daily Courier*, moreover, reported that "Judge George E. Taylor" published his *Negro Solicitor* in Ottumwa for five or six months early in 1904.[82]

But the documented record of this period in Taylor's life is remarkably sparse, amazingly so, considering the celebrity that he had obtained during the previous decade. Health issues continued to plague him, whether a consequence of long-term pulmonary problems or injuries sustained when he fell from his roof in 1896. Even so, both Albia and Ottumwa were logical places for Taylor to move. Both were sites of active Democratic Party machines and strong lodges of the Colored Masons and the Knights of Pythias, the latter organization to which Taylor had devoted significant efforts during the 1890s. Both were located alongside major railroads connecting directly with Chicago and points eastward. And both had large black populations from which Taylor could obtain the grounding, membership, and identity he wanted.

Between 1891 and 1900 Taylor had participated fully in the political process, and he did so during a period of significant turmoil in southern states. The Midwest itself had experienced a spike in "lynching" and other violence against blacks as the "White Hysteria" of the South had crept northward. During the 1900 presidential campaign the language of intolerance and alarm had even reached into Iowa's black press, which reported widely held and anxious sentiments.[83] The *Bystander* explicitly advised its readers: "We cannot see how any decent colored voter will support such a [Democratic] party."[84] Three lynchings were attempted even in Taylor's own Wapello and Monroe counties, with two of them directed against blacks.[85] The language of race and pseudoscientific racism had entered the lexicon of the northern popular press, but the black press, while universally condemning such expressions, tended to advocate patience, accommodation, and maneuvering within the "Grand Old Party" rather than separate action to advance a black agenda.[86] Other factors that surely influenced Taylor during this period included the obvious failures of his marriage to Cora and of his printing business.[87] Taylor's marriage to Cora did not survive his move to Hilton.

Taylor's return to a farming environment in Monroe County for a period before moving to Ottumwa early in 1904, however, displayed a need to rediscover his focus. That is what he may have experienced when faced with adversity in La Crosse in 1887. But this also was a time of significant discovery for many within the black community, including Taylor. Political choices that had been expected following the Civil War and Reconstruction were no longer so clearly defined, and blacks were confounded by options that included socialism and even alliances with Democrats that might result in opportunities and political appointments at the local level. By the beginning of the century the number of black-owned and black-edited newspapers had grown significantly, although most were directed to an urban, educated, and northern-based readership primarily linked to the Republican Party. Taylor had found himself and his newspaper no longer able to compete within that profession. As a dedicated student of black issues, Taylor likely found himself overwhelmed, or he perhaps simply needed to relax and regroup—and reconsider his options.

5

Taylor's Campaign to Become President

A Duty to Himself and His Race

At first Taylor was prone to decline the nomination but feeling that it was a duty to his race he accepted.

Daily Times-Tribune,
12 April 1907

Taylor's selection as standard-bearer of the National Negro Liberty Party in 1904 and his decision to leave the Democratic Party to accept that nomination doubtlessly mystified nearly everyone who had known him between 1892 and 1904. Yet Taylor's writings and actions demonstrate that he had changed course without advance notice before and that he certainly had been willing to consider options. From 1900 to the time of the National Negro Liberty Party Convention in St. Louis in July 1904, Taylor had participated within the Democratic Party as the president of its black satellite and bureau, which would not challenge the parent party at the polls.[1] At the 1904 National Democratic Convention, which also met in St. Louis, he was an assistant sergeant at arms, a largely honorary position that gave him status and recognition within the national party—at least to the degree possible for a black Democrat.[2] Early in 1904, however, Taylor apparently was ill, for he authorized James A. Ross, who was then secretary of the NNDL, to act as president in his place and to issue the league's convention call.[3] At the convention Taylor passed the torch of the NNDL leadership to Ross while retaining the chairmanship of the league's advisory board. Even St. Louis's Republican and black-edited *Palladium* applauded Taylor as "another gentleman whose political opinions have been formed from an honest conviction, and not for political gain."[4]

Taylor's decision to hand the reins of the NNDL leadership to Ross perhaps should have been enough to signal that Taylor was about to enter a new phase in his search for black leadership. Taylor's time as president of the NNDL from 1900 to 1904 had been neither happy nor rewarding years for him or for blacks in politics generally. Blacks had played crucial roles in securing election victories in some southern states through fusion politics, but nearly all of that occurred before 1900 and before blacks were systematically removed from southern voting rolls. In much of the South, voting numbers plummeted because of new voting requirements and because votes had become nearly meaningless in districts where Democrats outpolled Republicans by a factor of twenty to one.[5] Indeed, many black leaders had become increasingly concerned that neither Republicans nor Democrats could or would defend their interests, and these leaders also had begun to consider political options. Numerous state Liberty Leagues had coalesced into the National Liberty League (National Colored Personal Suffrage League) in December 1903, but even that movement was designed more to force changes in the Republican Party than to oppose it by proposing its own candidates.[6]

Still, the National Liberty League in 1904 claimed a national membership of 600,000 — certainly an exaggeration, but one that gave support to a thought that African American voters might sustain a separate movement if it provided them an option that promised to bring change to the platforms of one or both of the dominant parties.[7] The Negro Protective Party had even placed its candidate for governor on Ohio's official ballot in 1897 and, surprisingly, received nearly five thousand votes.[8] Certainly, Taylor believed that the black vote was larger than that reported in official censuses and that coalitions could influence election outcomes, even if coalitions generally failed. But whether that was a realistic expectation in 1904 was an entirely different matter. Most black voters continued to accept the Republican Party as the race's best hope and the national Democratic Party as unable to control the actions of its affiliated state parties in the South, most of which were demonizing African Americans.[9] Meanwhile, a small number of voters had given up on both national parties and were willing to consider the formation of a separate political party, even if it could never win a national election. Indeed, there were already options that might attract such disaffected voters, but none of these — whether Prohibition, Christian, People's, Union, Socialist, Communist, or others — were particularly friendly to Negro rights or to opposing rapidly deteriorating conditions within southern states. And there was that other option: "Refrain from political activity altogether."[10]

The National Negro Liberty Party had developed on a track entirely different from the one followed by Taylor once he left Wisconsin in 1890. It was the
outgrowth of at least a decade of efforts at state and regional levels across the
South to secure pensions for ex-slaves, a proposition that had been before Congress periodically since the end of the Civil War.[11] Over time, numerous bills
for that purpose had been introduced, but none had passed both houses.[12] The
issue of reparations had been largely ignored by Taylor and most northern
black activists because it was considered to be a southern and economic problem rather than a problem of race. The immediate antecedents for the Liberty
Party, which fielded a ticket in the 1904 presidential election, can be traced to
events in Arkansas. Arkansas had been one of the earliest and more enthusiastic states to curtail Negro rights, whether those occurred in relation to the expulsion of free blacks in 1859, or to voting restrictions, or to the use of common
facilities at the end of the century.[13] In 1897 Rev. Isaac L. Walton of Madison,
Arkansas, formed an organization called the Ex-Slave Petitioners' Assembly,
which was similar to numerous groups established throughout the South to
support passage of the bills.[14] In general terms these bills proposed that each
former slave would obtain a one-time payment (a bounty) and monthly payments (a pension) for the rest of his or her life. The amount of bounty and pension would differ, depending on the age of the ex-slave at the point of the bill's
passage.[15] Opposition to these bills within the black community came mainly
from the North and was grounded in the belief that federal funds should be
spent on education and public projects, assuming that bounties paid to individuals would amount to a one-time infusion of currency, thus "enriching southern businesses" without "uplifting the African-American community" in the
process.[16]

News of such bills before Congress, however, had spread quickly throughout the South, with the result that "fake associations" had formed to collect fees
from destitute rural blacks, who were told that they could qualify for benefits
only if they were certified members of these associations.[17] Both the federal
and state governments intervened numerous times to curb the activities of
such associations, accusing them of fraud and forbidding circulation of their
pamphlets through the mail.[18] The schemes generally involved chartering a
local branch association ($2.50), issuing certificates that qualified individuals to
receive the pension (25¢ each), and collecting monthly fees for overhead and
lobbying costs (10¢ per individual).[19] Such fees and dues commonly were a part
of the organizational structure of black society, whether they were attached to
insurance plans or fraternal organizations.

But, technically, there was no requirement for membership in any association, with the result that the federal courts found Walton and his assembly guilty of fraud. Walton consequently disbanded the assembly and formed a new organization in 1900 called the National Industrial Council of Ex-Slaves (National Independent Council), but that group also failed to escape fully from earlier legal challenges from state and federal governments.[20] To remove that stigma even further, Walton resigned as president of the council, likely at the time of the council's Washington, D.C., meeting in early January 1903, and Stanley P. Mitchell, a young newspaper editor in Memphis, Tennessee, was selected as the council's new president. At that conference Mitchell proposed the formation of a new political party to be known as the Civil Liberty Party that would combine the best elements of "republicanism as fostered by Lincoln and the principles of democracy as advocated by Thomas Jefferson." Mitchell envisioned the new party as leading to a "second emancipation of the colored race" and called for a conference to be held in Cincinnati in May to formalize such a party.[21] The actual beginning of the National Civil Liberty Party is unknown; no record was found for a May meeting in Cincinnati. But by mid-1904 there were state parties carrying either that name or that of the Personal Liberty Party in more than thirty states.

Mitchell was not new to the ex-slave pension movement. In 1902 he had submitted to Congress a request for pensions for ex-slaves who had served in the Union army during the Civil War. Soon after the 1903 meeting in which Mitchell was selected as the council's new president, Mitchell and "a deputation of colored men" met with President Theodore Roosevelt on 14 January 1903 to gain his support for bills then being prepared for introduction to both houses of Congress. Roosevelt reportedly "turned them down so hard that the leader of the deputation [Mitchell] went from the white house swearing vengeance upon President Roosevelt and declaring that they could control 300,000 votes in the close states in the north which would be thrown against Roosevelt in 1904."[22] Mitchell later claimed that Roosevelt had told them that "the negro had received enough from the government when he was set free."[23] Mitchell threatened that "unless the Republicans take up the old scheme, which has been before Congress year after year, the independent negro organization will be started again and the matter carried to the polls."[24]

Senator Marcus Hanna of Ohio, who was a favorite Republican senator in the black press and who was reported to be considering a run for the presidency in opposition to Roosevelt, agreed to reintroduce a new bill, which he did half-heartedly on 4 February 1903, but he introduced it "by request" of a constituent, which had the effect of indicating that he was only its sponsor and that even he might vote against the bill.[25] A Wisconsin newspaper accused Hanna of giving ex-slave pension advocates "a most mischievous and hurtful favor, a ghastly joke."[26] The bill failed to gain support in Congress, but even in its submission it generated enormous controversy within the northern black press, most of which denounced it and the entire idea as unproductive and humiliating.[27] William Benjamin Derrick, bishop of the New York Diocese of the African Methodist Episcopal Church and a Democrat, called the pension bill "an insult and prophesied political death for those who proposed it."[28]

At the National Industrial Council's second national convention, held in Memphis, Tennessee, in the summer of 1903, with three hundred delegates attending and representing constituents from thirty-four states, the council again championed passage of a pension bill and expanded its objectives to include other issues important to blacks in the Midwest as well as in the South.[29] Whatever its goals, that organization failed to remove the taint of fraud charges levied against its predecessor bodies, and it floundered without obtaining wide support. Perhaps in an attempt to move the agenda forward or perhaps only in frustration over its earlier efforts, the council essentially disbanded, and Mitchell placed his remaining trust in the still nonfunctioning National Civil Liberty Party. William T. Scott, who was a prominent leader of the Civil Liberty Party in Illinois, suggested that a meeting be held in St. Louis at the Douglass Hotel from 5 to 8 July 1904 (at the same time and in the same city as conventions scheduled for the National Negro Democratic League and the National Democratic Party) to form a national black party and select a separate ticket for the offices of president and vice president of the United States.[30]

The new party's convention in St. Louis was beset with confusion and division from the start. All of the more than three hundred delegates were dissatisfied with the treatment given them by the Democratic and Republican parties and were frustrated by disenfranchisement and the passage of Jim Crow laws. But that was about the only agreement among them. Some placed a small part of their trust in the National Democrats, and those delegates generally were those who had played roles in the National Negro Democratic League and the Anti-Imperialism League. Some continued to believe that the Republicans were their best opportunity for change, viewing Roosevelt as a "true friend of the negro."[31] And there were many who were interested only in supporting the platform of the National Industrial Council. But those who had convened the meeting had already announced in the black press that they hoped to create an entirely new party and to select Booker T. Washington as its standard-bearer, even though many delegates already had dismissed Washington as too accommodating to Roosevelt and as too conservative.[32] There also were those who had left both parties and were seeking a stage that was separate and solely African American upon which to rally black voters and plant a flag of independence, if only to gain the attention of both established parties and declare that blacks could not be easily ignored.[33]

The convention got off to a rocky start, despite the fact that its announcements stated that delegates (2,500 were projected) would "nominate candidates for president and vice president."[34] Some thought that W. Calvin Chase of the *Washington Bee* might be selected to lead the party.[35] Chase, however, failed to attend. The delegates instead nominated Bishop Alexander Walters of New Jersey (African Methodist Episcopal Zion Church and then ex-president of the National Afro-American Council [NAAC], which was scheduled to meet in St. Louis in September) for the office of president of the United States.[36] He declined, as did James Milton Turner of St. Louis, with both advocating that the convention endorse the candidacy of President Theodore Roosevelt, who was the choice of Booker T. Washington and who was seeking election on the Republican ticket, despite the fact that both Walters and Turner had expressed their dissatisfaction with Republican inaction and were unlikely supporters of the Republican Party.[37] The convention actually followed that advice on its first day and voted to endorse Roosevelt.[38] It was not uncommon at the turn of the century for new parties to emerge, declare their agendas to the general population, and fuse at the national level by endorsing the candidates of larger parties.

When the convention convened the next day, however, the first order of business was to reverse the decision made the day before and to proceed with production of a platform and nomination of a separate ticket under its own banner.[39] Fissures within the delegates must have been deep. The party adopted a platform that opposed imperialism, chastised the government for advancing a policy of paternalism over subject peoples, and supported an increase of black officers and regiments within the army. But the platform went further, condemning the gold standard and newly enacted laws in the South that restricted civil rights and advocating for public ownership of the nation's railroads and for payments of pensions to persons who survived from slavery times. Mitchell had retained his leadership within the convention and the party, but its platform had taken a visible step toward "democracy" and issues favored by Populists.[40]

With the stalwarts of the established parties bypassed, the convention proceeded to select William T. Scott of East St. Louis, Illinois, as its standard-bearer and Capt. W. C. Payne of Warrenton, West Virginia, as his running mate.[41] Scott was not without impressive although clearly midwestern and non-NAAC-endorsed credentials. Scott had been freeborn in 1844 near Cincinnati, Ohio, where he completed a high school education, an unusual accomplishment for the time. Scott volunteered in the U.S. Navy in 1863 and served as a wardroom steward aboard a warship on the Mississippi River. Stationed near Cairo, Illinois, Scott stayed in Cairo after his discharge and became known there for his business success and his participation in "[Democratic] ward politics."[42] From Cairo he drifted to East St. Louis and to its Denverside district, where he became a saloon and hotel owner (he called it a "summer resort") and a bondsman/bailsman, professions in which he "made considerable money."[43] He owned and operated the *Cairo Gazette* (1881–90), which he transformed into the nation's first black daily in 1882.[44] For a brief period Scott secured a contract to print official notices through his Democratic political contacts with the city of East St. Louis. From ca. 1892 he was editor of the *East St. Louis Herald*. He also was grand master of the Colored Masonic Fraternity of Illinois, a thirty-third-degree Mason, and a Shriner. For a time Scott was grand master of the Colored Odd Fellows of Illinois and international vice grand master of the Order of Twelve Knights and Daughters of Tabor. He became active in politics and was one of the founding members of the National Negro Democratic League (1888) and served as the latter's president from 1896 to 1898 and vice president from 1900 to 1902.[45] In 1899 Scott was a founding member of the National Negro Anti-Expansion, Anti-Imperialist, Anti-Trust, and Anti-Lynching League and was that league's first president.[46] He was president of the Illinois Negro Free Silver League and a cofounder of the Negro National Free Silver League of America. He also was a friend of George Edwin Taylor.

Unlike Taylor, however, Scott had severed his ties to the Democratic Party by 1903, and by 1904 he was firmly on a course to join a separate black party "committed to equality," knowing that such a race-specific party could never win an election at the national level.[47] He was a leader in the Illinois branch of the Civil Liberty Party in 1904, and it was mainly through his encouragement that the Liberty Party's national committee selected St. Louis to be the site for its first national convention.[48] Scott's tenure as nominee of the National Negro Liberty Party, however, was short-lived when it became known that he had been arrested eight years earlier for operating a "disorderly house," a charge that Scott then had denied. He nevertheless had paid a small fine ($50) and believed the issue to have been settled. Shortly after obtaining the party's nomination, however, he was rearrested, charged with having failed to pay his "full" fine ($149.80), and confined in the Belleville jail for twenty days, with the consequence that his selection as the party's standard-bearer was vacated.[49]

The National Negro Liberty Party was in disarray when its executive committee met in St. Louis on 20 July to select an alternative candidate.[50] In a letter written by Payne to the editor of the *Washington Bee* of that date, Payne blamed Calvin Chase for the party's "disrepute," informing him that had he attended the convention, he would have been nominated for president. Chase sarcastically responded: "Great Scott! . . . Great Caesar! . . . We shall certainly be present in 1908 if the United States are on earth at that time."[51] For a moment the committee considered Stanley Mitchell as the party's candidate, but he was only thirty-three years old and therefore unable constitutionally to serve as president.[52] Taylor, meanwhile, had attended the convention of the National Democratic Party and had relinquished his presidency of the National Negro Democratic League but retained a leading role in the league as chairman of its advisory board. He had not attended the July meeting of the National Negro Liberty Party in St. Louis, although while attending the National Democratic Convention in St. Louis he had held "several conferences with the leaders of the [new] party."[53] After all, Taylor and Scott had served together on several national boards and knew each other personally.

When the new party's executive committee approached Taylor, he was ready to take the next step in his political evolution. Although Taylor did not receive a formal invitation to lead the ticket until 26 July, his path forward was unambiguous as early as 21 July.[54] In a provocative letter to the editor of the *Chicago Tribune*, dated 1 August 1904 and published in the *Ottumwa Weekly Democrat* on 6 August, Taylor addressed the prominent issue of the day:

> In the first column of your issue of last Sunday I notice a discussion of the "Race Topic" by Senator [Albert Jarvis] Hopkins of Illinois [Republican, 1903–9]. It appears that the senator entered into this discussion soon after he left the conference with President Roosevelt and other distinguished party leaders at the White House, so it is fair to presume that he voiced the sentiments of the president and the republican party.
>
> The senator refers to the plank in the republican national platform, which deals with the disenfranchisement of blacks in certain states, making the following statement: "That plank is one to which no right thinking citizen, north or south can honestly object. The question suggested by that plank is one that lies at the foundation of representative government, and upon its right and righteous settlement depend in no small measure the liberty and prosperity of the American people." As a negro, and a citizen of the United States, I desire to briefly review the situation . . . as touching the issues raised by this plank and Senator Hopkins.
>
> It must truly be admitted by all intelligent people, that the present campaign is of the most vital importance to the negro, of any or all the campaigns that have intervened since the right of suffrage was first bestowed upon the race by Constitutional Amendment. Why? Because about one-fifth of the entire race have been disenfranchised in direct violation of the tenets, words and spirit of

the Declaration of Independence, and federal constitution, and the party in power makes no ta[n]gible effort to correct the wrong, but, on the contrary, endorses it by simply inserting a plank in its platform declaring that in lieu of such disenfranchisement, a penalty shall be assessed against the states involved reducing their representation in congress in proportion to the reduction of the general vote by reason of said disenfranchisement.[55] In other words, the republican party, according to Senator Hopkin's construction of their platform, propose to sell the citizenship rights of the negro for the paltry consideration of increased relative republican strength in congress. I would like to ask all honest Americans, Where do we Negroes come in? If this plank of the republican party is carried out to the letter, wherein will it benefit the negro? Can it be possible that the senator and his party assume that the ten million negroes of the country are still asleep, after forty years of contact with liberty-loving, free-thinking Americans?

Which is the greater wrong, to tax the two million and more people who are now disenfranchised, without allowing them the slightest semblance [of] representation, or permit the states involved to have more than their true representation in Congress? My contention is not that these states should not have their representation reduced, but that the administration, the republican party, should boldly and honestly deal with the proposition at issue, the constitutionality or unconstitutionality of the wholesale disenfranchisement of the race, and not dodge the issue by demanding simply a reduction of the congressional representation of these states. If this is the only penalty to be imposed for the disenfranchisement of the negro, what will hinder every state in the Union from entering into this disgraceful, gigantic, citizenship-steal?

Can it be that we are nearing another crisis in the history of our beloved country? God forbid. Can it be possible that universal public sentiment has at least surrendered to the defeated theory of "states rights?" I do not believe so. Can it be that the Declaration of Independence and the Federal Constitution are meaningless make-shifts. I shall not yield to such a conclusion. Then why not exact of every state equal opportunity under the law for all citizens of the United States? Why offer to compromise the suffrage rights (the only true rights) of ten million loyal, patriotic, liberty-loving people? There are today about 2,500,000 adult male negroes in the United States, decidedly the largest individual racial element of our citizenship, and we have no Congressional [seat] now, but offer no protest, so it seems to me very modest indeed to respect that this protest be filed.

Is it not clear that this negro plank of the republican platform sounds the key-note of the final elimination of the entire negro vote from the body politic of the country?

Yours respectively,

Geo. E. Taylor.

Ottumwa, Ia., Aug. 1.[56]

On 3 August Taylor's appointment to head the Liberty Party's ticket was confirmed, and he "prepared a synopsis of what the party is and what it stands for as outlined in its platform," which he shared with the editor of the *Ottumwa Courier*:

A STRONG PLATFORM.

"The committee on resolutions reported a strong platform declaring it expedient to nominate a national ticket and favoring the nomination of congressional tickets wherever the negro vote is strong enough to become a potent factor.

"The convention unanimously adopted the report and perfected the organization of the National Liberty party by the nomination of candidates for president and vice president and the selection of the necessary working committees.

THE PLATFORM.

"The platform declares for the full and unqualified enforcement of the constitution; equal opportunity for all American citizens against class legislation; against trusts and combines; condemns the attitude of numerous democratic leaders who advocated the disfranchisement of the negro on purely racial grounds; questions the sincerity of President Roosevelt's friendship for the race; brands the republican platform as bidding for the wholesale disfranchisement of the southern negro for the paltry consideration of 'reduced congressional and electoral representation from the south'; protests against taxation without representation; favors pensioning the ex-slave, absolute freedom of the Philippines, reduction of the tariff and condemns anarchy in all forms, classing lynching as acts of anarchists."[57]

It was not until 5 August that Taylor wrote to the National Negro Democratic League's new president, James A. Ross of Buffalo, New York. In that letter Taylor resigned from the league and from his chairmanship of its advisory board and memberships on "a number of committees."[58] In a letter to Taylor from Ross dated 9 August, Ross praised Taylor for his stewardship of the league, noting that "your ability as an organizer cannot be excelled" and expressing his sentiment that many within the NNDL might vote for him in the coming election.[59]

At a formal meeting at Ottumwa on 30 and 31 August, Taylor met with four members of the party's executive committee and its candidate for the vice presidency, W. C. Payne. This meeting had been called to develop a plan for the upcoming campaign and to determine the best method for announcing Taylor's appointment and acceptance of the party's nomination in order to guarantee the best newspaper coverage. At the turn of the century it was customary for party conventions to be held late in the summer and for candidates not to participate openly in the nomination process. In theory, a convention would select its candidate and only then contact its choices with invitations to become its presidential and vice presidential nominees. Formal letters would be exchanged, and all letters would be published widely in the national press. In effect, the actual campaign might last only a matter of weeks. Theodore Roosevelt had already indicated, for instance, that he would accept the party's nomination if it were offered, but he also stated that he would not deliver any speeches on his own behalf. Three items were confirmed at the Ottumwa meeting: a formal letter of appointment would be sent to Taylor within ten days; Taylor would reply with a formal letter of acceptance; and Taylor would meet with the party's full executive committee and the party's chairman, Stanley Mitchell, in St. Louis on 9 September to discuss other campaign issues.[60]

Taylor did not formally accept the new party's nomination until yet a week later, when he notified Mitchell and the nation with a letter of acceptance on 15 September, effectively leaving but seven weeks to campaign before the general election, scheduled for 8 November.[61] That letter was polemical and approximated in tone but certainly not in quality that of his 1887 period, when he encountered adversity in La Crosse. Perhaps it represented only a period of abdication or despair, but that is uncertain because only a fragment of the letter has survived. Taylor was angry and disappointed, and he was willing to express those feelings directly, openly, and thoughtfully. In his "National Appeal" of 1892 he had chastised the Republican Party for having surrendered to lily-white forces within the party, and he had shifted politically to the Democrats, whom he trusted would do the right thing in the long term. He understood southerners, but the migration northward of their deeply held sentiments regarding race had surprised him. By 1904 he obviously believed that he had made a bad choice, for his optimism had been replaced with gloom. Abandoned by the Democrats before 1904 and betrayed by the Republican "sell-out" of 1904, Taylor envisioned a future of agreement of the two on questions of race and the "Negro Problem." "We are doomed" so long as blacks did not take separate political action, a plan that the black press and most black politicians in 1904 dismissed as alarmist. "What, then, shall we do?" he asked, and he answered his question by recommending a new political option. For Taylor, the greater enemy was the "cloven-foot" Republicans, whom he now believed to have been party to a conspiracy to abandon blacks to their own fate. In effect, Taylor believed that only blacks would champion black interests. It is not surprising that no other paper printed Taylor's letter, which he shared with his Democratic friend who was editor of the *Ottumwa Weekly Democrat*:

"The only difference I am able to discern between the [Senator Benjamin] Tillman [of South Carolina] and [James] Vardaman [governor of Mississippi] school of democrats, and the present administration of [Theodore Roosevelt] republicans, as to the subject of disfranchisement is that the former are scrupulously honest in expressing their determination to defeat the evolution and progress of the Negro, law or no law, constitutional amendments to the contrary notwithstanding, while the latter are most unscrupulously dishonest—trying to run with the hounds, but sop with the coons.[62]

REMOVE THE MASK

"The enormity of this *disfranchisement crime* becomes more apparent when it is remembered that all the states that ever sent a Negro to either house of congress, or elevated one to a governor's chair, are included in the list quoted above. This forces the conclusion that in the disfranchisement already executed by these six southern states and confirmed by the present administration, the Supreme court and the recent republican national convention is equivalent to the practical disfranchisement of every Negro in the United States; for there is now no hope, no possibility of the election of a Negro to congress, or, in other words, *we are doomed* to submit to any and all measures of taxation without representation. *Can the race longer be conjured to the belief that the republicans are not now and have not for years been parties to this, the most stupendous citizenship steal known to modern history?*"

URGES A PARTY VOTE

". . . I perceive that *the national liberty party is purely a creature of necessity*. The time has come when all Negroes admit that something must be done, and, through this movement, that something can be done. Until 1892, ninety-nine per cent of the Negroes voted the republican ticket without a protest. At the general election that year about thirty per cent of the race voted against Harrison. Since then ninety per cent of the race have voted the republican ticket in and out of season, in the hope that something would turn up in consequence. But, alas! that something has fatally turned down instead. *What, then, shall we do?*

REPUBLICANS SELL BIRTHRIGHT

"Have not the republicans sold our birthright for the proverbial mess of pottage? If this statement is questioned I refer the critic to that plank in the republican national platform which touches the question of disfranchisement. Analyze this plank, and the completeness of this *sell-out* is made visible. So, there is no longer hope for the race in our fidelity to the party which once espoused the true principles of honest, just and equitable government as taught by our immortal Lincoln and exemplified by our lamented, sturdy, honest Grant. The time was when the Negro might have gained succor by affiliating directly with the democratic

118

party, but not now; that party has won a stronger ally in the person of the re-publican party. Whither then shall the race go, if not to the national liberty party. Shall you become populists or socialists? If so, what would you gain?"

OPPOSES PROTECTIVE TARIFF

". . . It has for many years been my opinion that a tariff for revenue only is the correct policy of political economy for this country to adopt. I am now more strongly than ever convinced that the unsubsidized competition of all lines of commerce and industry will best serve the interests of the masses. That the masses and not the classes are entitled to the earnest consideration of congress, the administration and the courts, is fundamental to our very system of government, is too well established to require argument. The Negro has never endorsed the protective tariff policy because of its merit, but simply because it has been the policy of the republican party. Now that this party has shown 'the cloven foot,' we are forced to resort to that unquenchable and unconquerable resource which is inherent with all civilized humanity, namely: reason, the mother of all investigation,—that we may measure our real interests in this or that political policy. Of all the people who comprise the vast population of this republic the Negro, it occurs to me, is the least benefited by the protective tariff policy."[63]

Interestingly, however, those who supported independent action through the Liberty Party were not alone in their dissatisfaction with the course of American politics at that time.[64] Only weeks before the NAAC was scheduled to hold its annual conference in St. Louis, another "Negro" party also convened in St. Louis to select candidates for the offices of president and vice president. This party was called the National Negro Lincoln Party, and it was affiliated with black members of the Republican Lincoln League, black Republicans who disagreed with specific issues supported by the national Republicans.[65] The liberal *Broad Ax* of Chicago announced this convention with the header "Silly! Yet, 'Tis Their Privilege." On its first day, 25 July 1904, the convention formed a committee to "interrogate Booker T. Washington, James Milton Turner and Bishop H[enry]. M. Turner to learn which one of them would accept to become a candidate."[66] Meanwhile, the party adopted a platform whose principal planks included "the pensioning of former slaves by the federal government," "freedom for every man, with special reference to the negro, Hawaiians and Porto Ricans," and unlimited coinage of silver, all issues that were ignored or opposed by the national Republicans.[67] The party's executive committee eventually selected E. P. Penn of Richmond to lead the ticket and Judge John G. Jones of Chicago to be his running mate.[68] Only nine references were found for this party or convention, but the fact that it occurred at all illustrated a high degree of discontent among African American voters during this election cycle and the willingness, for some few, to search for options on the ballot.[69] That two separate "Negro" parties might emerge from St. Louis within the span of a single month and somehow not commingle memberships seems incredible.

Taylor's decision to become the standard-bearer of the National Liberty Party must have been an agonizing choice. But surely Taylor knew the consequences of that option. In effect, this was a courageous decision, perhaps similar to that of a doctor who practices heroic medicine on a patient who is expected to perish regardless of treatment.[70] Even the convention's organizers had projected that the party was unlikely to obtain more than 500,000 votes in the coming election.[71] But the assertion of those numbers obviously was convincing enough to attract Taylor's interest and confirm his own belief about the leverage that blacks could exercise in elections. Southern turnout in the 1900 presidential election had been dismal at best, with 10 percent or fewer of total eligible voters casting ballots in Arkansas, Alabama, and Florida and 5 percent or fewer voting in Georgia, Louisiana, Mississippi, and South Carolina. If blacks had voted as a bloc, that alone might have determined several if not all of those contests.[72]

But Taylor was a realist. He admitted before 1 September that the new party had little chance to win the election. Taylor openly expressed that opinion to his colleague at the *Ottumwa Weekly Democrat*, indicating that the party planned to campaign aggressively in only "ten or twelve states, and to make a hard fight in about twenty congressional districts." Almost in resignation, Taylor added: "The campaign will be of an educational nature and will be confined largely to the distribution of literature rather than to the employment of speakers."[73]

Taylor must have known that his decision to lead the ticket would undermine if not poison whatever future roles he might play within the Democratic Party and various associations that were allied or friendly with the Democrats, assuming that there might have been a role for him to play there had he not accepted the party's nomination. But his letter of acceptance unmistakably contained his conviction, already known through his public pronouncements, that the national Democratic Party would fuse with Republicans if necessary to oppose enforcement of civil rights; in effect, any return to a meaningful position at the national level in any party would be unrealistic if not impossible—for him and for them. He knew that the ex-slave pension bill was ridiculed in nearly all black newspapers and that its passage by both houses of Congress was unlikely. And surely he knew that President Roosevelt opposed the bill. In effect, Taylor knew that his campaign likely would be the first and last of its kind.

But Taylor's choice was not entirely out of character with his previous ones. He had played significant roles in minor parties while in Wisconsin, and he had

George Edwin Taylor, portrait of a presidential candidate, 1904. *Voice of the Negro*, October 1904, 476.

switched parties earlier in his Iowa period. But winning the presidency of the United States as candidate of a solely black party—and one that expressed support for pensions for ex-slaves—was idealistic at best. Perhaps Taylor had simply tired of his lack of achievement in pressing an agenda within the Democratic Party, which was fueling "white hysteria" and spreading it nationwide.[74] Perhaps he assumed that he could give minimal lip service to the ex-slave pension plan while using his position to emphasize other issues that he considered more pressing within the black community and that certainly would not be discussed by white candidates.[75] Perhaps by 1904 he believed that his enemies within the party were both numerous and able to block any further progress for him or his supporters. Or perhaps he remembered an editorial he had written eighteen years earlier while in La Crosse in which he had admonished his supporters to "stand boldly for the principles of the party, labor earnestly to nominate a respectable and genuine state ticket and if it becomes necessary, bravely die the death of political defeat on election day, to be resurrected three years hence, rather than suffer yourselves to be made tools of to construct the Democratic ship." On that same date in 1886 Taylor had written: "Do not lose sight of the fact that all things have a beginning," and "success will perch upon our banner in the end."[76]

Once having made that choice and relying primarily on his own abilities to carry his campaign, Taylor attempted to accomplish the impossible. With his own hand and using carefully selected terms, Taylor produced an impressive broadside that explained the party's platform, and, using his contacts and reception for articles that he had written for other black newspapers, he distributed it nationwide. Only three major black newspapers published his material and welcomed his campaign, at least in the beginning. The *Voice of the Negro* of Atlanta and the *Independent* of Houston mildly supported Taylor's candidacy, and for a time the *Washington Bee* gave Taylor encouragement. Booker T. Washington, however, opposed all third-party efforts, believing that such action would damage whatever goodwill remained within the established parties and detract from his educational agenda. Those loyal to Washington's opinions, especially Washington, D.C.'s *Colored American* and the *Wichita Searchlight*, ridiculed Taylor's efforts, suggesting only that his candidacy provided "the humor of the campaign."[77] The *Racine Daily Journal*, a white paper, reminded the party's leaders that "had it not been for Abraham Lincoln there would have been no National Liberty party entirely free to do as they will, respecting, of course, the law," while the *Modesto Evening News* dismissed the party entirely with the observation that "all Reformers are funny, but none of them are quite as funny as the Reformers of the National Liberty Party."[78] The *Cedar Falls Gazette* less generously and certainly more ominously wrote that "if they attempt to push themselves too hard against the whites of the country, they will be snuffed out, politically speaking, like a candle. Let the negro stand for equal rights under the law, and they will always have proper sympathy, but we are not yet ready to turn the government over to them, and the fact that they are clamoring for this state of affairs is proof positive that they are incapable of enjoying what they have and wholly unable to control what they seek."[79]

Despite this opposition, the platform of the National Negro Liberty Party was progressive, if unattainable:

NATIONAL LIBERTY PLATFORM:
Adopted at St. Louis, MO., July 7, 1904.

We, the delegates of the National Liberty party of the United States, in convention assembled, declare our unalterable faith in the essential doctrine of human liberty, the fatherhood of God and the brotherhood of man.

Under no other doctrine can the people of this or any other country stand together in good friendship and perfect union. Equal liberty is the first concession that a republican form of government concedes to its people, and universal brotherhood is the cementing tie which binds a people to respect the laws.

It has always been so where caste existed and was recognized by law or by common consent, that the oppression of the weaker by the stronger has attained and a degree of human slavery been realized. Such a condition of affairs must necessarily exist where universal suffrage is not maintained and respected, and where one man considers that by nature he was born and by nature dies better than another.

The application of the fundamental principles of the rights of men is always the paramount issue before a people, and when they are strictly adhered to there is no disturbing element to the peace, prosperity, or to the great industrial body politic of the country.

We believe in the supremacy of the civil as against the military law, when and where the civil is respected. But when the civil law has been outraged and wrested from the hands of authority it should be understood that military law may be temporarily instituted.

Law and order should take the place of lynching and mob violence, and polygamy should not survive, but polygamy is more tolerable than lynching, and we regret that a great national party could overlook lynching, and yet denounce polygamy.

Citizens of a democracy should be non-partisan, always casting their votes for the safety of their country and for their best interests, individually and collectively.

The right of any American citizen to support any measure instead of party should not be questioned, and when men conform themselves to party instead of principles they become party slaves. There were 2,500,000 such slaves among our colored population in 1900, all voting strictly to party lines, regardless of their material welfare. We are satisfied that they did not serve their best interest in that section of the country in which the greater number of them live by doing so.

These being our thoughts and ideas of how the Government's affairs should be conducted, we most respectfully submit them to all liberty-loving and Christian-hearted people, that they may act upon them in a spirit of justice and equality, "with good will to all, malice toward none."

Suffrage.—We ask for universal suffrage, or qualification which does not discriminate against any reputable citizen on account of color or condition.

Citizenship.—We ask that the Federal Government enforce its guarantee to protect its citizens, and secure for them every right given under the Constitution of the United States, wherever and whenever it is necessary.

Lynch Law.—We appeal to all forms of Catholic and Protestant religions to assist us to awaken the Christian consciences of all classes of the American people, private citizens and officers, to wipe out the greatest shame known to civilized nations of the world, whose very root seems to have been planted in this, one of the most proud of all nations of its civilization—"lynch law," the pregna[n]ter of anarchism, the most dangerous system to revolutionize our Republic.

We ask that the national laws be so remedied as to give any citizen, being next of kin, the right to demand an indemnity of the National Government for the taking of life or the injuring of any citizen other than by due process of law. And that where the property of a citizen is willfully destroyed by the mob, the Federal Government shall be held to make restitution to the injured parties.

The Army.—We demand an increase of the regular army, making six negro regiments instead of four, and an equal chance to colored soldiers to become line officers.

We favor the adjustment of all grievances between the wage earner and the capitalist by equitable resources without injustice to either or by methods of coercion.

We firmly protest against interference of the Government in the Orient until paramount political issues of the races, capital and labor are settled and settled right at home.

Pensions for the Ex-Slaves.—We firmly believe that the ex-slave, who served the country for 246 years, filling the lap of the nation with wealth by their labor, should be pensioned from the overflowing treasury of the country to which they are and have been loyal, both on land and sea, as provided in the bill introduced in the Senate of the United States by Senator Hanna, of the State of Ohio.

Government Ownership and Public Carriers.—We ask that the general Government own and control all public carriers in the United States, so that the citizens of the United States could not be denied equal accommodations where they pay with the same lawful money provided by the Government as a circulating medium and as a legal tender for all obligations.

American Citizens Deprived of Self-Government.—The people of the District of Columbia, the capital of the nation, should be given the right to participate in the selection of President and Vice-President of the United States, and should be allowed representation in the two branches of Congress, and the election of a Governor, Mayor, City Council, and such other officers as necessary for the proper government of the District of Columbia. We indorse the Gallagher resolution looking to the establishment of self-government of the District of Columbia.[80]

In an editorial printed in *Voice of the Negro* (Atlanta) in October, the editors gave Taylor at least a small recommendation:

In politics he [Taylor] has always been an out spoken independent, proclaiming that the interests of his race are paramount to that of any political party. He has served two terms as Justice of the Peace in Monroe County, Iowa, and been often otherwise honored by his race.[81] . . . He is a natural leader, a fluent speaker and an advanced thinker. Mr. Taylor sets forth the principles of his party in an article following this sketch.[82] The editors of the *VOICE* invite our readers to give his article a careful perusal.[83]

Despite his efforts, however, few of Taylor's former colleagues in the Democratic Party chose to support his candidacy. McGhee of Saint Paul publicly endorsed the Democratic ticket, although McGhee later admitted that he had serious misgivings about the long-term future of blacks in that party after William Jennings Bryan stated in 1901 that "blacks in the South had not been denied any of their constitutional rights."[84] The reasons for the campaign's failure, however, were more than merely its lack of success in attracting voters from Democrats or Republicans. The party's St. Louis convention and its competing agenda had revealed that its platform had been assembled with disparate parts, all of which appealed to constituencies that had not worked together harmoniously previously but that recognized each other as oppressed and in need of leadership. But that was true of nearly all parties, whether Democratic, Republican, or other. The convention itself had been poorly planned and executed, and its membership perhaps reflected more a radical fringe and a leaderless and incoherent mass than a mainstream or even a moderate voice within the black community. Hastily called and without financial resources, the majority of its delegates represented midwestern states, even though representatives for thirty-seven states attended.[85] There was no grassroots party structure, and not a single newspaper sponsored or supported its platform with conviction. Nothing existed to carry the campaign and distribute its message once the national convention had completed its task.[86] Nor was the party truly national in its structure. Without newspapers to champion its cause, whatever

George Edwin Taylor, 1904 presidential poster. Eartha White Collection, Thomas G. Carpenter Library, University of North Florida.

enthusiasm may have existed for the party in St. Louis vanished within weeks as coverage of the Russo-Japanese War and long letters of acceptance from both Democratic and Republican nominees dominated the pages of black newspapers, almost all of which were Republican affiliated.

At first glance, however, it appeared even to such publishers as the *Washington Bee* that this new party might be able to have an impact upon the obviously negative course speeding through the South. Perhaps they assumed, as did Taylor, that the number of uncounted African Americans in previous censuses amounted to nearly 50 percent.[87] Perhaps Taylor trusted his own confidence (and that of those in the new party who convinced him to accept their nomination) that three hundred speakers would be put on the stump by 1 October to generate support and enthusiasm for his candidacy.[88] Taylor had been told in mid-July that the party had established committees in all states and that they were then "busy perfecting their state organizations."[89] There was also the implicit promise that there was sufficient time remaining to resolve legal and financial obstacles associated with placing the party on the election ballots of all the states and for selection of electors. Surely everyone knew that victory would not be achieved, but most believed that appearing as a separate party in a separate column on the ballot and even modest numbers in the election might deliver the message to both major parties that black votes could no longer be taken for granted. Perhaps Taylor and others in the party believed themselves able to obtain a "balance of power" between the two established parties or at least use the campaign as another stage for informing the nation of the impact of disenfranchisement on such a large part of America's citizens.[90]

The details of placing the party and its candidates on states' ballots, however, were costly, complicated by local regulations that had been enacted precisely to make it difficult for third parties to enter the contest. Perhaps these details had even been overlooked, for in the end few if any states had the party listed on their 1904 ballots.[91] William T. Scott later explained that even in his own state of Illinois, "it would have cost several thousand dollars to get the necessary petitions," an expense that neither the state nor the national parties could afford.[92] Even in Iowa, Taylor was unable to complete the process of adding the party to the ballot.[93] Surely Taylor's charisma and speaking ability would not have been expected to be sufficient to carry the entire campaign and negate the party's abysmal financial and grassroots vacuum. And yet, apparently, his party thought they could.[94] Even the enthusiasm of the convention evaporated following the debacle of Scott's rearrest in July. Few voters were even aware that a Negro party existed or that an African American was running for president: "His candidacy [simply] was not taken seriously."[95] Black newspapers championed the established candidates and ignored the others. And when they addressed the party at all, it was in indirect and negative terms:

> Much bugaboo is made by some colored men who wish to raise excitement about the American Negro being a "free being" and as having a right to vote for whom he may will. We do not dispute this, and neither does any, save the democrats, who denies that the Negro has a right to vote for whom he pleases, but they go so far as to even deny that the Negro has a right to vote at all. . . . Then again these colored men who aim to do great things by their ability to raise political excitement dote on reminding us that "they were born free." . . . The time is now passed when the colored man can be thrown into spasms over the exciting narratives of a few selfish politicians.[96]

The *Iowa State Bystander*, when describing parties contending in that election, bluntly gave this party an even more sinister and conspiratorial agenda:

> And lastly the national liberty party, headed by one Geo. E. Taylor of this state as its sponsor and candidate for president with no platform and but few principles stated in [his] letter of acceptance. This party was conceived by democrats [and] born in a democratic national convention recently held in St. Louis, operated and called by shrewd democratic leaders using a few colored men on the committees as tools. The expenses of this called meeting, we are informed, was borne by the national democratic committee, therefore the colored voter can have no faith in it.[97]

It is hardly astounding, then, that Taylor received only about two thousand write-in votes when votes were eventually tallied following the 8 November 1904 election (see appendix B for election data).[98] The 1904 election confirmed that between 1896 and 1904 a major shift in political power had occurred. The 1896 election had marked the beginning of a realignment of party constituencies, with urban, eastern, and business forces allying against rural, southern, western, and Populist supporters. That realignment, now completed, removed the threat of a third-party victory and would dominate the political landscape for more than three decades (except for Woodrow Wilson's two terms, which represented plurality rather than majority rule).[99]

The silence within the black community that followed the 1904 election was unambiguous. The election of Theodore Roosevelt was celebrated, and the plight of the National Liberty Party vanished from the humor section of newspapers. With the exception of an interview given by Taylor that was published in the *Sun* of New York soon after the 1904 election (see appendix A), Taylor's activities are largely unreported, although it was later noted that he had returned to his farm in Monroe Country, Iowa, for a brief time and then had moved back to Ottumwa, where he was reading law and receiving medical treatment.[100] He also had been accepted back into the Democratic fold, at least at the local level and to the degree that the party apparatus in Ottumwa readmitted him as "an avowed democrat"—"the Hilton Democrat"—and permitted him to campaign for its candidates in elections.[101] Taylor continued to write, although nothing from his pen between 1904 and 1908 has been found. Ottumwa in this decade, on the other hand, was a center of Democratic politics, with its mayor, Thomas J. Phillips, having run unsuccessfully for the governorship of Iowa in 1901. Taylor campaigned for Phillips in 1907, and with Phillips's election as mayor, Taylor was "admitted to the local political pie counter and handed out a policeman's job."[102] Political spoils of this sort were commonplace, and the national press delightfully reported it, conspicuously describing Taylor as the former candidate for president who had become little more than a night patrolman in Ottumwa's "tenderloin district," clearly a demotion and a pointed condemnation of his character and that of the party of which he had been standard-bearer.[103]

Only one instance suggests that Taylor remained active at the national level within the Democratic Party. That occurrence, however, was merely a comment that was distributed by news wire services in September 1908 and perhaps was of national interest only because its lead read: "Taylor in Ottumwa and Still Making News."[104] When James Ross, president of the National Negro Democratic League, convened its executive committee (fifty members) in Chicago on 6 and 7 August 1908, Taylor's name was absent. Ross announced that an important proclamation would soon be issued to "colored voters throughout the country" and that a full convention would meet in a month's time either in Chicago, Cleveland, Cincinnati, Columbus, or Buffalo. The league intended to focus its efforts in the Midwest and in New York State, New Jersey, Connecticut, and West Virginia.[105] Essentially, the league had abandoned its national agenda under Ross's leadership and had returned to the state-targeted focus of Ross's original association.

The National (Civil) Liberty Party limped on, but its fate remains unknown. W. T. Scott, who was chairman of the party's executive committee in 1908, summoned the party's members to meet in convention in Denver, Colorado, on 7 July, at the same time and location as the convention of the national Democratic Party. Scott indicated that the meeting would "consider their affiliations, and conditions, develop plans to change the political complexion of states wherein the negro vote is the balance of power," and "discuss the feasibility of nominating a candidate for president on the civil liberty ticket."[106] Delegates would decide then whether to select a separate ticket or endorse that of the Democratic Party. In either case, the party expected to issue an address to the nation.[107]

Taylor's demotion from presidential candidate to police patrolman must have been jarring. He had moved easily in national circles both before and after his selection to lead the Liberty Party ticket, but that ended with the conclusion of the 1904 election campaign. Issues of self-esteem and self-respect must have been acute. Taylor was, after all, the epitome of the "self-made man," the product of a frontier, a time, and a "success manual" so commonly followed at the turn of the century.[108] Taylor's encounter with an unbelieving and dismissive black press was itself unexpected and humbling. Many of its editors were his acquaintances, yet they had ignored and locked out his campaign. Taylor doubtless experienced the qualms about his adequacy and class membership that face those who rise too rapidly without sufficient social, intellectual, and political networks to support them. Bishop Derrick's prophecy—and Taylor's premonition—of "political death" was correct.

If Taylor's tenacity had been challenged by a poor showing at the polls in 1904, his self-esteem and that of nearly everyone else in his social and economic class had been damaged even more by legislative changes that had swept the South by 1910. That attack upon the status and self-esteem of black males, especially among those with little remaining capital except that given them by virtue of their gender, would have been fundamental to attitudes respecting self-worth. The world of 1910 was far different from that of 1890, when middle- and upper-class blacks worried more about the excesses of their own children than about the condition of the race. Many black males had used the Spanish-American War as an opportunity to both affirm and confirm their own manliness and show whites that blacks could be masters of their own houses and destinies. By 1910 that no longer was the case. Those chimerical claims of manhood had been dismissed, even to the point of being mocked.[109] Surely Taylor would have noticed and been affected by those changes.

What seems most intriguing, however, was Taylor's return to Ottumwa, even though he must have had opportunities to settle elsewhere. Little awaited him there except that which was known—the comfort of his farm and participation in local politics, even if that meant that he would be accepting demeaning patronage in the process. Taylor was well known and respected in Ottumwa, especially by S. B. Evans, editor of the *Ottumwa Democrat*, who in 1897 had described him as "one of the most notable Negroes of the northwest."[110] But there also remained the lingering issue of his health. Taylor had ended his studies at Wayland University for reasons of ill health and financial difficulty, and he had fallen from his roof in Oskaloosa, an accident that might have resulted in lasting injury. He had relinquished direct leadership of the NNDL early in 1904, likely for health reasons.[111] In Ross's letter to Taylor dated 9 August 1904, Ross had wished Taylor "good health," perhaps a reference to Taylor's handing effective direction of the NNDL to Ross earlier than necessary in 1904.[112] The *Ottumwa Daily Courier* had noted that Taylor had moved to Ottumwa early in 1904 to obtain medical treatment.[113] In April 1905, at the time of the death of his foster father in La Crosse, Taylor was interviewed by the *La Crosse Argus*, and at that time he indicated that he had abandoned his newspaper business in Iowa "on account of poor health."[114]

Equally interesting, Taylor's name, like countless others, was conspicuously absent from a historic assemblage of black leaders at Fort Erie, Ontario, Canada, from 11 to 13 July 1905.[115] That meeting had been called by W. E. B. Du Bois of Atlanta, Fredrick McGhee of St. Paul, and William Monroe Trotter of Boston to form a counterpoint to the moderate accommodating, self-help, and industrial education focus promoted by Booker T. Washington and followed fundamentally by Taylor until 1904. But that group was reacting to more than that. By 1905 the NAAC was essentially nonfunctional, and its national meetings consistently degenerated into shouting matches. Some of its committees operated well, but central leadership was inconsistent and ineffective. In the meantime, the surge of antiblack legislation in the South and inaction from Republicans in the North had led many newly educated black intellectuals by 1905 to doubt that Washington's plan or the council's leadership model were providing answers for America's worsening conditions. Taylor and McGhee had attempted to bring reform within the Democratic Party during the 1890s through the National Negro Democratic League, but Taylor had become dissatisfied with that course after 1900 and by 1904 had abandoned it entirely to stand as the National Negro Liberty Party's candidate for the presidency.

By 1905 differences between those known as Bookerites or the Tuskegee Machine and those who opposed Washington's vision at the national level had grown acute, with Trotter, editor of Boston's *Guardian* and leader of the Boston Gang, one of the most vocal among Washington's urban and northeastern critics. Calvin Chase of the *Washington Bee* was only slightly less anti-Washingtonian.[116] When Washington was scheduled to deliver a speech to Boston's branch of the National Negro Business League at Columbus Avenue AME Zion Church on 30 July 1903, Trotter was prepared to ask him nine accusatory questions.[117] Eleven policemen were present to maintain order, but even before Washington spoke the meeting disintegrated into fistfights, and at least one person was stabbed. Trotter, among others, was arrested and charged with "disturbing the peace" and spent thirty days in jail.[118] This "Boston Riot" of 1903 marked a turning point for many progressives and brought the debate between Washington and his critics to the front pages of black newspapers nationwide. It also led to a secret meeting called by Washington and held at Carnegie Hall in New York City from 6 to 8 January 1904 to find common ground between the two groups.[119] Du Bois, then professor of sociology at Atlanta University and author of *The Souls of Black Folk* (1903), McGhee of St. Paul, and Bishop Alexander Walters attended that meeting.[120] Du Bois later claimed that it was dominated by Bookerites and was attended by Andrew Carnegie and other "white millionaires" who treated its black participants like subordinates. This conference so embittered Du Bois that it "sealed the divisions in the black community and led to the founding of the Niagara Movement."[121]

According to Du Bois, fifty-four persons "signed a call" for the first meeting near Niagara Falls, but only twenty-nine actually attended.[122] Nearly all were from northern states and included ten lawyers, six teachers, five ministers, three editors, two government clerks, and a dentist, businessman, insurance company owner, and artist. Taylor did not attend. Except for McGhee (Democrat) and Du Bois and George Miller (socialists), all were Republicans. George Woodson, Taylor's good friend and former business partner from Buxton, Iowa, was one of the twenty-nine, and he became Iowa's state secretary.[123] All supported higher education, "racial militancy," and the top-down leadership model of a "Talented Tenth"—the "exceptional men" and an elitist "aristocracy of talent."[124] And all at that time supported litigation as the only promising path for guaranteeing or regaining civil rights for the race.[125]

If connection with the Niagara Movement was a marker for membership of a new vanguard within black society, Taylor clearly was physically as well as philosophically absent from that group, for he had supported a far different model.[126] Taylor's affiliation with the discredited ex-slave pension movement and his disaffection with McGhee may have been sufficient together to have disqualified him even from consideration.[127] Nor had Taylor and those who were listed within the leadership of the National Liberty Party been visible leaders or even prominent participants in the NAAC, which had come to dominate the national debate at the turn of the century.[128] Court rulings, whether at the national or state level, had brought successes and circumvented slow legislatures and referenda that seldom advanced civil rights. Taylor's candidacy for president, moreover, continued a tradition of aggressive political agitation, which the new leadership considered to be counterproductive, at least for that time. The Niagara Movement and the succeeding Constitutional League and National Negro American Political League signaled the demise of those with Populist and rural sentiments and confirmed the dominance of a far more

W. E. B. Du Bois. Du Bois, *The Souls of Black Folk* (1907).

professional, intellectually elitist, legal, and urban phase in African American political awareness.[129] These new groups rejected the premise that power flowed upward from grassroots associations and tended to view the leaderless masses as lacking "creative consciousness" and thoughtful deliberation or the ability to wait patiently.[130] Indeed, these new groups were themselves lacking in mass support and were composed of leaders who were described by Fortune as "an army of exalted generals."[131]

Of the new leaders, the most conspicuous was Du Bois, although McGhee was not far behind. Like Taylor, Du Bois had been raised in a largely white environment and believed himself to be a victim of marginalization, but, unlike Taylor, Du Bois had attended Fisk University, Harvard University, and the University of Berlin between 1885 and 1894, years during which Taylor was engaged in building political alliances. In 1905 Du Bois was teaching at Atlanta University, a center for building a top-down black leadership class.[132] Taylor's formative years were spent in the rural upper Midwest, while Du Bois, who was eleven years younger than Taylor, had lived his early years in Boston, where he had obtained a northeastern education and "'annexed the rich and well-to-do' as his natural companions."[133] Like Taylor, Du Bois had come to terms with his blackness only upon reaching his majority.[134] But Du Bois and those in the new leadership had never been printer's devils, and few had lived in small towns with boomtown mentalities. Indeed, Du Bois lacked any visible sign of compassion for the working classes, at least at the turn of the century.[135] Nor had he supported the ex-slave pension bill, as had Douglass in his later years.[136] Du Bois approached America's "Negro problem" intellectually from "outside of the American world, looking in."[137]

In significant contrast and perhaps marking the end of a period of African American political development, Taylor had represented a group composed mainly of pre-Populists, workingmen, farmers, and small business owners, all of whom might be linked by mutualistic self-benefit societies and by fraternal and ritualistic associations.[138] In that sense Taylor fit the typical Washingtonian supporter's characteristics of "early rural poverty and individual self help."[139] His generation and worldview were ones in which one's character, manliness, and physical accomplishments counted more than one's educational achievements. His was a world of conflict against exploitive capital interests and a promise of popular—albeit unstructured—reform and racial equality on the horizon. His world possessed "no precise map, no timetable, no all-knowing guide."[140] Nor had Taylor technically completed a certified high school or a college or university education.[141] Even if one considered his two-year period at Wayland University as a collegiate experience, that was distant in quality from that available to Du Bois or young black scholars two decades later. To be sure, Taylor, at the age of fifty, was reportedly reading law in Ottumwa in 1907, but other blacks in nearby Albia and Buxton were attending certified law schools in Iowa during those same years. Essentially, by 1908 a progressive and urban-based wing within African American society and an emerging black intellectual elite and black bourgeoisie had moved beyond Taylor and the fractured agrarian social and economic classes he had championed.[142]

6

Escape
to a Warm Place

Retreat and Reconstruct

George Taylor's last appearance in politics was in 1904, when he ran for
president of the United States on the national liberals ticket. . . . He
drifted into the white man's ways of seeking spoils of conquest and became so shifty that political leaders never were certain when they had
him or not. The republicans having lost him and the national liberals
having gone to an early grave, the Great Unwashed [Democrats] of
Ottumwa gathered him in. In the recent municipal campaign there the
democrats won, the lid was kicked higher than Gilroy's kite, and George
Taylor landed, not the consulate of which he had dreamed, but a more
appropriate if less aristocratic "job" as the supervisor of the morals of
the Ottumwa tenderloin.

La Crosse Tribune,
19 April 1907

It really grows wearisome to see so much "stuff" in the papers about
George Taylor, the Ottumwa candidate for president.

Cedar Rapids Gazette,
22 September 1904

Taylor maintained a lower profile while in Florida, but only to the degree
that he apparently neither sought national recognition nor received it.[1]
The reasons that led to his departure from Iowa are undocumented, although
changes within Ottumwa and the nation at the time suggest possible explanations. Taylor's political patron, Thomas J. Phillips, had been reelected in 1909 for

a second two-year term as Ottumwa's mayor, but by that date Phillips was being investigated by the assistant attorney general of the state of Iowa for permitting gambling houses and "resorts" to operate within Ottumwa, contrary to Iowa law. Surely Taylor would have recognized that whatever patronage he had obtained under Phillips might be short-lived and that it would be advantageous to seek employment elsewhere.[2]

Taylor also was obsessed with the belief that once again he had become a victim of being "put down" as an African American and as a person. A portion of his interview with the *Sun* of New York following his 1904 campaign focused on his conviction that some residents of Oskaloosa and other towns in Iowa had marginalized him and had jeopardized his future as a newspaper editor because of his financial success and his expenditures on basic personal comforts—for "putting on too many airs for a nigger."[3] To be sure, Taylor was a fancy dresser. Others, even black colleagues, had commented on his elaborate dress, with John Mitchell, Jr., editor of the *Richmond Planet*, writing: "He was always careful of his laundry and from the number of suits he produced from the capacious confines of trunk, silk hat included, one would have presumed that he was either a dancing master or a distant relative of the Prince of Wales."[4] Perhaps Taylor even believed himself "put down" by those East Coast black elites for having "put on too many airs" for a midwestern and minor voice who lacked both credentials and credibility and had embarrassed the nation's black community with his hopeless run for the presidency. Taylor's explanation in the *Sun* for the failures of his newspaper and his campaign sounded remarkably similar to his writing in 1887 regarding his circumstances in La Crosse and appeared nearly five years after the collapse of his newspaper venture in Oskaloosa, minimizing his own deficiencies, his argument with his own county party chairman, and the impact of more sophisticated coverage given readers by the *Iowa State Bystander*.

At another level, however, being pragmatic and well read undoubtedly influenced his decision to abandon efforts at the national level and to focus instead upon a small stage where he could obtain success. The nation's black leadership had ignored his campaign, almost to the point of dismissing it as a regional anomaly, an innocent and thoughtless expression of black powerlessness. Moreover, if Taylor had read Charlotte Gilman's provocative essay "A Suggestion on the Negro Problem," he might well have questioned whether America's white culture was prepared ever to tolerate equal black citizens, let alone to live alongside them. Gilman, a nationally recognized and respected thinker, recommended compulsory conscription of working-class blacks. They would be confined in special camps, where they would receive mandatory uplift through physical labor and education in types of "domestic service" before being released to rejoin the national population.[5] For Gilman, white people inherited a "racial memory" that blacks lacked, thereby leaving blacks physiologically and psychologically incapable of reaching higher stations.[6]

Indeed, the "Negro problem" had become a prominent topic of newspaper coverage between 1904 and 1910.[7] Thomas Dixon had published *The Leopard's Spots* (1902) and *The Clansman* (1905), two inflammatory novels that gained enormous nationwide popularity and generated pointed criticism within the black press.[8] Meanwhile, southern whites were engaged in a "white hysteria" and seemed intent upon moving blacks someplace (the "elimination theory"), whether that be Africa, the Philippines, Panama, or just any other state.[9] Bishop Turner of Atlanta had encouraged Congress to appropriate funds sufficient to remove all blacks who wished to leave the South, and many white southerners enthusiastically supported those notions.[10] Some argued that servile and freed blacks had reduced the price of labor and were obstacles to European migration, especially as that might relate to the region's economic development.[11] Others claimed that criminality increased with improved education and that racial hybridization defied Christian teaching.[12] Even Taylor at one point proposed "diffusion" or dispersal of blacks throughout the nation in small units that would be overwhelmed and transformed by superior numbers and superior culture.[13] Taylor may have known of Irving Garland Penn's belief that advantaged blacks should focus their attention solely within black communities and among black youths rather than expend fruitless efforts trying to convince whites of racial equality.[14]

But the "Negro problem" also had become more than simply a newspaper topic or a subject of intellectual discourse during that period. Only the most indifferent African Americans would not have noticed a dramatic and frightening change of demeanor toward their race then sweeping the country. In much of the South the degree of "white hysteria" against African Americans had intensified in the 1890s, and sentiments of racial inferiority had crept northward in the following decade as pseudoscientific fact. For many whites, blacks no longer were viewed as equals or near-equals. Instead, they were studied to learn the reasons for their deficiencies.[15] Whites became emboldened to attack blacks physically as well as verbally, with the consequence that a degree of rage and astonishment entered the national press with reports of blacks being "burnt alive" and of vigilante activities that seemed immune to legal restraint.[16] Taylor was not living in a vacuum.

Nor can one dismiss the probability that Taylor had come to accept that his beginnings and life course through Wisconsin and Iowa had been outside the mainstream of the black experience lived by those who increasingly exercised significant social and political influence within black society. Taylor had spent his formative years in a frontier and boomtown setting, neither of which was a part of the background of the race's new leadership. Taylor lacked the social and educational credentials of America's upper and even its professional middle class. Before 1905 he had been confident in describing himself as a waif, an orphan, and an underprivileged student who had worked his way through school. He had reveled in his "log-cabin-like" origins, his closeness to black miners and labor, and his willingness to call himself a "darkey." As a midwesterner with Populist and workingmen's roots, Taylor might have appealed to lower- and working-class blacks (or whites), but those self-descriptors would scarcely convert into influence among America's northern, urban, and increasingly well-educated African Americans. Taylor was well read but not respected by those destined to lead a black renaissance.[17] His origins and life history were very different from those of John Mitchell, Jr., for instance, who, while born to working-class parents, had "grown up amid the wealth of [Richmond's] Grace Street" and had enjoyed the benefits of a Freedmen's Bureau education.[18] Taylor's health also may have been an impediment to travel within an expanded lecture circuit. Surely he would have recognized those deficits by 1910.

Moving from coal country in Iowa to Florida would have represented a major change of environment, but even that move was entirely reasonable in Taylor's case. He had traveled widely during his tenures as presidents of various national organizations, and by 1905 he was known as an accomplished and entertaining lecturer, even in "southern educational circles."[19] He had served as grand chancellor of the Iowa Knights of Pythias and president of the National Negro Knights of Pythias and had attended the national convention of the (Prince Hall) Free and Accepted Masons in Jacksonville in 1900 as a leader within Iowa's "colored" order.[20] Without doubt, by 1910 he would have made useful acquaintances in Florida within the Masonic and journalistic fraternities, friendships that might have translated into employment opportunities. Tampa as well as Jacksonville and St. Augustine to its north all had thriving black communities in 1910. Tampa's black population in 1900 was 9,000 of a total of 26,000, accounting for a third of the city's population.[21] Census records for Jacksonville from 1880 to 1910 listed blacks as the statistical majority of its population (29,293 of 57,622 in 1910). Blacks there had been well represented in government, at least until the tide of disenfranchisement legislation swept the South at the turn of the century and moved into Florida.[22] Florida's eastern coast also was known nationally for its "health resorts" and its numerous "sulphur springs," with a "marvelous reputation for healing."[23]

Taylor's first appearance in Florida records is a single entry of 21 April 1910 in the federal census for Tampa (Hillsborough County), where he was listed as a boarder at 610 Kay Street, as unmarried, and as a journalist working for a "daily paper," likely the *Florida Reporter*, but no issues of that paper have survived.[24] The *Florida Reporter* in 1910 was owned and operated by Rev. Y. K. Meeks, who two decades earlier had lived in St. Augustine and who by 1910 was a prominent member of Tampa's branch of the recently formed National Negro Business League.[25] Taylor remained in Tampa for little more than a year, for in 1911 and 1912 he was described as "organizer," "promoter," and "secretary and manager" of the Magnolia Remedy Company of St. Augustine.[26] While service in such a company would have been unusual for Taylor, it was not outside his antecedents. White Beaver Powell of La Crosse, Wisconsin, who had been Taylor's principal supporter during his introduction into political activism, had been involved in such ventures, producing nostrums, salves, and medicinal remedies to cure most known and imagined illnesses. Taylor, moreover, had sold advertisements in his *Wisconsin Labor Advocate* to numerous companies producing and hawking such items nationwide. Nearly a third of the pages of the *Albia Republican* (Taylor lived near Albia between 1901 and 1904) were filled with extravagant advertisements for miraculous cures—all guaranteed, of course, with testimonies to prove their claims. One of the concoctions distributed by the Magnolia firm was Brown's New Consumption Remedy, which it represented "as a remedy for consumption, pneumonia, la grippe, etc."[27] St. Augustine also promoted its sulphur springs as having miraculous healing properties, a promise that might have appealed to Taylor for personal reasons. Perhaps Taylor accepted the "buyer beware" attitude of turn-of-the-century America, for nostrums and extravagant promises were prominently advertised in newspapers and even in the Sears catalog at that time. While in St. Augustine, Taylor also engaged in a degree of self-promotion, entering his name in *Successful Americans of Our Day*, where he commended himself for writing a book titled "Remove the Mask" and for his "lecture on Backward Steps [that] has made him famous."[28]

While neither the book nor the lecture has been located, the book title alone indicates that Taylor had not capitulated completely as of 1911 to the passive role of disinterested spectator in national debates on disenfranchisement or the "Negro problem."[29] In 1904 Taylor had argued that Republicans—white or black—who had constructed platform planks to oppose disenfranchisement in the South were either unknowing and naive or disingenuous and deceitful.[30] What Taylor demanded was clarity and honesty from both parties, especially the Republican Party, which the majority of blacks continued to support. If the party could remove the "mask" of pretending to support equal voting rights and equal opportunity for all of its citizens, Taylor believed that the national debate on race would advance. The greater opponents of black progress were southern Democrats and lily-white Republicans, but those in the North who spoke with one voice while minimizing the long-term implications of disen-franchisement nationwide were, for Taylor, equally at fault and perhaps even more dangerous.

Taylor remained in St. Augustine only one year. He moved to Jacksonville late in 1912, where he was listed in the 1913 city directory as the manager of the Promotion Publishing Company. This firm printed the *Daily Promoter*, a news-paper that contained advertisements for items of interest to the black commu-nity.[31] Taylor's specific activities of early 1914 are largely unknown, except that the city directory listed him as "lecturer," a description that would have been reasonable in his case. In August 1914 he became the secretary of the Colored AME/YMCA (African Methodist Episcopal/Young Men's Christian Associa-tion) of Jacksonville, a position that in 1914 was the equivalent of "executive di-rector" and confirmed both his organizational abilities and a significant degree of acceptance within Jacksonville's established black community.[32]

By 1916 Taylor had become president of the board of commissioners of the Most Worshipful Union Grand Lodge of the Prince Hall Free and Accepted Masons, a position that placed him squarely in the center of Jacksonville's black establishment.[33] Indeed, in 1912 this lodge had commenced the construction of a magnificent new headquarters at 410 Broad Street. Taylor's acceptance within the Masonic organizational structure includes an unambiguous recognition that he had arrived in Jacksonville sufficiently known within the fraternity and that he rose quickly within its local hierarchy. Arriving already in Florida as a thirty-third-degree Mason, Taylor perhaps was unusual, for that degree gener-ally was held only by grand masters of lodges. Within Jacksonville, moreover, the central Masonic lodge exercised significant influence, perhaps only ex-ceeded by that of the "Negro church."[34]

Why Jacksonville? Once having moved to Florida and with two years' expe-rience there, Taylor surely recognized that Jacksonville held more opportunities for him than did either Tampa or St. Augustine. In 1910 nearly one-tenth of Florida's state population was located in Duval County, and more than half of that number consisted of African Americans, of which 85 percent were liter-ate.[35] Black migration from rural areas to Jacksonville, moreover, had already reached a mature stage by 1910. A massive fire destroyed 146 city blocks and nearly 2,350 of Jacksonville's wooden structures in May 1901, and a major re-building effort had followed.[36] The consequence was a fully employed city and a people that presented the black newcomer with the outward appearance of progress, improvement, and optimism, despite significant setbacks in voting rights then sweeping Florida as in other southern states.

By 1910 much of the city had been reconstructed and to a degree transformed. That makeover began earlier in Jacksonville than in many southern cities, primarily because of the necessity to rebuild after the 1901 fire.[37] By 1912 Jacksonville's center even included two ten-story "skyscrapers."[38] It had become a "bustling, go-getter, money-mad city," much like La Crosse in the 1880s.[39] Improvements in clearing swamps and controlling mosquitoes were significantly better than elsewhere in the South.[40] For its black citizens, Jacksonville contained sixty-four churches, two segregated parks (Mason and Lincoln, with the latter having a roller coaster, dance pavilion, and facilities for vaudeville shows and concerts), Manhattan Beach, two theaters, thirty-three elementary schools, two newspapers, two banks, eight drugstores, and at least "342 small businesses owned by blacks."[41] James Weldon Johnson, who returned to Jacksonville in 1912 after a decade's absence, described it as a city captured by "get-rich-quick fever," with "marvelous tales of fortunes suddenly made" and where "colored men lived in finer houses than were occupied by anybody, except the quite rich white citizens."[42] The city was home to "thirteen black [Masonic] lodges, seven black Knights of Pythias lodges, and several mutual aid societies."[43] Jacksonville also was the site of the B. F. Lee Theological Seminary, Cookman Institute, Edward Waters College, Florida Baptist Academy/College, Walker National Business College, Boylan-Haven Home Industrial Training School for Girls, and Stanton Night School, all secondary or post–high school level schools operated by or for African Americans.[44] Jacksonville headquartered the Afro-American Life Insurance Company, founded in 1901 as the Afro-American Industrial and Benefit Association and destined to become one of the nation's premier African American insurance companies.[45] The city even contained the exclusive black Lincoln Golf and Country Club, which catered to its wealthiest black citizens.[46] There was a black upper class in Jacksonville, but the majority of Jacksonville's blacks worked, shopped, and studied in businesses that were black owned or black operated.[47]

Against those advances there existed significant drawbacks. Jacksonville remained a "wide-open town" where "saloons, brothels, and opium dens" flourished.[48] A majority of Jacksonville's black population was concentrated in the city's northwestern section, called Hansontown, an area that lacked sewers and that accounted for "three-fourths of the [city's] typhoid fever cases."[49] While 59 percent of whites held white-collar jobs, 76 percent of blacks were occupied in semiskilled or unskilled professions and "at the bottom of the economic ladder."[50] Black schools were separate and significantly underfunded relative to white ones, but many schools were new in consequence of the 1901 fire. Newly passed Jim Crow laws had ended by 1910 the assertion of integration and had segregated the city's population more visibly than a decade before. Jacksonville had developed into "two cities in the years after the fire, one white and one black."[51]

For Taylor, however, Jacksonville, unlike Wisconsin or Iowa, represented a significant improvement, and it provided him with a new stage upon which to rebuild his reputation. Taylor could now participate in a majority urban population as an African American. He had arrived in Jacksonville with credentials as an articulate speaker and writer, an editor, a business owner and manager, an organizer, an insurance salesman, a "judge," an accomplished Mason and Pythian, and a former presidential candidate. He had attended Wayland University and had studied law, although informally while recuperating in Ottumwa.

Jacksonville likely provided Taylor with an opportunity to start anew. He arrived without a wife and with good credentials. The record of his initial years in Jacksonville indicates that he obtained a level of acceptance that recognized both his abilities and his former accomplishments. He obtained middle-class confirmation by working for black-owned and black-operated organizations but at a managerial rank that would have separated him from the city's working class.[52] He was neither "well bred" nor "well born" and therefore lacked admission to the city's "natural aristocracy," which considered even the newly formed NAACP as "too grassroots for people like us."[53] In effect, Taylor obtained status and position without assuming significant risk, as was the case when he ran for the office of president of the United States. To a degree, Taylor assumed the role of a noteworthy and financially rewarding player within a small, controlled environment. This was not the national platform upon which he had effectively performed before 1904 and that clearly had moved beyond him by 1910, but he could play this role upon a stage and within a setting that would bring him success.

Taylor returned to the publishing field in 1917, at least to the degree that he became the editor of the "colored" section of the *Florida Times-Union*, the city's most important newspaper and certainly the one with the largest black readership in Florida. Two editions of the paper were printed daily. One had a black star at the top of the first page; the other did not. The "black star edition" contained an additional section titled "News for and about the Colored People of Jacksonville" that could be inserted into papers delivered to black residents. That section contained mainly local news concerning churches, schools, and fraternal organizations. It also covered the city's social life, sports events, weddings and engagements, and obligatory obituaries.[54]

How long Taylor remained employed with the *Florida Times-Union* is uncertain, but it is known that he maintained an office at the Walker National Business College (417½ West Broad) in 1918. Walker was privately owned and operated, and it focused on business skills (typing, bookkeeping, business letter writing, secretarial, salesmanship) and vocational training (tailoring, hairdressing, printing, blueprint reading, design, and others), essentially following the formula advanced by the Tuskegee Institute. It maintained a dormitory and provided board and was considered one of the largest privately funded black schools of its type in the United States.[55]

During this same period Jacksonville experienced significant economic recovery from a difficult downturn that had occurred between 1914 and 1916. The city had overbuilt in the decade following the great fire of 1901, and that bubble burst in 1914, with nearly a third of the commercial buildings, half of the houses, and two-thirds of office space unsold or underused. Recovery came with the beginning of World War I, when Jacksonville's prosperity became linked to food exports to Europe, shipbuilding, and service to nearby military campsites. Nearly 32,000 of Duval County's men were conscripted into military units, and high government-generated demands for civilian labor produced "enormous wages" for those who remained behind.[56] Nearly all of Jacksonville's office space, for instance, was occupied by government agencies by 1918.

War and the presence of nearby military encampments, however, also had its downside. In September 1918 Jacksonville encountered its first cases of Spanish influenza, and the epidemic reached its peak in late October, when more than 5,000 whites and 11,000 blacks contracted the virus.[57] Spanish influenza assaulted the United States basically in three waves. The second occurred in the early winter of 1918–19, and it was likely this wave that accounted for the high number of cases in October 1918. The third wave arrived in March 1919, and it was equally invasive, although many of its victims were those from the second wave who had not recovered fully from their earlier illness. During its peak, businesses, theaters, popular venues, and sports events were strictly regulated to minimize crowds and viral exposure.

It is perhaps not surprising that Taylor vanished from Jacksonville's city directory for three years, from 1919 to 1922, especially if he suffered from chronic pulmonary difficulties throughout his life. The 1920 census placed him in the Thirty-second Arlington Precinct of Duval County (Magnolia), where he was operating a "poultry farm" along with his new wife, Marion M. Tillinghast (born in March 1888 and the daughter of James P. and Sarah Tillinghast of Green Cove Springs, Clay County, Florida).[58] A January 1926 newspaper notice after his death late in 1925 reported erroneously that Taylor's "farm" was located near Green Cove Springs, Florida.[59] Green Cove Springs was famous even before the Civil War as a destination for medical treatment, and its popularity increased steadily for the remainder of the nineteenth century. It was known for "a warm sulphur spring noted for its medicinal properties."[60] Jacksonville and Green Cove Springs (thirty miles apart) were well served, with three trains daily.[61]

Taylor reappeared in the Jacksonville city directory in 1922, this time as a cofounder and organizer for the Progressive Order of Men and Women. This order was affiliated with the Free and Ancient Masons and was considered the "latest" fraternal organization to arrive in Jacksonville and one of its most "secret" ones.[62] Its objectives and memberships were unique if not altogether apparent from its name. Its founders included Jacksonville's leading citizens, among whom were two presidents of women's lodges:

> The Progressive Order of Men and Women register[s] a significant and unique name on the catalogue of Fraternal organizations. Moreover it has in it those inherent principles and qualities that give it an honored place among the societies of the country. It will live and grow because of its adapt[at]ion and fitness to meet the growing demands of this strenuous age. We, as a race, are casting about for societies in which to invest our money, and devote our time in a successful and pleasant way. Such an opportunity is offered among the class of individuals who make up the Fraternal membership of this Order. We find them in possession of one of the world's leading principles, perpetual progress for wives, husbands, sons and daughters, which come through its benefit department, hence, something is left beside the regalia and uniform that could rightly be put away close beside [the] sleeping one, who has served his society so faithfully during his or her life time. The marching out of the Progressives upon the Fraternal Arena marks a new epoch in society life of the race that is destined to bring about more beneficial change, taking its members out of the ruts of the dim and dusty past, planting their feet in a straight and plain path, fixing the eye upon the golden Star of Hope, which means much to a people whose ancestry has been the dupes and prey to the unscrupulous organizer of many petty secret societies that might have done much in uniting the races, instead of arousing suspicion and mistrust, thereby keeping them out of many good things that might have proven to be the instrument of their mutual uplift. Suspicion, superstition and jealousy are among the greatest burdens of the age. We need to have implicit confidence in our leader else the dark cloud that may arise will have no silver lining to shed a ray of hope.[63]

That it contained a "benefit department" indicates that the organization sold memberships and collected dues and that benefits were paid out to survivors.

The duration of his employment with the Progressive Order is unclear, except that by 1923–24 Taylor also had become editor of the *Florida Sentinel*, a progressive weekly newspaper that in 1912 had moved to Jacksonville from Pensacola.[64] The latter employment was significant, for the *Sentinel* covered agrarian Populist issues, and Taylor's midwestern roots and his editorial experience would have made him eminently qualified for such a position. Additionally, Taylor returned from a three-year absence from Jacksonville without having suffered diminished status; the reverse seems to have been the case. In May 1923, for example, Taylor delivered the commencement address for the graduating class of Walker National Business College, an honor given generally to one of Jacksonville's leading black citizens.[65]

Taylor's activities in 1925 are largely unknown, with the exception of his death on 23 December. Jacksonville's city directory for 1925 lists only his address and the name of his wife, Marion.[66] The announcement of his death and funeral was brief. A single obituary, published in Albuquerque's *Southwest Review*, reported that he had been found dead in his house on Duval Street in Jacksonville, that his funeral "was widely attended by citizens of all walks of life and the passing of the dapper old man was mourned by persons far and wide," and that he was "survived by a wife, Mrs. Marie [Marion] Taylor now of Arlando," likely referring to the residence of a relative, Viola Tillinghast, who was married to Rev. Hezekiah K. Hill, pastor of the Zion Missionary Baptist Church in Orlando.[67] Taylor was sixty-eight years of age. Marion Tillinghast Taylor was listed in the 1930 federal census and the 1935 Florida census as a teacher and widow living with her parents in Clay County, Florida, where Green Cove Springs was the county seat.[68]

Conclusion

Taylor's political activism at the national level was remarkably brief, but what an impressive thirteen years it was. That Taylor was able to appear from nowhere and within two years rise to become president of one of black America's few national nonpartisan forums, the National Colored Men's Protective Association, says much about his innate abilities, which separated him from those around him, and about his internal drive to attempt and accomplish great things. In those first two years, 1891–93, black leaders in the national Republican Party recognized this newcomer as an emergent voice with leadership potential, but he bolted that party in a public display and then wrote a dazzling broadside, actions that brought him serious censure and probably would have destroyed the political potential of a person of lesser drive and ability. Within his first three years, moreover, Taylor led the National Colored Men's Protective Association to perhaps its most influential period, hosting in 1893 a conference of three hundred delegates and six hundred attendees in Chicago (the Congress of Negroes) during the World's Columbian Exposition. A significant number of America's black political thinkers attended that meeting and enthusiastically joined its mission, and Taylor addressed them all as the association's president. Within six years he was president of both the Negro National Free Silver League and the Negro (Midwestern) Inter-State Free Silver League. Within seven years he had captured a leadership role in the National Negro Democratic League and within nine was president of NNDL and founder and president of the National Knights of Pythias. He traveled the country in support of these organizations and became an accomplished orator who charmed his audiences with wit and eloquence. He was rising rapidly.

Taylor's political and nonpartisan activities at the state level were significant as well, although perhaps never reaching the prominence of his national accomplishments. He published a newspaper that lasted from 1893 to 1898, married for a second time, and served as a delegate—of sorts—for both state-based Republican and Democratic parties at their national conventions. He founded and was president of statewide nonpartisan forums, and he participated widely in all groups that professed to champion progress in the black community. He was cofounder of a cooperative commercial venture along with persons with divergent political views and socioeconomic backgrounds. And he was a frequent lecturer who appeared throughout the state to celebrate black solidarity and self-help.

But that he was able to accomplish so much in a short period also says something significant about the condition of black activism during this crucial time in black political history. Between 1891, when Taylor surfaced after his time in the "West," and 1904, when effectively he left political activism following his very public and failed presidential election campaign, black activists were alarmed by the rapid dismantling of voting rights that accompanied redemptive white rule in southern states. To that were added certain and accelerating waves of violence against blacks across the South through lynching and terrorist raids, a spread of "white hysteria" northward into states that bordered the Old South, and an emergence of "scientific racism" that justified for many whites those latent prejudices already existing within the nation's population. For black activists, the prominent issues were no longer simply those of patronage, of integration and full participation within the whole of American life, or of obtaining civil equality. Instead, the question then was how to stop the steady slide into an abyss and a status of new servitude, separateness, and racial inferiority. For all practical purposes, that battle had been lost in the South after the Hayes-Tilden Compromise of 1877 and especially after the Supreme Court's ruling in *Civil Rights Cases* in 1883.

Indeed, a vast majority of black political activists following the Civil War had expected the Republican Party to protect those it had liberated during the war. That had happened so long as the Radical Republicans remained in control of national and state administrations, but that support group was leaving politics through death or defeat, and the emergent class of leaders was not interested in revisiting old battlefields. The country increasingly was divided between Democrats, who profited when splinter groups formed as advocates of special interests, and Republicans, who championed business, capital, and the old themes of protecting the country against the radicals who were increasing in labor's ranks. Blacks found options in other parties, although it was hard to break an old habit of voting Republican. By 1891 even the long dominance of Republicans at the national level had been interrupted by the election of Grover Cleveland as president in 1884, and new opportunities opened for alienated black Republicans who felt affinity to sections of the Democratic agenda and who changed parties for that reason as well as for patronage options available from the other party. Continued Republican rule was no longer a certainty, and the possibility of other Democratic victories at the national level sent shock waves and insecurity through the black community.

By 1891 black Republicans had split into several factions: first, the old guard, or those who had participated in southern Reconstruction and who had become prominent voices in bureaucracy at the national level; second, those in the middle, who had come of age in the 1870s, who had participated in state-based struggles in the North to obtain rights, and who expected patronage and influence but found that path obstructed if not occupied already by members of the old guard; and last, latecomers from the mid-1880s, who found themselves embattled primarily with issues of retaining rights and privileges gained through struggle during the preceding quarter century. Most had remained loyal to the party of Lincoln and Sumner, but a sizeable number had declared themselves Democrats, and some had even become socialists. Everyone knew that the South had been lost, but the question was how to bring solidarity and usefulness to a group of black activists who themselves had splintered into nearly warring factions.

Effectively, this was a chaotic period of almost frantic organizing into "anti-lynching leagues," desperate rearguard attempts to find a consensus that would halt the violence. Such nonpartisan leagues ideally would be expected to end bickering between factions and bridge widening gaps between those who proposed acceptance and slow progress through education and self-help schemes, those who advocated aggressive approaches through political activism and "constant agitation," and those who placed their trust in litigation and the courts. The legal system had at least a chance of countering mob rule and violence, which appeared to be gaining ground nationwide. Few trusted the leaderless masses, but whether guidance would come from an educated "talented tenth" or from grassroots agitation was still undecided.

Taylor entered this scene as a new voice, one unencumbered by a history of involvement in any of these groups. Perhaps that and his ability to organize and lead were his attractions to those who wished for nonpartisan forums but were unable to guide them because of identification with one cause or another. As a new voice, and as one with remarkable organizational skills learned through labor agitation, Taylor provided that ideal neutral choice in providing guidance and direction. Fortune, for instance, had envisioned that his National Afro-American League would be led by someone untainted by patronage—a heavy burden to find in 1887 or 1890. The National Negro Democratic League had limped through its early years primarily because strong personalities controlled it, and they argued incessantly and essentially avoided consensus even among black Democrats. The National Colored Men's Protective Association required leadership and organizational skills, although, frankly, little of its activities are known because the press printed only reports of its conventions, its objectives as announced publicly, and lists of its officers.

By 1900 and 1904, however, all of these groups were in disarray. The South had disenfranchised its black population, segregation was being put into place, and the contagion of antiblack rhetoric was creeping northward, and nothing seemed able to stop it. The Republican Party in 1900 and 1904 had won impressive national elections, and the country effectively had split into two sections. The anomaly of Democratic victories at the national level had passed, and except for the failed administration of Woodrow Wilson during World War I, Republicans would retain control of the national government until 1933. Black voters, who had been courted before and whom both parties had considered potential swing voters, turning elections in either direction, were no longer regarded as relevant or important for political victory. And black issues were ignored.

Perhaps Taylor recognized that reality before 1904, but the Republican landslide of 1904 essentially confirmed it and relegated Taylor and his dream of black leverage in the electoral process to the dustbin of history. Most of these national organizations limped forward, but if they survived at all it was at the state and city levels, for their objectives and relevance at the national level were now disregarded. Taylor must have comprehended that fact while recouping in Ottumwa following his election loss in 1904. Taylor ended an era with his run for the presidency in 1904. In 1903 Trotter of Boston had fired the first volleys in a new approach for black solidarity with a different leadership style and with new objectives that would lead eventually to the founding of NAACP in 1909. Taylor's campaign in 1904 was the last one in the old approach. He was the last of his class and surely a man before his time.

On a more personal level, Taylor was largely the captive of his own time and place. Born before the beginning of the Civil War in a slave state, it is doubtful that Taylor had any memory of his early years in those circumstances. But he would have remembered the confusion and insecurity that accompanied his mother's move from Arkansas to Alton and the uncertainty and trauma that followed her death there. One can only imagine what emotional and physiological scars were left upon a four- or five-year-old who found himself abandoned by the death of a parent, living alone in "dry goods boxes" and without a sponsor. He was on a river-based frontier during a period of war, and people around him were moving ever westward or along the Mississippi River in search of an

149

unknown place and future. Taylor followed that flow, whether by choice or by circumstance, to the boomtown of La Crosse, where he found a patron, a gentle but politically savvy farmer who went far beyond what was expected to care for Taylor and others taken under his charge.

In a large sense Taylor was fortunate. Orphans or fostered children often were exploited mercilessly and abused in an age when opportunities were great but circumstances were constricting. Taylor obtained not only loving attention but also a laudable education for his time and place. While Wayland University might not have equated with institutions in the Yankee Northeast or with Freedmen's Bureau colleges specifically established to produce an African American leadership class, it provided him an education steeped in classical studies and an appreciation for oratory and grammar. He was intelligent and a quick learner, and he became an excellent organizer.

In his time and place, doors were open for a well-read and educated African American. That was not true everywhere. Blacks had played important service roles in La Crosse since its founding in the 1840s, and by the time of Taylor's arrival there in 1865—and by the time he finished his studies at Wayland in 1879—blacks were included in the membership of La Crosse's exclusive Old Settlers Association. Black barbers had dominated that trade for decades, and a few of its more successful members had accumulated sizeable assets through land speculation and property development. Blacks lived scattered throughout La Crosse, with some living on the estates of wealthy families and acting as coachmen, horse tenders, and household staff. Others of the working class labored in the river and railroad trades as cooks, stewards, and waiters. The record indicates that, despite the color line, numerous mixed-racial marriages were recorded officially in the city. La Crosse was basically a Yankee-based frontier city and a boomtown, and it reflected many of those attitudes of northern towns toward black residents—so long as the latter remained a minor segment of the population.

Frontier life also influenced Taylor's life and thinking—in his time and location. The 1870s and 1880s were decades of massive migration, with larger than average personalities leading the way. Yankee settlers had dominated post–Civil War migration patterns, but those models were changing rapidly as newly arrived Europeans competed for space and livelihoods in the upper Midwest. Old money still counted on the frontier, but a new spirit of adventure and get-rich-quick schemes flourished, with high-risk takers aplenty. La Crosse and Taylor's early years were filled with flamboyant characters (Brick Pomeroy, White Beaver Powell, and Buffalo Bill) who promised magical cures, unrealistic dreams, and spectacular entertainment. But a frontier world, where Judge Lynch could survive alongside robber barons who purchased influence freely and cheaply within the established political parties, also came at a price and a re-action. It was only reasonable that Taylor, who reached his age of majority in a rural and smallish industrial center, might find his guides or mentors among those who had obtained success through showy behavior and extravagant dress and might respond against big capital and champion workingmen's causes. The frontier also was a place of increasing nativistic sentiments, blaming problems on newly arrived settlers, whether strike-breaking mill workers from the South or newly arrived immigrants from Europe.

At the same time, however, Taylor was restricted in his worldview. He was black in a predominantly white and midwestern world to which he had gained entry through effort and skill and to no small degree through acceptance by others regardless of his race. He certainly knew that he was black and experi-enced the color line in La Crosse, but to what degree he was fully aware of the full condition of his race before he left La Crosse is unanswered. He was mar-ginal with regard to his birth, his status as a child who had been raised by some-one other than his biological parents, his race, and his level of skill. He had no class standing, except that of a willing follower who conformed to whatever status he was given. Still, he was not average by any means. He had been the re-cipient of crucial opportunities at important points in his life course. If he hoped to retain his acceptance in La Crosse, however, his attention would be re-stricted to a small space and to small issues. As soon as he moved beyond that small space he lost degrees of acceptance at an increasing rate.

Taylor's move from Wisconsin to an unknown "West" and then to Iowa demonstrates that he also was a risk taker or at least was not terrified by the pros-pect of uprooting and moving to another location. Whether that risk taking came as a consequence of believing that he had been "put down" as an African American or whether his behavior or his elaborate and "dapper" wardrobe had increased his own marginality remains unclear. At the same time he was willing to think unconventionally and to act upon new opportunities when they be-came open to him. He was adventurous enough to make a major environmental change with his move to Iowa and his even more dramatic one to Florida two decades later. One might argue that he made few risky decisions while living in La Crosse, but investing in and operating a printing business does not demon-strate risk aversion, nor do his "spicy" editorials against his former patrons and allies, despite the fact that all editors for the time tended to be intemperate. That was perhaps not a wise course to follow, but he must have known the potential consequences of an immoderate pen, and still he was willing to take that risk. Perhaps he deliberately burned bridges when confronting adversity.

Either before he arrived in Iowa or during his three-year hiatus between 1887 and 1891, Taylor changed and reinvented himself, and he never again returned

151

to clear the wreckage left in La Crosse. Likely even before moving to Iowa, Taylor had abandoned his labor activism while retaining much of its objectives and methods. He took risks by involving himself in numerous state and national associations that focused exclusively upon African American issues, a remarkable change from his earlier period in Wisconsin. He allied himself with the Republican Party only to find that his agenda was more akin to that of the Democrats, at least that part of the party in the North. He championed Democratic causes in an age when the overwhelming majority of voting African Americans were loyal to the Republican Party, unless they were agrarian Populists, of course. He married—again. He started a newspaper to support his agenda. And he traveled widely on a lecture circuit, always speaking to black audiences and encouraging support for several national organizations of which he was often president. He was a superb multitasker, able to engage in numerous activities at the same time and accomplish moderate success in nearly all of them.

His greatest risk, however, was not really a risk at all—his candidacy within the National Negro Liberty Party. Yet he seemed knowingly to discount prudence in favor of a cause that had no chance of victory. Perhaps Taylor, even before his selection to lead the Liberty Party's ticket, had reached a crossroads and had obtained an appreciation that his generation and persons of his status were being overtaken by other currents within the national and increasingly the newly emerging urban black community. That analysis may reward Taylor with more foresight than he deserves or than is reasonable. Taylor was not naive. Apparently, he also was not healthy in 1904. By then he had relinquished leadership roles in the National Negro Democratic League and the Colored People's National Protective Association and perhaps in others that are unknown. He had retreated from his newspaper business, at least to the degree that he had followed it as both owner and editor from the mid-1880s. But success as editor of a nationally recognized black newspaper had eluded him, likely because he lacked the social class status and the historical and educational backgrounds found among America's leading black editors. Equally likely, however, Taylor had obtained great success in initiating organizations and businesses but lacked the personal drive and perhaps physical stamina necessary to insure continuity over the long term. And he was without both social and economic capital upon which to call for support when facing adversity. His roots were founded in an agrarian Populist and boomtown context, and both were declining at the beginning of the twentieth century with the growth of large industrialized cities and the emergence of a progressive wing within the Republican Party.

Taylor's run as candidate of the National Liberty Party in 1904 probably ended permanently his risk-taking phase and brought the "political death" that he had envisioned and others had promised. But it also may have brought an appreciation for a new concept of time and place and the limits of his physical well-being. Perhaps Taylor had missed major adversity during the preceding years, as though two marriages were not to be defined as setbacks or to have raised deep-set issues of abandonment and self-worth. But assuming that one of those marriages ended with the death of a spouse and the second through divorce, Taylor recovered sufficiently to permit them neither to handicap nor to immobilize him permanently.

Abandonment and betrayal were not small issues in Taylor's life course. Whether Taylor believed himself abandoned by the death of his mother or the exit of the Southalls in 1868 is perhaps a minor point. But he surely thought himself betrayed by workingmen who failed to support his Union Labor Party in 1887 and by his patron, White Beaver Powell, in that same election cycle. Even Brick Pomeroy, his guide, had left him behind in La Crosse when he moved to Denver in 1880. Taylor had placed his trust in the Republican Party, only to believe himself betrayed in 1892 for having placed his faith in its promise of protection of black civil rights. At least one wife and perhaps two betrayed him before he moved eventually to Florida. To be sure, his newspaper readers abandoned him in 1898, whether because he failed to maintain their interest or because they "put him down" on account of his race. Certainly, the Democratic Party betrayed him, despite his commitment to its general platform. And even the Liberty Party betrayed him in 1904 by promising a lively campaign when it was fully unable and unwilling to deliver on that pledge.

In large part, Taylor's moves to Iowa and Florida provided opportunities for reinvention within a context where people around him did not expect miracles to result from his efforts. In 1910 Florida was distant from Iowa and from his upper midwestern heritage. Florida gave Taylor yet a third chance to create himself, and yet it permitted him to call upon his past experiences and accomplishments to provide him with sufficient capital for success and employment. None of the positions he held in Florida were insignificant ones, for certainly all of Taylor's employers believed him to be competent to lead their enterprises and bring them success. Taylor was not beyond flaunting his abilities, however, and selling himself to employers. But none of those employments represented major risk taking in the conventional sense of the term. Perhaps the only risk taken was Taylor's decision to marry for yet a third time.

Florida also represented for Taylor his first opportunity to be fully engaged in an increasingly segregated and urban African American world and to confront it as a near equal. If one assumes that before Florida he had been above average among those with whom he maneuvered, his circumstances in Tampa,

St. Augustine, and Jacksonville were very different. Perhaps it was only there that Taylor had been forced to confront his true negritude and his diminished position within it. Jacksonville had a black upper class, at least the beginnings of a "natural aristocracy" to which Taylor could never belong. Nor did he possess financial resources sufficient to gain recognition in its upper middle class. His skills, celebrity, memberships in fraternal organizations, and reputation as a superb organizer were his capital, as they had been in Wisconsin and Iowa, and he could call only upon them for support to carry him through his mature years.

Taylor was the agent of his own successes and deficiencies. Only when it became clear to him that race was a dominating factor did Taylor make the attempt to join the black community as a fully participating member. Most of his efforts before 1891 can be viewed in terms of a white-dominated world, and in that world his successes were remarkable. He was articulate, accepting of its norms, and willing to acquiesce to its demands. That changed dramatically with his geographical and philosophical move to Iowa, where his involvement as an African American took form. There his organizational skills, his intellectual abilities, and his literary talents were applied to issues important to the black community and gained him national recognition as a political thinker and up-and-coming leader. He was one of few who could fuse the language of labor agitator to that of Washingtonian "uplift" and make it address the needs of the common folk. That was no mean accomplishment, for Booker T. Washington had opposed political protest, and that issue was the one that most separated him from his critics. But Taylor abandoned that world with his move to Florida, where he settled for a contained urban environment and for a degree of normality that provided success and yet permitted him to express himself successfully within a diminished context.

In a speech in Keokuk, Iowa, in 1898 Taylor had borrowed from Washington to illustrate his belief that black Americans should look first to their own improvement and personal interests, noting that Washington had asked his audience to "put down thy bucket here." Taylor did that several times.

A Postscript

Muriel Tillinghast, Taylor's niece by marriage and daughter of John Tillinghast, Marion Tillinghast Taylor's younger brother, was Ralph Nader's running mate on the Green Party ticket (New York State ballot) for vice president of the United States in the 1996 election cycle. Tillinghast lives in Brooklyn, New York, where she is active in political and social reform.

Appendix A

Taylor's Interview with the *Sun* after the 1904 Election

This interview was given by George E. Taylor to the *Sun* in New York City a few days after the election of 1904.* Taylor reminisced about his last years in Iowa and reasons for the failure of his campaign. He also delivered a warning to the effect that African Americans could exercise a balance of power with their votes, a lesson learned most recently in the election of 2008.

Negroes Seek Recognition.

Hold the balance of power, says ex-candidate Taylor.

Aims of the Party That Nominated Him for President. He thinks there are 5,000,000 more Negroes in the country than the census reported.

The night before election, one of the Presidential candidates sat in the little office of a Sixth avenue saloon in the heart of the Tenderloin negro colony. Few persons knew of his presence in the city. Though he had been regularly nominated by his party, any one voting for him had to use the free-for-all column on the extreme right hand side of the ballot.

The candidate was George E. Taylor of the National Negro Liberty party. After election day he spoke of the aims and hopes of his supporters.

*Sun (New York City), 20 November 1904, sec. 3, 7.

155

"Yes, I know most white folks take me as a joke," said Mr. Taylor. "Frequently when I was introduced as one of the Presidential candidates, I saw people pass the wink around. They didn't think I saw it, but I want to tell you the colored man is beginning to see a lot of things that the white folks do not give him credit for seeing. He's beginning to see that he has got to take care of his own interests, and what's more, that he has the power to do it.

"There are few people that know just what the negroes' power is. In spite of the census, even their numerical strength is not known. The special bulletin on the negro issued this year by the census bureau credits the colored man with being a little over nine million strong. If the census-takers had added about five million more to that number they would have been nearer the truth.

"Those are startling figures, but they are based on facts that are hard to get around. When I started the *Negro Solicitor* in Oskaloosa, Ia., a few years ago, I wanted to find out for advertising and publishing reasons the exact number of negroes in each town and country district of Iowa and the surrounding States.

"Intelligent negroes were picked out in each district, and they made a personal canvass for me. The returns showed a negro population 50 per cent, in excess of that returned in the official United States census.

"Two explanations may be given for this tremendous discrepancy. One is that the authorities do not want to let the negro know his numerical strength. The other reason, and the one I think by far the more likely, is that the negro is one of the hardest of people to get census information from.

"A black mammy can't understand why any one, particularly a white stranger, should want to know how many children she has. If any reason at all comes into her head it is that the authorities want to find out if she is sending all her children to school. She knows that she can be arrested if she isn't. So in nine cases out of ten she will lie as to the size of her family.

"If this lack of accuracy existed in the census returns from Northern States like Iowa, it is more than likely that it extended to the returns from the Southern States, where the negroes are not so well educated and where as a consequence they are more distrustful and uncommunicative.

"Fourteen millions of people make a mass that would cause some serious reckoning if once it were awakened to activity. In the south to-day there are places where in spite of disfranchisement the negro has a sufficient vote to elect local officers of his own race. There are even districts where he could send his own representatives to Congress. In the North there are some districts where he has a similar power.

"But by being scattered in large colonies throughout the Union the negroes have something more than the mere power of numbers. An examination of the census and of the election returns will reveal a surprising number of places in which the negro holds the balance of power.

"There are districts, counties and even States where the negro vote is largely in excess of the normal Republican or Democratic plurality. Now, if this negro vote were controlled by an independent party organization so that it could be swung into the Democratic or the Republican line, the negro vote could be made to determine who would fill many of our public offices. Except in the event of a landslide, that vote could even determine the Presidential election.

"To get the negroes into an independent party of this kind is the end toward which I am now working. It was for that purpose that the National Negro Liberty party was organized.

"We may not have done much this election, but the party is only in its infancy. At the election next year we expect to run a number of candidates for local offices through the country.

"When the party managers see colored men getting into office they will wake up to the fact that the negro vote is a new factor in national politics. Each party will be striving to secure the balance of power held by the colored man. Then we will have what we never had before from any party—consideration of the rights of the colored man, concessions, inducements.

"It is not going to be as difficult to organize this independent party as some may think. The negro is beginning to see that his present political attitude brings him nothing. The Republicans think that to vote the Republican ticket is one of the tenets of the negro's religion, so they do not think it necessary to offer any inducements. The Democrats think that the negro is inseparably linked to the Republican party; so, expecting nothing, they give nothing.

"When the negro sees what Republicanism is allowing Democracy, or rather rebelism, to do in the South, he asks himself why he should continue to make his cross under the eagle.

"Roosevelt asked a negro to dine with him, and from the fuss made over it one would have thought that he had done a great thing. But the negro cannot see it that way.

"He cannot see why a mere difference in complexion should make the colored man an outcast race. Had the White House guest been a Jew or an Italian nothing would have been said about it.

"Any ignorant foreigner can come to this country and he has an even chance with the white man, but 'the nigger must be kept down.' He's all right so long as he's a laborer; but let him get a little education, a little money, a little success in his community, and he's all wrong. White folks whom he has passed industrially, financially, will say:

" 'That nigger begins to think he's better than white people. He ought to be kept down.'

"I know what the keeping-down process is. I've been through it.

"When I started the *Negro Solicitor* in Oskaloosa I had very little money. I had to secure advertisements, boom circulation, write articles and do some of the printing. I had to put in sixteen or eighteen hours a day.

"But I was working like a nigger, and I was all right. White folks bought my paper and gave me their advertisements.

"As the paper was gradually made to pay, I was able to begin to take things easier. I began to secure such comforts as a white man in my position would have done.

"I added a story to my house, put in bath tubs, and cooked on a gas stove. Then I got a horse and a rubber-tired trap. When I was buying a horse I thought I might as well get a good one. I bought a horse that could pass anything in town.

"My wife got hats and silk dresses and we used to drive out in the afternoons. When our friends visited us we would take them to the best restaurants in town.

"Then my advertisements and circulation began to fall off. The paper was soon run at a loss. I went to a white man who was a friend of mine and asked what was the trouble.

" 'Well, if you want me to tell you,' he said, 'people think that you are putting on too many airs for a nigger. They think that if you have so much money you can do without theirs.'

"The end was that I had to sell out my paper at a loss. I had been kept down.

"Booker Washington and his plans are good enough in their way, but they will never secure the redemption of the negro race. The negro must do that himself at the polls. When the negro by an independent party organization proves and secures his equality at the polls, then perhaps there will not be so much talk about 'keeping the nigger down.'

"There is one important fact that the white man must keep in mind when he calculates our fighting chance at the polls in the future. The white race is standing still while the black is growing.

"The whites no longer have large families, but the blacks are breeding fast. To be sure, the census shows that there has been a greater increase in the number of whites than the blacks. But there are two facts that discount that showing.

"One is that the negro conceals his numbers, as I have already said. The other is that the whites are receiving immense yearly accessions from Europe, while the colored race is growing only through its birth rate."

Appendix B

Election Data for Nine Political Parties and Candidates in the 1904 Election

Presidential Candidate	Vice Presidential Candidate	Political Party	Popular Vote[1]
Theodore Roosevelt	Charles Fairbanks	Republican	7,630,557
Alton Parker	Henry Davis	Democratic	5,083,880
Eugene Debs	Benjamin Hanford	Socialist	402,810
Silas Swallow	George Carroll	Prohibition	259,103
Thomas Watson	Thomas Tibbles	Populist/People's	114,062
Charles H. Corregan	William Wesley Cox	Socialist Labor	34,683
Austin Holcomb	A. King	Continental (Labor)	33,454
George Edwin Taylor	W. C. Payne	National Liberty (Negro)[2]	Not recorded
E. P. Penn	John J. Jones	Lincoln Party (Negro)	Not recorded

Source: *Galveston Daily News*, 1 November 1904, 7.

Note: Total vote 13,525,002; 1,229 unaccounted for.

1. Http://uselectionatlas.org/RESULTS/index.html (accessed 23 April 2009). This record does not indicate whether the final vote totals include only valid ballots or include "write-in" votes.

2. The *Galveston Daily News*, in a datelined article for New York on 31 October, indicated that nine conventions had been held and that only six had completed electoral tickets: "The two negro parties, however, apparently ended their work when the National convention adjourned, as no electors have been selected, or at least none will appear on any official ballot; and the Continental party seems to be confined to Illinois, and, perhaps, to Chicago, the place of its origin" (1 November 1904, 7).

Appendix C

Chart of George Edwin Taylor's Life

Primary Residence	Inclusive Dates	Events, Occupation, Dates
Little Rock, AR	1857–59	Place of birth (4 August 1857)
Alton, IL	1860–65	Mother's death, a "waif" Travel to La Crosse onboard the *Hawkeye State* (May 1865)
La Crosse, WI	1865–68	Household of Henry and Agnes Southall Took on Southall name Attended La Crosse school
West Salem, WI	1868–79	Household of Nathan and Sarah Smith "Bound out" to Smith until twenty years old Used both the Southall and Taylor surnames Kinney or Waterloo school Student at Wayland University (1877–79) First mention of health issues (1879) Printer's devil at *La Crosse Democrat* (before 1879)
La Crosse, WI	1879–87	City editor for *Pomeroy's Democrat* (1879–80)? Writer for *Morning Chronicle, Daily Republican and Leader, Chicago Inter Ocean* Married Mary Hall (15 October 1885)

(table continued on next page)

Primary Residence	Inclusive Dates	Events, Occupation, Dates
		Writer and editor for *La Crosse Evening Star* (1885–86)
		Active in "White Beaver" Powell's mayoralty (1885–87)
		Labor activist, secretary of Workingmen's Party of La Crosse (1885–86)
		Owner/editor *Wisconsin Labor Advocate* (20 August 1886–ca. 1887), owner of printing company
		Secretary of Wisconsin People's Party (1886–87)
		La Crosse Convention (13 July 1886)
		Neenah Convention (17 September 1886)
		Cincinnati Conference of Union Labor (22–24 February 1887), delivered speech
		April 1887 La Crosse City elections
La Crosse, West Salem, the "West"?	1887–90	Reflection Newspaper work in the "West"?
Oskaloosa, IA	1891–1900	Arrival on 1 January 1891
		Owner/editor of *Negro Solicitor* (13 February 1893–August 1898), owner of printing company
		Married Cora Cooper Buckner (25 August 1894)
		Contributed articles to *Sunday Des Moines Leader* (Republican) (August–December 1898)
		Second mention of health issues (1899)
		Divorce from Cora Taylor (after 1900 census)
		Insurance agent (1901)
		National-level activities:
		National Republican Party (1891–92)
		National Democratic Party (1892–1904)
		National Colored Men's Protective Association, president (1892–?)
		Chicago Congress (June 1893)
		National Negro Democratic League, secretary and temporary chair (1898–1900), president (1900–1904)

Primary Residence	Inclusive Dates	Events, Occupation, Dates
		National Knights of Pythias, president (1899–?)
		Negro National Free Silver League, vice president (1896–97), president (1897–?)
		Negro Inter-State Free Silver League, president (1897–?)
		State-level activities:
		Iowa Afro-American Association/League, president (1894–?)
		Iowa State Negro Protective League/ Association, president (1998)
		Iowa Knights of Pythias, grand chancellor (1895–1900), supreme lodge representative (1899), attended Richmond, VA, national convention (1899)
		Iowa Colored Congress (1898)
		Prince Hall Masons, attended Jacksonville, FL, convention (1900)
		Local-level activities:
		Negro Protective Association of Oskaloosa, chairman (1897–98)
		Afro-American League/Council—Oskaloosa branch (1898)
Coalfield, IA	1899–1900?	Superintendent of mines, A. B. Little & Company (1899–1900)
Albia, Monroe Township, IA	1900?–1904	Farmer/owner near Hilton, Iowa, four years "Hilton Democrat," two terms as justice of the peace
Ottumwa, IA	1904–10	Four- to six-month run of *Negro Solicitor* (1904) Third mention of health issue (1904)

(table continued on next page)

Primary Residence	Inclusive Dates	Events, Occupation, Dates
		Conventions of National Democratic Party, National Negro Democratic League, and National Negro Liberty Party in St. Louis (early July 1904)
		Selected as candidate of National Liberty Party (late July 1904)
		Resigned from National Negro Democratic League (5 August 1904)
		Presidential election (8 November 1904)
		Fourth mention of health issue (1905)
		Ottumwa Police Department (1907–10)
		Slight involvement in National Democratic Party politics (1908)
Tampa, FL	1910–11	Reporter for *Florida Reporter*
St. Augustine, FL	1911–12	Manager of Magnolia Remedy Company
		Author of "Remove the Mask," "Backward Steps"
Jacksonville, FL	1912–?	Editor of *Daily Promoter*, Promotion Publishing Company (1912–13)
		Secretary of "Colored" YMCA (August 1914–?)
		Board of Commissioners of Masonic Lodge (1916–?)
		Editor of "Black Star" edition of *Florida Times-Union* (1917–?)
		Walker National Business College (1918–?)
Green Cove Springs, Clay County, FL	1919?–21?	Marriage to Marion Tillinghast of Green Cove Springs, FL (date uncertain)
		Engaged in "poultry" farming (1920)
		Fifth mention of health issue (date uncertain)
Jacksonville, FL	1921?–25	Organizer/director of Progressive Order of Men and Women (1922)
		Editor of *Florida Sentinel* (1923–24)

Primary Residence	Inclusive Dates	Events, Occupation, Dates
		Commencement address at Walker National Business College (May 1923)
		Death (23 December 1925)

Notes

Introduction

1. *Iowa State Bystander*, 12 August 1898, 1. Keokuk was a Mississippi River town with a large black population. Schwalm (*Emancipation's Diaspora*, 198) described Keokuk as Iowa's largest city at the end of the Civil War.

2. Mouser, *Black La Crosse*, 117–19; Vollmar, "Negro in a Midwest Frontier City," 24; Gerber, *Black Ohio*, 70–71; Cooper, *Black Settlers*, 5–6; Taylor, "The Blacks," 73–91; Gallaher and Throne, "The Negro in Iowa," 3–90; Kremer, *James Milton Turner*, 106–15; Schwalm, *Emancipation's Diaspora*.

3. See Petty, "History of the South."

4. See *United States Statutes at Large*, 43rd Cong., 2nd sess., 1874–75, chapter 114, 335–37. See also Higginbotham, *Shades of Freedom*, 81–93.

5. Schwalm, "Overrun with Free Negroes"; Schwalm, *Emancipation's Diaspora*, 177.

6. Squibb, "Roads to Plessy," 1–2.

7. For these sentiments, see Kremer, *James Milton Turner*, 5, 12.

8. Fishel, "Wisconsin and Negro Suffrage," 183–96; Squibb, "Roads to Plessy," 57–60; Current, *History of Wisconsin*, 145–48, 570–73; Schwalm, *Emancipation's Diaspora*, 182–83. See also Smith, *History of Wisconsin*, 635, 665–69.

9. Squibb, "Roads to Plessy," 1–2, 20. See also *Dodge County Citizen*, 19 February 1863, 1, for similar sentiments.

10. Tucker, "M. M. 'Brick' Pomeroy," 139–43. See also the *Prairie du Chien Courier* for reports that the La Crosse and St. Paul Packet Line intended to import "contraband labor" from the South. That report also warned: "If whitemen will not submit to the grasp of capitalists, who set a price on fellow-man's labor, they will all inevitably be made to feel the effects of *Negro competition*" (26 June 1862, 2).

11. *Prairie du Chien Courier*, 5 June 1862, 2; *Republican Journal*, 27 December 1860, 2; Lofton, "Northern Labor," 251–54. See Klement for Wisconsin fears that a flood of freed blacks would bring "impoverishment and annihilation" ("Midwestern Opposition," 176). See also Fleming, *Deportation and Colonization*, 13, for governmental attempts to allay fears of migration northward. The *Grant County Herald* wrote: "They [contrabands] will continue to come, possibly in great numbers, until the Proclamation is carried through and the war closed, after which they will return to their old homes, where their preferred climate is, and where their labor is most wanted" (10 February 1863, 2).

12. Tucker, "M. M. 'Brick' Pomeroy," 144–45; Hirshheimer, "La Crosse River History," 269, 271. Pomeroy claimed that Davidson brought in three hundred workers and described them as "dirty, lice-devoured, and filth-besmeared" (*La Crosse Daily Democrat*, 9 August 1866, 1).

13. Cited in Tucker, "M. M. 'Brick' Pomeroy," 144. See also Schwalm, *Emancipation's Diaspora*, 83–89, for similar reports.

14. Schwalm, *Emancipation's Diaspora*, 86–87.

15. Tucker, "M. M. 'Brick' Pomeroy," 145–46; *La Crosse Democrat*, 10 June 1865.

16. Mouser, *Black La Crosse*.

17. Sanford and Hirshheimer, *History of La Crosse*, 154–56; Canuteson, "The Lumbering Industry," 22–29; Plain, "The Black River Boom," 549–55; Bristow, "Early Steamboat and Packet Lines," 32. Morser ("Manufacturing Pioneers," 131) listed thirty-two sawmills operating in La Crosse between 1841 and 1900.

18. The most complete study of La Crosse migration is Wingate, "Settlement Patterns."

19. Brown, "Lodging in La Crosse," 5–6.

20. For an excellent overview of La Crosse during this period, see Rausch and Zeitlin, *Historic La Crosse*, 2–8.

21. See any of the city's directories for lists of manufacturers and businesses. See also "La Crosse History Unbound," http://lacrossehistory.org, a cooperative venture of the La Crosse Public Library and Murphy Library at the University of Wisconsin–La Crosse to digitize and place online original reports, student papers, theses, city and county records, monographs, and personal papers that directly relate to La Crosse and its history.

22. Cooper, *Black Settlers*, 5. Those who migrated to Pleasant Ridge and Mount Tabor came mainly as fugitive and freed slaves. Rosser Taylor (*Free Negro*, 21–22) wrote that many free blacks had never been slaves and that some had free ancestors who had fought in the Revolutionary War. The terms "Waldens" and "old issue" were applied to this group. Many owned farms that could be converted into cash. In North Carolina a clear distinction was drawn between "old issue" and manumitted blacks. Waldron was a common surname among black settlers at Hillsboro, Wisconsin.

23. See excellent articles in the *Grant County Herald* (10 February 1863, 2, and 3 March 1863, 2) that provide detailed descriptions of these early settlements.

24. *Weekly Gazette and Free Press*, 21 June 1861, 4. See Mouser, *Black La Crosse*, 41–42, 81, 129, for Samuel Thompson, who was born in Virginia in 1846, served as a barber with a military unit from La Crosse, and accompanied his troop back to La Crosse in 1864. In 1865 Thompson volunteered and served in the Twenty-ninth Regiment of Colored Troops. After the war he returned to La Crosse, where he remained a barber until 1885. See also Schwalm, *Emancipation's Diaspora*, 68–72.

25. See Schwalm, *Emancipation's Diaspora*, 81–106, for extensive discussion of this phase of migration.

26. Current, *History of Wisconsin*, 389–91; Schwalm, *Emancipation's Diaspora*, 45, 74–76.

27. For migration patterns, see Mouser, *Black La Crosse*, 95–99.

28. Ibid., 93–110, 124–30. Schwalm (*Emancipation's Diaspora*, 100) noted that more than half of Iowa's white men of military age either enlisted or were drafted during the Civil War.

29. "Christian Taugott Ficker's Advice," 473.

30. See Mouser, *Black La Crosse*, 93–110, for statistical data relating to La Crosse's black entrepreneurs and workers.

Chapter 1. From Orphaned Black to Printer's Devil

1. "Sketch of Iowa Negro Presidential Candidate," *Lincoln Evening News*, 5 September 1904 (accessed online through several databases, including NewspaperArchive). For similar announcements, see "Negro Candidate for President of U.S.," *Logansport Daily Reporter*, 10 August 1904; "Sketch of George Edwin Taylor: The Only Colored Man Ever Nominated for the Presidency," *Voice of the Negro*, October 1904, 476–81. The terms "free black" and "free Negro" substituted directly in Arkansas with the term "freeborn." That Taylor was able to provide a certain date for his birth likely only reflected a selected date, for most former slaves did not know the date or year of their birth. Washington (*Up from Slavery*, 2) wrote that he was born in either 1858 or 1859 and that he did not know any further information. That was likely common.

2. See Taylor, *Negro Slavery*, 189–202, for discussion of Arkansas laws respecting unions between African Americans during the pre–Civil War period and of the fragile nature of family construction under the system prevailing in Arkansas at that time.

3. Ibid., 256–57.

4. Ibid., 257. See also Stockley, *Ruled by Race*, 37. Other states had debated the question of expelling free blacks, but Arkansas was the only state to pass such legislation.

5. Taylor, *Negro Slavery*, 257. The act provided that money earned by those youths who were "hired out" would be placed in a special account and given to the youth upon reaching his or her twenty-first birthday.

6. *Iowa State Bystander*, 23 December 1898, 2; *Milwaukee Journal*, 15 October 1904, 12. The *Daily Alaska Dispatch* (31 August 1904, 2) reported that George was one of twelve children to flee from Arkansas with Amanda Hines. If that were the case, she would have taken some of her children illegally from Arkansas.

7. *Iowa State Bystander*, 23 December 1898, 2. In "Sketch of George Edwin Taylor," Taylor claimed that his mother had moved to Alton, located approximately twenty-five miles north of St. Louis and upon the Mississippi River, where she was befriended by Hiram Lovejoy. This is likely an error in memory, for it was Owen and Joseph Lovejoy who operated a printing company in that city.

8. See "Sketch of Iowa Negro Presidential Candidate."

9. The *Hawkeye State* was a side paddle wheeler owned and operated by the Northern Packet Company of Dubuque, Iowa, which ran boats between St. Louis and St. Paul. In 1865 La Crosse was ranked third in riverboat dockings along the Mississippi after New Orleans and St. Louis. Three railroads linked La Crosse to Chicago, and many believed

then that permafrost would prohibit further railroad expansion northward, with the consequence that La Crosse positioned itself as a gateway city. It expected to expand commercially and in numbers commensurate with its importance as a terminus of immigrant migrations.

10. Mouser, *Black La Crosse*, 79 -81. The *La Crosse County Countryman* (17 June 1993, 8) resolved this confusion simply by concluding that both Taylor and Southall had sought the presidency and that Smith was unique in having two sons to seek that high office.

11. Assuming that Taylor's father and mother were unmarried, he could have taken any surname, and perhaps he picked the one that suited him at the moment.

12. *La Crosse Tribune*, 22 November 1953, 3. The source for this account mentioned several children by name: Frank Butterfield (white), Kelly Vaughn (black), George Southall (black), and Sam Baltimore (black). The author also noted that several small children from La Crosse were under Sarah Smith's care. Only Butterfield was formally adopted by the Smiths. Kindschy (*Leonard's Dream*, 38 -39) deleted Southall's name and added George Taylor to this list. The federal census for 1880 lists only four persons in the household of Nathan Smith: Nathan, Sara, "George Southall (22 years of age) and attending school," and Joseph Louis. The *Times Picayune* (12 August 1900, 22) reported that Taylor had been "bound out" to a farmer. That term generally implies legal foster-age and indicates that Smith may have received payments from the county for Taylor's care. Taylor later remarked that he was required to remain with Smith until he reached the age of twenty.

13. No school records exist for this period.

14. Haas, "George Edwin Taylor," 1.

15. Curti, when describing the treatment of orphans in neighboring Trempeleau County, noted that orphaned "children were always useful on a farm" (*Making of an American Community*, 314).

16. Heider, *Along the Waterloo Road*, 67 -68, 83.

17. Mouser, *Black La Crosse*, 37 -38.

18. Harman ("A Look at History") argues that Nathan Smith originally came from Mississippi and suggests that Smith may have fled northward along the Mississippi in consequence of a failed slave insurrection that occurred in the mid-1830s. Census records, from information provided only by those being enumerated, indicate consistently that both Smiths claimed to have been born in Tennessee.

19. Mouser, *Black La Crosse*, 42 -43; Goldbloom, "Black Added His Bit."

20. *History of Northern Wisconsin — 1881*, 1058 -62. Galesville University accepted its first students in 1859 and continued under various religious managements until 1894, when its name was changed to Gale College. Between 1876 and 1894 it was under the management of the Presbytery of Chippewa, during which time it modeled itself after the prestigious Phillips Academy (Phillips Andover and Andover) of Andover, Massachusetts, near Boston, which had positioned itself as a feeder school for Yale, Harvard, and Princeton.

21. Wichman, *Wayland Story*, 1, 35 -44.

22. Ferris, *Jerry at the Academy*, 67–68, 90. Names of students attending in 1877–78 were recorded in *The Annual Catalogue*, 6–9.

23. Ferris, *Jerry at the Academy*. *The Annual Catalogue* (17) listed room rent as 25¢ per week, incidentals at 15¢ per week, board in the Academic Club at $2 per week, and laundry at 60¢ per dozen. All charges were to be paid in advance.

24. Wayland's financial ledger shows that George Edward Taylor of West Salem lived in the dorm during two terms, fall of 1877 and fall of 1878, and that he paid fees amounting to $72.40 during his two-year attendance. When meal charges are added, that approximates the figure suggested by Ferris. Approximate comparison of dollar values indicates that $1 of 1877 currency would equal $21.21 of 2008 currency, or a projected cost of $3,381 per year.

25. *The Annual Catalogue* specifically noted that "board and rooms can be had with private families on very reasonable terms" (17).

26. Ferris, *Jerry at the Academy*, 26, 49, 63–74, 80, 84–94.

27. Ferris (*Jerry at the Academy*, 5) wrote about a Billy Waldron from Hillsboro, Wisconsin, and it is possible that Ferris substituted Waldron's name for Taylor. The 1878–79 catalogue specifically lists Ferris and Taylor as members of the Junior Class of fourteen students.

28. *Iowa State Bystander*, 23 December 1898, 2; "Sketch of George Edwin Taylor." Unfortunately, neither these nor future references to Taylor's health indicate physical symptoms. A financial ledger from that time indicates that Taylor paid fees to Wayland in 1877, January 1878, February 1878, December 1878, January 1879, and April 1879. Those six payments amounted to $72.40 ($1,535.76 in 2008 dollars) for charges that included tuition, a library fee, incidentals, and room. Ferris had estimated board or meals at $2.50 per week, or $97.50 ($2,068.10) per year.

29. Tucker claimed that the *La Crosse Democrat* at one time had "a larger circulation than any other newspaper in the country" ("M. M. 'Brick' Pomeroy," 1).

30. Klement, "'Brick' Pomeroy," 106–7, 156. See also Avrich, *Haymarket Tragedy*, 4, for a detailed transformation of the eight-hour movement "from socialism to anarchism."

31. Pomeroy and A. S. Foote operated the *La Crosse Daily Democrat* (a weekly) from 27 May 1879 into mid-1880. See the *La Crosse Daily Democrat*, 29 October 1879, 2; Oehlerts, *Guide to Wisconsin Newspapers*, 128; *Morrissey & Bunn's La Crosse City Directory, 1880–81*, 136, 191.

32. Doolen, "'Brick' Pomeroy," 445–49; Coate, "Early La Crosse County Authors"; "'Brick' Pomeroy: Fiery La Crosse Editor Urged Assassination of Abraham Lincoln," *La Crosse Tribune*, 4 June 1967; Moore, "Pomeroy Build an Empire." Usher (*Greenback Movement*, 56–59) noted that 57,530 votes out of a total state vote of 206,318 supported Greenback candidates for Congress in Wisconsin in the election of 1878, that Greenbackers received nearly 1.25 million votes nationwide that year, and that Pomeroy had campaigned heavily with "annoying activities" in Wisconsin for the party's nomination for the presidency before the party's 1880 convention.

33. *Ottumwa Daily Courier*, 22 July 1904, 6; *La Crosse Leader-Press*, 12 October 1904, 5; *Milwaukee Journal*, 15 October 1904, 12.

34. Tucker, "M. M. 'Brick' Pomeroy," 2, 64–66, 120–28, 131, 240.

35. Ibid., chap. 11, "Workingmen's Advocate."

36. Pomeroy, *Reminiscences and Recollections*, 162. For La Crosse views of Pomeroy, see Hebberd, "Marcus 'Brick' Pomeroy," 1–3; *La Crosse Tribune*, 28 July 1911, 3, and 21 July 1938; Tucker, "M. M. 'Brick' Pomeroy," 146–47.

37. Tucker, "M. M. 'Brick' Pomeroy," 23, 38, 39, 122, 123, 127–28, 271–73, 164.

38. *Weekly Argus*, 6 June 1896.

39. Langston ("African-American Legacy," 343) suggests that Taylor was a "Lincoln Republican" in his youth. Bertha Kinney, a classmate in West Salem, suggested that he had given speeches in support of the Republican Party, and Taylor wrote in his "National Appeal" of 1892 (see chapter 3) that he had voted Republican before he became a labor advocate, but no additional documentation substantiates that claim. The *La Crosse County Countryman* described Smith, Taylor's foster father, however, as "a radical in the Farmer Labor Party" (17 June 1993, 8).

40. Ozanne, *Labor Movement*, 18.

41. Ibid., 7–8; Morser, "Manufacturing Pioneers," 219.

42. Ozanne, "Lumber Industry Strikes," 22.

43. Morser, "Manufacturing Pioneers," 220–21.

44. *La Crosse Morning Chronicle*, 29 July 1881, 2.

45. "Sketch of George Edwin Taylor." For *Inter Ocean*, see *Iowa State Bystander*, 15 April 1897, 4.

46. For standard but detailed histories of Populist movements, see Rayback, *History of American Labor*; Fine, *Labor and Farmer Parties*. The Greenback Party was most active in the upper Midwest between 1874 and 1884. The party encouraged "easy money" based on a promise to pay the bearer of the greenback. In 1878 it sent twenty-one members to Congress. The Order of Patrons of Husbandry was the basis of the Granger movement, a party of agricultural cooperatives and associations. It became the most active after the Panic of 1873, which was particularly difficult for farmers. This party became a significant force in Iowa, Minnesota, Wisconsin, and Illinois. It emphasized cooperative ventures, with farmer and community cooperation. Greenbackers and Grangers fused with Farmers' Alliances and farmer/labor groups in the 1880s and with the Populists in the 1890s.

47. *La Crosse News*, 26 December 1885 and 9 January 1886.

48. Drago, "Black Press & Populism," 100. In 1885 these included the *Western Appeal* and the *Broad Axe* of St. Paul, Minnesota, the *Chicago Eagle*, the *Indianapolis Freeman*, the *Bulletin* of Louisville, Kentucky, the *Cairo Gazette*, and the *Colored Citizen* of Cincinnati, Ohio, among those immediately accessible by the Ohio and Mississippi rivers.

49. Lewinson, *Race, Class, and Party*, 69.

50. Sorg, *Doctor, Lawyer, Indian Chief*, 5–10, 18, 24–27; Schlicht, "Political Career," 4–6. See also *La Crosse Tribune*, 9 May 1906, 3, for an article reviewing Powell's life. Sorg is Powell's unofficial biographer, and much of the data here relating to Powell comes from his work.

51. *La Crosse Tribune*, 7 May 1906, 1.

52. These included White Beaver's Cough Cream, which was advertised to heal diseased lungs and cure coughs and colds; Yosemite Yarrow was to cure rheumatic pains, "neuralgic sides," and headaches; and White Beaver's Wonder Worker was supposed to cure cholera and rheumatism. His major claim was his guarantee of "no cure, no pay." For the above, see Holmlund, "Office Safe." Sorg (*Doctor, Lawyer, Indian Chief*, 59) noted that Powell was known in Lanesboro as "Fancy Frank," obviously referring to his flamboyant dress and manner, and suggested that his name White Beaver did not become commonly used until he arrived in La Crosse.

53. Sorg, *Doctor, Lawyer, Indian Chief*, 79–80. Buffalo Bill's novels are *White Beaver's Still Hunt*; *The Wizard Brothers: or White Beaver's Trail*; and *White Beaver: The Exile of the Platt*.

54. Sorg, *Doctor, Lawyer, Indian Chief*, 18, 74–77, 86.

55. Mouser, *Black La Crosse*, 10–12.

Chapter 2. Labor Agitator, Newspaper Editor, and Political Novice

1. *La Crosse County Countryman*, 17 June 1993, 8. The term "printer's devil" generally refers to an apprentice typesetter, someone who is at the most junior level of apprenticeship.

2. Bryant, *Memoirs*, 120, noted that La Crosse had a reputation "for racy editorial writers."

3. Moe, "Pleasant Memories," 103; Sanford and Hirshheimer, *History of La Crosse*, 209–10. See also *La Crosse Argus*, 1 April 1905, 3; *La Crosse Tribune*, 27 March 1905, 1, 27 May 1934, 7, 29 March 1936, 24 April 1938, 5, and 26 March 1959; *La Crosse Daily Republican and Leader*, 17 October 1884, 1; *La Crosse News*, 19 October 1884, 4.

4. Sorg, *Doctor, Lawyer, Indian Chief*, 81.

5. "Sketch of George Edwin Taylor"; *Iowa State Bystander*, 23 December 1898, 2. For Powell's investment in the *Evening Star*, see Sorg, *Doctor, Lawyer, Indian Chief*, 18.

6. State of Wisconsin, Crawford County, Marriages, vol. 6, 142.

7. In *Ottumwa Daily Courier*, 22 July 1904, 6, Taylor claimed to be a widower. The term "grass widow" or "grass widower," however, is used in Iowa to refer to a divorced person and is considered less negatively than the term "divorced."

8. *Oshkosh Daily Northwestern*, 4 November 1885, 4.

9. Morser, "Manufacturing Pioneers," 223–27.

10. *La Crosse News*, 26 December 1885, 2 January 1886, and 9 January 1886, 2.

11. *La Crosse News*, 30 January 1886, 2, and 27 February 1886, 3.

12. *La Crosse News*, 27 February 1886, 2.

13. *La Crosse News*, 31 July 1866, 2.

14. Katz, *Vignettes*, 58; Bryant, *Memoirs*, 120; *Wisconsin Labor Advocate*, 1 April 1887, 4.

15. Sorg, "Media Savvy."

16. *La Crosse News*, 10 April 1886, 2. See also Morser, "Manufacturing Pioneers," 230–32.

17. Organized labor within La Crosse was caught up, as were workers elsewhere, in the debate of whether the Knights of Labor should remain involved "only" in labor issues or whether it should participate actively in the political process as an official party. In La Crosse this split in labor was manifested in the positions taken by the *Free Press*, the *Evening Star*, and the *News*. That became especially evident following Powell's election in 1886, when Taylor left the *Star* to form his own newspaper.

18. A significant fire on the waterfront had broken out on election day, and many workingmen voters were involved in extinguishing the fire. The quality of the microfilm of this issue of the *Evening Star* (7 April 1886) is poor, and the original no longer exists. The *La Crosse County Record* (16 July 1886, 2) described Powell's paper as "really pathetic."

19. Sorg, "Media Savvy."

20. For fuller treatment of Powell's activities in 1885–86, see Sorg, *Doctor, Lawyer, Indian Chief*, 82–102, 115. Nugent noted: "Populism like any other American reform movement of large proportions had many voices and comprised a broad spectrum of groups and individuals" (*Tolerant Populists*, 104).

21. Ozanne, *Labor Movement*, 6–7. See also Ginger, *Altgeld's America*, 42–44, for this same period and ideal in Chicago.

22. Gurda, "When Bay View Strike Turned to Bloodshed."

23. Ozanne, *Labor Movement*, 8–11. For details of Knights of Labor activities in Milwaukee and events preceding the 1886 crisis, see Fink, "Knights of Labor in Milwaukee," 26–33; Nesbit, "Bay View Tragedy," 34–46. For the Haymarket massacre, see Green, *Death in the Haymarket*, 160–91; Mittelman, "Chicago Labor," 417–18.

24. Interestingly, many Democratic newspapers supported Rush's actions and assumed initially that to do otherwise would undermine the rule of law. For one such example, see *Sparta Democrat*, 12 June 1886, 2. On 3 July 1886, however, the *Sparta Democrat* wrote: "In the light of a judicial investigation it would be very questionable whether any exigencies existed in the troubles in Milwaukee which the courts with a thoroughly active and vigilant police force were not able to cope with. At all events it would have been judicious in a humane point of view to have exhausted the ordinary legal remedies before resorting to unusual and dangerous expedients."

25. *La Crosse News*, 5 June 1886, 2.

26. *La Crosse News*, 29 May 1886, 2.

27. *La Crosse News*, 26 June 1886, 2.

28. *La Crosse Morning Chronicle*, 13 July 1886, 2; *La Crosse News*, 26 June 1886, 2, and 10 July 1886, 2. Wyman noted that Wisconsin Populism came "not out of agrarian distress but from socialist-oriented labor union radicalism" ("Agrarian or Working-Class Radicalism?" 825).

29. These delegate counts relate more closely to the numbers of workers eligible for membership in the Knights of Labor and not a ratio based on the cities' populations. See also the account in the *Oshkosh Daily Northwestern*, 14 July 1886, 1.

30. *La Crosse County Record*, 16 July 1886, 2; *La Crosse Morning Chronicle*, 13 July 1886, 2.

31. *Oshkosh Daily Northwestern*, 14 July 1886, 1.

32. Ibid.; *La Crosse Daily Republican*, 13 July 1886, 1, and 14 July 1886, 1.

33. *La Crosse News*, 17 July 1886, 2; *La Crosse County Record*, 16 July 1886, 2. The full text of resolutions from the 1886 La Crosse Convention is available at http://murphy library.uwlax.edu/digital/TaylorGeorge/6LaCrosseConv86.pdf.

34. "Dr. Powell's bright prospects for governor of the state have faded somewhat since the Labor Convention in La Crosse last week. It seems the Milwaukee delegation under the leadership of Carl [*sic*] Schilling was strong enough to control the convention and an adjournment was made to Neenah Aug. 14th, at which time it is expected that a straight labor ticket will be nominated but it is hardly probable that the name of Dr. Powell will decorate the head" (*Galesville Independent*, 22 July 1886, 4). The *La Crosse County Record* warned his supporters, however, "to beware of the trap into which they are apt to be led this fall at the Neenah convention." The editor of the *Record* noted that Powell's criticisms of the Republican Party were "very mild, so much so in fact, that one would not be surprised to see him assume the dignities of an official in their ranks" (13 August 1886, 2).

35. The word "his" was likely a typographical error that should have read "high."

36. *Wisconsin Labor Advocate*, 20 August 1886; Mouser, *Black La Crosse*, 131–36. The full first year's run of the *Wisconsin Labor Advocate* is available online at http://murphy library.uwlax.edu/digital/lacrosse/WiscLaborAdv/n01p01.html.

37. Drago, "Black Press," 98. The black press of the late nineteenth century was very different from the black press that preceded the Civil War. For a discussion of the earlier period, see Bullock, *Afro-American Periodical Press*; Foster, "Narrative," 714–40. Washburn reviewed literature regarding black newspapers printed during this period, noting that 1,200 black newspapers likely had been founded between 1866 and 1907, with many coming and going "by the score, like foot soldiers storming a fortress" (*African American Newspaper*, 49). Small newspapers were notorious for emerging at little cost. Many were subcontracted to printing firms at small cost and represented minimal capital investment, with the consequence that they survived only as long as advertisers were willing to patronize them.

38. See Detweiler, *Negro Press*, 53–61. Penn (*Afro-American Press*, 112–14) found only ten black newspapers printed ca. 1870, with a total of thirty-one printed by ca. 1880. Penn noted, however, that the number had increased rapidly by 1890, with 154 newspapers in print. For more on the *Washington Bee* and early black newspapers in the upper Midwest, see Pride and Wilson, *History*, 98–104.

39. See similar sentiments in Woods, "C. H. J. Taylor," 125.

40. *Wisconsin Labor Advocate*, 27 August 1886, 2.

41. Ibid. One of the visible manifestations of typesetting was the presence of black fingernails from ink used in the printing process.

42. *Wisconsin Labor Advocate*, 27 August 1886, 2.

43. *Wisconsin Labor Advocate*, 3 September 1886, 1.

44. Ibid., 2.

45. A "wire-puller" was a secret manipulator or intriguer who stood in the background but manipulated the puppets—the public personae—onstage like a puppeteer.

46. *Wisconsin Labor Advocate*, 10 September 1886, 2, emphasis added. Robert Schilling was the leader of the Knights of Labor in Milwaukee who had been arrested and then released after the Bay View Massacre of 5 May 1886. In this instance, however, Taylor cleverly positioned a double meaning for the use of this name by referring instead to British currency and suggesting that Labor should defend itself against having its votes bought either with eloquent speakers or with shillings or dollars.

47. *La Crosse Daily Republican*, 16 September 1886, 1.

48. *La Crosse Daily Republican*, 17 September 1886, 1; *Oshkosh Morning News*, 17 September 1886, 1; Sorg, *Doctor, Lawyer, Indian Chief*, 105; Wyman, "Agrarian or Working-Class Radicalism?" 828; Sorg, "Powell Keeps Fighting"; *Wisconsin Labor Advocate*, 17 September 1886, 2; *Sparta Democrat*, 18 September 1886, 2. Fink dismissively described Powell as a "patent medicine salesman and an alleged former prairie bandit" (*Workingmen's Democracy*, 196).

49. *Wisconsin Labor Advocate*, 17 September 1886, 2.

50. *Wisconsin Labor Advocate*, 24 September 1886, 2. A transcription of the Neenah Platform is available at http://murphylibrary.uwlax.edu/digital/TaylorGeorge/9Neenah Conv86.pdf.

51. *Wisconsin Labor Advocate*, 15 October 1886, 3. Philpot (*Race, Republicans*, 39) noted that Lynch had been the "temporary chairman" of the 1884 National Republican Party Convention. See also Turkel, *Heroes*, for biographical sketches of Bruce, Lynch, and Smalls.

52. *Wisconsin Labor Advocate*, 29 October 1886, 2.

53. *Wisconsin Labor Advocate*, 4 November 1886, 2. Milwaukee was often considered to be a socialist and labor stronghold in the early twentieth century. Wyman ("Agrarian or Working-Class Radicalism?" 829–30) wrote that Schilling attempted to broaden the party's appeal by again running a Granger for the position of governor but that the effort to merge agrarian and labor radicalism was unsuccessful. In consequence, the center of Labor influence remained solely in Milwaukee.

54. *Wisconsin Labor Advocate*, 14 January 1887, 2. Taylor reproduced a broadside supposedly distributed by Read: "The demagogues who are so actively engaged in securing delegates to Cincinnati, are not acting in the interests of the Knights. It may even be doubted whether they are members of the Order or not. If they are or ever have been, they do not understand the A.B.C. of its teachings" (*Wisconsin Labor Advocate*, 18 February 1887, 2).

55. There is an unexplained reference in the *Wisconsin Labor Advocate* (28 January 1887, 3) to the effect that Taylor had been selected as a state delegate to the Cincinnati convention at a district convention held at Sparta, Wisconsin, during the preceding days. On 5 February 1887 Taylor complained that few delegates were planning to attend the Cincinnati convention and that Read had not mentioned the convention in the *La Crosse News*, suggesting that "the working classes of the state must suffer, because of some near sighted whim, or jealous notion of a fossil editor of a so-called labor paper."

56. For the 1886 election, see Gardner, "Frustrated Minority," 83–84, 94.

57. In the election of 1888, Alson Jenness Streeter of New Windsor, Illinois, was the nominee of the Union Labor Party and received 145,115 votes nationwide, nearly 1.3 percent of the popular vote. Charles E. Cunningham of Arkansas was the party's vice presidential candidate in that election.

58. *Weekly Fort Wayne Sentinel*, 23 February 1887, 1; Haynes ("Collapse," 149) wrote that the Cincinnati meeting had attempted to form a Greenback Labor Party that would combine agrarian groups with city trades-union organizations but that the fusion was not successful. He also claimed that this new party failed to connect with populist movements in the South and the West.

59. *Wisconsin Labor Advocate*, 4 March 1887, 2; *Decatur Daily Republican*, 24 February 1887, 2; *Marion Daily Star*, 24 February 1887, 1. See also *Appletons' Annual Cyclopaedia*, 778. The *Oshkosh Daily Northwestern* (24 February 1887, 2) contains a summary of the convention and an abbreviated version of its platform. See also Ali, *In the Balance of Power*, 76–77, for roles played by Colored Wheels and the Colored Alliance in the Union Labor Party. Mittelman ("Chicago Labor," 422–23) wrote that this platform was too moderate for Chicago labor in 1887. A transcription of the Cincinnati Platform is found at http://murphylibrary.uwlax.edu/digital/TaylorGeorge/2Cincinnatiplatform87.pdf.

60. *Oshkosh Daily Northwestern*, 25 February 1887, 2.

61. *Wisconsin Labor Advocate*, 4 March 1887, 2.

62. *Wisconsin Labor Advocate*, 11 March 1887, 2.

63. *La Crosse News*, 5 March 1887, 3, and 12 March 1887, 3. It is likely that Read was referring to the *Oshkosh Daily Northwestern*, whose editor enthusiastically reported activities of the new labor party. The *Northwestern* was one of the earliest newspapers in the state, having been established in 1867.

64. *Wisconsin Labor Advocate*, 25 February 1887, 2.

65. Sorg, *Doctor, Lawyer, Indian Chief*, 108–9.

66. Morser, "Manufacturing Pioneers," 238–40.

67. *La Crosse News*, 2 April 1887, 3; *Wisconsin Labor Advocate*, 1 April 1887, 2.

68. *Wisconsin Labor Advocate*, 18 March 1887, 2, emphasis in original.

69. *Wisconsin Labor Advocate*, 8 April 1887, 4.

70. *La Crosse Morning Chronicle*, 19 April 1887. Neither Marsh nor Reed mentioned in the editorial is identified.

71. Sorg, *Doctor, Lawyer, Indian Chief*, 112. For similar conclusions, see *La Crosse County Record*, 5 November 1886, 2.

72. Powell had called Taylor his brother's "dusky tool" (*La Crosse Morning Chronicle*, 19 April 1887, 1). Taylor may have considered this to be an even more demeaning slur.

73. *Wisconsin Labor Advocate*, 22 April 1887, 4.

74. The *La Crosse News* (22 January 1887, 3) referred to the *Advocate* as "the nigger in the fence."

75. *Wisconsin Labor Advocate*, 22 April 1887 and 17 June 1887.

76. *Wisconsin Labor Advocate*, 29 April 1887, 1.

77. As quoted in *Wisconsin Labor Advocate*, 2 July 1887, 4.

78. *Wisconsin Labor Advocate*, 9 July 1887, 4.

79. Only one full year of the *Advocate* has survived, perhaps because it was sent directly and without cost to the Young Men's Library Association of La Crosse, which at the time was trying to establish a public library. Luckily, this association and its members dismissed the *Advocate* as unworthy and apparently failed even to remove these issues from their original wrappers. In 1984 I discovered this cache of copies in the archive of the La Crosse Public Library in a storage area where it had remained unopened.

80. *Wisconsin Labor Advocate*, 11 March 1887, 2.

81. *Wisconsin Labor Advocate*, 17 June 1887, 4. The references to labor inactivity in Wisconsin increase significantly as Taylor reported on labor successes in neighboring states.

82. *Iowa State Bystander*, 23 December 1898, 2. The *Bystander* described itself as the official newspaper of the Afro-American Protective Association of Iowa and the Most Worshipful United Grand Lodge of Iowa AF&AM (Ancient Free and Accepted Masons). The *Milwaukee Journal* (15 October 1904, 12) reported that Taylor left La Crosse in 1888.

83. The *Waterloo Times-Tribune* (12 April 1907, 1) noted that Taylor had lived in St. Paul "for years" before moving to Oskaloosa in 1891. That account, however, contained numerous errors, leaving questions about its accuracy.

84. For La Crosse views of Pomeroy, see Hebberd, "Marcus 'Brick' Pomeroy," 1–3; *La Crosse Tribune*, 21 July 1938 and 28 July 1911, 3.

85. *Blue Book*, 397.

86. See Meier, *Negro Thought*, 53–58, for discussion of popular ideas current among America's black leaders at the end of the century.

Chapter 3. Emergence of a Black Activist

1 In regard to the quote Taylor used in his 10 August 1898 speech, Washington wrote that he had actually said: "Cast down your bucket where you are" (*Up from Slavery*, 219). See Bayor, *Columbia Documentary History*, 356–58, for the full text of Washington's 1885 speech.

2. Aptheker, "Negro Who Ran for President," 64. Aptheker's article contains many events and dates that have not been confirmed in this research. See also "Sketch of George Edwin Taylor" for the exact date of Taylor's arrival at Oskaloosa.

3. See http://www.jimcrowhistory.org/scripts/jimcrow/press.cgi?state=Iowa (accessed 6 January 2009). No issues of that newspaper have survived.

4. *Oskaloosa Daily Herald*, 3 July 1950, 13.

5. Schwieder, Hraba, and Schwieder, *Buxton*. For a more specific study of mining in southeastern Iowa, see Hickenlooper, *Illustrated History*. For meatpacking, see *Iowa State Bystander*, 25 June 1897, 1.

6. Hoffmann, *Oskaloosa*, 124. For census population data for Mahaska, Marion, Monroe, and Wapello counties for 1880, 1890, and 1900, see Bergmann, "Negro in Iowa," 34–35; Goudy, "Selected Demographics," 29; Schwieder, Hraba, and Schwieder, *Buxton*, 38.

7. *Negro Solicitor*, 18 February 1893. No copies of this newspaper have survived, but clippings from it are found in scrapbooks, and items from the paper were reprinted in

other newspapers. This clipping from the 18 February 1893 issue was provided by the Mahaska County Genealogical Society.

8. Penn College was the first higher institution in Iowa to hire an African American as a full-time professor. Penn's personnel and student records for this early period no longer exist. Student names are included only in the college's annual catalogs.

9. Ostler, *Prairie Populism*, chaps. 8 and 9; Shambaugh, *James B. Weaver*, 294–98; *Wisconsin Labor Advocate*, 25 June 1887, 4. The *Albia Union* (11 November 1904, 1) noted that miners in one part of Monroe County had given a plurality to Eugene Debs's So-cialist Party in the 1904 presidential election. See also Haynes, *Third Party Movements*, 308–20, for the success of the Union Labor and Greenback parties in influencing Iowa politics during the 1889–91 period. Haynes (ibid., 305) amusingly noted that it was pos-sible in Iowa to be a Greenbacker, a Populist, a Union Labor advocate, a Prohibitionist, a Republican, and a Christian all at the same time. And it was helpful and acceptable to ally with Democrats if convenient. See also Hild, *Greenbackers*, for a careful review of interactions between southern agrarian alliances and national Union Labor, People's, and Populist movements.

10. *Iowa State Bystander*, 7 February 1896, 1. See Bergmann, "Negro in Iowa," and Beran, "Diamonds in Iowa," 56–69, for a detailed description of black migration into the coal-producing regions of south-central Iowa.

11. Numerous issues of the *Albia Republican* were used in this reconstruction. See also the *Ottumwa Daily Courier*, 15 January 1910; *Ead's Illustrated History*, 42. The "Carlsbad" claim refers to the famed mineral springs of Carlsbad (Karlovy Vary), Czech Republic, which became well known in the fourteenth century.

12. Quoted in Higginbotham, *Shades of Freedom*, 106, emphasis added. See also Tom-lins, *United States Supreme Court*, 132.

13. Blaustein and Zangrando, *Civil Rights*, 268–69; Scaturro, *Supreme Court's Retreat*, 70–76; Richardson, *Death of Reconstruction*, chap. 4; Higginbotham, *Shades of Freedom*, chap. 8. For Douglass's reactions to the decision, see Douglass, *Life and Times*, 652–59.

14. For an excellent and brief description of conditions of this period, see Alexander, "Vengeance without Justice," 117–18.

15. Taylor, "John Quincy Adams," 284. See also Penn, *Afro-American Press*, 238, for early history of the *Western Appeal*.

16. Taylor, "John Quincy Adams," 287–88.

17. Ibid., 289.

18. Ibid., 291–92. The 2008 value of $25 in 1887 was $580.

19. Ibid., 291–92. Nelson noted that McGhee was known for his "caustic wit" (*Fredrick L. McGhee*, 93). See also *Landmark*, 8 December 1887, 3.

20. Taylor, "John Quincy Adams," 292–93; *Landmark*, 8 December 1887, 3.

21. Fishel, "Genesis," 324–27.

22. Petty, "History of the South."

23. See Woods, "C. H. J. Taylor." Chafe noted that blacks joined the Populist move-ment for protective rather than economic reasons, for "protection from violence," and for "a secure place in the community" ("Negro and Populism," 404).

24. Quoted in the *Piqua Daily Leader*, 17 January 1890, 1.

25. Abramowitz, "Negro in the Populist Movement."

26. Meier, *Negro Thought*, 28.

27. Watson, "Black Phalanx," 3, 7. For the logic of disenfranchisement in Mississippi, see McMillen, *Dark Journey*, 35–71. For similar treatment, see "Vortex of Racial Disenfranchisement," in Valelly, *Two Reconstructions*, 121–48.

28. Justesen, *Broken Brotherhood*, x; Beatty, *Revolution Gone Backward*, 140–48. See also Swan, "Thomas McCants Stewart," 103–5, for Stewart's conversion to Democracy in 1884, and chap. 4, "Political Mission of the Talented Tenth," in ibid.

29. Fishel, "Negro in Northern Politics," 483–86; Schwalm, *Emancipation's Diaspora*, 213–14. See also Thornbrough, *T. Thomas Fortune*, chap. 4, for detailed treatment of the founding of the NAAL. For a recent treatment of the first Afro-American League and its problems, see Alexander, "We Know Our Rights," 13–97.

30. Doherty, "Voices of Protest," 47.

31. Ibid.

32. Moreno, *Black Americans*, 56; Doherty, "Voices of Protest," 47.

33. Doherty, "Voices of Protest," 47. See Fredrickson, *Black Image*, 32, for Fortune's devotion to democracy and his ambivalence toward Henry George when George ran for mayor of New York City in 1886. Fredrickson indicated also that Fortune believed in self-help and the Tuskegee formula while using labor rhetoric in explaining and supporting it. Fortune believed that blacks and other underrepresented persons should first prepare for the ballot before exercising their right to vote. See also King and Tuck, "Decentring the South," 213.

34. Seraile, "Political Views," 17.

35. Doherty, "Voices of Protest," 48.

36. See also Swan, "Thomas McCants Stewart," 145–46, for a detailed description of New York politics and the role that events there played in the failure of Fortune's first effort to establish a National Afro-American League. See also Alexander, "We Know Our Rights," 21–52.

37. Miller, "This Worldly Mission," 161–62. Others who cosigned the call included John Mitchell, Jr., of Richmond, W. Calvin Chase of Washington, D.C., and William Pledger of Georgia. See also Thornbrough, *T. Thomas Fortune*, 111, and Penn, *Afro-American Press*, 530–31, for names of cosigners.

38. Taylor, "John Quincy Adams," 293.

39. Fishel, "Genesis," 328–29. A civil rights bill was finally passed and signed into law on 20 April 1895, but only after both houses of Wisconsin's legislature were in Republican hands.

40. Fishel, "Negro in Northern Politics," 485–86. See also Penn, *Afro-American Press*, 532–33, for the NAAL's organizational structure.

41. *Galveston Daily News*, 18 January 1890, 16; *Decatur Daily Republican*, 17 January 1890, 2; *Piqua Daily Leader*, 17 January 1890, 1; *Salem Daily News*, 16 January 1890, 1; *Fitchburg Sentinel*, 18 January 1890, 1; *Daily Republican*, 17 January 1890, 2. For more on the reformed League, see Thornbrough, "National Afro-American League," 494–512;

Salley, *Black 100*, 216–18; Reed, *Black Chicago's First Century*, 311–13; Fortune, "Negro's Place," 216; Goldstein, "Preface"; Meier, *Negro Thought*, 70–71. The humorous high point at that meeting, however, was a resolution that passed unanimously and that read: "Resolved, That we do petition the Honorable Congress of the United States to make an appropriation of $100,000,000 to furnish the unhappy white citizens of those States [Alabama, South Carolina, Louisiana] who may desire to settle elsewhere in other favored States, free from Afro-American majorities, the means to do so" (see *Decatur Daily Republican*, 17 January 1890, 2). Alexander's ("We Know Our Rights," 35–97) treatment of the NAAL's first years is exhaustive and documents the activities of northern leagues and emergence of rival associations, such as the American Citizen's Equal Rights Association, the Minnesota Civil Rights Committee, and the National Civil Rights Association, which competed for similar membership and funding.

42. Thornbrough (*T. Thomas Fortune*, 117) mentioned another group, the American Citizens Civil Rights Association, which met in Washington, D.C., in 1890, but that association's meeting was attended only by federal officials or blacks then holding patronage positions. That group agreed to hold annual meetings.

43. Lovett (*African-American History*, 95) noted that the national association was formed by northern blacks whose objective was "to fight violence with violence," likely an incorrect characterization. Lovett indicated that a similar group was formed in Nashville at the same time.

44. Reed wrote that the association had been formed "evidently as an alternative to T. Thomas Fortune's declining Afro-American Council" (*All the World Is Here!* 127). Beatty identified the National Colored Men's Protective Association as formed by "a small group of black Democrats" (*Revolution Gone Backward*, 136–37). The name of the NCMPA had changed to Colored People's National Protective Association (CPNPA) by 1896. It is undetermined that this is the same organization named by Justesen, *Broken Brotherhood*, xi, as the National Racial Protective Association. The *Chicago Evening Post* (27 June 1893, 2) reported that the NCMPA held its first national convention in Chicago on 4 June 1892. The *Evening Post* issue for 26 June 1893 specified instead that the 1893 meeting was the association's third annual conference, organized in Chicago in 1891.

45. Reed, *Black Chicago's First Century*, 313.

46. See Swan, "Thomas McCants Stewart," 190–92, for a detailed description of circumstances leading to the Indianapolis meeting. Swan listed the leaders of black democracy at that time as Stewart, Fortune, Peter H. Clark of Ohio, J. Milton Turner of Missouri, George T. Downing of Rhode Island, Theophile T. Allain of Louisiana, and Charles H. J. Taylor of Kansas. Stewart did not attend the Indianapolis meeting because he argued that such a league only parroted similar organizations set up by Republicans. Chicago, Indianapolis, Cleveland, St. Louis, Detroit, and Kansas City each had significant black populations by the late nineteenth century, and each community was large enough to host conventions by black organizations and provide delegates with sufficient hotels, restaurants, entertainment, and so forth. Those were not unnecessary considerations during this period.

47. Beatty, *Revolution Gone Backward*, 145; *Newark Daily Advocate*, 28 July 1888, 2.

48. The *Weekly Fort Wayne Sentinel* (1 August 1888, 1) indicated that J. M. Vana and a T. T. Brown also were among the organizers. See the *New York Tribune*, 7 July 1904, 3, for Clark's role in the 1904 convention.

49. Woods, "C. H. J. Taylor," 128; Swan, "Thomas McCants Stewart," 191.

50. *Republican-Freeman*, 26 July 1888, 1; *Indianapolis Freeman*, 28 July 1888. Attending the executive meeting were James Milton Turner, T. Thomas Fortune, Charles M. Shelton, Noah Plummer, Peter H. Clark, E. A. Payne, Joseph Houser, Charles H. J. Taylor, William T. Scott, J. T. V. Hill, Edward Brown, Ogilby, and "a half dozen others." See also Kremer, *James Milton Turner*, 146–53; Grossman, *Democratic Party*, 144–45; Woods, "C. H. J. Taylor," 124–28.

51. The *Newark Daily Advocate* reported that the conference was attended by delegates from Indiana, Illinois, Ohio, Pennsylvania, New York, "and several of the southern and other northern states" (26 July 1888, 1).

52. Woods, "C. H. J. Taylor," 130; Beatty, *Revolution Gone Backward*, 142; *Broad Ax* (Salt Lake City), 6 August 1898, 1; *Adams County Union*, 6 September 1894, 4; *Evening Gazette*, 21 June 1892, 1; *Iowa State Bystander*, 14 August 1896, 4; *New York Times*, 10 August 1898. Beatty noted that the league was most active during election years, that "most prominent black Democrats were members," but also that the Democrats were seldom united in their objectives. In 1892, for instance, C. H. J. Taylor and H. C. C. Astwood contended for control of the league. A publication, the *National Democrat*, supposedly was launched by this league. For Clark, see Gutman, "Peter H. Clark," 413–18.

53. Swan, "Thomas McCants Stewart," 207; Beatty, *Revolution Gone Backward*, 98.

54. Beatty, *Revolution Gone Backward*, 142. The *Galveston Daily News* (27 September 1894, 1) reported that Astwood resigned as chairman of the NNDL's executive committee and joined the Republican Party. See also *World*, 21 August 1894, 3, for a simmering dispute among leaders in the NNDL.

55. Beatty, *Revolution Gone Backward*, 148–52.

56. *Atlanta Constitution*, 14 May 1893, 1.

57. Woods, "C. H. J. Taylor," 126–27.

58. *Daily Mail*, 25 July 1908, 4. The *Fitchburg Sentinel* (24 August 1893, 8) indicated that it also was called the National Negro Democratic Association.

59. Swan described this league as basically a New York State–based organization that had been established by A. B. Upshaw of the Democratic National Committee in 1892. James A. Ross "edited their organ, the *National Negro Democrat*" (Swan, "Thomas McCants Stewart," 203–4).

60. Beatty, *Revolution Gone Backward*, 143.

61. *Iowa Postal Card*, 12 August 1897, 6; *Cedar Rapids Evening Gazette*, 11 January 1894, 4.

62. See *Moberly Daily Monitor*, 27 July 1904, 3; *Tyrone Herald*, 18 August 1904, 8; *Rake Register*, 4 November 1904, 3; *Galveston Daily News*, 1 November 1904, 7; *Anacanda Standard*, 1 November 1904, 3; *Indiana Democrat*, 9 November 1904, 2; *Altamont Enterprise*, 19 August 1904, 1; *Daily Times*, 17 August 1904, 2; *Albia Union*, 4 November 1904, 1;

Rising Sun, 5 August 1904, 4. Nicolay and Hay mentioned that numerous pamphlets were printed in Minneapolis by the Lincoln Republicans, who were described as "anti-imperialist partisans" (*Complete Works*, 264). They also were called Silver Republicans.

63. McKerley, "Citizen and Strangers," 203–6; Swan, "Thomas McCants Stewart," 188.

64. Reed, *Black Chicago's First Century*, 360; *Daily Inter Ocean*, 27 June 1893, 13. "Sketch of Iowa Negro Presidential Candidate," published in the *Lincoln Evening News*, gave his election as president as 4 June 1892 at its Chicago convention. The *Decatur Daily Republican* (23 September 1892, 1) contrarily noted that Taylor had been elected the association's president in May 1892 at its Chicago meeting, at which time Knox, editor of the *Indianapolis Freeman*, had been elected secretary. By the time of the 23 September meeting, however, Knox, who was then supporting Harrison's reelection, had concluded that the association was a "democratic scheme."

65. The *Logansport Daily Pharos* (18 March 1892, 1) listed Taylor as first alternate "delegate-at-large" for the "liberal element" of the Iowa party. See also *Cedar Rapids Evening Gazette*, 22 August 1892, 4; *Union Star*, 1 April 1892, 2; and *Williamsburg Journal Tribune*, 25 March 1892, 8, for his appointment.

66. Philpot, *Race, Republicans*, 39.

67. See the *Iowa State Bystander* for John Thompson's characterization of Taylor as a "deep thinker and able writer" (23 December 1898, 2). Also in that newspaper, Thompson described Taylor as "an able editor a bright man, intellectually and a hard democratic worker" (22 July 1898, 1). Taylor humbly and amusingly described himself: "I believe that George Taylor is the greatest Negro editor in the world and on account of that, I will never be any greater than I am" (*Iowa State Bystander*, 12 August 1898, 1).

68. See Grossman, *Democratic Party*, 148–72, and Nathanson, "African Americans," 77, for the 1892 campaign and discontent with Harrison. See also King and Tuck, "Decentring the South," 244–45.

69. "Sketch of Iowa Negro Presidential Candidate." Logan drew a significant difference between Douglass and Booker T. Washington, suggesting that Washington's view was one of acceptance of "a subordinate position for Southern Negroes," while Douglass's was one of an "unequivocal standard for equal citizenship" (*Betrayal*, 280). Charles M. Ferguson, a Texas Republican, was a delegate to the Republican National Conventions in 1888, 1892, 1896, and 1900. Harlan and Smock (*Booker T. Washington Papers*, 7:523) indicated that Washington had been told of these suggestions, that he had asked that they be considered by the platform committee, but that he did not want his name attached to them in any fashion.

70. Logan (*Betrayal*, 75–76, 85–87) claimed that Harrison's policy was to do little to oppose disenfranchisement efforts in the South. See Beatty, *Revolution Gone Backward*, 105–25, for black disenchantment with Harrison's first term. See *Cedar Rapids Evening Gazette*, 8 June 1892, 1, for the Afro-American League's demands for a "new force bill."

71. Aptheker, "Negro Who Ran for President," 66. Meier (*Negro Thought*, 33–34) noted that Douglass also was critical of the Republicans during this period but that he believed that "the Republican party was the deck, all else the sea," a clear suggestion that the Democratic Party was not a viable option for progress. Beatty mentioned only that

"most black Republicans again closed ranks behind the ticket" (*Revolution Gone Backward*, 134). The *Milwaukee Journal* described Taylor: "He virtually walked out of the convention and became a bolter" (15 October 1904, 12). The *Iowa State Bystander* wrote of the "woeful mistake of four years ago" in obvious reference to Taylor's performance at the convention and of the embarrassment that he brought to Iowa's black Republicans (21 February 1896, 1); it later spoke of the "sad" lesson of 1892 and termed Taylor "a renegade" (28 February 1896, 1). On 13 March 1896 the *Bystander* less generously described Taylor as the "'Nigger' democrat and traitor" (1). Nathanson wrote that black Republicans "left Minneapolis [in 1892] unsure of their future role in the Republican Party" ("African Americans," 81).

72. Beatty, *Revolution Gone Backward*, 137.

73. According to the *Negro Year Book* (148), in 1912 the following numbers of lynchings per year occurred: 184 (1885), 138 (1886), 122 (1887), 142 (1889), 176 (1889), 127 (1890), 192 (1891), and 255 (1892). Of the total lynchings, 80 to 90 percent of them were in southern states and directed against African Americans. But there is another use of this term. "Judge Lynch" was used often to refer to "extralegal justice" as practiced on the frontier. For the latter, see Waldrep, *Many Faces*, 23; Pfeifer, *Rough Justice*, 91–93; White, *Rope & Faggot*.

74. Bishop J. Milton Turner, a leader in the African Methodist Church (AME), was a strong proponent of migration to Liberia in West Africa, a movement (Back to Africa) that was championed by the American Colonization Society and in the 1920s by Marcus Garvey. For more on this period and Turner, see Woods, "C. H. J. Taylor," 122; Barnes, *Journey of Hope*; Redkey, *Black Exodus*. The *Palladium* quoted Turner: "I have no apology to make for my well-known position on the subject of Negro emigration to Africa. God sent us here to this great white race to learn civilization and then go back and show to the world that we are a people" (14 May 1904, 1). In 1899 Turner would propose to ship seven million African Americans "to Liberia for a mere $15 apiece. . . . He planned to ask Congress for $105 million to accomplish this goal. . . . 'The white race either rules or exterminates'" (Justesen, *Broken Brotherhood*, 43). Here Taylor displayed his use of language and his knowledge of geography in a clever way. Clearly, Taylor knew that there was a Black Sea dividing Europe from Asia Minor, but his reference here was to an African homeland, where black Americans would find themselves surrounded by masses of Africans with whom they had no affinity. Taylor was not interested in finding a black paradise in Africa—his world remained in America and in the promise granted in the Constitution. In 1892 Fortune had argued that "if every one of the 8,000,000 Afro-Americans should go to Africa, would they swallow up the 100,000,000 natives, or would they be swallowed up? Jonah could not swallow the whale, and, therefore, the whale swallowed Jonah." To Fortune, "Afro-Americans are not Africans" (Alexander, *T. Thomas Fortune*, 266–67).

75. The word "tocsin" was a popular term used in the 1890s to refer to a "warning" or an "alarm." See Killian, "Bishop Daniel A. Payne," 181–82.

76. Clarkson, editor of the *Des Moines Register* in 1892, also was chairman of the Republican National Committee. It is likely that Clarkson had been instrumental in

Taylor's selection as an alternate at-large delegate for the convention. For Clarkson's and Taylor's selection at the Iowa State Convention, see *Cedar Rapids Evening Gazette*, 18 March 1892, 1, and 22 August 1892, 1.

77. The complete text of Taylor's "National Appeal" of 1892 is part of the Library of Congress series African American Perspectives: Pamphlets from the Daniel A. P. Murray Collection, 1818–1907, and is available at http://hdl.loc.gov/loc.rbc/lcrbmrp.toc03 or http://murphylibrary.uwlax.edu/digital/TaylorGeorge/7NationalAppea192.pdf. The italics and (?) appear as they do in the Library of Congress copy. The *Cedar Rapids Evening Gazette* did not appreciate Taylor's appeal: "In politics he uses his razor with more vigor than good judgment, and he has been taken up by the slack of the pants and scruff of the neck by the prophets of the faith in Iowa, and has been cast over the battlements into outer darkness. And there shall be, in fact there is at the present writing wailing and gnashing of teeth. Fault is found because Taylor is accused of selling himself to the democrats. If the charge is true his purchasers lack business judgment as much as he lacks honesty. It would be reckless extravagance to pay fifteen cents a crate for such 'leaders,' and it will not be generally believed that the democrats bought him if they had to take him at the republican state convention's appraisement" (22 August 1892, 4). The *Alton Democrat* praised Taylor, noting that he "is out in a card [an appeal] saying he cannot support Harrison and advising his race to follow him in supporting Cleveland" (27 August 1892, 4).

78. See *Marshfield Times*, 7 October 1892, 2; *Los Angeles Times*, 23 September 1892, 1.

79. *Landmark*, 22 September 1892, 3; *Carroll Sentinel*, 30 September 1892, 5.

80. "Colored Men in Session," *New York Times*, 23 September 1892.

81. Reed, *Black Chicago's First Century*, 364.

82. Rudwick and Meier, "Black Man in the 'White City,'" 360. Peavler noted that Douglass had envisioned the Chicago Exposition as the proper platform for the inauguration of a national forum such as the National Colored Men's Protective Association, which was intended to serve as a "grand convention or congress of colored men" ("African Americans in Omaha," 354). The *Marshville Times* (7 July 1893, 2) reported that this meeting also decided that Chicago would be the site of the association's national headquarters.

83. Alexander, "We Know Our Rights," 97. Walters (*My Life and Work*, 97–98) indicated that the Knoxville, Tennessee, meeting in 1891 was the last of this revived NAAL.

84. *Daily Inter Ocean*, 8 July 1893, 5.

85. *Logansport Pharos*, 26 June 1903, 1, and 27 June 1903, 1; *Trenton Times*, 26 June 1903, 6.

86. The *Taylor County Democrat* wrote: "Mr. Taylor is the coming Fred Douglass of America, but with very different political attachments, and Iowa democracy is proud of him" (27 July 1893, 1).

87. *Daily Inter Ocean*, 27 June 1893, 13, and 28 June 1893, 7; *Weekly Inter Ocean*, 4 July 1893, 2; Reed, *All the World Is Here!* 127–28. See also Kennedy, "Racial Overtones," 266–75. Roberts described Downing as "a leader in the National Colored People's Protective Association" and chairman of its executive committee in 1893 ("Lost Theaters," 272,

282n21). Roberts also indicated that "Ida B. Wells and Frances E. W. Harper were appointed to the [association's] Ladies' Auxiliary Board" (ibid., 282n21). The *Weekly Inter Ocean* listed officers as "president, George E. Taylor, Iowa; vice presidents T. T. Allan, Louisiana; J. E. Knox, Arkansas; W. H. Sinclair, South Carolina; M. M. McCloud, Mississippi; Miss Ida B. Wells, Tennessee; recording secretary, J. H. Porter, Illinois; corresponding secretary, A. G. Plummer, Minnesota; statistician, C. H. Shotwell, Louisiana; treasurer, H. M. B. Spencer, Kansas; national organizer, R. A. Dawson, Illinois; attorney, W. R. Morris, Minnesota" (4 July 1893, 2). Henry Francis Downing was chairman of the NCMPA's executive committee.

88. *Inter Ocean*, 8 July 1993, 5. Ida Wells came from Tennessee, but in 1893 she was working in New York City.

89. *Weekly Inter Ocean*, 4 July 1893, 2.

90. Ibid.; *Daily Inter Ocean*, 28 June 1893, 7.

91. For a brief description of the exposition and the "Negro" congresses that met in that city at the same time, see Reed, "Black Presence at 'White City.'" For a detailed version, see Reed, *All the World Is Here!*

92. *Iowa State Bystander*, 24 August 1894. In Texas, for instance, the Populist/People's Party obtained nearly 34 percent of statewide votes for its presidential candidate in the 1892 general election. Ali ("Making of a Black Populist") noted that the People's Party of North Carolina, of which the Colored Farmers' Alliance was a part, fused with the Republicans during the 1894 election, and together they seized a majority of the state legislature. Marszalek (*Black Congressman*, 20–67) described a similar circumstance in South Carolina, where George Murray and black South Carolinians carefully took advantage of a split among Democrats to win a major victory, sending Murray to Washington as the only black member of Congress in 1891.

93. The *Moberly Evening Democrat* described Taylor as "president of the Colored People's National Protective Association of America" (9 March 1899, 3). Marszalek (*Black Congressman*, 114–15) suggests a different sequence and circumstance for the Protective Association during this period. In Marszalek's reconstruction a Negro National Protective Association had been formed in Washington in May 1897 by George W. Murray of South Carolina. John Cromwell of Washington was the group's national secretary, with T. Thomas Fortune of New York and John Mitchell, Jr., of Virginia acting as state secretaries. Calvin Chase was "president of the Washington branch." A constitution was adopted in 1898 for a "National Racial Protective Association," but Marszalek claimed that this group "became part of the 1898 revival" of NAAL in the form of the National Afro-American Council. Taylor's name does not appear in Marszalek's reconstruction.

94. Alexander, "We Know Our Rights," 108.

95. Perry ("History of the South," n.p.) noted that the Colored Farmers' National Alliance and Cooperative Union had spread throughout the South by 1891 and that it claimed a membership of 1.2 million, of which 150,000 were men under the age of twenty-one and 750,000 were adult men. Perry suggested that it was the largest organization of blacks during the nineteenth century and that its platform was "more radical" than its white-dominated counterpart, the Southern Alliance. For the Colored Alliance,

see also Holmes, "Demise"; Ali, *Balance of Power*, 74–100; Ali, "Independent Black Voices," 4–5; Gaither, *Blacks and the Populist Movement*, 162–77. Ali ("Independent Black Voices," 7) wrote that black activists in the South regularly fused with the Republican Party on ballots and that blacks accounted for nearly 400,000 members of the Populist Party by 1892.

96. *New York Times*, 4 August 1894, 1.

97. *Moberly Evening Democrat*, 9 March 1899, 3; *Richmond Planet*, 14 October 1899.

98. Alexander, "We Know Our Rights," 116–23.

99. Quoted in ibid., 125.

100. Marszalek, *Black Congressman*, 114–15. See also Alexander, "We Know Our Rights," 110–16.

101. *New York Times*, 21 December 1898, 4.

102. *New Era*, 5 February 1890, 2.

103. *Iowa State Bystander*, 6 July 1893, 1. See also the *Negro Solicitor*, 18 February 1893, for an announcement regarding a "call" for "leading Negroes from different parts of the state" to convene in Des Moines. Oskaloosa had been appointed to send five delegates and five alternates to the convention. Schwalm noted that in an issue dated 20 January 1893 a "new [but short-lived] black newspaper, the *Weekly Avalanche*" of Des Moines, had announced itself to be the official organ of the "Afro-American Protective Association of Iowa" (*Emancipation's Diaspora*, 214). The *Weekly Avalanche* was published between 1891 and 1895 and was edited by A. S. Barnett. Only one issue has survived, that of 20 January 1893. Barnett was described as a "pleasing speaker" and a Republican. For Barnett, see *Burlington Hawk-Eye*, 9 October 1892, 1; *Milford Mail*, 23 August 1894, 2; *Cedar Rapids Evening Gazette*, 25 October 1892, 2.

104. *Iowa State Bystander*, 6 July 1894, 1.

105. Ibid.

106. The *Oskaloosa Daily Herald* of 3 July 1950 contains a picture of the header for the first issue of the *Negro Solicitor*, the only clipping from that issue that survived. *Colman's City Directory, Oskaloosa, Iowa, 1898–1899*, identified the *Solicitor* as a "(dem) weekly." The paper sold for five cents per issue, or a subscription price of $1.50 per year. For the newspaper's end, see *Daily Iowa Capital*, 21 April 1899, 5; *Iowa State Bystander*, 23 December 1898, 2. Morris ("Black Media," 287, 299) estimated that Taylor had 1,700 subscribers during the tenure of the *Negro Solicitor*. That figure is unlikely, however, because newspapers and their owners frequently elevated such numbers to retain advertisers, for no business would place ads in newspapers known to have small readerships. Herringshaw described the *Solicitor* as "a national journal" (*Herringshaw's Encyclopedia* [1901], 916).

107. *Iowa State Bystander*, 24 August 1894, 1, 7 September 1894, 1, and 5 October 1894, 1.

108. *Iowa State Bystander*, 5 October 1894, 1.

109. Ibid.

110. *Iowa State Bystander*, 22 March 1895, 1. Suggs wrote that "Taylor was active in local politics and used the *Negro Solicitor* as his campaign organ" (*Black Press*, 74).

111. *Iowa State Bystander*, 29 March 1895, 1, and 31 May 1895, 1.

112. *Iowa State Bystander*, 5 July 1895, 1.

113. *Iowa State Bystander*, 3 July 1896, 1, 10 July 1896, 1, and 13 November 1896, 1.

114. The Slavery Abolition Act of 1833 took effect and ended slavery in the British Empire on 1 August 1834. In the upper Midwest, Emancipation Day was celebrated generally on 1 August and involved music, a parade, many speeches, a picnic, and an evening ball. Over time, however, these celebrations also became opportunities for speeches that dealt with aspirations for the race, for self-reliance, and for assimilation with the ideals of American society. For a detailed description, see Schwalm, "Emancipation Day Celebrations," 291–332. Schwalm (ibid., 297, 303) indicates that these celebrations dated to the pre–Civil War period and continued after it because blacks believed themselves unwelcome to celebrate the Fourth of July alongside whites. Bontemps and Conroy (*Anyplace but Here*, 93) noted that many ex-slaves used the term "War of Emancipation" rather than "Civil War." See also Schwalm, *Emancipation's Diaspora*, 224–34, for an updated interpretation of Emancipation Day celebrations. For Taylor's activities in the Lodge, see *Iowa State Bystander*, 2 November 1894, 2, and 13 July 1900, 1. See *Iowa State Bystander*, 18 January 1901, 8, for the First International Council of Grand Master Masons, Colored, which met in Jacksonville on 27 December 1900.

115. "Sketch of George Edwin Taylor"; *Moberly Evening Democrat*, 9 March 1899, 3; "Sketch of Iowa Negro Presidential Candidate"; *Iowa State Bystander*, 26 March 1897, 1, and 9 April 1897, 1; *Broad Ax* (Chicago), 21 July 1900, 1. For a brief survey of the Knights of Pythias and Taylor's role as grand chancellor commander of the order in Iowa, see Walker-Webster, "Social, Fraternal, Cultural, and Civic Organizations," 408. For degree sequences in major Masonic orders, see Carnes, *Secret Rituals and Manhood*, 166–67. See also *Iowa State Bystander*, 26 March 1897, 1, and 9 April 1897, 1, and *Cedar Rapids Evening Gazette*, 22 July 1897, 4, for Taylor's office within the Knights.

116. *Quincy Daily Journal*, 26 August 1897, 8; *Planet*, 14 October 1899. The *Planet*'s editor praised Taylor: "His suave manner, graceful deliberation made friends for him even among his late antagonists and all hands agreed that he had done the best he could. . . . We forgot to state it—Mr. Taylor, unfortunately (from our standpoint) is a Democrat." He also described Taylor's wife: "His Madame is one of the best stenographers and typewriters in the United States."

117. See Schwalm, *Emancipation's Diaspora*, 160–74, for the spread of Prince Hall Masonry in the Midwest, its struggle to obtain recognition for existing black lodges as a part of regular Masonry, and its internal debates regarding leadership issues.

118. Trotter, "African American Fraternal Associations," 356. See also Liazos and Ganz, "Duty to the Race," 486; Skocpol and Oser, "Organization Despite Adversity," 369; Kuyk, "African Derivation," 559; *Atlanta Constitution*, 4 February 1900, 24. Fahey noted that black societies in the 1920s had large memberships—Odd Fellows (304,000), Knights of Pythias (250,000), Prince Hall Masons (150,000), and Elks (70,000)—and that "the sixty-odd leading black fraternal societies had about 2,500,000 members and property worth about $20,000,000" in the 1930s (*Black Lodge*, 10–11). Alexander (*Race Man*, 150–53) claimed that the Knights of Pythias of Richmond, Virginia, led by John Mitchell, Jr., was primarily an insurance scheme, with members paying fifty cents in

dues per month and receiving three dollars per week if sick. Benefits included payments for illnesses, death, and burial expenses.

119. Schwalm, *Emancipation's Diaspora*, 157–58.

120. *Cedar Rapids Gazette*, 23 June 1897, 1; *Burlington Hawk-Eye*, 23 June 1897, 3.

121. *Iowa State Bystander*, 8 April 1897, 1, 23 April 1897, 4, and 21 May 1897, 4. Whether Taylor and Woodson considered this model as restricted to Iowa or whether they believed it to be a brand that could be expanded nationwide is unclear, partly because only three references to this corporation have been found in the literature, perhaps suggesting that it was unsuccessful or never was realized. In 1898 currency $125,000 would have had the purchasing power of $3.3 million in 2008 dollars.

122. *Iowa State Bystander*, 20 November 1896, 1, and 12 February 1897, 4.

123. By 1899 even the *Iowa State Bystander*, which otherwise had supported the league and its successor council after 1898, reported: "It is said that the Afro-American Council that was held in Washington was noted for noise and that common sense, decency and sobriety were conspicuous because of their absence; such meetings will hardly help the Negro" and are "disgraceful" (20 January 1899, 4). Chase, editor of the *Washington Bee*, described the council as "A National Fraud" (11 July 1903, 4). See also Miller, "This Worldly Mission," 164–95, for a description of the council's activities under the leadership of Walters.

124. Nelson, *Fredrick L. McGhee*, 80.

Chapter 4. Taylor as the National Democrat

1. *Broad Ax* (Chicago), 8 September 1900; *Times Picayune*, 12 August 1900.

2. *Cedar Rapids Evening Gazette*, 22 August 1892, 4.

3. Miller, "Alexander Walters," 180–81.

4. See Squibb, "Roads to Plessy," 85–86, for a discussion of impediments to northward migration of disenfranchisement and Jim Crow laws.

5. Walton, *Black Political Parties*, 32–33, 36; Woods, "C. H. J. Taylor," 126–28; Meier, "Negroes and the Democratic Party." See also Walton, *Negro in Third Party Politics*, 38–45, for the rise and collapse of the Populist parties and the difficult symbiosis of white and "colored" farmers' alliances. Taylor consistently argued that the black population was 50 percent larger than that reported in official census announcements.

6. Abramowitz, "Negro in the Populist Movement." Miller ("This Worldly Mission," 182) noted that there was discussion in 1900 about the possibility of launching a "black political party" but that nothing resulted from that notion.

7. Woods ("C. H. J. Taylor," 127–28) explained this as an issue of state rather than national party success. If, for instance, enough black voters could be drawn away from the Republican Party in crucial states in the North, Democratic elections would be possible. The price for that cooperation would be patronage. Woods indicated that Grover Cleveland's administration was particularly attuned to this reasoning.

8. It is unlikely that any African American would have been recognized in the convention in 1896 as a delegate. This was a time when southern delegates to nearly all national conventions protested the presence of blacks and regularly threatened to leave

conventions en masse until their demands were met. The claim that Taylor had been selected as a delegate to the 1896 Democratic Convention appears in two editions of *Herringshaw's Encyclopedia*, 1898 (916) and 1901 (916). That claim may have been submitted to editors by Taylor. Neither Dickinson, *Official Proceedings*, nor Bensel, *Passion and Preference*, lists Taylor as a delegate or mentions his name, nor do they indicate that an African American attended that convention as a listed delegate. *Iowa State Bystander*, 22 May 1896, 2, reported the proceedings of the Iowa State Democratic Convention, and it also failed to list Taylor as one of the four at-large delegates selected to attend the national convention. That the state Democratic Convention had failed to select any black to represent Iowa at the national convention became a subject of much discussion in Iowa's Republican newspapers in 1896.

9. Justesen, *Broken Brotherhood*, 5, 8 –33; Woods, "C. H. J. Taylor," 128. See also *Iowa State Bystander*, 7 August 1896, 4, for Taylor's attendance at the NNDL's 1896 meeting in Chicago.

10. Herringshaw, *Herringshaw's Encyclopedia* [1901], 916; Beatty, *Revolution Gone Backward*, 166 –67. In the article "Our Ticket for President," the *Broad Ax* (Chicago) wrote on 8 September 1900: "Mr. Taylor was a delegate to the Democratic National Convention of 1896 and seconded the nomination of Col. Wm. J. Bryan. He made many speeches for him." For a detailed treatment of the 1896 convention, see Bensel, *Passion and Preferences*, 279. It is interesting that Bensel, in this most recent study of the convention, failed to mention the name of a single African American participant or any role played by the National Negro Democratic League. For a deputation from W. T. Scott, president of the League, to Bryan in September 1896, see *New York Times*, 8 September 1896, 2.

11. Pinchney Benton Steward Pinchback was governor of Louisiana from 1872 to 1873; John Mercer Langston, Virginia, lawyer, was a congressman in 1890–91, dean of Howard University's law school, and president of Virginia State University; Norris Wright Cuney, Texas, was a high official in the Republican Party and grand master of the Free Masons of Galveston; William Pledger, Georgia, editor, supported Populist Party candidates in the mid-1890s and had been instrumental in the formation of Fortune's Afro-American League in 1890; Col. Perry Carson was appointed district inspector of Washington, D.C., and was known as the "political boss in the District of Columbia."

12. The complete text of Taylor's "National Appeal" of 1896 is part of the Library of Congress series African American Perspectives: Pamphlets from the Daniel A. P. Murray Collection, 1818 –1907, and is available at http://hdl.loc.gov/loc.rbc/lcrbmrp.t0c02 or http://murphylibrary.uwlax.edu/digital/TaylorGeorge/8NationalAppea196.pdf. The full text contains 9,116 words.

13. *Weekly Argus*, 6 June 1896. Taylor's motto is taken from his 1892 "National Appeal," in the section titled "To Exterminate the Negro."

14. *Quincy Daily Journal*, 30 July 1897, 5.

15. *Quincy Daily Journal*, 27 July 1896, 5, and 25 August 1897, 7.

16. *Quincy Daily Journal*, 18 August 1897, 5.

17. *Quincy Daily Journal*, 27 July 1896, 5, and 30 July 1897, 5. Those attending the Oskaloosa meeting included Prof. Harry R. Graham of Kansas City, Missouri; T. L. Allen

of Quincy, Illinois; Cyrus Bell of Omaha, Nebraska; and others. Taylor was selected as the league's first president. For the Colored Free Silver League, see *Iowa State Bystander*, 13 August 1897, 1; *Carroll Sentinel*, 9 August 1897, 4.

18. Those attending sessions in Quincy included McGhee from St. Paul; A. E. Manning, who was editor of the *Indianapolis World* and president of the National Negro Democratic League; Cyrus Bell, editor of Omaha's *Afro-American Sentinel*; William T. Scott, president of the Illinois Negro Free Silver League; C. W. Lear of Clarksville, Missouri, principal of Clarksville School; F. O. Allen of Burlington; Harry R. Graham, editor of Kansas City's *Rising Sun*; James A. Ross of Buffalo and editor of Buffalo's *Globe*.

19. *Quincy Morning Whig*, 27 August 1897, 8.

20. *Quincy Daily Journal*, 25 August 1897, 7.

21. Ibid.

22. *Quincy Daily Journal*, 26 August 1897, 8.

23. Ibid.

24. "Negro Democratic League," *Washington Post*, 10 August 1898. "The Negro National Democratic League official convention call," 23 June 1900, indicated that Edward E. Lee served as president of the league before Taylor and that terms of office were for two years. Conventions of the league also were called to coincide with the meetings of the Democratic National Convention, with delegates recessing while the DNC was in session.

25. The Supreme Court ruling in *Plessy v. Ferguson* (1896) essentially legitimized the doctrine of "separate but equal," a notion that remained in force until *Brown v. Board of Education, Topeka, Kansas* (1954). Blight (*Frederick Douglass' Civil War*, 222–24) noted that Douglass believed that the American people are "destitute of political memory," that they are willing to forget the past or reinvent it. Blight engages in an interesting discussion of historical memory as a problem of passage of time versus a "struggle between rival versions of the past," with extremes attempting to "manipulate its meaning." See King and Tuck, "De-centring the South," 237–39, for the impact of *Plessy v. Ferguson*.

26. See Gatewood, "Black Americans," 557–60 and passim; Mitchell, "Black Man's Burden," 89–90. See also Blight, *Race and Reunion*, 348–49, for a discussion of black opposition to the war.

27. See http://www.antiimperialist.com/1626.html (accessed 9 January 2009). See also Krenn, *Race and U.S. Foreign Policy*, 366, for a list of members of the league's executive committee: William T. Scott of Cairo, Illinois, president; Lawrence Newby, secretary; C. F. Armsted of Gallopolis, Ohio; T. C. Brown of Baltimore, Maryland; Edward Clark of San Francisco; Charles Croswalt of Nashville; A. B. Davidson of Newark; George Downing of Rhode Island; F. W. Ernst of Detroit; D. T. Freemont of Virginia; William Gross of New York City; J. T. Hill of Indianapolis; Joseph Houser, editor of the *Negro World* of St. Paul, Minnesota; J. H. Howard of Philadelphia; W. T. Peyton of Louisville, Kentucky; Jerome Riley of Seattle; James Ross, editor of Buffalo's *Globe & Freeman*; Rev. T. B. Stamps of New Orleans; George E. Taylor of Oskaloosa, Iowa; James Milton Turner of St. Louis, Missouri; and John Vashon of St. Louis, Missouri. Krenn also noted that "in this period the Negro press was filled with accounts of lynchings,

mutilations, and other outrages and the Negroes' protests against them. Many petitions were addressed to [President] McKinley by the Afro-American Council and other groups, but the President did nothing about enforcing civil rights laws" (ibid., 369).

28. *Broad Ax* (Chicago), 30 September 1899, 1.

29. *Monroe County News* (n.d.) mentions three railroads that passed through Albia: Chicago Burlington and Quincy, Iowa Central Railroad, and Wabash.

30. Suzann Holland to Bruce Mouser, 23 January 2009, Mouser file, Area Research Center, University of Wisconsin–La Crosse. State of Iowa, Mahaska County, Marriage Record, 1889–97, 121, recorded that Cora E. Cooper had been married previously to Grant Buckner (21 July 1887), that she was twenty-one years of age at the time of her marriage to Taylor (25 August 1894), that she was "colored," and that she had been born in Iowa. The *Iowa State Bystander* described her as "one of Oskaloosa's fairest and best educated young ladies" (31 August 1894, 1). Cora Cooper was self-described as "Miss Buckner" in July 1894 when she accompanied Taylor to Ottumwa to attend a meeting of the Afro-American Association as a delegate from Oskaloosa.

31. *Broad Ax* (Chicago), 7 July 1900, 1.

32. A transcript of the surviving portion of Cora Taylor's editorial is available at http://murphylibrary.uwlax.edu/digital/TaylorGeorge/4CoraTeditNS96.pdf.

33. *Waterloo Daily Courier*, 12 August 1896, 4. The *Iowa State Bystander* (7 August 1896, 4) indicated that he injured his right ankle and foot and his right hip and left arm.

34. "Our Ticket for President," *Broad Ax* (Chicago), 8 September 1900. Only one such editorial has been found.

35. "State Disfranchisement," *Broad Ax* (Salt Lake City), 30 April 1898, 4.

36. See Kelly for the middle-class attitude that the black poor were "lazy, self-destructive, and prone to criminal behavior" ("We Are Not What We Seem," 80). See *Iowa State Bystander*, 12 August 1898, 1, for similar sentiments given by Taylor at a speech in Keokuk, Iowa, on 4 August. See also Saunders, "Black American Conservatism," 13, for Washington's "tendency to blame Negroes for their condition."

37. Moore, *Booker T. Washington*, 128. Logan directly concluded that Washington "accepted a subordinate place for Negroes in American life" (*Betrayal*, 276).

38. Logan, *Betrayal*, 305. In 1895 Washington had said: "As a rule, I believe in universal, free suffrage, but I believe that in the South we are confronted with peculiar conditions that justify the protection of the ballot in many of the states, for a while at least, either by an educational test, a property test, or by both combined; but whatever tests are required, they should be made to apply with equal and exact justice to both races" (*Up from Slavery*, 237).

39. Peavler ("African Americans in Omaha," 337–61) described a "Congress of Representative White and Colored Americans" that met in Omaha from 17 to 19 August 1898 and a subsequent meeting of the Western Negro Press Association, to which Taylor was appointed an official representative from the state of Iowa. One of the goals of the congress was to form a "Representative White and Colored American Association" that would reflect a biracial effort to support civil rights. The *Iowa State Bystander* (21 May 1897, 4) noted that Taylor also attempted to secure an Iowa exhibit at the Tennessee

Centennial Exposition, which was then "in progress." The report of "The Negro Department" (in Justi, *Official History*, 193 –204) is an extraordinary document in its simplistic approach to the "Negro Problem," its appeal for "industrial education," and its premise that the South was the black man's "natural home" and "its people, though once his master, are his natural friends." Eighty-five cities sent exhibits (ibid., 203 –4). The exposition lasted from 1 May to 30 October 1897.

40. See also Fahey, *Black Lodge*, 19 –20, for the failure of the Readjusters, the "failed dreams of black politicians," and the rise of the "True Reformer" insurance organization. For a detailed description of black Populism, see Ali, *In the Balance of Power*, chap. 4, and Abramowitz, "Negro in the Populist Movement." For the Readjusters movement, see Dailey, "Limits of Liberalism," 88 –114. Woodward (*Strange Career of Jim Crow*, 31–66) reviews the period between Reconstruction and disenfranchisement and the complicated cooperative ventures made to bring black voters into the Populist movement. Nugent (*From Centennial to World War*, chap. 4) traced the source of these cooperative ventures to the agricultural depression of 1893 –97, which fell most heavily on poor farmers in the South and the Midwest.

41. Ali, "Independent Black Voices," 5.

42. Gerteis, "Populism, Race, and Political Interest," 197 –227; Meier, *Negro Thought*, 37 –38; Meier, "The Negro and the Democratic Party," 17; Walton, *Black Political Parties*, 32 –33, 36; Mjagkij, *Organizing Black America*, 601. For the reaction to black Populism, see Mendelberg, *Race Card*, 66. See also Gaither, *Blacks and the Populist Movement*, and Ali, *In the Balance of Power*, for "Colored Alliance" organizations that existed at the turn of the century.

43. Harris, *Something Within*, 90 –91; Lewinson, *Race, Class, and Party*, 74. Shofner concluded that while the era of Reconstruction had ended with the withdrawal of federal troops in 1877, cultural patterns had remained unchanged: "Reconstruction ended before Negroes [had] secured a place in society" (*Nor Is It Over Yet*, 344). Logan described the change: "A specter of a new era of Negro 'domination' once again swept the South" (*Betrayal*, 95).

44. *Broad Ax* (Salt Lake City), 5 March 1898, 1.

45. *National Newspaper Directory & Gazetteer*, 185.

46. *Iowa State Bystander*, 23 December 1898, 2.

47. *Iowa State Bystander*, 15 April 1898.

48. In 1904 Taylor claimed that he had ceased publication of the *Negro Solicitor* because he was accused of "putting on too many airs for a nigger," a likely mischaracterization of his circumstances in 1898. The more likely explanation is that the *Iowa State Bystander* advanced in format and coverage at a time when Taylor was busy with other projects and when he neglected his newspaper. For Taylor's explanation, see appendix A.

49. When Pomeroy's *Democrat* was most popular and had its largest circulation, many of its pages were filled with letters from loyal subscribers, all of whom used his newspaper as a sounding board for their agenda. Pomeroy was critical of Reconstruction, and nearly all published letters were from southern readers. Unfortunately, no copies of the *Negro Solicitor* have survived. If Taylor followed the success formula used by Pomeroy,

the high number of subscribers might have reflected a strong base of southern support among black Populists. That support base also would have collapsed in 1898, the same year that brought the end of the *Negro Solicitor*.

50. This editorial, "A Man or a Monkey," was found in George Woodson's scrapbook, and it was amongst a group of clippings from the early August 1898 period. A copy of the editorial is available at http://murphylibrary.uwlax.edu/digital/TaylorGeorge/17Manora Monkey98.pdf. All remaining quotations in this paragraph come from this editorial.

51. Ibid.

52. *Iowa State Bystander*, 30 September 1898, 1. The *Bystander* characterized his political efforts in the East as "Missionary work."

53. *Iowa State Bystander*, 23 December 1898, 2. None of these articles has been found.

54. *Mine, Quarry and Metallurgical Record*, 463; *Daily Iowa Capital*, 21 April 1899, 5; *Ottumwa Daily Courier*, 22 July 1904, 6. Coalfield was described as a village of two to three hundred persons located approximately nine miles northwest of Albia, Iowa.

55. *Daily Iowa Capital*, 21 April 1899, 5; *Moberly Evening Democrat*, March 1899, 3. The *Lincoln Evening News* (5 September 1904) reported that Taylor's employment with Little lasted "nearly a year."

56. *Broad Ax* (Chicago), 18 August 1900.

57. *Colman's City Directory, Oskaloosa, Iowa, 1900–1901*, n.p.

58. *Colman's City Directory, Oskaloosa, Iowa, 1904–1905*, n.p. The Iowa census for 1905 placed "Mrs. Cora Taylor" in Mahaska County (Oskaloosa) and George Taylor in Wapello County (Ottumwa). In 1899 Cora Taylor accompanied Taylor to Richmond, Virginia, where she was praised by John Mitchell, Jr., editor of the *Richmond Planet*. See the *Broad Ax* (Chicago) for a description of Cora Taylor: "Mrs. Taylor is well educated and being handsome posses[ses] all the qualifications which go to make up a true woman" (7 July 1900, 1).

59. *Broad Ax* (Chicago), 23 June 1900, 2, and 7 July 1900, 1.

60. *New York Times*, 1 July 1900.

61. Nelson, *Fredrick L. McGhee*, 81.

62. Quoted in ibid., 84. Chicago's *Broad Ax* (23 June 1900) indicated that Taylor as secretary of the league had convened its national convention while noting that Edward E. Lee had been president of the league since 1898. Taylor had received his selection of secretary on 10 August 1898. It was commonly expected that the position of secretary was a stepping stone to the presidency of any organization.

63. Meier, *Negro Thought*, 241–42. For McGhee at the 1900 National Afro-American Council meeting, see Justesen, *Broken Brotherhood*, 64; see Alexander, "We Know Our Rights," 124, for McGhee's activities in the National Afro-American Council.

64. *Iowa State Bystander*, 25 August 1899, 1.

65. Nelson, *Fredrick L. McGhee*, 85.

66. *Broad Ax* (Chicago), 18 August 1900. On 30 July 1900 Taylor wrote to George Knox, editor of the *Indianapolis Freeman*, explaining his reasons for supporting Bryan: "Negro voters of the country are today arrayed with the Democratic party, no well informed person can deny. And, in order that our Republican brothers may know why we

cherish the faith that is within us, I desire to say through the *Freeman*, that we believe that imperialism leads to despotism, and we consider that the present administration has strong imperialistic tendencies; we also believe in the rights of all men to govern themselves, hence we oppose the policy of the administration towards the Philippines; we are firm believers in the Monroe Doctrine, and since the present administration has practically annulled this doctrine we oppose the action; we are opposed to the propagation of private trusts and such; we in no wise feel benefited by the Dingley tariff, hence we oppose it; we are unalterably opposed to the present 'gold standard' policy, believing that it tends to contract the currency of the country, thus hampering our chances for sustenance; hence, it is apparent that we stand for the principles of the Democratic Party and for Bryan, as against the principles of the present Republican Party and McKinley" (Aptheker, *Documentary History*, 1:819–20).

67. *Broad Ax* (Chicago), 21 July 1900. This appeal appears to lack the quality of language and skill evident in Taylor's earlier writing, with the suggestion that it likely came from the pen of another member of the league. In this instance McGhee is listed as "Chairman Committee on Addresses," perhaps indicating that it was his responsibility to compose it. A transcription of this appeal is available at http://murphylibrary .uwlax.edu/digital/TaylorGeorge/10NegroesforBryan00.pdf. See also Nelson, *Fredrick L. McGhee*, 85–86.

68. *Dallas Morning News*, 23 August 1900, 8; *Savannah Tribune*, 8 September 1900, 48.

69. *Savannah Tribune*, 8 September 1900, 48. Copeland ("Republocrats") claimed that Bryan had met with Turner and W. R. McAllister, the latter describing himself as president of the Afro-American Protective League. Interestingly, Kremer, in his authoritative biography of *James Milton Turner*, does not mention this event. Justesen traced Turner's conversion from Republican to Democrat to 1888, indicating that he "would leave the [Democratic] party for good in 1903, declaring allegiance to Theodore Roosevelt in 1904" (*Broken Brotherhood*, 70–71). Chicago's *Broad Ax* noted that many blacks considered Turner a "has been" who should have known that "it is impossible to run the mill with the water that has past" (8 September 1900).

70. *Savannah Tribune*, 27 August 1898, 2.

71. *New York Times*, 23 August 1900, 3; *Iowa State Bystander*, 24 August 1900; *Times Picayune*, 23 August 1900, 2.

72. *Dallas Morning News*, 23 August 1900, 8. Chicago's *Broad Ax* published a critical "open letter" to Jones on 15 September 1900, asking him "to drop J. Milton Turner, and his gang of unsavory followers the same as you would drop a red-hot potato." The author of this letter accused Turner of informing the members of the convention that the Democratic National Committee "had no funds to make any grand stand plays, and owing to this fact, the chances were twenty to one that no money would be or could be expended for opening and maintaining National headquarters for the colored Democrats" while knowing that DNC already had decided otherwise. See also *New York Times* (23 August 1900, 3) for the dispute and the issue of the Negro Bureau within the national party.

73. *Dubuque Daily Herald*, 16 August 1900, 1. This party may have represented the earliest forms of the National Liberty Party, which was organized in June 1904.

74. *Dubuque Daily Herald*, 16 August 1900, 1.

75. The *Washington Bee* (17 September 1904, 4) noted that in 1904, members of the National Negro Democratic League were preparing a list of appointments for themselves just in case the Democratic national ticket was elected.

76. In 1900 he had become president of the Negro Knights of America. See *Cedar Rapids Evening Gazette*, 21 May 1900, 6, and *Semi-Weekly Cedar Falls Gazette*, 8 June 1900, 2.

77. *Ottumwa Evening Democrat*, 27 May 1934, 7. For the duties of a justice of the peace in Monroe County, see Hickenlooper, *Illustrated History*, 23. Hickenlooper (ibid., 274–75, 187) mentioned that Albia had an active African Methodist Episcopal Church (formed in 1873) but also noted that many black miners had been brought into Albia from Missouri during the early 1880s as strikebreakers, with the consequence that many in Albia's white community resented their recruitment and the existence of blacks in the area. Taylor sought election to the office of justice of the peace only in November 1901 in Monroe Township of Monroe County, and he lost that election. At that time Monroe Township was divided into two precincts, Hilton and Foster. If Taylor were a justice of the peace at Hilton, it likely would have been an appointive position. The *Herald* (Oskaloosa) reported only that Taylor had been a resident of Hilton, "where he served a term as a justice of the peace" (28 July 1904, 7).

78. *Ottumwa Daily Courier*, 22 July 1904, 6. Even his farming venture was controversial, however. In 1904, while campaigning on the East Coast, Taylor was sued (*Ackely Phonograph*, 1 October 1904, 6) by Fisher Bros. of Albia, Iowa, for failing to make payments on farm equipment he had purchased, all of which was duly reported in the press as perhaps the only time that a presidential candidate had been sued while campaigning.

79. For Taylor's production of articles, see *Broad Ax* (Chicago), 8 September 1900.

80. Smith, *Emancipation*, 453; Schwieder, Hraba, and Schwieder, *Buxton*, 27, 33, 61; *Iowa State Bystander*, 27 November 1896, 3. Woodson, born in Virginia in 1866, graduated from Petersburg College in 1890 and Howard University's law school in 1896. Woodson served in Iowa with the U.S. Army's Twenty-fifth Infantry before establishing a law practice in Oskaloosa, Muchakinock, and Buxton. Woodson was a founder of the Iowa Negro Bar and the National Bar Association. He also was one of the original members of the Niagara Movement. For Woodson, see Bergmann, "Negro in Iowa," 43–44; and Talbert, *Sons of Allen*, 80–81.

81. *Ottumwa Daily Courier*, 22 July 1904, 6. There are no surviving police or disbursement records for Ottumwa during this period.

82. *Ottumwa Daily Courier*, 21 July 1904; *Herald*, 28 July 1904, 7. The *La Crosse Argus* reported that Taylor was "engaged in farming at Ottumwa, Ia., recently having retired from the newspaper business on account of poor health" (1 April 1905, 3).

83. "The nation today is in the throes of a great crisis—a crisis that will be more disastrous in its results than the civil war. We are threatened with a reign of terror, of injustice, of disfranchisement and of anarchism" (*Iowa State Bystander*, 19 October 1900, 5). See also King and Tuck, "De-centring the South," 226–31, 235, for the spread of violence into northern states.

84. *Iowa State Bystander*, 28 September 1900, 1. Other remarks were included in the *Bystander*: "The Bryan democracy of to-day is the same as the Jeff Davis democracy of 1864" (31 August 1900, 1); "The colored man that has any race pride will not be long in making up his mind with which party to cast his vote, at the coming election. He will never vote with the party that is trying to rob him of his elective franchise" (14 September 1900, 1); "Disfranchisement is the first step into a new slavery" (21 September 1900, 5).

85. Black, "Attempted Lynchings in Iowa," 279–83; Pfeifer, *Rough Justice*, 91–92.

86. Meier, *Negro Thought*, 245–47; *Iowa State Bystander*, 28 September 1900, 1. See also Postel, *Populist Vision*, chap. 4, for the racial dilemma in southern Populism and the relationship of scientific racism to cooperation between poor blacks and poor whites in the South.

87. State of Iowa, Mahaska County, Marriage Record, 1889–97, 121. There also is a bit of mystery regarding Taylor's second marriage—he claimed, for instance, that his marriage to Cora was his first, although that might be easily explained as an attempt to avoid revisiting his failed or short-lived marriage with Mary Hall a decade earlier.

Chapter 5. Taylor's Campaign to Become President

1. Walton, *Black Political Parties*, 5. See *Washington Bee*, 12 September 1903, 4, for an editorial on scientific racial ideas in the press.

2. *Ottumwa Daily Courier*, 22 July 1904, 6.

3. *Fort Wayne Journal-Gazette*, 25 February 1904, 7.

4. The *Palladium* characterized Ross as "sincere" and a "first class democratic gentleman" (16 July 1904, 1). Ross was editor of the *Globe & Freeman* of Buffalo (later changing its name to *Gazetteer & Guide*, a monthly magazine). The *Washington Bee* (5 September 1903, 1) noted that Ross had edited the *Western Recorder* in Seattle in the 1890s. Ross also was described as one of the first prominent Democrats in upper New York State and as a "lawyer, publisher, journalist, news dealer, editor, tobacconist and magazine publisher in a short eight-year period, from 1896 through 1903" (http://wings .buffalo.edu/uncrownedqueens/C/history/black_faces/james_ross.html [accessed 9 March 2009]). The *New York Times* (1 July 1900) mentioned that Ross had been the chairman of the National Executive Committee of the National Association of Negro Democratic Clubs in 1900. For another account of the 1904 convention, see *Appeal*, 9 July 1904, 2.

5. See Hild, *Greenbackers*, 80–90, 120–38, for labor and agrarian alliances in Arkansas and for the greatest successes for Union Labor in the 1888 and 1890 elections. Hild noted that "in some ways the campaigns of 1892 marked the last hurrah of both the Southern and Northern Farmers' Alliances as well as the Knights of Labor. . . . After the elections of 1892 none of the three organizations would ever again figure prominently in national politics or as farmer or labor organizations" (ibid., 175). Ali dates 1892 and 1894 as the peak in influence for third parties, noting that "not since the advent of the Republican Party . . . had a third party grown so rapidly and posed such a threat to the established political order" ("Independent Black Voices," 5). Still, Ali agreed that by 1900 "the electoral arena all but closed to Black independents" (ibid., 13).

6. Watson, "Black Phalanx," 4–5. Harbaugh ("Election of 1904," 1969) noted that Theodore Roosevelt had opposed a strong suffrage plank, but, over his objections, the following language was contained in the party's 1904 platform: "We favor such Congressional action as shall determine whether by special discrimination the elective franchise in any State has been unconstitutionally limited, and, if such is the case, we demand that representation in Congress and in the electoral college shall be proportionately reduced as directed by the Constitution of the United States" (ibid., 2005). Woodward (*Strange Career of Jim Crow*, 85) recorded that black registered voters in Louisiana had fallen from 130,334 in 1896 to 1,342 in 1904. The *Lincoln Evening News* reported on 4 January 1901 that the National Colored Personal Liberty League (H. C. Hawkins, president; L. A. Wiles, secretary; and Charles C. Curtis, national organizer) claimed by 1901 to have a national membership of more than 100,000, with 2,000 in Nebraska alone.

7. See *Negro Solicitor*, ca. 12 May 1898 (Woodson scrapbook), for a convention of the National Personal Liberty League called for Oskaloosa for 11 July 1898. A note in the *Washington Post* (1 August 1904, 17) and authored by officers of the Civil Liberty Party observed that a national convention of the National Colored Personal Liberty League had been held in St. Louis. The Civil Liberty Party disavowed any connection with the National Colored Personal Liberty League and noted that the Civil Liberty Party supported the Republican ticket.

8. Watson, "Black Phalanx." Much of the following regarding the party is taken from Watson's reconstruction. For the Negro protectionists, see *New York Times*, 25 September 1897, 1.

9. Watson, "Black Phalanx," 5–6. See also Link, "Negro as a Factor," 82.

10. Beatty, *Revolution Gone Backward*, 176.

11. Hill ("Ex-Slave Pension Movement," 9) identified six organizations that emerged to support pension bills: National Ex-Slave Mutual Relief, Bounty and Benefit Association; Ex-Slave Petitioners' Assembly (Arkansas); Western Division Association; Great National Ex-Slave Union, Congressional, Legislative, and Pension Association of U.S.A.; Ex-Slave Pension Association of Texas; and Ex-Slave Pension Association of Kansas.

12. See U.S. House, HR 11119, 51st Cong., 1st sess., 24 June 1890 (Mr. Connell), *Cong. Rec.* 21 (1889–90): 6464; U.S. Senate, S. 1389, 53rd Cong., 2d sess., 8 January 1894 (Mr. Cullom), *Cong. Rec.* 26 (1894–95): 519; U.S. House, HR 8479, 55th Cong., 2d sess., 21 February 1898 (Mr. Curtis), *Cong. Rec.* 31 (1898–99): 2010; U.S. Senate, S. 1176, 56th Cong., 1st sess., 11 December 1899 (Mr. Pettus), *Cong. Rec.* 33, pt. 1 (1899–1900): 180–84; U.S. House, HR 11404, 57th Cong., 1st sess., 17 February 1902 (Mr. Blackburn), *Cong. Rec.* 35, pt. 4 (1901–2): 1841. The provisions of these bills were identical. See also "M2110—Correspondence and Case Files of the Bureau of Pensions pertaining to the Ex-slave Pension Movement, 1892–1922," National Archives and Records Administration, Washington, D.C., 2006, http://www.archives.gov/research/microfilm/m2110.pdf (accessed 7 May 2009). A copy of S. 1176 (1899) is reproduced at http://murphylibrary.uwlax.edu/digital/TaylorGeorge/18Senate.jpg.

13. Watson, "Black Phalanx," 5–6.

14. Fleming wrote that "Walton, the secretary, published a newspaper called the *Ex-Slave Assembly*, in which he printed regularly the old pension bills making it appear that they were laws. He announced that he had accepted the agency for the slave pension business and authorized his agents to collect from each member twenty-five cents and to forward each name with ten cents to him. . . . The usual procedure was as follows: an agent, usually a 'professor' or a 'reverend,' went into a negro community, made a speech in the negro church to announce his business, and then proceeded to organize the ex-slaves into a club which paid $2.50 for a charter, and each member paid twenty-five cents entrance fee and monthly dues of ten cents. A portion of the fees and dues was sent to the headquarters of the organization" (*Ex-Slave Petition Frauds*, 7–8). The Arkansas-based organization was not affiliated with the National Ex-Slave Mutual Relief, Bounty, and Pension Association or the Ex-Slave Pension Association founded by Caillie House. For discussion of House and other pension groups, see Henry, *Long Overdue*, 46–57.

15. The *Atlanta Constitution* (5 February 1903, 1) indicated that the bill submitted to Congress on 4 February 1903 included the following provisions: ex-slaves over seventy would receive a bounty of $500 and a pension of $15 per month; ex-slaves sixty to seventy would receive a bounty of $300 and $12 per month; ex-slaves fifty to sixty would receive a bounty of $100 and $8 per month; and ex-slaves under fifty would receive $4 per month until they reached the age of fifty, at which time they would receive $8 per month.

16. Berry, *My Face Is Black Is True*, 42. Berry also indicated that Douglass had supported the earliest pension bills (ibid., 39). The *Semi Weekly Iowa State Reporter* reported sentiments to the effect that Hanna's bill would "promote darkey immigration to the United States" (19 February 1903, 4).

17. *Atlanta Constitution*, 5 February 1903, 1, and 6 February 1904, 6; *Denton Journal*, 29 August 1903, 2.

18. Berry, *My Face Is Black Is True*, chaps. 3 and 5. See Smythe, *Obsolete American Securities*, 362, for legal action to bar associations from use of U.S. mail. The Ex-Slave Petitioners' Assembly was banned on 11 August 1899.

19. The *New York Times* indicated on 30 November 1900 that approximately 100,000 blacks were subscribers to such schemes in 1900.

20. Berry, "Reparations for Freedmen," 224–25. For official records regarding fraud charges, see http://www.archives.gov/research/microfilm/m2110.pdf (accessed 9 March 2009). For a newspaper account, see *Alton Evening Telegraph*, 23 September 1899, 4. The *Tyrone Daily Herald* (28 February 1901, 10) noted that the association claimed a membership of 250,000 in 1901.

21. *Richwood Gazette*, 8 January 1903, 1. For reports of the Washington conference, see *Davenport Daily Republican*, 7 January 1903, 2; *New York Times*, 11 January 1903, 13.

22. *Atlanta Constitution*, 5 February 1903, 1. The *Atlanta Constitution* (6 February 1904, 6) reported that Mitchell argued that the lily-white movement among southern Republicans would encourage black voters to switch parties in the 1904 election and that the key to Republican victory in the presidential election would be in New York, New

Jersey, West Virginia, Indiana, and Kansas, where the numbers of black voters were significant. If 300,000 voters in those five states refused to vote for the Republican candidate, the Democratic Party would win the presidency. See also Logue and Blanck, "Benefit of the Doubt," 377–99, for detailed discussion of attempts to secure pensions for black veterans.

23. *Washington Bee*, 3 September 1904, 1. A similar sentiment was noted by Judge Albion W. Tourgee, who stated: "Candidly, I do not think the American people will give the blacks the opportunities they now need or pay any considerable part of the debt now due" (*New York Times*, 20 August 1888).

24. *New York Times*, 15 January 1903, 1. Turner noted that in the 1920s the ex-slave pension movement was "the largest social movement among African Americans before the formation of Garvey's Universal New Improvement Association" ("Caillie House," 309).

25. U.S. Senate, S. 7254, 57th Cong., 2d sess., 4 February 1903 (Mr. Hanna), *Cong. Rec.* 36, pt. 7 (1902–3): 1673. For Hanna's motives, see *Daily Nevada State Journal*, 8 November 1903, 2; *Fort Wayne News*, 30 October 1903, 8; *Hamilton Evening Sun*, 12 February 1903, 8. The *Atlanta Constitution* suggested that Hanna had introduced the bill to "stir up a warm and friendly feeling among the old former slaves and their descendants" (5 February 1903, 1).

26. *Eau Claire Leader*, 26 February 1903, 4.

27. See Berry, "Reparations for Freedmen," 223–24, 226–27, for the opposition of African American politicians and black press and for Hanna's submission of the Ex-Slave Pension Bill to Congress. Hine wrote: "Many black newspaper publishers refused to support the pension bill. They had their own agenda and they desired greater protection for the right to vote and more funding for public education" ("From the Margins," 314). See Masci for the sentiment that reparation payments would "drive a new wedge between blacks and whites, leading to greater polarization" ("Reparations Movement," 531). Walter Williams of George Mason University argued: "I can't think of a better fortification for racism than reparations for blacks" (ibid., 535). Masci also noted that many believed reparations to be a waste of resources at a time "when so much needs to be done in education and other issues" and that reparations would "cheapen their [the slaves'] suffering" (ibid., 532–33).

28. *Atlanta Constitution*, 29 March 1903, 18. Washington (Harlan and Smock, *Booker T. Washington Papers*, 8:29) had characterized Derrick as a "volcanic" speaker. The *New York Times* noted on 15 March 1904 that Derrick was an enthusiastic supporter of immigration to Africa, having declared that "this is no country for us." The *New York Times* also observed: "These slave pension bills are absurd on their face" (16 February 1903, 8). The *Cleveland Gazette* noted on 14 February 1903 that "there is no more chance of the passage by congress of such a bill than there is of his [Hanna's] going to Heaven as he is, should he die," and on 7 March 1903 declared that Hanna's action of introducing the bill was "extremely fraudulent and reprehensible."

29. *Atlanta Constitution*, 27 July 1903, 1.

30. *Courier*, 31 March 1904, 8; Watson, "Black Phalanx," 11–12; Aptheker, *Documentary History*, 1:852–53; "A Negro for President," *New York Times*, 31 March 1904.

An account of Stanley Mitchell and the beginnings of the National Liberty Party is found also in the *Washington Bee*, 3 September 1904, 1.

31. "Indorse Roosevelt: Negro Convention Names Two Men for Presidency but Both of Them Decline," *Logansport Reporter*, 7 July 1904, 2; "[Roosevelt] Is the Friend of the Negro," *Wichita Searchlight*, 2 July 1904, 1.

32. *Atlanta Constitution*, 12 May 1904, 4. Goldstein noted that Washington, at the Indianapolis Convention of the Afro-American Council in 1899, had "exhorted the gathering to remember that 'friction with whites is unnecessary'" ("Preface," 90). This position would have been rejected by nearly all attending the 1904 St. Louis meeting. Goldstein also noted that during the Roosevelt administration Washington "was quickly becoming the official dispenser of practically all national patronage allotted to blacks," which might have been a significant incentive for the 1904 convention to offer him leadership of the new party.

33. See Flewellen, "National Black Independent Political Party," 94. An abundance of examples might be cited here, but illustrative of attitudes commonly accepted within progressive circles were those expressed by Freeman: "The whole negro race has come to seriously doubt the intentions of the (white) Republican party, North and South. They are throwing off on the negro with increasing frequency and boldness. This is said, not for political advantage—good or bad—but because it is true and must be headed off to save the negro's complete political overthrow. Again, there is no use to enumerate the difficulties that obstruct our pathway to progress. Let it suffice to say, that the whole world is out of harmony, if not out of sympathy with the negro as a race and as a citizen" (*Devil*, 254).

34. "National Liberty Party," *Marysville Tribune*, 5 May 1904, 1.

35. *Washington Bee*, 21 May 1904, 4, and 30 July 1904, 4; Meier, "Negroes and the Democratic Party," 177. Chase began to deliver warnings to the Republican Party in the editorial page of the *Washington Bee* as early as August 1903. For the latter, see issues for 8 August, 29 August, 5 September, and 19 December 1903, and 6 February 1904, 4.

36. Bishop Walters (1858 –1917) was an activist, a politician, and a progressive. Elected bishop in 1892, Walters was a close colleague of Timothy Fortune and was an early member of the National Afro-American League, which had been founded to oppose lynching and racial discrimination. He was one of the founders of the National Afro-American Council and was elected its first president, and he continued in that office from 1898 until 1902, during which time he advocated an "active agenda" within existing parties. At its 1900 national meeting Walters had "stopped short of threatening a mass exodus from the Republican Party, although he noted that '[s]ome of us have signified to the Democratic Party our willingness to unite with it wherever and whenever it will make it advantageous to our cause to do so'" (Justesen, *Broken Brotherhood*, 62–63). When the National Afro-American Council changed that agenda after 1902, Walters sought an alternative. He was a known and popular speaker who traveled widely in the United States, Africa, and Europe (he had been one of the primary organizers and the chair of the Pan-African Conference held in London in 1900; he also was its first president). He would have been considered to become the nominee of the National Liberty Party in

1904, if he had chosen to accept it. For Walters, see also Martin, *For God and Race*, 186–87.

37. *Indiana Progress*, 13 July 1904, 8; "Indorse Roosevelt," *Logansport Reporter*, 7 July 1904. See *Freeman*, 17 September 1904, 1, for coverage of the NAAC meeting in St. Louis.

38. *Daily Huronite*, 8 July 1904, 3; *Eau Claire Leader*, 8 July 1904, 6.

39. *Newport Mercury*, 9 July 1904, 5; *Iowa Recorder*, 13 July 1904, 6; *Salt Lake Tribune*, 9 July 1904, 2; *Ogden Standard*, 8 July 1904, 6.

40. Goldstein argued that those who supported independent action on either the state or national level had reached "complete failure" by 1904 and that "the future belonged not to the independent agitator but to the shrewd black party politician who could adeptly manipulate those structures" ("Preface," 99).

41. The *Colored American Magazine* noted that Payne had been a "long time connected with the Naval Observatory" (3 September 1904, 6). The *Landmark* reported that Payne was "a new issue negro and is only 37 years old" (22 July 1904, 2). The *East St. Louis Daily Journal* reported on 8 July 1904 that Payne had "attended Wayland Seminary" in Washington, D.C. Several Baptist groups had established Wayland in 1865 to prepare freedmen for the ministry. The *Oxford Mirror* (14 July 1904, 3) reported that Mitchell had been offered the nomination for president, but that he had "declined." The *Voice of the Negro* (August 1904, 298–99) merely reported the event and the fact that "someone" had been nominated to lead the ticket.

42. *Appeal*, 23 July 1904, 2. The *Landmark* (22 July 1904, 2) indicated that Scott had been born of "free parents in Newark, Ohio" and that he was sixty years old in 1904. The *East St. Louis Daily Journal* reported on 8 July 1904 that Scott also had "learned the barber trade." See also the *Daily Miami Metropolis* (16 July 1904, 1), which indicated that Scott had briefly operated a saloon in St. Louis, Missouri, and was known for "his diamond and gold-filled teeth" and as "the only Democratic negro in the State of Illinois." Cairo's population in 1865 was approximately 8,500, of which more than 2,000 were blacks. Of 10,388 residents in 1890, 3,689 were blacks.

43. "Ran for President to Win Place as Janitor," *Lincoln Evening News*, 30 January 1905, 2. According to Lumpkins (*American Pogrom*, 62), Scott claimed to have served as a colonel in the Spanish-American War alongside Roosevelt during the Cuban phase. Blight (*Race and Reunion*, 348) reported that nearly ten thousand blacks had volunteered during the Spanish-American War but also noted that Mitchell, editor of the *Richmond Planet*, had opposed participation by using the slogan "No Officers, No Fight!" Scott was a leader of the General Maceo Club, named after a Latin leader who fought for Cuban independence. See also "Our City Has a Citizen Who Has Been Nominated for the Presidency," *East St. Louis Daily Journal*, 8 July 1904, 1.

44. Penn, *Afro-American Press*, 128.

45. Beatty (*Revolution Gone Backward*, 167) noted that Charles H. J. Taylor had served as president of the National Negro Democratic League from 1888 to 1896. The best treatment of the league's uncertain history is described in Beatty. In "Ran for President," *Lincoln Evening News*, 30 January 1905, 2, Scott erroneously claimed that he had been president of the league for eight years and that A. E. Manning had followed him as

the league's president from 1896 to 1900, after which George Taylor assumed the league's presidency from 1900 to July 1904. No copies of the *Cairo Gazette* or the *East St. Louis Leader* have survived. For the International Order of Twelve Knights and Daughters of Tabor, see Schwalm, *Emancipation's Diaspora*, 159–60.

46. See http://www.antiimperialist.com/webroot/PEOPLEdocuments/Membership/ NatNegroAExpAImpATrusALynch.html. This announcement indicated that "many of its members supported William Jennings Bryan in the 1900 election alienating themselves from most other African-Americans. Even so, the establishment of the League represented a voice for those who felt sidelined by the Republican Party."

47. For more details regarding Scott, see Lumpkins, *American Pogrom*, 60–63.

48. *Daily Review*, 26 May 1904, 9; *Cedar Rapids Evening Gazette*, 31 March 1904, 7; *Courier*, 31 March 1904, 8. Another reason for selecting St. Louis was because the Louisiana Purchase Exposition was scheduled in St. Louis for the summer of 1904, and many national associations intended to arrange their meetings to meet in the same city and at the same time as major events at the exposition.

49. "To Run for President," *Ottumwa Daily Courier*, 21 July 1904; "Candidate in Jail, Ottumwa Man Named," *Ottumwa Evening Democrat*, 21 July 1904; *Waterloo Times-Tribune*, 26 July 1904; *Oskaloosa Daily Herald*, 22 July 1904; *Washington Post*, 21 July 1904; *Galveston Daily News*, 14 July 1904, 3; *New York Times*, 14 July 1904, 1. The *Palladium* identified Scott as an "old man" and an "objectionable Negro" and reported that he was "serving out $99.80 of a fine and costs" (16 July 1904, 1). Mitchell claimed that when the convention ended Scott was arrested by "white Republicans without warrant or cause" and that Scott had withdrawn his name "over the protest of the [executive] committee." The *Galveston Daily News* questioned: "What is the matter with his campaign manager, that he has failed to raise funds to keep the ticket out of jail?" (27 July 1904, 6).

50. *Modesto Evening News*, 4 August 1904; *Washington Bee*, 30 July 1904, 1.

51. *Washington Bee*, 30 July 1904, 1, 4.

52. *Grand Rapids Tribune*, 13 July 1904, 6; *Janesville Daily Gazette*, 8 July 1904, 8. Chase, in the *Washington Bee*, described Mitchell as "a young man of ability and one of the most independent and fearless men in this country" (3 September 1904, 4).

53. *Ottumwa Daily Courier*, 22 July 1904, 6.

54. *Moberly Evening Democrat*, 27 July 1904, 3; *North Adams Evening Transcript*, 23 July 1904, 4. The *Oskaloosa Daily Herald* reported on 22 July 1904 that by that date, "Judge George E. Taylor, of Ottumwa, Iowa, [had] been chosen to fill the place made vacant by disposing [of] Scott." For other accounts of his appointment, see *Grand Forks Herald*, 21 July 1904, 8; *Omaha World Herald*, 21 July 1904, 2; *Pawtucket Times*, 21 July 1904, 8; *Springfield Republican*, 21 July 1904, 12.

55. Miller ("This Worldly Mission," 191–93) noted that Walters had recommended a reduction of representation for southern states that disenfranchised black voters as early as 1901.

56. *Ottumwa Weekly Democrat*, 6 August 1904, 5. This is the only known location for this letter.

57. *Ottumwa Courier*, 3 August 1904. No other copy of this synopsis was located in other newspapers. The *Ottumwa Courier* included commentary with Taylor's words; a full copy of that article is available at http://murphylibrary.uwlax.edu/digital/Taylor George/16Whatthepartyis04.pdf.

58. *Cedar Rapids Evening Gazette*, 11 August 1904. See also *Waterloo Semi-Weekly Courier*, 16 September 1904, 8.

59. "Geo. E. Taylor, Presidential Candidate, Withdraws from Democratic League," *Ottumwa Courier*, 16 August 1904. Meier (*Negro Thought*, 34) noted in contrast that the period between 1904 and 1912 was the high point of support for Democrats. Meier also noted that black activists changed positions often during this period. A transcript of Ross's letter to Taylor, dated 9 August 1904, is available at http://murphylibrary.uwlax .edu/digital/TaylorGeorge/13RosstoTaylor04.pdf.

60. *Cedar Rapids Republican*, 3 September 1904, 2; *Ottumwa Weekly Democrat*, 1 September 1904, 1; *Des Moines Daily Capital*, 2 September 1904, 8. The four members of the executive committee who met with Taylor on 1 September were E. L. Edmunson of Kentucky, S. Y. Jones of Missouri, James Hill of Indiana, and R. Grayham of Illinois.

61. *Waterloo Semi-Weekly Courier*, 16 September 1904, 8; *Ottumwa Weekly Democrat*, 1 September 1904, 1, and 15 September 1904, 1.

62. For more on the Second Mississippian plan, which led to disenfranchisement and Senator Benjamin Tillman's assertion that South Carolina and Mississippi "were the only Southern states to avoid a strong challenge from the third party," see Woodward, *Origins of the New South*, chap. 12. Logan quoted Tillman (South Carolina): "We have done our level best [to disenfranchise blacks]. We have scratched our heads to find out how we could eliminate the last one of them. We stuffed ballot boxes. We shot them. WE ARE NOT ASHAMED OF IT" (*Betrayal*, 99 –100). In the *Mills County Tribune* (20 August 1907, 5), Tillman claimed that South Carolina's population was composed of 750,000 blacks and 500,000 whites. Chicago's *Broad Ax* described Tillman as "half devil and half beast" and reported that Tillman said: "Yes we keep the colored man under restraint down there. We have too. We want to live" (22 October 1904, 3). For the return of white rule in South Carolina, see also Simkin, *Pitchfork Ben Tillman*, and Kantrowitz, *Ben Tillman*.

63. *Ottumwa Weekly Democrat*, 15 September 1904, 1, emphasis added. The full text of this article is available at http://murphylibrary.uwlax.edu/digital/TaylorGeorge/ 5LAcceptance04.pdf. Aside from the *Waterloo Daily Courier* (4 October 1904, 4), which reproduced an even more abbreviated version, no other newspaper is known to have published any portion of this letter. The *Logansport Pharos* described it as "bitter in its arraignment of both the Democrats and Republicans, and it holds the latter especially responsible for the failure of the negro to get full civil recognition. He accuses the Republicans of having betrayed the negro while holding out false inducements to him" (15 September 1904, 1). But the *Pharos* did not print any portion of the letter. A similar report appeared in the *Montgomery Advertiser* (15 September 1904, 5).

64. St. Louis in late July and early August 1904 was also host to a number of national fraternal conventions, among them the "African Grand encampment of Knights Templar of the United States and Canada" (*Palladium*, 6 August 1904, 1) and the International

Congress of Colored Masons (*Palladium*, 13 August 1904, 1). The National Afro-American Council was scheduled to meet in St. Louis in September.

65. See *Rising Sun*, 5 August 1904, 4. The Lincoln Republican League published numerous pamphlets from its base in Minneapolis. In 1900 it published a pamphlet, "Empire or Republic," in which it "express[ed] opposition to U.S. Policy" in the Philippines. Nicolay and Hay mentioned that numerous pamphlets were printed in Minneapolis by the Lincoln Republicans, who were described as "anti-imperialist partisans" (*Complete Works of Abraham Lincoln*, 11:264).

66. *Broad Ax* (Chicago), 6 August 1904, 1. See also *Moberly Daily Monitor*, 27 July 1904, 3, for a brief report of the convention.

67. *Moberly Daily Monitor*, 27 July 1904, 3; *Tyrone Herald*, 18 August 1904, 8.

68. *Rake Register*, 4 November 1904, 3; *Galveston Daily News*, 1 November 1904, 7; *Anacanda Standard*, 1 November 1904, 3; *Indiana Democrat*, 9 November 1904, 2; *Altamont Enterprise*, 19 August 1904, 1; *Daily Times*, 17 August 1904, 2; *Albia Union*, 4 November 1904, 1. The *Broad Ax* on 6 August 1904 listed national committee members to include E. P. Penn of Richmond, Virginia, chairman; J. W. Smith of New York; Samuel Martin of Chicago; Louis Walker of New Orleans; S. S. Scott of Wheeling, West Virginia; W. F. Taylor of Detroit; P. J. Montgomery of Vicksburg, Mississippi; W. J. Smith of Galveston, Texas; and J. B. Evans of Charleston, South Carolina. An executive committee included W. J. Smith, J. B. Evans, Samuel Martin, Louis Walker, James W. Smith, S. S. Scott, P. J. Montgomery, and W. F. Taylor. W. R. Vaughan of St. Louis was appointed an "ex-officio member of both the national and executive committees. A. Mayer, J. B. Hoffman and Milton Turner were appointed on a committee to co-operate with the national and executive committees and in the selection of candidates to be placed on the party ticket.— *The Sentinel*, East St. Louis." The *Iowa State Bystander* printed a letter that it received from Judge Jones dated 18 October 1904: "I desire to state that I am not a candidate for Presidency or Vice Presidency of the United States by the Lincoln Party and no other party, and that my name has been used by them in that direction without my consent knowledge or sanction whatever, and I wish to be thoroughly and correctly understood by all as it will forever set at rest all inquiries on that matter that I am a Republican and belong to the great Republican party and have always been a Republican and I am working for the election and shall cast my vote for President Theodore Roosevelt and Fairbanks for President and Vice President of the United States and I advise all colored men in the United States to cast their vote on election day for Roosevelt and Fairbanks for President and Vice President of the United States" (4 November 1904, 1).

69. Childs described the sudden emergence of two "Negro" parties as a product of "the blind fury of the oppressed, passion without thought, action without necessary structure" (*Leadership, Conflict, and Cooperation*, 12–13).

70. In 1920 a prominent editor of the *Negro World* commented: "No one pretends, of course, that the votes of Negroes can elect a Negro to the high office of president of the United States. Nor would anyone expect that the votes of white people will be forthcoming to assist them in such a project. The only way in which a Negro could be elected President of the United States would be by virtue of the voters not knowing that the particular

205

candidate was of Negro ancestry" (19 June 1920, 2, reproduced in Perry, *Hubert Harrison Reader*, 149).

71. *Daily Progress*, 6 May 1904, 1. This announcement included the names of three organizers (Con A. Rideout of New York City, Rev. D. A. Tayman of West Virginia, and J. J. Jones of St. Louis) and indicated that the party expected to obtain "half a million" votes and to concentrate its "fight in New York, Pennsylvania, West Virginia, Indiana, Illinois and Missouri."

72. Noll, *God and Race*, 5.

73. *Ottumwa Weekly Democrat*, 1 September 1904, 1.

74. The degree to which the notion of a "black peril" was addressed nationwide—most often within the context of Darwinian theory—is discussed in Fredrickson, *Black Image*, 244–82; Degler, *In Search of Human Nature*, chap. 1; Rose, *Slavery and Its Aftermath*, 71–81. See also Tillinghast, *Negro in Africa and America*, for a representative sample of scholarly literature of the 1900–1905 period.

75. Of the 946 words found in the party's platform, only 72 were devoted to the issue of the ex-slave pension proposal.

76. *Wisconsin Labor Advocate*, 10 September 1886, 2.

77. Cited in Watson, "Black Phalanx," 16. See *Colored American*, 23 July 1904; *Wichita Searchlight*, 2 July 1904, 1; *Washington Bee*, 11 June 1904. The *Voice of the Negro* (Atlanta) sent readers different messages. On page 476 of the October 1904 edition it published a positive biographical sketch of Taylor, but on page 491 it recommended that readers vote Republican in the coming election. The *Wichita Searchlight* did not wait until the convention to ridicule the party and Taylor's candidacy: "It is to be regretted that a few of our men are inclined to use their political privileges in a way that is not at all credited to the principles of manhood. They bob up in every campaign, whether it be national or municipal, and [are] interested in selfish aggrandizement, [they] assume to be leaders and lay in wait for some one out of whom [they] may fleece a few paltry dollars and for some reason their game is easily caught, as a result the entire Negro family is besmirched by the narrow-minded who declare that the entire Negro vote can be bought for a song, and for that reason the entire Negro population should be disfranchised" (2 July 1904).

78. *Racine Daily Journal*, 26 September 1904; *Modesto Evening News*, 4 August 1904, 3.

79. *Cedar Falls Gazette*, 5 April 1904, 4.

80. Brown and Strauss, *Dictionary of American Politics*, 585–87. For a summary of the platform, see *East St. Louis Daily Journal*, 8 July 1904. The platform also is printed in Stanwood, *History of the Presidency*, 2:127–29. The *Landmark* (22 July 1904, 2) listed the "non-interference" in the affairs of the Far East as one of the five most important issues of the campaign.

81. The official record in Monroe County, Iowa, shows only that Taylor ran unsuccessfully for office in one election cycle.

82. See "Sketch of George Edwin Taylor."

83. *Voice of the Negro*, October 1904, 478.

84. Nelson, *Fredrick L. McGhee*, 90; Meier, "Negro and the Democratic Party," 183. Smith described McGhee as "one of the few blacks in the nation to join the Democratic

Party," surely an exaggeration, unless Smith was referring only to lawyers (*Emancipation*, 461). In a letter from McGhee to Booker T. Washington dated 14 September 1904 (Harlan and Smock, *Booker T. Washington Papers*, 8:66–69), McGhee informed Washington that he intended to vote for Roosevelt in 1904, that he could not "afford" to campaign openly for Roosevelt because of his alliances within the Farmer/Labor (Democratic) Party in Minnesota, and that he was certain that within the national Democratic Party there was an "anti-Negro sentiment that seems to dominate it." See also *Washington Bee*, 10 September 1904, 4, for an "address" from the National Negro Democratic League, in which McGhee was a prominent signatory.

85. *Atlanta Constitution*, 13 April 1913. See also Flewellen, "National Black Independent Political Party," 96–98, for a discussion of stages involved in "building a party" and the concurrent need for financial resources.

86. Goldstein ("Preface," 98) bluntly critiqued both the Afro-American League and the Afro-American Council as being "virtually devoid of grass roots," a criticism that would apply similarly to the National Negro Liberty Party in 1904. Goldstein concluded that by 1904 federal protection of black civil rights "had all but disappeared" and that black politicians were then faced with "declining rewards and increasing isolation from the mainstream of national political life" (ibid., 97).

87. *Sun*, 20 November 1904, sec. 3, 7. A transcript of Taylor's interview is located in appendix A. James Lance Taylor ("Black Politics," 148–49) engages in a compelling discussion of the concept of "political party neutrality." He notes that "the Black vote would become strengthened as an electoral commodity, and simultaneously, it could potentially force into retreat the disinterest and racial animus that had been directed toward them by the Republican North and the Democratic South" (ibid., 149). He essentially describes the thesis advanced by George Edwin Taylor in 1904.

88. *Washington Bee*, 3 September 1904, 1.

89. *Ottumwa Daily Courier*, 22 July 1904, 6. Frye noted that "independent black political parties tend to rise . . . [when] accompanied by a rising political consciousness within the national black community as well as in the specific county or state where the parties are established" (*Black Parties*, 5). That had not occurred nationwide in 1904.

90. *Kansas City Star*, 14 October 1904, 10. For more on the theory of "balance of power," see Walters, *Black Presidential Politics*, xiii, 5–10, 110–15, 184–85. The *Emmetsburg Democrat* reported that "as the candidate for presidency on the national liberty party Mr. Taylor and his associates believe that they may hold the balance of power which will decide who will be president" (14 September 1904, 7).

91. Watson ("Black Phalanx," 15) wrote that the party was registered officially in no state. The *Tri-City Star* of Davenport, Iowa, reported on 11 October 1904 that the National Liberty Party had neglected to complete the necessary forms to place the party on the Iowa ballot, with the consequence that Taylor could not even be listed in his own state. The *Waterloo Daily Times-Tribune* reported on 12 April 1907 that Taylor's name had been on the ballot only "in several states in the union in the last election," with reports in the *Washington Post* (12 April 1907) and *Colorado Transcript* (9 May 1907, 2) noting that the National Liberty Party was on the ballot of seven states. The *Galveston*

Daily News noted that for both Negro parties, "no electors [had been] selected, or at least none will appear on any official ballot" (1 November 1904, 7).

92. "Ran for President," 2.

93. *Semi Weekly Reporter*, 11 October 1904, 5; *Tri-City Evening Star*, October 1904, 2.

94. Only one reference was found for Taylor's engagement in a lecture tour. The *Post Standard* (14 October 1904, 4) indicated that Taylor was interviewed by the editor of the *Independent*, which was headquartered in Houston.

95. Luker, *Social Gospel*, 242. The editor of the *St. Paul Appeal* (23 July 1904, 2) dismissed the party as little more than a "Democratic scheme" to siphon sufficient African American votes from Republican candidates in southern Indiana and Illinois to turn those elections to the Democratic Party. A similar sentiment was noted by the *Albia Republican*: "The democrats hope to use George, and the party nominating him, for the highest office in the land, to benefit the democrats in an effort to get the colored people to forsake the republican party. The colored people are too well informed to be fooled by such peanut politics" (28 July 1904, 2). The *Cleveland Gazette*, in an article titled "Stanley Mitchell, the Negro Traitor," wrote: "The democracy of the south is in desperate straits and is using every effort foul and fair in order to win in the coming national election. It has induced a few crazy Negroes to organize a 'black man's party' who would send out speakers to espouse the cause of their candidates. The act is a villainous imposition upon the 'colored' people of the country and deserves not only prompt exposure but our hearty and unqualified condemnation. Stanley Mitchell, the black 'Judas' is very active in promoting the ends of this dirty scheme. . . . The Afro-Americans of the north, to a man, are for Roosevelt and Fairbanks—as they ought to be" (24 August 1904, 2).

96. *Wichita Searchlight*, 8 October 1904, 1. The issue dated 12 November 1904 noted that 98 percent of blacks in Wichita had voted Republican in the 1904 election, and there was no mention of Taylor or the National Liberty Party in that issue.

97. *Iowa State Bystander*, 23 September 1904, 1. The *Palestine Daily Herald* (11 April 1904, 2) reported a different objective for the party's leaders. That account suggested that the party convention had been called and announcements were made precisely to alarm the Republican Party that the new party intended to contest heavily in New York, New Jersey, Connecticut, and Indiana, where the black vote was high, and to indicate that it could be bribed to fuse its ticket with that of the Republican Party.

98. Walton (*Black Political Parties*, 249) cites this figure of 2,000 votes but does not provide documentation. J. L. Taylor ("Black Politics," 177) reported that "less than 5,000 votes" were obtained. Scott ("Ran for President," 2) claimed that the party received nearly 60,000 votes in Tennessee, West Virginia, and Alabama. In fact, however, personnel at the state archives of Tennessee, Alabama, and West Virginia confirmed that neither Taylor's name nor his party had appeared on the 1904 election ballots in their state. The *Colorado Transcript* (9 May 1907, 2) reported that Taylor's name had appeared on the ballots of seven states and "his supporters numbered over 300,000." This account also appeared in *l'Abeille de la Nouvelle-Orléans* on 23 May 1907. State archival personnel in Texas, Arkansas, Kentucky, Virginia, South Carolina, Iowa, Pennsylvania, New York, New Jersey, Indiana, and Illinois also confirmed that the Negro Liberty Party did not appear

on their state's ballots. The *Logansport Reporter* reported that "the two negro parties, however, apparently ended their work when the national conventions adjourned, as no electors have been selected, or at least none will appear on any official ballot" (1 November 1904, 2).

99. Maisel, *Parties and Elections*, 48–52. Mazmanian (*Third Parties*, 82–85) argued instead that it was the 1892 election that signaled the end of third-party influence. Mazmanian also contended that a statistical study of elections suggested that those who had voted for third parties would not have changed election results if third parties had not existed on ballots.

100. *Sun*, 20 November 1904, sec. 3, 7 (see appendix A).

101. *Fort Wayne Journal-Gazette*, 19 January 1908, 10.

102. *Washington Post*, 12 April 1907, 1. For Phillips's 1901 campaign for governor, see *New York Times*, 22 August 1901, 3. *McCoy's Ottumwa's City Directory, 1907–1908* (277) noted Taylor's profession as "police" and indicated that he boarded at 224 E. 4th. Taylor also was listed as a policeman in the 1910–11 directory, although data for this edition would have been collected late in 1909 or early in 1910.

103. *Bismarck Daily Tribune*, 30 April 1907, 2; *Washington Post*, 12 April 1907, 1; *Oxford Mirror*, 25 April 1907, 2; *Waterloo Daily Times-Tribune*, 12 April 1907; *Colorado Transcript*, 9 May 1907, 2.

104. *Daily Mail*, 16 September 1908, 2.

105. *Logansport Pharos*, 3 August 1908; *Cedar Rapids Evening Gazette*, 7 August 1908, 1; *Nebraska State Journal*, 7 August 1908, 1; *Van Wert Daily Bulletin*, 7 August 1908, 1; *Emporia Gazette*, 6 August 1908, 1; *Daily Mail*, 25 July 1908, 4. Interestingly, in the *Alaska Citizen* (27 January 1913, 16), under the heading "All Coontown Will Be There," an announcement was made that an inaugural ball sponsored by the "National Negro Democratic League" to celebrate the election of Woodrow Wilson would be held in Washington, D.C., on 5 March 1913.

106. *Evening News*, 27 June 1908, 3. No report was found regarding this conference. The *Vindicator and Republican* reported that Scott had been selected as "a candidate for the position of minister to the negro republic of Haiti" (11 June 1913, 4).

107. *Cedar Rapids Evening Gazette*, 27 June 1908, 1; *Hopkinsville Kentuckian*, 4 August 1908, 4. The *Galveston Daily News* (3 August 1908, 1) and the *Ogden Standard* (3 August 1908, 3) mentioned that the Liberty Party was scheduled to meet in Wheeling, West Virginia, on 3 and 4 August and was to select candidates for president and vice president. The call was issued to "all members of the National Liberty League and other individuals interested in the welfare of the negro race." The *Wheeling Intelligencer* (4 August 1908) attempted to locate the meeting and reported that it had interviewed Thomas Norris, a leader in the local community, who denied that a meeting was being held and added: "Of course there are always a few who want to buck and talk of starting new parties, but they, too, generally fall in line and vote the sentiments of the majority when it comes to the election." No report of an address to the nation has been found.

108. Summers, *Manliness and Its Discontents*, 1–2.

109. Gilmore, *Gender and Jim Crow*, 75–84; Schwalm, *Emancipation's Diaspora*, 216; Mitchell, "Black Man's Burden," 80–84, 87. See also Cha-Jua, "Warlike Demonstration," for issues of "manhood" as they related to political agency taken against lynchings that had occurred in Illinois.

110. *Ottumwa Democrat*, 14 April 1897.

111. *Fort Wayne Journal-Gazette*, 25 February 1904, 7.

112. A transcript of Ross's letter to Taylor is available at http://murphylibrary.uwlax .edu/digital/TaylorGeorge/13RosstoTaylor04.pdf.

113. *Ottumwa Daily Courier*, 16 July 1904, 6; *La Crosse Argus*, 1 April 1905, 3.

114. *La Crosse Argus*, 1 April 1905, 3. See also *La Crosse Tribune* (27 March 1905, 1) for Taylor's visit in La Crosse following his foster father's death. According to the latter account, Nathan Smith had willed his farm to La Crosse County, "to be used as the county thought best. Unappreciative, and immune to the sentiments which activated the old darkie the county sold it, for a paltry sum."

115. Niagara Movement Archive, http://www.library.umass.edu/spcoll/dubois/?page _id=896 (accessed 15 February 2009).

116. Howard-Pitney, "Calvin Chase's *Washington Bee*," 89–91. Fox contrasted Trotter and Washington, describing Trotter as a product of Hyde Park, New York, and as having "won scholarships at Harvard" (*Guardian of Boston*, 32–34). Trotter declared bluntly: "The policy of compromise has failed." Even more openly, Trotter insisted that Washington "must be stopped" (ibid., 35).

117. See Fox (*Guardian of Boston*, 49–51) for the nine questions, which Fox characterized as "challenges."

118. Harlan and Smock, *Booker T. Washington*, 44–49; *Guardian*, 1 August 1903, 1; *Washington Bee*, 8 August 1903, 1, 4; *Washington Bee*, 17 October 1903, 1; *Marble Rock Journal*, 13 August 1903, 6; Mjagkij, *Organizing Black America*, 523.

119. *Washington Bee*, 23 January 1904, 1; Justesen, *Broken Brotherhood*, 138–42. See also Norrell, *House I Live In*, chap. 2 ("The New and Improved Negro"), for a lively discussion of Washingtonian versus Du Boisian philosophies. See Alexander, "We Know Our Rights," 362–66, for a detailed description of the conference.

120. Miller, "This Worldly Mission," 244. The *Palladium* identified Du Bois as "the most scholarly Negro in the United States" (May 1904, 8). Fox (*Guardian of Boston*, 83) listed other "anti-Bookerites" who attended the meeting. For a critique of *Souls*, see Watkins, "Between Slavery and Freedom." See also Thornbrough, *T. Thomas Fortune*, 248–50, for Fortune's view of the January 1904 meeting.

121. Bennett, "Niagara Movement," 134. See also Harlan, *Booker T. Washington*, for this critical period. Nelson noted that McGhee was in contact with Trotter by early 1903 and that by mid-1903 McGhee "had concluded that the [National Afro-American] Council must free itself from the dominion of Booker Washington or die" (*Fredrick L. McGhee*, 108–9). In effect, by late 1903 McGhee was firmly in the camp of the anti-Washingtonians. See also ibid., 122–27, for McGhee's interpretation of the New York meeting. For a list of those attending the January meeting, see *Washington Bee*, 23 January 1904 and 30 January 1904.

122. Du Bois, *Autobiography*, 248; Mjagkij, *Organizing Black America*, 523–25.

123. For Taylor's relationship to Woodson, see *Negro Solicitor*, 13 February 1897, 6 March 1897, 4 December 1897, 20 January 1898, 3 February 1898, 24 March 1898, and 18 April 1898; and *Broad Ax* (Chicago), 28 July 1900, 1.

124. Du Bois, *Souls of Black Folk*, 33. James (*Transcending the Talented Tenth*, 18–33) includes a provocative discussion of Du Bois's change of mind about the "talented tenth" concept as it was applied after 1930. Scott described these elites as "a rather smugly superior group" who tended to support issues that were "dearest to their own social class" ("Their Faces Were Black," 318–19).

125. Bennett, "Niagara Movement," 134.

126. Childs (*Leadership*, 3–30) discussed a "vanguard perspective" versus a "mutualistic perspective." The former indicated a preference for a core or dominant center, and from that center flowed power and influence. The center accepted few contributions from the periphery, believing that it was devoid of substance and was materialistic. In contrast, a "talented" center would act as the vanguard, with a single voice for the whole, and would seek idealized progress. The "mutualistic perspective" was characterized by chaotic encounters within the hinterland, much of which was without direction, leadership, or a promise of profit. Childs's *Leadership* is a complex treatment with multiple "vanguard groups," but his principal focus was that led by the Du Boisians. He was also willing to link "mutualism" to the foundational works of Merville Herskovitz, George Ellis, and Arthur Schomburg, all of whom published on topics of African mutual aid and voluntary associations. Childs's argument is compelling: "Washington constructed a vanguard in his own image. He was knowledgeable about technology, conversant with industrialists, and understanding of the spirit of capitalism. In contrast, Du Bois's vanguard, like him [i.e., Du Bois], would be highly literate, cosmopolitan, and well-versed in the world's high culture. Both men envisioned their vanguard groups in ways that would privilege a particular portion of the black elite and exclude others. Both men essentially excluded the black masses. The issue for them was which portion of the black elite was to occupy the main leadership positions. The possibility of local grass-roots leadership, arising from many sources, was not considered" (ibid., 19–20).

127. Scott wrote that "virtually all [within this group] agreed that political organization around reparations was not worthy of consideration." Rather than become involved in the ex-slave pension movement, "they chose not to enter the fray. . . . [T]hey were distrustful of the movement's leadership, suspecting the motives of those who advocated reparations" ("Their Faces Were Black," 318–19).

128. Justesen, *Broken Brotherhood*, chap. 3.

129. J. L. Taylor, "Black Politics," 42–43.

130. Turner argued that the ex-slave pension movement was clearly not leaderless and that "Caillie House's organizational style was based on the philosophy of 'bottom-up' leadership, and that she encouraged social and political activism at the grassroots level" ("Caillie House," 308). Turner also characterized House as "a populist" and as one who "facilitated agency."

131. Quoted in Alexander, "We Know Our Rights," 101.

132. For the role played by the American Missionary Association, see Jewell, *American Missionary Association and Black America*.

133. Lewis, *Biography of a Race*, 31. See also Nelson, *Rise and Fall*, 20–30, for a brief review of Du Bois's education and rise within America's intellectual community.

134. Du Bois, *On Sociology*, 1–6; White, *Black Leadership*, 51–55; Marable, *Black Radical Democrat*, 6–10. See also Pattillo-McCoy for a discussion of attitudes held by black Yankees with respect to "phenotypical, spatial, and cultural proximity to the white upper class" (*Black Picket Fences*, 16–17).

135. Childs, *Leadership*, 8. Ottumwa's estimated population was 18,000 in 1900 and 22,000 in 1910 (Munsell and Meagher, *Ottumwa Yesterday and Today*, 21).

136. See the article on Carrie House at http://tennesseeencyclopedia.net/imagegallery.php?EntryID=C005a (accessed 3 May 2009).

137. Du Bois, *Autobiography*, 157.

138. Ali, *In the Balance of Power*, 74–76, 104–5. See also Summers, *Manliness and Its Discontents*.

139. Cunnigen, "Du Bois–Washington Debate," 13.

140. Childs, *Leadership*, 6.

141. The *Moberly Evening Democrat* (27 July 1904, 4) reported that Taylor was "a college graduate," although that is not substantiated in any known record.

142. Muraskin explained that his marginal status as a Jew allowed him "to understand a key facet of black experience: the black middle class is simultaneously attracted to and repelled by *both* the white middle class and the black lower class" (*Middle-Class Blacks*, ix). Childs cleverly described the evolution of the "cooperative union," which existed without a leading group, noting that the objective of the "mutuality" model "is not to develop a leading group. Rather, it is to expand the mutual recognition and interaction of a multitude of groups, all of whom have undergone oppression" (*Leadership*, 7–8).

Chapter 6. Escape to a Warm Place

1. Only one reference was found to suggest that Taylor may have sought a patronage appointment at the national level. The *Cedar Rapids Evening Gazette* (9 January 1893, 2) reported that Taylor was "being boomed by his friends for registrar of deeds at Washington," a position generally held by a black person after the Civil War.

2. For Phillips's removal from office on 19 August 1910, see *New York Times*, 20 August 1910; *La Grand Reporter*, 26 August 1910, 2. The precise meaning of the word "resort" is unclear. The same term was used with reference to a "disorderly house," usually nomenclature applied to a place associated with prostitution (Waterman, *History of Wapello County*, 123).

3. *Sun*, 20 November 1904, sec. 3, 7. A small portion of that interview was reprinted in the *Washington Bee* on 26 November 1904. A full transcript of Taylor's interview appears in appendix A.

4. *Planet*, 14 October 1899. Kelly noted that "seeing oneself and others 'dressed up' was important to constructing a collective identity based on something other than wage

work, presenting a public challenge to the dominant stereotypes of the black body, and shoring up a sense of dignity that was perpetually under assault" ("We Are Not What We Seem," 86). A year earlier the *Iowa State Bystander* critically and yet sarcastically addressed the issue of clothes: the Negro "will make only $5.00 a week and yet he and his wife will dress like a man who makes $50.00 per week and who has been free all his life" (5 August 1898, 4).

5. Gilman, "Suggestion," 78–85.

6. Gilman, *Human Works*, 31–32; Pittenger, *American Socialists*, 85–87.

7. See Newkirk, *Within the Veil*, chap. 2, for a discussion of newspaper accounts regarding black crimes between 1890 and 1910.

8. Everett, *Returning the Gaze*, 60–66.

9. Grossman quoted South Carolina senator Wad Hampton as suggesting that blacks "go off or settle in New England" (*Democratic Party*, 147). O'Brien noted that Fortune had proposed to President Roosevelt that America could supply "the Philippines with 'a competent labor population' of 5 million U.S. blacks" ("Blacks in All Quarters," 264). For Fortune's views on colonization in Asia, see Thornbrough, *T. Thomas Fortune*, 235–40. See also Mitchell, "Black Man's Burden," 90–94, for a discussion of race, racial redemption, manhood, and African American attitudes about black settlements in the Philippines.

10. See *Iowa State Bystander* for a speech by Senator John T. Morgan (D-AL) in which he stated that the "evil" of black enfranchisement "would end only when the United States had provided a home for the negro race suited to their traits," a clear implication that such a home was not in the United States (12 January 1900, 1).

11. *Atlanta Constitution*, 28 October 1906, 12. See *New Age*, 16 July 1904, 4, for mention of sending black Americans to Panama. See also Stokes, *Birth of a Nation*, 37–47, for a summary of both novels. Stokes states that *The Leopard's Spots* had as great an impact on American society and its attitudes as had Harriet Beecher Stowe's *Uncle Tom's Cabin* a half century earlier (ibid., 41).

12. *Galveston Daily News*, 20 August 1905, 17. Dixon wrote that "amalgamation simply meant Africanisation," that "two such races, counting millions in numbers, cannot live together under a Democracy," and that "*the future American must be an Anglo-Saxon or a Mulatoo*" (*The Leopard's Spots*, 386–87, emphasis in original).

13. *Nebraska State Journal*, 11 June 1909, 7.

14. *Atlanta Constitution*, 19 June 1910, 34. Taylor surely would have read Penn's *Afro-American Press*. Spear (*Black Chicago*, 53–56) argues that 1900 marked a watershed between a period when—at least in the case of Chicago—a promise of integration into the mainstream of American society was replaced by an appeal to racial solidarity and self-help. Spear noted that those who supported separate and parallel development within the black community had integrated Washington's premise of self-help in a modern context of voluntary exclusion.

15. See Tillinghast, *Negro in Africa and America*, for an excellent example of this genre of literature.

16. *Iowa State Bystander*, 25 January 1901, 12.

17. For an excellent description of attitudes held by this upper class, see Graham, *Our Kind of People*, 2–15.

18. Alexander (*Race Man*, 13) noted that Mitchell was "better educated than most Virginians of his day."

19. *La Crosse Tribune*, 27 May 1905, 1. The *Iowa State Bystander* complimented Taylor on a speech that he had given to celebrate emancipation, describing it as a "fine address, which by his wit and humor held the audience" (12 August 1898, 1). The *Bystander's* editor may not have considered that a compliment, because he may have believed that Taylor's liberal views were unacceptable to the audience.

20. *Lincoln Evening News*, 5 September 1904, 8. Alexander (*Race Man*, 153) noted that national meetings of fraternal organizations were occasions for establishing "networks" and "long-lasting friendships."

21. *Proceedings . . . 1900*, 239.

22. Bartley, *Keeping the Faith*, 5–8. The *Washington Bee* (8 August 1903, 2) specifically listed Jacksonville as experiencing significant in-migration during the 1890s. See also the introduction to Trotter, *Great Migration*, for a review of changing attitudes about migration and migrants over the past century.

23. Halloran ("Florida as a Health Resort," 486–88) described the superior health advantages of St. Augustine and Jacksonville and contrasted them with other cities in the South. Halloran especially noted St. Augustine as a favored destination for those seeking relief from consumption, chronic bronchitis, asthma, and chronic rheumatism, concluding that "Florida appears to offer more attractions and advantages as a winter resort of invalids than any other State in the Union. The temperature is favorable, the mean relative humidity is peculiarly adapted to the treatment of all forms of pulmonary disease; the air is salubrious, and in a large portion of the State dry and bracing; atmospheric changes are infrequent, and not so great as in other sections east of the Rocky Mountains" (ibid., 487).

24. 1910 United States Federal Census, Florida, Hillsborough County, Tampa (Ward 5), roll T624, 162, 10B. Taylor's name did not appear in Tampa's city directory. I am indebted to Gary Mormino, Rodney Kite-Powell, and Leland Hawes of Tampa, Florida (Hillsborough County), for information regarding the *Florida Reporter*, which was published between 1901 and 1919 and edited by Y. K. Meeks (1910) and F. B. Davis (1913). See *Proceedings . . . 1900*, 237–42, for a description of Tampa, the "largest city in South Florida."

25. *Old and New Testament Student* 11, no. 6 (1890): 403. Meeks had moved to Tampa by 1896. See Saunders, "Black American Conservatism," chap. 1, for the role played by the National Negro Business League in promoting self-sufficiency in small urban settings.

26. *Successful Americans*, 394. See Colburn, *Racial Change*, chap. 2. There is only one reference to a George Taylor in the St. Augustine *R. L. Polk & Co.'s City Directory, 1911–12* (202), but that person was listed as a real estate agent, and he may not have been the Taylor of this narrative. There was no listing for the Magnolia Remedy Company.

27. Cramp, *Nostrums and Quackery*, 88.

28. *Successful Americans*, 394. Compilations of this type were common at the turn of the century. Generally, one could have oneself listed for the price of the book's purchase. The phrase "Remove the Mask" first appears in a letter from Taylor to Mitchell in which he accepted his selection as nominee of the National Liberty Party (*Ottumwa Weekly Democrat*, 15 September 1904, 1). In that letter Taylor used the phrase in reference to Republican claims to be in opposition to black disenfranchisement while including in their 1904 platform language that Taylor considered as "equivalent to the practical disfranchisement of every Negro in the United States." The phrase "backward steps" was used between 1908 and 1910 in Republican politics by progressives who accused "standpatters" of accepting then-current legal changes in the South. Progressives considered such acceptance as "backward steps." Brown wrote a utopian-like essay, projecting a world of "one mind," "no conflicting warring, inharmonious entities," and "one universal struggle for the uplifting of all. . . . No backward steps will be taken" (*Iowa Unionist*, 21 December 1906, 2). The *Iowa Unionist* was a paper that Taylor likely would have read. The *Galveston Daily News* (10 May 1904, 2) reported that Booker Washington had given a speech at the AME conference in Chicago in which he had said that "there had been no backward steps in the education of the colored man." The *Iowa State Bystander* (5 August 1898, 1) had used the phrase with reference to American attitudes regarding the ability of Filipinos to rule themselves. In this case the author suggested that the United States had made "forward steps" in liberating the Filipinos from unjust rulers and exploitative business interests and that by refusing to permit the Filipinos to rule themselves the U.S. government was making "backward steps" that would enable old ruling classes and capital to exploit them once again.

29. The survival of either of these items would represent a major addition to the narrative of Taylor's life course.

30. *Ottumwa Weekly Democrat*, 15 September 1904, 1. See also *Ottumwa Weekly Democrat*, 4 August 1904, 5, for a letter from Taylor to the editor of the *Chicago Tribune* regarding an article written by Senator Albert Jarvis Hopkins of Illinois and published the previous week.

31. C. H. Harris to Bruce Mouser, 13 February 1984, enclosed list from city directories. No copies of the *Promoter* have survived.

32. Ibid. Information regarding the YMCA at Jacksonville appears in *Age*, 21 August 1914, 4, and 23 February 1915.

33. Bartley noted that the new headquarters for Jacksonville's "Most Worshipful Grand Lodge" was completed in 1913 and that this lodge remains "the wealthiest institution known among the group in the state" (*Keeping the Faith*, 13).

34. Skocpol, Liazos, and Ganz, *What a Mighty Power*, 8. For extensive treatment of the importance of religious and social institutions, see Du Bois, *Negro Church*, and Dittmer, *Black Georgia*, 50–71.

35. Ortiz, *Emancipation Betrayed*, 47; Bartley, *Keeping the Faith*, 3. See also Richardson, "History of Blacks," for black achievements between 1888 and 1895 and the importance of benevolent associations in the city's development. See also Johnson, *Along This Way*, for a view of growing up in Jacksonville before 1900.

36. Crooks, "Changing Face," 441; Davis, *History of Jacksonville*, 225.

37. Crooks, *Jacksonville*, 2–6.

38. Davis, *History of Jacksonville*, 244.

39. Johnson, *Along This Way*, 297.

40. Crooks, *Jacksonville*, 50–52.

41. Crooks, "Changing Face," 446, 449–50, 455, 462; Sokol, "Black Journalist." Thomas ("Present Day Story," n.p.) listed six hundred businesses by 1926.

42. Johnson, *Along This Way*, 297.

43. Crooks, "Changing Face," 440. Crooks (*Jacksonville*, 88–94) described numerous clubs, societies, churches, and leaders who were active during the decade. Thomas ("Present Day Story," n.p.) reported that in 1926 there were "no less than forty [fraternal] organization" in Jacksonville with an estimate of "at least twenty thousand" members.

44. Bartley, *Keeping the Faith*, 4. See also http://brokert10.fcla.edu/DLData/NF/NF00000085/file41.pdf (accessed 16 March 2009).

45. Stuart, *Economic Detour*, 109–17. Neyland (*Twelve Black Floridians*, 56) indicated that this company began as a health and burial insurance provider.

46. Stuart, *Economic Detour*, 10.

47. Thomas ("Present Day Story," n.p.) estimated that of Jacksonville's population in 1926 of 138,688, "approximately 50,000" were blacks, or "about one-third the total population." Nearly six hundred commercial establishments then were owned and operated by blacks, and there were more than one hundred black churches. See Richardson, "History of Blacks," 131.

48. Crooks, "Changing Face," 451.

49. Ibid., 453.

50. Crooks, *Jacksonville*, 35.

51. Ibid., 43. Tindall (*Emergence of the New South*, 145) noted that by 1910 Jim Crow legislation had moved to the municipal level with attempts to establish "residential segregation" as well.

52. For an excellent discussion of middle-class attitudes at the turn of the century, see the introduction to Summers, *Manliness and Its Discontents*.

53. Graham, *Our Kind of People*, 12. See Thompson, *Black Elite*, 3–4, for a discussion of the notion of a black elite and Du Bois's concept of the "talented tenth." Gatewood (*Aristocrats of Color*) identified Washington, D.C., as the center of that culture and Du Bois as one of its most prominent members. This group was known by the terms "colored aristocracy," "black 400," "the old black upper class," "upper reaches," "upper tens," and "best society" (ibid., ix). Gatewood also noted that the station of membership within this group could be carried from city to city (ibid., 107).

54. Hurst, *It Was Never about a Hotdog*, 19–20; Crooks, *Jacksonville*, 100. Sokol ("Black Journalist") noted that the "star edition" was also known as "the Jim Crow pages" and that no copies of that section of the paper for that period were preserved.

55. Harrison, *Colored Girls and Boys*, 111–12.

56. Davis, *History of Jacksonville*, 250–62, 269–70.

57. Ibid., 273.

58. I am indebted to Sharon C. Avery, archivist for the State Historical Society of Iowa, who supplied this information. The 1910 federal census, Florida, Clay County, precinct 1, identified James and Sarah Tillinghast as operating a "general farm" and Marion and her sister Nellie as teachers in a "public school." See also http://genforum.genealogy.com/tillinghast/messages/242.html (accessed 16 May 2009), for information about the James Tillinghast family of Green Cove Springs, Florida. The Tillinghast family had moved from South Carolina to Orange (likely Orange Park), Florida, and then Green Cove Springs, Florida, between 1890 and 1893. No record of the marriage between Taylor and Marion Tillinghast has been found. Arlington is located across the St. Johns River from downtown Jacksonville and is now considered a part of the city.

59. The *Southwest Review* (16 January 1926, 1) in an article with a dateline of "Jacksonville, Fla., Jan. 8, 1926," reported that Taylor had been "one of the foremost and most patriotic Negroes in the field of journalism," that he had lived on Duval Street, that he had lived on a farm near Green Cove Springs, and that he was survived by his wife, Mrs. Marie Taylor of "Arlando."

60. *Encyclopedia Americana*, entry for Green Cove Springs. See also *Guide to Florida*, 93.

61. Lee, *Tourist's Guide*, 115–16.

62. Wright, *Centennial Encyclopaedia*, 33.

63. Holloway, *Daughter's Memento*, 38–39. The leaders of this organization were called "organizers," although that term generally refers to persons who sold memberships or collected dues.

64. Mather, *Who's Who*, 176. John Simms had preceded Taylor as editor of the *Florida Sentinel* beginning in 1921 (Harrison, *Colored Girls and Boys*, 2). The *Sentinel* was published in Jacksonville until 1931. See Neyland, *Twelve Black Floridians*, 13, for Mathew Lewey's management of the *Sentinel*. The sole surviving copy of the *Florida Sentinel* (19 April 1919, 4) contains an intriguing article about the National Nonpartisan League (NNPL), headquartered in Minneapolis, perhaps suggesting that the *Sentinel* and its editor, N. K. McGill, were friendly to agrarian Populist movements. The National Nonpartisan League had been formed in North Dakota in 1915 by Arthur Townley and had expanded its influence throughout the upper Midwest and the Northwest. It rejected third-party affiliation but supported candidates of established parties who championed its program of ownership of agricultural cooperatives. It officially affiliated with the Democratic Party in 1956. The Democratic Party in Minnesota, partly as a consequence of the prominent influence of the NNPL, is called the Farmer Labor Party. The author of a letter to the *Sentinel* dated 18 March 1919 wrote: "We have no doubt that the Republican party can do little or nothing for the Negro. In fact we are convinced that it has no intention of doing anything for him. A party whose record is positive proof of hostility to [the] white worker cannot claim to be a friend of the colored worker."

65. Taylor was known to have given a speech titled "Remarks on Behalf of Business Men" at the college's commencement program on 2 May 1923.

66. List from city directories provided by the Historical Society of Jacksonville, Florida, and enclosed in C. H. Harris to Bruce L. Mouser, 13 February 1984 (copy in Area Research Center, University of Wisconsin–La Crosse).

67. *Southwest Review*, 17 January 1926, 1. According to http://genforum.genealogy.com/tillinghast/messages/245.html (accessed 17 May 2009), the Hill-Tillinghast house in Orlando was located at 626 W. Washington Street, and it "served as a meeting place for famous people, including educator Mary McLeod Bethune and aviator Bessie Coleman." For the Hill-Tillinghast house, see McCarthy, *African American Sites*, 198.

68. I am indebted to Sharon C. Avery, archivist for the State Historical Society of Iowa, who supplied this information.

Bibliography

Documents relating to this study are posted online by Murphy Library, University of Wisconsin–La Crosse: http://murphylibrary.uwlax.edu/digital/TaylorGeorge/.

Manuscript Collections (Archives)

Iowa State Historical Society, Des Moines. George H. Woodson Scrapbook, ca. 1895–1902, microfilm.

Ottumwa, Iowa, Public Library. Newspaper Clippings File.

University of Wisconsin–La Crosse, Area Research Center. Mouser's Black La Crosse File.

Wayland Academy, Archive. Beaver Dam, WI.

Government Publications

United States Statutes at Large. 43rd Cong., 2nd sess., 1874–75.

U.S. House. HR 8479. 55th Cong., 2d sess., 1898–99. *Congressional Record* 31 (21 February 1898): 2010.

———. HR 11119. 51st Cong., 1st sess., 1889–90. *Congressional Record* 21 (24 June 1890): 6464.

———. HR 11404. 57th Cong., 1st sess., 1901–2. *Congressional Record* 4, pt. 4 (17 February 1902): 1841.

U.S. Senate. S. 1176. 56th Cong., 1st sess., 1899–1900. *Congressional Record* 33, pt. 1 (11 December 1899): 180–84.

———. S. 1389. 53rd Cong., 2d sess., 1894–95. *Congressional Record* 26 (8 January 1894): 519.

———. S. 7254. 57th Cong., 2d sess., 1902–3. *Congressional Record* 36, pt. 7 (4 February 1903): 1673.

Newspapers

L'Abeille de la Nouvelle-Orléans, New Orleans, LA
Ackely Phonograph, Ackely, IA
Adams County Union, Corning, IA
Age, New York, NY
Alaska Citizen, Fairbanks, AK

Albia Republican, Albia, IA
Albia Union, Albia, IA
Altamont Enterprise, Altamont, NY
Alton Democrat, Alton, IA
Alton Evening Telegraph, Alton, IL
Anacanda Standard, Anacanda, MT
Appeal, St. Paul, MN
Atlanta Constitution, Atlanta, GA
Bismarck Daily Tribune, Bismarck, ND
Broad Ax, Chicago, IL
Broad Ax, Salt Lake City, UT
Burlington Hawk-Eye, Burlington, IA
Carroll Sentinel, Carroll, IA
Cedar Rapids Evening Gazette, Cedar Rapids, IA
Cedar Rapids Gazette, Cedar Rapids, IA
Cedar Rapids Republican, Cedar Rapids, IA
Chicago Evening Post, Chicago, IL
Cleveland Gazette, Cleveland, OH
Colorado Transcript, Golden, CO
Colored American, Washington, DC
Courier, Connellsville, PA
Daily Alaska Dispatch, Juneau, AK
Daily Citizen, Iowa City, IA
Daily Huronite, Huron, SD
Daily Inter Ocean, Chicago, IL
Daily Iowa Capital, Des Moines, IA
Daily Mail, Hagerstown, MD
Daily Miami Metropolis, Miami, FL
Daily Nevada State Journal, Reno, NV
Daily Progress, Petersburg, VA
Daily Republican, Decatur, IL
Daily Review, Decatur, IL
Daily Times, New Brunswick, NJ
Daily Times-Tribune, Waterloo, IA
Dallas Morning News, Dallas, TX
Davenport Tribune, Davenport, IA
Decatur Daily Republican, Decatur, IL
Denton Journal, Denton, MD
Des Moines Daily Capital, Des Moines, IA
Dodge County Citizen, Beaver Dam, WI
Dubuque Daily Herald, Dubuque, IA
Dubuque Herald, Dubuque, IA
East St. Louis Daily Journal, East St. Louis, IL

Eau Claire Leader, Eau Claire, WI
Emmetsburg Democrat, Emmetsburg, IA
Emporia Gazette, Emporia, KS
Evening Gazette, Sterling, IL
Evening News, Ada, OK
Evening Star, La Crosse, WI
Fitchburg Daily Sentinel, Fitchburg, MA
Fitchburg Sentinel, Fitchburg, MA
Florida Sentinel, Jacksonville, FL
Florida Times-Union, Jacksonville, FL
Fort Wayne Journal-Gazette, Fort Wayne, IN
Fort Wayne News, Fort Wayne, IN
Galesville Independent, Galesville, WI
Galveston Daily News, Galveston, TX
Grand Forks Herald, Grand Forks, ND
Grand Rapids Tribune, Grand Rapids, WI
Grant County Herald, Lancaster, WI
Guardian, Boston, MA
Hamilton Evening Sun, Hamilton, OH
Herald, Oskaloosa, IA
Hopkinsville Kentuckian, Hopkinsville, KY
Independent, Houston, TX
Indiana Democrat, Indiana, PA
Indianapolis Freeman, Indianapolis, IN
Indiana Progress, Indiana, PA
Iowa Postal Card, Fayette, IA
Iowa Recorder, Greene, IA
Iowa State Bystander, Des Moines, IA
Iowa Unionist, Des Moines, IA
Janesville Daily Gazette, Janesville, WI
Kansas City Star, Kansas City, MO
La Crosse Argus, La Crosse, WI
La Crosse County Countryman, West Salem, WI
La Crosse County Record, Onalaska, WI
La Crosse Daily Democrat, La Crosse, WI
La Crosse Daily Republican, La Crosse, WI
La Crosse Daily Republican and Leader, La Crosse, WI
La Crosse Democrat, La Crosse, WI
La Crosse Leader-Press, La Crosse, WI
La Crosse Morning Chronicle, La Crosse, WI
La Crosse News, La Crosse, WI
La Crosse Tribune, La Crosse, WI
La Grand Reporter, La Grand, IA

Landmark, Statesville, NC
Lincoln Evening News, Lincoln, NE
Logansport Daily Pharos, Logansport, IN
Logansport Daily Reporter, Logansport, IN
Logansport Pharos, Logansport, IN
Logansport Reporter, Logansport, IN
Los Angeles Times, Los Angeles, CA
Marble Rock Journal, Marble Rock, IA
Marion Daily Star, Marion, OH
Marshville Times, Marshville, WI
Marysville Tribune, Marysville, OH
Middleton Daily News, Galveston, TX
Milford Mail, Milford, IA
Mills County Tribune, Glenwood, IA
Milwaukee Journal, Milwaukee, WI
Milwaukee Journal Sentinel, Milwaukee, WI
Moberly Daily Monitor, Moberly, MO
Moberly Evening Democrat, Moberly, MO
Modesto Evening News, Modesto, CA
Monroe County News, Albia, IA
Montgomery Advertiser, Montgomery, AL
Morning News, Hagerstown, MD
Nebraska State Journal, Lincoln, NE
Negro Solicitor, Oskaloosa, IA
New Age, Portland, OR
Newark Daily Advocate, Newark, OH
New Era, Humeston, IA
Newport Mercury, Newport, RI
News, Frederick, MD
New York Times, New York, NY
New York Tribune, New York, NY
North Adams Evening Transcript, North Adams, MA
Ogden Standard, Ogden City, UT
Omaha World Herald, Omaha, NE
Oshkosh Daily Northwestern, Oshkosh, WI
Oshkosh Morning News, Oshkosh, WI
Oskaloosa Daily Herald, Oskaloosa, IA
Ottumwa Courier, Ottumwa, IA
Ottumwa Daily Courier, Ottumwa, IA
Ottumwa Democrat, Ottumwa, IA
Ottumwa Evening Democrat, Ottumwa, IA
Oxford Mirror, Oxford Junction, IA
Oxford Public Ledger, Oxford, NC

Palestine Daily Herald, Palestine, TX
Palladium, St. Louis, MO
Pawtucket Times, Pawtucket, RI
Piqua Daily Leader, Piqua, OH
Planet, Richmond, VA
Post Standard, Syracuse, NY
Prairie du Chien Courier, Prairie du Chien, WI
Quincy Daily Journal, Quincy, IL
Quincy Morning Whig, Quincy, IL
Racine Daily Journal, Racine, WI
Rake Register, Rake, IA
Republican-Freeman, Waukesha, WI
Republican Journal, Columbus, WI
Richwood Gazette, Richwood, OH
Rising Sun, Kansas City, MO
St. Paul Pioneer Press, St. Paul, MN
Salem Daily News, Salem, OH
Salt Lake Tribune, Salt Lake City, UT
Savannah Tribune, Savannah, GA
Semi-Weekly Cedar Falls Gazette, Cedar Falls, IA
Semi-Weekly Inter Ocean, Chicago, IL
Semi Weekly Iowa State Reporter, Waterloo, IA
Semi Weekly Reporter, Waterloo, IA
Southwest Review, Albuquerque, NM
Sparta Democrat, Sparta, WI
Springfield Republican, Springfield, MA
Sun, New York, NY
Taylor County Democrat, Bedford, IA
Times Picayune, New Orleans, LA
Trenton Times, Trenton, NJ
Tri-City Evening Star, Davenport, IA
Tri-City Star, Davenport, IA
Tuesday and Friday Union, Albia, IA
Tyrone Daily Herald, Tyrone, PA
Tyrone Herald, Tyrone, PA
Union Star, Union, IA
Van Wert Daily Bulletin, Van Wert, OH
Vindicator and Republican, Estherville, IA
Voice of the Negro, Atlanta, GA
Washington Bee, Washington, DC
Washington Post, Washington, DC
Waterloo Daily Courier, Waterloo, IA
Waterloo Daily Times-Tribune, Waterloo, IA

Waterloo Semi-Weekly Courier, Waterloo, IA
Waterloo Times-Tribune, Waterloo, IA
Weekly Argus, La Crosse, WI
Weekly Fort Wayne Sentinel, Fort Wayne, IN
Weekly Gazette and Free Press, Janesville, WI
Weekly Inter Ocean, Chicago, IL
Wheeling Intelligencer, Wheeling, WV
Wichita Searchlight, Wichita, KS
Williamsburg Journal Tribune, Williamsburg, IA
Wisconsin Labor Advocate, La Crosse, WI
World, New York, NY

Books, Articles, Theses, and Dissertations

Abramowitz, Jack. "The Negro in the Populist Movement." *Journal of Negro History* 38, no. 3 (1953): 257–89.

Alexander, Ann Field. *Race Man: The Rise and Fall of the "Fighting Editor," John Mitchell, Jr.* Charlottesville: University of Virginia Press, 2002.

Alexander, Shawn Leigh, ed. *T. Thomas Fortune, the Afro-American Agitator: A Collection of Writings, 1880–1928.* Gainesville: University Press of Florida, 2008.

———. "Vengeance without Justice, Injustice without Retribution: The Afro-American Council's Struggle against Racial Violence." *Great Plains Quarterly* 27, no. 2 (2007): 117–34.

———. "'We know our rights and have the courage to defend them': The Spirit of Agitation in the Age of Accommodation, 1883–1909." PhD diss., University of Massachusetts, Amherst, 2004.

Ali, Omar H. "Independent Black Voices from the Late Nineteenth Century: Black Populists and the Struggle against the Southern Democracy." *Souls: A Critical Journal of Black Politics, Culture, and Society* 7, no. 2 (2005): 4–18.

———. *In the Balance of Power: Independent Black Politics and Third-Party Movements in the United States.* Athens: Ohio University Press, 2008.

———. "The Making of a Black Populist: A Tribute to the Rev. Walter A. Pattillo." *Oxford (NC) Public Ledger*, 28 March 2002.

The Annual Catalogue of the Officers and Students in the Academic Department of Wayland University. Waupun, WI: P. M. Pryor, 1878.

Appletons' Annual Cyclopaedia and Register of Important Events . . . 1888. New York: Appleton, 1889.

Aptheker, Herbert, ed. *A Documentary History of the Negro People of the United States.* New York: Citadel Press, 1951.

———. "The Negro Who Ran for President." *Negro Digest*, March 1947, 64–67.

Avrich, Paul. *The Haymarket Tragedy.* Princeton, NJ: Princeton University Press, 1984.

Barnes, Kenneth C. *Journey of Hope: The Back-to-Africa Movement in Arkansas in the Late 1800s.* Chapel Hill: University of North Carolina Press, 2004.

Bartley, Abel A. *Keeping the Faith: Race, Politics, and Social Development in Jacksonville, Florida, 1940–1970.* Westport, CT: Greenwood Press, 2000.

Bayor, Ronald H., ed. *The Columbia Documentary History of Race and Ethnicity in America.* New York: Columbia University Press, 2004.

Beatty, Bess. *A Revolution Gone Backward: The Black Response to National Politics, 1876–1896.* New York: Greenwood Press, 1987.

Bennett, Lerone, Jr. "The Niagara Movement." *Ebony,* May 1976, 130–40.

Bensel, Richard Franklin. *Passion and Preferences: William Jennings Bryan and the 1896 Democratic National Convention.* New York: Cambridge University Press, 2008.

Beran, Janice. "Diamonds in Iowa: Blacks, Buxton, and Baseball." *Journal of African American History* 87, no. 1 (2002): 56–69.

Bergmann, Leola Nelson. "The Negro in Iowa." *Iowa Journal of History and Politics* 66 (1948): 3–90.

Berry, Mary Frances. *My Face Is Black Is True: Callie House and the Struggle for Ex-slave Reparations.* New York: Alfred A. Knopf, 2005.

———. "Reparations for Freedmen, 1890–1916: Fraudulent Practices or Justice Deferred?" *Journal of Negro History* 57, no. 3 (1972): 219–30.

Black, Paul Walton. "Attempted Lynchings in Iowa." *Annals of Iowa* 11, no. 4 (1914): 279–83.

Blaustein, Albert P., and Robert L. Zangrando, eds. *Civil Rights and the American Negro: A Documentary History.* New York: Trident Press, 1968.

Blight, David W. *Race and Reunion: The Civil War in American Memory.* Cambridge, MA: Harvard University Press, 2001.

The Blue Book of the State of Wisconsin. Milwaukee: Thomas Cunningham, 1893.

Bontemps, Arna Wendell, and Jack Conroy. *Anyplace but Here.* New York: Hill and Wang, 1966.

Bristow, Ruth. "Early Steamboat and Packet Lines." In *La Crosse County Historical Sketches,* ser. 1, 31–34. La Crosse, WI: Liesenfeld Press, 1931.

Brown, Everit, and Albert Strauss. *A Dictionary of American Politics.* New York: A. L. Burt, 1907.

Brown, Richard W. "Lodging in La Crosse, Wisconsin, 1880s." Undergraduate paper, University of Wisconsin–La Crosse, 1992.

Bryant, Benjamin F. *Memoirs of La Crosse County.* Madison, WI: Western Historical Association, 1907.

Buffalo Bill [William Cody]. *White Beaver: The Exile of the Platt.* New York: Beadle & Adams, 1886.

———. *White Beaver's Still Hunt.* New York: Beadle & Adams, 1880.

———. *The Wizard Brothers: Or White Beaver's Red Tail.* New York: Beadle & Adams, 1886.

Bullock, Penelope. *The Afro-American Periodical Press, 1838–1909.* Baton Rouge: Louisiana State University Press, 1981.

Canuteson, Richard Lewis. "The Lumbering Industry of the Black River." Bachelor's thesis, University of Wisconsin–Madison, 1925.

Carnes, Mark C. *Secret Rituals and Manhood in Victorian America*. New Haven, CT: Yale University Press, 1989.

Chafe, William H. "The Negro and Populism: A Kansas Case Study." *Journal of Southern History* 34, no. 3 (1968): 402–19.

Cha-Jua, Sundiata Keita. "'A Warlike Demonstration': Legalism, Violent Self-help, and Electoral Politics in Decatur, Illinois, 1894–1898." *Journal of Urban History* 26 (2000): 591–629.

Childs, John Brown. *Leadership, Conflict, and Cooperation in Afro-American Social Thought*. Philadelphia: Temple University Press, 1989.

Coate, D. O. "Early La Crosse County Authors and Their Works." *La Crosse (WI) Tribune*, 2 April 1929.

Colburn, David R. *Racial Change and Community Crisis: St. Augustine, Florida, 1877–1980*. New York: Columbia University Press, 1985.

Colman's City Directory, Oskaloosa, Iowa, 1898–1899. Oskaloosa, IA: Herald Print, 1898.

Colman's City Directory, Oskaloosa, Iowa, 1900–1901. Oskaloosa, IA: Herald Print, 1900.

Colman's City Directory, Oskaloosa, Iowa, 1904–1905. Oskaloosa, IA: Herald Presses, 1905.

Cooper, Zachary. *Black Settlers in Rural Wisconsin*. Madison: State Historical Society of Wisconsin, 1977.

Copeland, Vince. "The Republocrats, Part 18: Imperialism Abroad, Reform at Home." http://www.preterhuman.net/texts/politics/capitalist.rule.18 (accessed 17 November 2009).

Cramp, Arthur J. *Nostrums and Quackery*. Chicago: American Medical Association, 1921.

Crooks, James B. "Changing Face of Jacksonville, Florida: 1900–1910." *Florida Historical Quarterly* 62, no. 4 (1984): 439–63.

———. *Jacksonville after the Fire, 1901–1919*. Jacksonville: University of North Florida Press, 1991.

Cunnigen, Donald. "The Du Bois–Washington Debate in the 21st Century: Multiculturalism and the African American Community." In *The New Politics of Race: From Du Bois to the 21st Century*, edited by Marlese Durr, 5–22. Westport, CT: Praeger, 2002.

Current, Richard N. *The History of Wisconsin: The Civil War Era, 1848–1873*. Madison: State Historical Society of Wisconsin, 1976.

Curti, Merle. *The Making of an American Community: A Case Study of Democracy in a Frontier County*. Stanford, CA: Stanford University Press, 1959.

Dailey, Jane. "The Limits of Liberalism in the New South: The Politics of Race, Sex, and Patronage in Virginia, 1879–1883." In *Jumpin' Jim Crow: Southern Politics from Civil War to Civil Rights*, edited by Jane Dailey, Glenda Elizabeth Gilmore, and Bryant Simon, 88–114. Princeton, NJ: Princeton University Press, 2000.

Davis, Thomas F. *History of Jacksonville, Florida and Vicinity, 1513 to 1924*. Reproduction of 1925 ed. Gainesville: University of Florida Press, 1964.

Degler, Carl N. *In Search of Human Nature: The Decline and Revival of Darwinism in American Social Thought*. New York: Oxford University Press, 1991.

Detweiler, Frederick G. *The Negro Press in the United States*. College Park, MD: McGrath Publishing, 1968.

Dickinson, Edward B. *Official Proceedings of the Democratic National Convention: Held in Chicago, Ill., July 7th, 8th, 9th, 10th and 11th, 1896.* Logansport, IN: Wilson, Humphrey & Company, 1896.

Dittmer, John. *Black Georgia in the Progressive Era.* Urbana: University of Illinois Press, 1977.

Dixon, Thomas. *The Leopard's Spots.* New York: Grosset & Dunlap, 1902.

Doherty, Herbert, Jr. "Voices of Protest from the New South." *Mississippi Valley Historical Review* 42, no. 1 (1955): 45–66.

Doolen, Richard M. "'Brick' Pomeroy and the Greenback Clubs." *Journal of the Illinois State Historical Society* 65, no. 4 (1972): 434–50.

Douglass, Frederick. *Life and Times of Frederick Douglass.* Boston: De Wolfe & Fiske, 1892.

Drago, Edmund L. "The Black Press & Populism, 1890/1896." *San Jose Studies* 1, no. 1 (1975): 97–103.

Du Bois, W. E. B. *The Autobiography of W. E. B. Du Bois.* New York: International Publishers, 1968.

———. *The Negro Church.* Atlanta University Publications no. 8. Atlanta, GA, 1898.

———. *On Sociology and the Black Community*, edited by Dan S. Green and Edwin D. Driver. Chicago: University of Chicago Press, 1987.

———. *The Souls of Black Folk.* New York: Modern Library, 2003.

Ead's Illustrated History of Ottumwa. Ottumwa, IA: A. B. Eads Publishers, 1885.

The Encyclopedia Americana. New York: Encyclopedia Americana Corporation, 1919.

Everett, Anna. *Returning the Gaze: A Genealogy of Black Film Criticism, 1909–1949.* Durham, NC: Duke University Press, 2001.

Fahey, David M. *The Black Lodge in White America: "True Reformer" Browne and His Economic Strategy.* Dayton, OH: Wright State University Press, 1994.

Ferris, Elmer E. *Jerry at the Academy.* Garden City, NY: Doubleday, 1940.

Fine, Nathan. *Labor and Farmer Parties in the United States, 1828–1928.* New York: Russell & Russell, 1961.

Fink, Leon. "The Knights of Labor in Milwaukee." In *Workers and Unions in Wisconsin: A Labor History Anthology*, edited by Darryl Holter, 26–33. Madison: State Historical Society of Wisconsin, 1999.

———. *Workingmen's Democracy: The Knights of Labor and American Politics.* Urbana: University of Illinois Press, 1983.

Fishel, Leslie H., Jr. "The Genesis of the First Wisconsin Civil Rights Act." *Wisconsin Magazine of History* 49 (1966): 324–33.

———. "The Negro in Northern Politics." *Mississippi Valley Historical Review* 42, no. 3 (1955): 466–89.

———. "Wisconsin and Negro Suffrage." *Wisconsin Magazine of History* 46, no. 3 (1963): 180–96.

Fleming, Walter L. *Deportation and Colonization: An Attempted Solution of the Race Problem.* New York: N.p., 1914.

———. *Ex-Slave Petition Frauds.* Baton Rouge, LA: Ortlieb's Printing, 1910.

Flewellen, Kathryn. "The National Black Independent Political Party: Will History Repeat?" *Freedomways* 21, no. 2 (1981): 93–105.

Fortune, T. Thomas. "The Negro's Place in American Life at the Present Day." In *The Negro Problem*, edited by August Meier, 213–34. New York: Arno Press, 1969.

Foster, Frances Smith. "A Narrative of the Interesting Origins and (Somewhat) Surprising Developments of African-American Print Culture." *American Literary History* 17, no. 4 (2005): 714–40.

Fox, Stephen R. *The Guardian of Boston: William Monroe Trotter*. New York: Atheneum, 1970.

Fredrickson, George M. *The Black Image in the White Mind: The Debate on Afro-American Character and Destiny, 1817–1914*. New York: Harper & Row, 1971.

Freeman, W. A. *The Devil between the White Man and the Negro*. St. Louis: Freeman-Norwood Publishing, 1907.

Frye, Hardy T. *Black Parties and Political Power: A Case Study*. Boston: G. K. Hall, 1980.

Gaither, Gerald H. *Blacks and the Populist Movement: Ballots and Bigotry in the "New South."* Tuscaloosa: University of Alabama Press, 2005.

Gallaher, Ruth A., and Mildred Throne. "The Negro in Iowa." *Iowa Journal of History and Politics* 46, no. 1 (1948): 3–90.

Gardner, Robert Wallace. "A Frustrated Minority: The Negro and New York City Politics of the 1880's as Typified by the Mayoralty Election of 1886." *Negro History Bulletin* 29, no. 4 (1966): 83–84, 94.

Gatewood, Willard B., Jr. *Aristocrats of Color: The Black Elite, 1880–1920*. Bloomington: Indiana University Press, 1990.

———. "Black Americans and the Quest for Empire, 1898–1903." *Journal of Southern History* 38, no. 4 (1972): 545–66.

Gerber, David A. *Black Ohio and the Color Line 1860–1915*. Urbana: University of Illinois Press, 1976.

Gerteis, Joseph. "Populism, Race, and Political Interest in Virginia." *Social Science History* 27, no. 2 (2003): 197–227.

Gilman, Charlotte Perkins. *Human Works*. New York: McClure, Phillips & Company, 1904.

———. "A Suggestion on the Negro Problem." *American Journal of Sociology* 14, no. 1 (1908): 78–85.

Gilmore, Glenda Elizabeth. *Gender and Jim Crow: Women and the Politics of White Supremacy in North Carolina, 1896–1920*. Chapel Hill: University of North Carolina Press, 1996.

Ginger, Ray. *Altgeld's America: The Lincoln Ideal versus Changing Realities*. New York: Funk & Wagnalls, 1958.

Goldbloom, Shelley. "Black Added His Bit to Wisconsin's History." *Milwaukee Journal*, 19 April 1981.

Goldstein, Michael. "Preface to the Rise of Booker T. Washington: A View from New York City of the Demise of Independent Black Politics, 1889–1902." *Journal of Negro History* 62, no. 1 (1977): 81–99.

Goudy, Willis. "Selected Demographics: Iowa's African-American Residents, 1840–2000." In *Outside In: African-American History in Iowa, 1838–2000,* edited by Bill Silag, Susan Bridgford, and Hal Chase, 22–43. Des Moines: State Historical Society of Iowa, 2001.

Graham, Lawrence Otis. *Our Kind of People: Inside America's Black Upper Class.* New York: HarperCollins, 1999.

Green, James. *Death in the Haymarket.* New York: Pantheon Books, 2006.

Grossman, Lawrence. *The Democratic Party and the Negro: Northern and National Politics, 1868–92.* Urbana: University of Illinois Press, 1976.

Guide to Florida by "Rambler." New York: American News Company, 1873.

Gurda, John. "When Bay View Strike Turned to Bloodshed." *Milwaukee Journal Sentinel,* 30 April 1995.

Gutman, Herbert G. "Peter H. Clark: Pioneer Negro Socialist, 1877." *Journal of Negro Education* 34, no. 4 (1965): 413–18.

Haas, Charles. "George Edwin Taylor: The Black Presidential Candidate with the La Crosse Connection." *Past, Present and Future: Magazine of the La Crosse County Historical Society* 30, no. 4 (2008): 1–3.

Halloran, M. J. "Florida as a Health Resort." In *The Medical and Surgical Reporter: A Weekly Journal,* edited by D. G. Brinton and Joseph F. Edwards, 486–88. Philadelphia: N.p., 1884.

Harbaugh, William H. "Election of 1904." In *History of American Presidential Elections, 1789–1968,* edited by Arthur Schlesinger, Jr., 3:1965–2046. New York: McGraw-Hill, 1971.

Harlan, Louis R. *Booker T. Washington: The Wizard of Tuskegee, 1901–1915.* New York: Oxford University Press, 1983.

Harlan, Louis, and Raymond Smock, eds. *The Booker T. Washington Papers.* 14 vols. Urbana: University of Illinois Press, 1972–89.

Harman, Donald J. "A Look at History: The Further Legacy of Nathan Smith." *La Crosse Tribune,* 26 March 2006.

Harris, Fredrick C. *Something Within: Religion in African-American Political Activism.* New York: Oxford University Press, 1999.

Harrison, William Henry, Jr. *Colored Girls and Boys Inspiring United States History.* Allentown, PA: Searle & Dressler, 1921.

Haynes, Fred E. "The Collapse of the Farmer-Labor Bloc." *Social Forces* 4, no. 1 (1925): 148–56.

———. *Third Party Movements Since the Civil War, with a Special Reference to Iowa; A Study in Social Politics.* Iowa City: The State Historical Society of Iowa, 1916.

Hebberd, Mary. "Marcus 'Brick' Pomeroy: 'Copperhead' Editor." *Historical Notes [of the] La Crosse County Historical Society* 2, no. 1 (1975): 1–3.

Heider, Hazel Rahn. *Along the Waterloo Road.* West Salem, WI: Heider, 1981.

Henry, Charles P. *Long Overdue: The Politics of Racial Reparations.* New York: New York University Press, 2007.

Herringshaw, Thomas. *Herringshaw's Encyclopedia of American Biography.* Chicago: American Publishers' Association, 1898.

————. *Herringshaw's Encyclopedia of American Biography*. Chicago: American Publishers' Association, 1901.

Hickenlooper, Frank. *An Illustrated History of Monroe County, Iowa*. Marceline, IA: Walsworth Publishing Company, 1976.

Higgenbotham, A. Leon, Jr. *Shades of Freedom: Racial Politics and Presumptions of the American Legal Process*. New York: Oxford University Press, 1996.

Hild, Matthew. *Greenbackers, Knights of Labor, and Populists: Farmer-Labor Insurgency in the Late-Nineteenth-Century South*. Athens: University of Georgia Press, 2007.

Hill, Walter B., Jr. "The Ex-Slave Pension Movement: Some Historical and Genealogical Notes." *Negro History Bulletin* 59, no. 4 (1996): 7–11.

Hine, Darlene Clark. "From the Margins to the Center: Callie House and the Ex-Slave Pension Movement." *Journal of African American History* 91, no. 3 (2006): 311–17.

Hirshheimer, H. J. "La Crosse River History and the Davidsons." *Wisconsin Magazine of History* 28, no. 3 (1945): 263–76.

History of Northern Wisconsin—1881. Chicago: Western Historical Company, 1881.

Hoffmann, Phil. *Oskaloosa: Or the First One Hundred Years in a Mid-West Town*. Cedar Rapids, IA: Torch Press, 1942.

Holloway, M. M. *A Daughter's Memento*. Jacksonville: Edward Waters College Press, 1920.

Holmes, William F. "The Demise of the Colored Farmers' Alliance." *Journal of Southern History* 41, no. 2 (1975): 187–200.

Holmlund, Jim. "Office Safe Yields Early Relationship." *St. Paul Pioneer Press*, 28 October 1973.

Holter, Darryl. *Workers and Unions in Wisconsin: A Labor History Anthology*. Madison: State Historical Society of Wisconsin, 1999.

Howard-Pitney, David. "Calvin Chase's *Washington Bee* and Black Middle-Class Ideology, 1882–1900." *Journalism Quarterly* 63, no. 1 (1986): 89–97.

Hurst, Rodney L., Sr. *It Was Never about a Hotdog and a Coke!* Livermore, CA: Wingspan Press, 2008.

James, Joy. *Transcending the Talented Tenth: Black Leaders and American Intellectuals*. New York: Routledge, 1997.

Jewell, Joseph O. *Race, Social Reform, and the Making of a Middle Class: The American Missionary Association and Black America, 1870–1900*. New York: Rowman & Littlefield, 2007.

Johnson, Dorothy Sagen. "Lumbering on the Black River at Onalaska, Wisconsin, 1852–1902." Master's thesis, University of Wisconsin–La Crosse, 1974.

Johnson, James Weldon. *Along This Way: The Autobiography of James Weldon Johnson*. New York: Da Capo Press, 1973.

Justesen, Benjamin R. *Broken Brotherhood: The Rise and Fall of the National Afro-American Council*. Carbondale: Southern Illinois University Press, 2008.

Justi, Herman, ed. *Official History of the Tennessee Centennial Exposition*. Nashville: Brandon Printing, 1898.

Kantrowitz, Stephen. *Ben Tillman and the Reconstruction of White Supremacy*. Chapel Hill: University of North Carolina Press, 2000.

Katz, Mayer. *Vignettes of Historic La Crosse.* La Crosse, WI: La Crosse Foundation, 1985.

Kelly, Robin D. G. "'We are not what we seem': Rethinking Black Working-Class Opposition in the Jim Crow South." *Journal of American History* 80, no. 1 (1993): 75–112.

Kennedy, Philip. "The Racial Overtones of Imperialism as a Campaign Issue, 1900." *Mid-America* 48 (1966): 196–205.

Killian, Charles Denmore. "Bishop Daniel A. Payne: Black Spokesman for Reform." PhD diss., Indiana University, 1971.

Kindschy, Errol. *Leonard's Dream: A History of West Salem.* Shawnee Mission, KS: Inter-Collegiate Press, 1981.

King, Desmond, and Stephen Tuck. "De-centring the South: America's Nationwide White Supremacist Order after Reconstruction." *Past and Present*, February 2007, 213–53.

Klement, Frank L. "'Brick' Pomeroy: Copperhead and Curmudgeon." *Wisconsin Magazine of History* 35, no. 2 (1951–52): 106–13, 156–57.

———. "Midwestern Opposition to Lincoln's Emancipation Policy." *Journal of Negro History* 49, no. 3 (1964): 169–83.

Kremer, Gary R. *James Milton Turner and the Promise of America: The Public Life of a Post–Civil War Black Leader.* Columbia: University of Missouri Press, 1991.

Krenn, Michael, ed. *Race and U.S. Foreign Policy in the Ages of Territorial and Market Expansion, 1840 to 1900.* New York: Garland Publishing, 1998.

Kuyk, Betty M. "The African Derivation of Black Fraternal Orders in the United States." *Comparative Studies in Society and History* 25, no. 4 (1983): 559–92.

Langston, Ronald. "The African-American Legacy in Iowa Politics." In *Outside In: African-American History in Iowa, 1838–2000*, edited by Bill Silag, Susan Bridgford, and Hal Chase, 341–63. Des Moines: State Historical Society of Iowa, 2001.

Lee, Henry. *The Tourist's Guide of Florida.* New York: Leve & Alden, 1885.

Lewinson, Paul. *Race, Class, and Party: A History of Negro Suffrage and White Politics in the South.* New York: Grosset & Dunlap, 1965.

Lewis, David L. *W. E. B. Du Bois, Biography of a Race, 1868–1919.* New York: Holt, 1993.

Liazos, Ariane, and Marshall Ganz. "Duty to the Race: African American Fraternal Orders and the Legal Defense of the Right to Organize." *Social Science History* 28, no. 3 (2004): 485–534.

Link, Arthur S. "The Negro as a Factor in the Campaign of 1912." *Journal of Negro History* 32, no. 1 (1947): 81–99.

Lofton, Williston H. "Northern Labor and the Negro during the Civil War." *Journal of Negro History* 34, no. 3 (1949): 251–73.

Logan, Rayford Whittingham. *Betrayal of the Negro, from Rutherford B. Hayes to Woodrow Wilson.* New York: Collier Books, 1965.

Logue, Larry M., and Peter Blanck. "'Benefit of the Doubt': African-American Civil War Veterans and Pensions." *Journal of Interdisciplinary History* 38, no. 3 (2008): 377–99.

Lovett, Bobby L. *The African-American History of Nashville, Tennessee, 1780–1930.* Fayetteville: University of Arkansas Press, 1999.

Luker, Ralph. *The Social Gospel in Black and White*. Chapel Hill: University of North Carolina Press, 1991.

Lumpkins, Charles L. *American Pogrom: The East St. Louis Race Riot and Black Politics*. Athens: Ohio University Press, 2008.

Maisel, L. Sandy. *Parties and Elections in America*. New York: Rowman & Littlefield, 2002.

Marable, Manning. *W. E. B. Du Bois: Black Radical Democrat*. Boston: Twayne Publishers, 1986.

Marszalek, John F. *A Black Congressman in the Age of Jim Crow*. Gainesville: University Press of Florida, 2006.

Martin, Sandy D. *For God and Race*. Columbia: University of South Carolina Press, 1999.

Masci, David. "Reparations Movement." *CQResearcher Online*, 22 June 2001, 529 –52 (accessed 16 June 2009).

Mather, Frank L. *Who's Who of the Colored Race . . . 1915*. Chicago: Frank Mather, 1915.

Mazmanian, Daniel A. *Third Parties in Presidential Elections*. Washington, DC: Brookings Institution, 1974.

McCarthy, Kevin M. *African American Sites in Florida*. Sarasota, FL: Pineapple Press, 2007.

McCoy's Ottumwa's City Directory, 1907–1908. Keokuk, IA: McCoy Directory Company, 1908.

McKerley, John W. "Citizen and Strangers: The Politics of Race in Missouri from Slavery to the Era of Jim Crow." PhD diss., University of Iowa, 2008.

McMillen, Neil R. *Dark Journey: Black Mississippians in the Age of Jim Crow*. Urbana: University of Illinois Press, 1989.

Meier, August. "The Negro and the Democratic Party, 1875 –1915." *Phylon* 17, no. 2 (1956): 173 –91.

———, ed. *The Negro Problem*. New York: Arno Press, 1969.

———. *Negro Thought in America, 1880–1915*. Ann Arbor: University of Michigan Press, 1963.

Mendelberg, Tali. *The Race Card: Campaign Strategy, Implicit Messages, and the Norm of Equality*. Princeton, NJ: Princeton University Press, 2001.

Miller, George Mason. "'This Worldly Mission': The Life and Career of Alexander Walters (1857 –1917)." PhD diss., State University of New York at Stony Brook, 1984.

The Mine, Quarry and Metallurgical Record of the United States, Canada and Mexico. Chicago: Mine and Quarry New Bureau, 1897.

Mitchell, Michele. "'Black Man's Burden': African Americans, Imperialism, and Notions of Racial Manhood 1890–1910." *International Review of Social History* 44, supp. 7 (1999): 77 –99.

Mittelman, Edward B. "Chicago Labor in Politics, 1877 –96." *Journal of Political Economy* 28, no. 5 (1920): 407 –27.

Mjagkij, Nina, ed. *Organizing Black America: An Encyclopedia of African American Associations*. New York: Garland Publishing, 2001.

Moe, Wesley S. "Pleasant Memories." In *La Crosse County Historical Sketches*, ser. 7, edited by Albert H. Sanford, 103 –6. La Crosse: La Crosse County Historical Society, 1945.

Moore, Jacqueline M. *Booker T. Washington, W. E. B. Du Bois, and the Struggle for Racial Uplift*. Wilmington, DE: Scholarly Resources, 2003.

Moore, Pat. "Pomeroy Build an Empire by Publishing." *La Crosse Tribune*, 30 April 1992.

Moreno, Paul D. *Black Americans and Organized Labor: A New History*. Baton Rouge: Louisiana State University Press, 2006.

Morris, Robert. "The Black Media in Iowa, 1868 –2000." In *Outside In: African-American History in Iowa, 1838–2000*, edited by Bill Silag, Susan Bridgford, and Hal Chase, 284 – 301. Des Moines: State Historical Society of Iowa, 2001.

Morrissey & Bunn's La Crosse City Directory, 1880–81. La Crosse, WI: Morrisey & Bunn, 1880.

Morser, Eric John. "Manufacturing Pioneers: Commerce, Government, and Manhood in La Crosse, Wisconsin, 1840–1900." PhD diss., University of Wisconsin–Madison, 2003.

Mouser, Bruce L. "Black La Crosse: From Trading Post to Frontier Boomtown, 1850– 1865, Part 1." *Past, Present, & Future: The Magazine of the La Crosse County Historical Society* 20, no. 6 (1998): 1, 3 –7.

———. "Black La Crosse: From Trading Post to Frontier Boomtown, 1850–1865, Part 2." *Past, Present, & Future: The Magazine of the La Crosse County Historical Society* 21, no. 1 (1999): 1, 3 –7.

———. "Black La Crosse: From Trading Post to Frontier Boomtown, 1850–1865, Part 3." *Past, Present, & Future: The Magazine of the La Crosse County Historical Society* 21, no. 2 (1999): 1, 3 –7.

———. *Black La Crosse, Wisconsin, 1850–1906: Settlers, Entrepreneurs, & Exodusers*. La Crosse, WI: La Crosse County Historical Society, 2002.

———. "Discovering Local History." *Past, Present, & Future: The Magazine of the La Crosse County Historical Society* 20, no. 5 (1998): 1, 3 –7.

———. "Lots of Women's History Out There, if You Are Willing to Look for It: Black Women in La Crosse." *Feminist Collections* 7, no. 2 (1986): 4 –9.

———. "The 'Wisconsin Labor Advocate' of La Crosse, the Knights of Labor, and George Edwin Taylor." *Past, Present, & Future: The Magazine of the La Crosse County Historical Society* 20, no. 3 (1998): 3 –7.

Munsell, Harry, and Glenn Meagher. *Ottumwa Yesterday and Today*. Ottumwa, IA: Meagher and Munsell, 1923.

Muraskin, William A. *Middle-Class Blacks in a White Society: Price Hall Freemasonry in America*. Berkeley: University of California Press, 1975.

Nathanson, Iris. "African Americans and the 1892 Republican National Convention, Minneapolis." *Minnesota History* 61, no. 2 (2008): 76 –82.

National Newspaper Directory & Gazetteer. Boston: Pettingill & Company, 1899.

Negro Year Book. Tuskegee, AL: Negro Year Book Company, 1912.

Nelson, H. Viscount "Berky." *The Rise and Fall of Modern Black Leadership*. Lanham, MD: University Press of America, 2003.

Nelson, Paul D. *Fredrick L. McGhee: A Life on the Color Line, 1861–1912*. St. Paul: Minnesota Historical Society, 2002.

Nesbit, Robert. "The Bay View Tragedy." In *Workers and Unions in Wisconsin: A Labor History Anthology*, edited by Darryl Holter, 34–46. Madison: State Historical Society of Wisconsin, 1999.

Newkirk, Pamela. *Within the Veil: Black Journalist, White Media*. New York: New York University Press, 2000.

Neyland, Leedell W. *Twelve Black Floridians*. Tallahassee: Florida Agricultural and Mechanical University Foundation, 1970.

Nicolay, John G., and John Hay, eds. *Complete Works of Abraham Lincoln*. 12 vols. New York: Francis Tandy Company, 1905.

Noll, Mark A. *God and Race in American Politics*. Princeton, NJ: Princeton University Press, 2008.

Norrell, Robert J. *The House I Live In: Race in the American Century*. New York: Oxford University Press, 2005.

Nugent, Walter T. *From Centennial to World War: American Society 1876–1917*. Indianapolis: Bobbs-Merrill Company, 1977.

———. *The Tolerant Populists: Kansas Populism and Nativism*. Chicago: University of Chicago Press, 1963.

O'Brien, Colleen C. "'Blacks in All Quarters of the Globe': Anti-imperialism, Insurgent Cosmopolitanism, and International Labor in Pauline Hopkins's Literary Journalism." *American Quarterly* 61, no. 2 (2008): 245–70.

Oehlerts, Donald E., ed. *Guide to Wisconsin Newspapers, 1833–1957*. Madison: State Historical Society of Wisconsin, 1958.

Old and New Testament Student 11, no. 6 (1890).

Ortiz, Paul. *Emancipation Betrayed: The Hidden History of Black Organizing and White Violence in Florida from Reconstruction to the Bloody Election of 1920*. Berkeley: University of California Press, 2005.

Ostler, Jeffrey. *Prairie Populism: The Fate of Agrarian Radicalism in Kansas, Nebraska, and Iowa, 1880–1892*. Lawrence: University Press of Kansas, 1993.

Ozanne, Robert. *The Labor Movement in Wisconsin: A History*. Madison: State Historical Society of Wisconsin, 1984.

———. "Lumber Industry Strikes: Eau Claire, Marinette, Ashland, La Crosse." In *Workers and Unions in Wisconsin*, edited by Darryl Holter, 22–25. Madison: State Historical Society of Wisconsin, 1999.

Pattillo-McCoy, Mary. *Black Picket Fences: Privilege and Peril among the Black Middle Class*. Chicago: University of Chicago Press, 1999.

Peavler, David J. "African Americans in Omaha and the 1898 Trans-Mississippi and International Exposition." *Journal of African American History* 93, no. 3 (2008): 337–61.

Penn, Irving. *The Afro-American Press and Its Editors*. Springfield, MA: Willey & Company, 1891.

Perry, Jeffrey B., ed. *A Hubert Harrison Reader*. Middleton, CT: Wesleyan University Press, 2001.

Petty, Adrienne. "History of the South: The Southern Revolt." Guest lecture, December 1998, Columbia University. http://www.geocities.com/salika_2000/ap.html?20092 (accessed 1 October 2009).

Pfeifer, Michael. *Rough Justice: Lynching and American Society, 1874–1947*. Urbana: University of Illinois Press, 2004.

Philpot, Tasha. *Race, Republicans and the Return of the Party of Lincoln*. Ann Arbor: University of Michigan Press, 2007.

Pittenger, Mark. *American Socialists and Evolutionary Thought, 1870–1920*. Madison: University of Wisconsin Press, 1993.

Plain, Hannibal. "The Black River Boom." *American Magazine*, March 1888, 549 –55.

Pomeroy, Mark. *Reminiscences and Recollections of "Brick" Pomeroy*. New York: Advance Thought Company, 1890.

Postel, Charles. *The Populist Vision*. London: Oxford University Press, 2007.

Pride, Armistead, and Clint Wilson II. *A History of the Black Press*. Washington, DC: Howard University Press, 1997.

Proceedings of the National Negro Business League . . . 1900. Boston: J. R. Hamm, 1901.

Quarles, Benjamin. *Black Mosaic*. Amherst: University of Massachusetts Press, 1988.

Rausch, Joan M., and Richard Zeitlin. *Historic La Crosse: Architectural and Historic Record*. La Crosse: Architectural Resources, 1984.

Rayback, Joseph. *A History of American Labor*. New York: Macmillan Company, 1971.

Redkey, Edwin S. *Black Exodus: Black Nationalist and Back-to-Africa Movements, 1890– 1910*. New Haven, CT: Yale University Press, 1969.

Reed, Christopher Robert. *"All the World Is Here!" The Black Presence at White City*. Bloomington: Indiana University Press, 2000.

———. *Black Chicago's First Century*. Columbia: University of Missouri Press, 2005.

Richardson, Barbara Ann. "A History of Blacks in Jacksonville, Florida, 1860–1895: A Socio-economic and Political Survey." Doctorate of Arts diss., Carnegie Mellon University, 1975.

Richardson, Heather Cox. *The Death of Reconstruction: Race, Labor, and Politics in the Post–Civil War North, 1865–1900*. Cambridge, MA: Harvard University Press, 2001.

R. L. Polk & Co.'s City Directory, 1911–12. Jacksonville, FL: Polk & Company, 1912.

Roberts, Brian Russell. "Lost Theaters of African American Internationalism: Diplomacy and Henry Francis Downing in Luanda and London." *African American Review* 42, no. 2 (2008): 269 –86.

Rose, Peter Isaac. *Slavery and Its Aftermath*. New York: Atherton, 1970.

Rudwick, Elliott M., and August Meier. "Black Man in the 'White City': Negroes and the Columbian Exposition, 1893." *Phylon* 26, no. 4 (1965): 354 –61.

Salley, Columbus. *The Black 100*. Secaucus, NJ: Carol Publishing Group, 1999.

Sanford, Albert H., and H. J. Hirshheimer. *A History of La Crosse, Wisconsin, 1841–1900*. La Crosse, WI: La Crosse County Historical Society, 1951.

Saunders, Robert. "Black American Conservatism in the Twentieth Century." Master's thesis, University of Wisconsin–Milwaukee, 1989.

Scaturro, Frank J. *The Supreme Court's Retreat from Reconstruction: A Distortion of Constitutional Jurisprudence.* Westport, CT: Greenwood Press, 2000.

Schafer, Joseph, trans. "Christian Taugott Ficker's Advice to Emigrants." *Wisconsin Magazine of History* 25 (September 1941–June 1942): 456–75.

Schlesinger, Arthur Jr., ed. *History of American Presidential Elections, 1789–1968.* 4 vols. New York: McGraw-Hill, 1971.

Schlicht, Clarence L. "The Political Career of White Beaver Powell, Mayor of La Crosse, Wisconsin." Master's thesis, Wisconsin State University-La Crosse, 1966.

Schwalm, Leslie A. "Emancipation Day Celebrations: Former Slaves in the Upper Midwest." *Annals of Iowa* 62 (Summer 2003): 291–332.

———. *Emancipation's Diaspora: Race and Reconstruction in the Upper Midwest.* Chapel Hill: University of North Carolina Press, 2009.

———. "'Overrun with Free Negroes': Emancipation and Wartime Migration in the Upper Midwest." *Civil War History* 50, no. 2 (2004): 145–74.

Schwieder, Dorothy, Joseph Hraba, and Elmer Schwieder. *Buxton: A Black Utopia in the Heartland.* Expanded ed. Iowa City: University of Iowa Press, 2003.

Scott, Daryl Michael. "Their Faces Were Black, but the Elites Were Untrue." *Journal of African American History* 91, no. 3 (2006): 318–22.

Seraile, William. "The Political Views of Timothy Thomas Fortune: Father of Black Political Independence." *Afro-Americans in New York Life and History* 2, no. 2 (1978): 15–28.

Shambaugh, Benjamin. *Iowa Biographical Series: James B. Weaver.* Iowa City: State Historical Society of Iowa, 1919.

Shofner, Jerrell H. *Nor Is It Over Yet: Florida in the Era of Reconstruction, 1863–1877.* Gainesville: University Presses of Florida, 1974.

Silag, Bill, Susan Bridgford, and Hal Chase, eds. *Outside In: African-American History in Iowa, 1838–2000.* Des Moines: State Historical Society of Iowa, 2001.

Simkin, Francis Butler. *Pitchfork Ben Tillman: South Carolinian.* Baton Rouge: Louisiana State University Press, 1944.

Simmons, William J. *Men of Mark: Eminent, Progressive and Rising.* Cleveland, OH: George M. Rewell, 1887.

"Sketch of George Edwin Taylor: The Only Colored Man Ever Nominated for the Presidency." *Voice of the Negro,* October 1904, 476–81.

"Sketch of Iowa Negro Presidential Candidate." *Lincoln Evening News,* 5 September 1904.

Skocpol, Theda, and Jennifer Oser. "Organization Despite Adversity." *Social Science History* 28, no. 3 (2004): 367–437.

Skocpol, Theda, Ariane Liazos, and Marshall Ganz. *What a Mighty Power We Can Be: African American Fraternal Groups and the Struggle for Racial Equality.* Princeton, NJ: Princeton University Press, 2006.

Smith, Alice E. *History of Wisconsin: From Exploration to Statehood.* Madison: State Historical Society of Wisconsin, 1973.

Smith, J. Clay, Jr. *Emancipation: The Making of the Black Lawyer, 1844–1944.* Philadelphia: University of Pennsylvania Press, 1993.

Smythe, Ronald Mulville. *Obsolete American Securities and Corporations.* New York: Trow Press, 1911.

Sokol, Marlene. "Black Journalist Wrote and Politicked for Change." *Florida Times-Union,* Jacksonville, FL, 27 February 1984.

Sorg, Eric V. *Doctor, Lawyer, Indian Chief: The Life of White Beaver Powell, Buffalo Bill's Blood Brother.* Austin, TX: Eakin Press, 2002.

———. "Media Savvy Helped 'Quack' Become Mayor." *La Crosse Tribune,* 26 May 1997.

———. "Powell Keeps Fighting." *La Crosse Tribune,* 27 May 1997, 8.

Spear, Allan H. *Black Chicago: The Making of a Negro Ghetto, 1890–1920.* Chicago: University of Chicago Press, 1967.

Squibb, John Roy. "Roads to Plessy: Blacks and the Law in the Old Northwest: 1860–1896." PhD diss., University of Wisconsin–Madison, 1992.

Stanwood, Edward. *A History of the Presidency.* 2 vols. New York: Houghton Mifflin, 1916.

Stockley, Grif. *Ruled by Race: Black/White Relations in Arkansas from Slavery to the Present.* Fayetteville: University of Arkansas Press, 2009.

Stokes, Melvyn. *D. W. Griffith's "The Birth of a Nation": A History of "The Most Controversial Motion Picture of All Time."* New York: Oxford University Press, 2007.

Stuart, M. S. *An Economic Detour: A History of Insurance in the Lives of American Negroes.* College Park, MD: McGrath Publishing, 1969.

Successful Americans of Our Day. Chicago: Successful Americans, 1912.

Suggs, Henry Lewis. *Black Press in the Middle West, 1865–1985.* Westport, CT: Greenwood Press, 1996.

Summers, Martin. *Manliness and Its Discontents: The Black Middle Class and the Transformation of Masculinity, 1900–1930.* Chapel Hill: University of North Carolina Press, 2004.

Swan, Robert J. "Thomas McCants Stewart and the Failure of the Mission of the Talented Tenth in Black America, 1880–1923." PhD diss., New York University, 1990.

Talbert, Horace. *Sons of Allen: Together with a Sketch of the Rise and Progress of Wilberforce University, Wilberforce, Ohio.* Xenia, OH: Aldine Press, 1906.

Taylor, David Vassar. "The Blacks." In *They Chose Minnesota: A Survey of the State's Ethnic Groups,* edited by June Holmquist, 73–91. St. Paul: Minnesota Historical Society Press, 1981.

———. "John Quincy Adams: St. Paul Editor and Black Leader." *Minnesota History* 43, no. 8 (1973): 283–96.

Taylor, James Lance. "Black Politics in Transition: From Protest to Politics to Political Neutrality?" PhD diss., University of Southern California, 1999.

Taylor, Orville W. *Negro Slavery in Arkansas.* Durham, NC: Duke University Press, 1958.

Taylor, Rosser H. *The Free Negro in North Carolina.* Chapel Hill: University of North Carolina Press, 1920.

Thomas, J. A. "The Present Day Story of the Negro in Jacksonville." In *Negro Blue Book (Jacksonville).* Jacksonville: Florida Blue Book Publishing Company, 1926.

Thompson, Daniel C. *A Black Elite: A Profile of Graduates of UNCF Colleges*. New York: Greenwood Press, 1986.

Thornbrough, Emma Lou. "The National Afro-American League, 1887–1908." *Journal of Southern History* 27, no. 4 (1961): 494–512.

———. *T. Thomas Fortune: Militant Journalist*. Chicago: University of Chicago Press, 1972.

Tillinghast, Joseph Alexander. *The Negro in Africa and America*. 1902. Reprint, New York: Negro Universities Press, 1968.

Tindall, George Brown. *The Emergence of the New South, 1913–1945*. Baton Rouge: Louisiana State University Press, 1967.

Tomlins, Christopher L. *The United States Supreme Court: The Pursuit of Justice*. Boston: Houghton Mifflin Company, 2005.

Trotter, Joe W. "African American Fraternal Associations in American History: An Introduction." *Social Science History* 28, no. 3 (2004): 355–66.

———, ed. *The Great Migration in Historical Perspective: New Dimensions of Race, Class, and Gender*. Bloomington: Indiana University Press, 1991.

Tucker, Ruth Anne. "M. M. 'Brick' Pomeroy: Forgotten Man of the Nineteenth Century." PhD diss., Northern Illinois University, 1979.

Turkel, Stanley. *Heroes of the American Reconstruction*. Jefferson, NC: McFarland & Company, 2005.

Turner, James. "Caillie House: The Pursuit of Reparations as a Means of Social Justice." *Journal of African American History* 19, no. 3 (2006): 305–10.

Usher, Baker. *The Greenback Movement of 1875–1884 and Wisconsin's Part in It*. Milwaukee: E. B. Usher, 1911.

Valelly, Richard M. *The Two Reconstructions: The Struggle for Black Enfranchisement*. Chicago: University of Chicago Press, 2004.

Vollmar, William J. "The Negro in a Midwest Frontier City, Milwaukee, 1835–1870." Master's thesis, Marquette University, 1968.

Waldrep, Christopher. *The Many Faces of Judge Lynch*. New York: Macmillan, 2002.

Walker-Webster, Lynda. "Social, Fraternal, Cultural, and Civic Organizations." In *Outside In: African-American History in Iowa, 1838–2000*, edited by Bill Silag, Susan Bridgford, and Hal Chase, 402–63. Des Moines: State Historical Society of Iowa, 2001.

Walters, Alexander. *My Life and Work*. New York: Fleming H. Revell, 1917.

Walters, Ronald W. *Black Presidential Politics in America: A Strategic Approach*. Albany: State University of New York Press, 1988.

Walton, Hanes, Jr. *Black Political Parties*. New York: Free Press, 1972.

———. *Black Politics: A Theoretical and Structural Analysis*. Philadelphia: Lippincott, 1972.

———. *The Negro in Third Party Politics*. Philadelphia: Dorrance & Company, 1969.

Walton, Hanes, Jr., and Ronald Clark. "Black Presidential Candidates: Past and Present." *New South* 27 (Spring 1972): 14–22.

Washburn, Patrick S. *The African American Newspaper: Voice of Freedom*. Evanston, IL: Northwestern University Press, 2006.

Washington, Booker T. *Up from Slavery: An Autobiography.* New York: Doubleday, 1904.

Waterman, Harrison Lyman, ed. *History of Wapello County, Iowa.* Chicago: S. J. Clarke Publishing, 1914.

Watkins, Ralph. "Between Slavery and Freedom: A Reflection on *The Souls of Black Folk* during the Ninetieth Anniversary of Its Publication." *Afro-Americans in New York Life and History,* 31 January 1994, 73–91.

Watson, Bobby. "'Black Phalanx': The National Liberty Party of 1904." MSS 00-10, Series VI—Law and Politics, A–B, box 1, file 12. Tom D. Dillard Arkansiana Collection, University of Arkansas Library.

White, John. *Black Leadership in America: From Booker T. Washington to Jesse Jackson.* London: Longman, 1990.

White, Walter Francis. *Rope and Faggot: A Biography of Judge Lynch.* New York: A. A. Knopf, 1929.

Wichman, Alton Edward. *Wayland Story: Centennial History of Wayland Academy, 1855–1955.* Beaver Dam, WI: Wayland Academy, 1954.

Wingate, Robert George. "Settlement Patterns of La Crosse County, Wisconsin 1850–1875." PhD diss., University of Minnesota, 1975.

Woods, Randall B. "C. H. J. Taylor and the Movement for Black Political Independence, 1882–1896." *Journal of Negro History* 67, no. 2 (1982): 122–35.

Woodward, C. Vann. *Origins of the New South 1877–1913.* Baton Rouge: Louisiana State University Press, 1951.

———. *The Strange Career of Jim Crow.* New York: Oxford University Press, 1966.

Wright, Richard R., Jr. *Centennial Encyclopaedia of the Farican American Episcopal Church . . .* Philadelphia: N.p., 1916.

Wyman, Roger E. "Agrarian or Working-Class Radicalism? The Electoral Basis of Populism in Wisconsin." *Political Science Quarterly* 89, no. 4 (1974–75): 825–47.

Index

Note: Page numbers in italics refer to illustrations.

AACI. *See* Afro-American Council of Iowa

AALI. *See* Afro-American League of Iowa

AAPAI. *See* Afro-American Protective Association of Iowa

Adams, John Quincy, *61*; cofounder of Afro-American League of St. Paul (1889), 66; editor of *Appeal* (St. Paul), 60, 66; lawsuit against Clarendon Hotel, 60–62; at National Afro-American League meeting (Jan. 1890), 66; and organization of Protective and Industrial League, 62

Afro-American Council of Iowa (AACI), objectives of, 84–85

Afro-American League. *See* Fortune, T. Thomas; National Afro-American League

Afro-American League of Iowa (AALI): founded (1890), 81; objectives of, 85

Afro-American League of St. Paul, 66; founded by John Quincy Adams and Fredrick McGhee (1889), 66

Afro-American Protective Association of Iowa (AAPAI), 81, 83; *Iowa State Bystander*, official organ, 81; objectives of, 85; President T. L. Smith, 81; *Weekly Avalanche*, 81

Age (New York), edited by T. Thomas Fortune, 64

Agricultural Wheelers, 63; at Cincinnati Conference, 47; Colored Wheels, 177n59

Alabama: Jim Crow laws, 74; Knights of the White Shield, 75

Albia, IA, railroad lines, 96

Allan, Theophile T., vice president of National Colored Men's Protective Association (NCMPA) (1893), 77, 186n87

Allen, F. O., 191n18

Allen, T. L., 190n17

Alton, IL, 15, 149; Taylor in Alton, 15, 161, 169n7

American Negro Industrial and Commercial Incorporation, founded by George E. Taylor, George H. Woodson, L. A. Wills, and F. P. Davis (1898), 84, 105

anarchism, 24, 32, 35, 39, 44, 116, 124, 171n30, 196n83

Appeal (St. Paul): edited by John Quincy Adams, 60; lawsuit against Clarendon Hotel, 60–62; Republican, 60; *Western Appeal* (1885), 60

"Appeal to the American Negro . . . 1892" (Taylor), 71–77, 86, 93, 117, 172n39; description of, 71–72, 117, 185n77; transcription in text, 73–76

"Appeal to the American Negro . . . 1896" (Taylor), 88–89, 93, 190n12; transcription of, 89–92

Arkansas: birthplace of George E. Taylor, ix, 4, 14, 149; Free Negro Expulsion Act, 15, 169n4; Jim Crow laws in, 74; laws

241

Arkansas (*continued*)
respecting free blacks, 15, 169n1; laws respecting marriage among slaves, 14–15; Little Rock, 14; pensions for ex-slaves, 109, 198n11, 199n14. *See also* Cunningham, Charles E.; Knox, J. E.; Walton, Rev. Isaac L.

Armsted, C. F., member of executive committee of National Negro Anti-Expansion, Anti-Imperialist, Anti-Trust, and Anti-Lynching League, 191n27

barbering: apprenticeships within, 12; demand for, 11–12; extended family, 12; in La Crosse, 4, 6, 11, 27, 150, 168n24; ranking, 12; social class, 12, 150

Barnett, A. S., editor of *Weekly Advocate* (Des Moines), 187n103

Beaver Dam, WI: destination of contraband slaves, 10; Wayland University/Academy, 16, 18, 54

Bell, Cyrus, 191n17; editor of *Afro-American Sentinel* (Omaha), 191n18

Birney, John, barber, 27

black migration: to Africa, 184n74, 200n28; black Yankees, 5, 10–11; Civil War, 6, 10; colonization in Asia, 137, 213n9; colonization in Midwest, 77; contraband slaves, 10, 167n10, 167n11; free blacks/Waldens/"old issue," 168n22; to Iowa, 179n10; to Liberia, 75, 103, 184n74; out of the South, 66, 103; pre–Civil War, 6, 10; refugees, 10; South as "natural home," 193n39; to Wisconsin, 6, 10–11

black Populism, 79–80, 193n40, 193n42

Black Sea, 73, 184n74

black strike breakers. *See* strike breakers

black Yankees, 5, 10–11; characteristics of, 10–11, 212n134; skills, 11

Boies, Horace, ex-governor (IA), 88

Brown, Edward, 182n50

Brown, Samuel Joseph, lawyer, 105. *See also* Woodson, George H.

Brown, T. C., 191n27

Bruce, Senator Blanche K. (MS), 45, 176n51

Bryan, William Jennings, 88, 93, 104, 125, 195n66, 203n46; and free silver, 94; supported by Taylor, 88–89, 91, 190n10, 194n66, 195n67

Burt, Albert and Elizabeth: steamboat cook and steward, 15; boarding house operator, 15

Butterfield, Frank, 170n12

Carnegie, Andrew, 80, 132; Carnegie Hall, 132; "Carnegie strikers," 75

Carson, Col. Perry, 89; "Boss in the District [of Washington]," 190n11

census undercount: 1900 census, 108, 127; *Sun* interview, 156–58

Chase, W. Calvin, 69; anti-Bookerite, 131; call for revival of National Afro-American League, 80; Democrat, 69; editor of *Washington Bee*, 68; "Great Scott!" 114; possible candidate of National Negro Liberty Party (1904), 112, 201n35

Chase, Salmon, 74

Chicago Columbian Exposition. *See* Congress of Negroes; National Colored Men's Protective Association

child labor, 35, 44

Cincinnati convention (1887), 47, 55, 77, 88, 176n54, 176n55, 177n58, 177n59; industrial labor interests discussed at, 47

Civil Liberty Party of Illinois, 111; President William T. Scott, 111

Civil Rights Act of 1875, 5, 59

Civil Rights Cases (1883), 59–62, 147; dismissed "special favorite" treatment, 59; Justice Joseph Bradley opinion, 59

The Clansman (Thomas Dixon, 1905), ix, 137

Clark, Edward, 191n27

Clark, Herbert A., Democrat, early supporter of National Negro Democratic League, 67

Clark, Peter H., Socialist, educator, first president of National Negro Democratic League (1888–90), 68, 181n46, 182n50

Clarkson, J. S., editor of *Des Moines Register*, chairman of Republican National Committee (1892), 74, 184n76

Cleveland, Grover, president of United States (1885–89), 63–64, 67–68, 76, 78, 86, 88, 147, 185n77

Coalfield, IA: A. B. Little Co., 101, 163, 194n54; without Cora Taylor, 102

Cochrane, John, 43; a Granger, 43; gubernatorial candidate, 43

color line, 5–6, 22; in La Crosse, 5–7, 22, 150–51; in Minnesota, 60, 62; in Wisconsin, 6

Colored Farmers' Alliance, 99–100, 172n46, 186n92, 189n5. *See also* black Populism

Colored Farmer's National Alliance and Cooperative Union, 186n95

"Colored men," at Cincinnati convention, 47

Colored National Anti-Imperialism League, combined with National Negro Anti-Expansion, Anti-Imperialist, Anti-Trust and Anti-Lynching League (1899), 96

Congress of Negroes, 76–77, 146. *See also* National Colored Men's Protective Association

contraband. *See* black migration

convict labor, opposed by La Crosse convention resolutions, 35

Cooper/Buckner, Cora E. *See* Taylor, Cora E.

Corn-Growers, at Cincinnati convention, 47

Crosthwaite, William A., anti-Taylor (1900), 103

Croswalt, Charles, 191n27

Cuney, Norris W., 89; Grand Master of Free Masons of Galveston, 190n11

Cunningham, Charles E., 177n57

Curtis, Charles C.: member of National Colored Men's Protective Association, 76; national organizer of National Colored Personal Liberty League (1901), 198n6

Davidson, A. B., 191n27

Davis, F. P., business partner of George Edwin Taylor, 84

Davis, Jefferson, president of the Confederacy, 86, 197n84

Dawson, R. A., 186n87

Democratic National Party conventions: in 1896, 87–88, 189n8, 190n10; in 1900, 102, 104, 191n24; in 1904, 107, 128; in 1908, 129

Derrick, Bishop William Benjamin, of New York Diocese of African Methodist Episcopal Church, 111, 130; condemned pensions for ex-slaves, 111; "political death," 111, 130; supported migration to Africa, 200n28; "volcanic speaker," 200n28

Dingley Tariff, 195n66

Dixon, Thomas (*The Leopard's Spots* [1902] and *The Clansman* [1905]), ix, 137, 213n11, 213n12

Douglass, Frederick, x, 45, 72, 86, 99, 185n86, 191n25; at Congress of Negroes (1893), 77, 185n82; died (1895), 79, 99; at Minneapolis convention (1892), 71; "Republican party is the deck; all else is the sea," 85, 183n71; restrictions on voting, 183n69; supported pension scheme, 134, 199n16

Douglass Hotel, 111

Downing, George T., 181n46, 185n87, 191n27

Du Bois, W. E. B., x, 131–32, *133*, 134, 210n120; New York meeting (1904), 132; the Niagara 29, 131–32; Socialist, 132; *The Souls of Black Folk* (1903), 132; youth and education, 134. *See also* Talented Tenth

Eau Claire lumber strike of 1881, 23–24

Edmunson, E. L., executive committee of National Negro Liberty Party, 204n60

eight-hour workday movement, 19, 23–24, 30–33, 171n30; "Eight-Hour Day Explosion of 1886," 32; "Eight-Hour League," 32; Massacre at Haymarket Square, 32

Emancipation Day Celebration: at Keokuk, IA, 3; origins of, 3, 83, 188n114

Ernst, F. W., 191n27

Evans, S. B., editor of *Ottumwa Democrat*, 130

ex-slave pensions. *See* pensions for ex-slaves

Ex-Slave Petitioners' Assembly: dissolved, 199n18; formed in Arkansas (1897), 109, 198n11; formed by Isaac L. Walton, 109;

Ex-Slave Petitioners' Assembly (*continued*)
publication of *Ex-Slave Assembly*, 199n14;
purpose of, 109. *See also* National Industrial Council of Ex-Slaves

Ferguson, Charles M., at Minneapolis conven-
tion (1892), 71, 183n69
Ferris, Elmer (*Jerry at the Academy* [1940]),
18–19
Fifteenth Amendment, 4, 59, 96, 118; and *Civil
Rights Cases*, 59
"first born," 90
Florida Reporter (Tampa): owned by Y. K.
Meeks, 139, 214n24; Taylor worked for,
139, 164
Florida Sentinel (Jacksonville), 144–45, 164,
217n64; affiliation with National Non-
Partisan League, headquartered in
Minneapolis, 217n64
Florida Times-Union, Black Star Edition,
Taylor as editor, 142–43, 164
Fond du Lac, WI, destination of contraband
slaves, 10
Fortune, T. Thomas, 65; *Black and White* (1884),
64; editor of *Freeman, Globe*, and *Age*
(New York), 63–64; education of, 64;
National Afro-American League, 66, 77,
148; *Negro in Politics* (1885), 65; Negro
National Protective Association, 186n93;
opposed migration to Africa, 184n74;
origins in Florida, 64; supported migra-
tion to Philippines, 213n9
fosterage, 15–16, 170n12; "bound out," 15–16,
161. *See also* Smith, Nathan and Sarah
Fourteenth Amendment, 4, 59, 95; *Civil Rights
Cases*, 59
Freemont, D. T., 191n27
Fritz, Theo, Labor candidate elected to Wisconsin Senate (1887), 46

Gale University, 16–17, 170n20. *See also*
Vaughn, Kelly
Garrison, William, 74

Garvey, Marcus, 184n74, 200n24
George, Henry, 45, 47, 64–65, 180n33; "chat-
tel slavery," 46; at Cincinnati convention (1887), 47; "Landlords Must Go," 48;
leader of New York People's Party, 45;
speech by, 46; and Taylor, 88
Gillespie v. Palmer et al. (1866), 5
Graham, Harry R.: editor of *Rising Sun*, 191n18;
president of Missouri Negro Free Silver
League (1897), 94; professor in Kansas
City, MO, 190n17
Granger movement, Patrons of Husbandry,
24, 27, 63, 172n46, 176n53; at Cincinnati
convention (1887), 47
Grant, Ulysses S., president of United States
(1869–77), 74, 118
Grayham, R., executive committee of National
Negro Liberty Party, 204n60
Greenbackers, 19, 43; at Cincinnati conven-
tion (1887), 47, 177n58; at 1880 convention, 19; in 1878 election, 171n32,
172n46; Greenback era, 24, 55; Greenback Party, 19, 94; Ohio Greenback
Party, 33; and "Brick" Pomeroy, 19–
20; Wisconsin Union Greenback Labor Party, 19
Griffon, Isabella and Joseph, steamboat
porter, 15
Gross, William, 191n27

Hall, Mary, 29; marriage to George Edwin
Taylor (1885), 29, 161, 197n87
Hanna, Senator Marcus (OH), Republican,
110; Ex-Slave Pension Bill, 110–11, 124,
199n16, 200n25, 200n27, 200n28
Harper, Frances E. W., 186n87
Harrison, Benjamin, president of United
States (1889–93), 67, 71, 78, 86, 118,
183n64, 183n68, 183n70, 185n77
Harvard University, 64, 134, 170n20, 210n116
Hawaiian annexation, 78, 119
Hawkeye State (side paddle wheeler), 15, 161,
169n9

Hayes, Rutherford B., president of United States (1877–81), 5, 147

Hill, James T., 204n60; member of executive committee of National Negro Liberty Party (1904), 204n60

Hill, J. T. V., 182n50

Hines, Amanda, George E. Taylor's mother, 14–15; free black, 14; flight to Alton, IL, 15; twelve children, 169n6

House, Caillie, 199n14; Ex-Slave Pension Association, 199n14, 211n130

Houser, Joseph, editor of *Negro World*, 182n50, 191n27

Howard, J. H., 191n27

Howard University, 64, 190n11, 196n80

Howell v. Litt (1889), 62

Hyde, R. N., 81

income tax, graduated, x, 19; La Crosse convention resolutions, 35; People's Party platform, 44

Jacksonville, FL: characteristics of, 140–42; *Daily Promoter*, 140, 164; *Florida Times-Union*, 142–43; Walker Business College, 143; World War I and impact, 143

Jerry at the Academy (Ferris [1940]), 18–19

Jim Crow: Jim Crow pages, 216n54; in Kentucky, 74; legislation, ix, 66, 78, 111, 142; in Tennessee, 74; in Texas, 74

Jones, Judge John G., selected to ticket of National Negro Lincoln Party (1904), 119; letter to *Bystander*, 205n68

Jones, Senator J. K. (IL), anti-Taylor (1900), 103

Jones, S. Y., executive committee of National Negro Liberty Party, 204n60

"Judge Lynch," 73, 150, 184n73

Keokuk, IA, 3, 57, 81, 167n1; Emancipation day speech (1898), 3, 57, 154, 192n36

Kinney, Bertha, 14

Knights of Labor: at Cincinnati convention (1887), 47; in La Crosse, 24, 29–30, 39, 174n17; Powderly mentioned, 24, 47; Taylor's criticism of, 39, 47–48; in Wisconsin, 32–34, 39

Knights of Pythias (Colored): Columbus (OH) convention (1897), 83; Negro Knights of Pythias of America, 105, 146, 163; Richmond, VA, convention (1899), 83; service role, 83–84; Taylor as Grand Chancellor of Iowa Knights, 83, 87, 105, 138, 163, 188n115

Knights of the White Shield, Alabama, 75

Knox, George, editor of *Indianapolis Freeman*, 67, 183n64, 194n66

Knox, J. E., vice president of National Colored Men's Protective Association (1893), 77, 186n87

labor newspapers in La Crosse: *La Crosse Evening Star*, 29–31, 36, 48, 162, 173n5, 174n17; *La Crosse Free Press*, 29, 31, 174n17; *La Crosse News*, 28–29; *Sunday News*, 28–29

labor parties: Workingmen's Party, 33, 162; People's Party, 33; Union Labor, 33

La Crosse, WI: bird's-eye view, 9; black residents in, 10–11; boomtown, 7, 12, 54, 138; and Civil War, 7; class structure, 11–12; education in, 11; immigration to, 8; manufacturing, 9; physical setting, 8–10; railroad center, 9; ship building, 7–10; timber industry, 7–10. *See also* black Yankees

La Crosse and St. Paul Packet Line, 167n10

La Crosse convention (1886), 34–36

La Crosse Democrat, edited by Marcus "Brick" Pomeroy, 6, 20

La Crosse Evening Star: ended publication (1886), 36; labor newspaper, 29, 174n17; Taylor as "Brains of the *Star*," 30

La Crosse Free Press, labor newspaper, 29, 31, 174n17

La Crosse News, edited by George M. Read, 28–29, 174n17

Langston, John Mercer, 89; dean of Howard University Law School, 190n11; president of Virginia State University, 190n11

lawsuits. See *Gillespie v. Palmer et al.* (1866); *Howell v. Litt* (1889); *Scott v. Sandford* (1857)

Lear, C. W., principal of Clarksville School, 191n18

Lee, Edward E., chair of United Colored Democracy of New York and president of National Negro Democratic League (1898–1900), 68; NNDL election of 1900, 102, 191n24, 192n62

The Leopard's Spots (Dixon, 1902), ix, 137, 213n11, 213n12

Liberty Leagues: claimed 600,000 members, 108; National Colored Personal Suffrage League, 108; National Liberty League, 108

lily-white Republicans, 63, 87, 117, 140, 199n22

Lincoln, Abraham: president of United States (1861–65), 19, 64–65, 73–74, 88, 90–92, 99, 103, 110, 118, 122, 148, 172n39, 183n62; Lincoln League, 70, 119, 159, 205n65, 205n68; "Voice of God," 73, 91; "Widow Maker," 19

Lovejoy, Owen, 15, 169n7; underground railroad, 15

Little, A. B., Coal Company: Coalfield, IA, 101–2, 105, 163; Taylor's employer, 101–2

Lynch, John R., congressman (MS), 45, 89, 176n51

lynching in La Crosse, 29; of Frank Burton, 29

Magnolia Remedy Company (St. Augustine), 139; Brown's New Consumption Remedy, 139; George E. Taylor as "organizer," "promoter," and "secretary and manager," 139, 164

Mahaska County, IA, 57–58, 82; large black population, 57–58, 100–101; mining, 57; "'Mitey' Mahaska editor," 82

Manning, A. E.: editor of *World*, 68, 191n18; leader of anti-Taylor faction in National Negro Democratic League (1900), 102–3; president of National Negro Democratic League (1896–98), 68, 202n45

marginality, 52, 54–55, 134, 136, 151

marriage: among slaves in Arkansas, 14; status of children among slaves, 14

McCloud, M. M., vice president of National Colored Men's Protective Association (1893), 77, 186n87

McGhee, Fredrick L.: anti-Taylor (1900), 102–4; "caustic wit," 179n19; champion of Protective and Industrial League, 62; from Chicago, 62; cofounder of Afro-American League of St. Paul (1889), 66; and free silver, 94, 102, 191n18; lawyer and Republican, 62; lawyer in National Afro-American Council, 102, 194n63; left Republicans (1893), 94, 206n84; member of National Negro Anti-Imperialism League, 102–3; member of Niagara group, 132, 210n121; at National Afro-American League meeting (Jan. 1890), 66; and National Negro Democratic League election (1900), 102–3

McKinley, William, president of United States (1897–1901): 1896 campaign, 91; at Minneapolis convention (1892), 71

Meeks, Y. K., owner of *Florida Reporter*, 139, 214n24

migration. See black migration

Miller, George, socialist, member of Niagara 29, 132

Miller, William, anti-Taylor (1900), 103

Missouri Negro Free Silver League, Harry Graham, president, 94, 190n17, 191n18

Mitchell, John Jr.: editor of *Planet*, 81, 83, 136, 138, 180n37, 194n58; Knights of Pythias, role in, 188n118; Negro National Protective Association, 186n93

Mitchell, Stanley P.: "black 'Judas,'" 208n95; editor, 110, 114; met with Taylor, 117; "one of the most independent and fearless men in this country," 203n52; "Negro Traitor," 208n95; president of National Industrial Council of Ex-Slaves (1903), 110; proposed Civil Liberty Party (1903), 110; as a "young man," 203n52

Morris, W. R., attorney, 186n87

Moss, Zacharias, barber, 27

Murray, George, congressman (SC), 80, 186n92, 186n93

National Afro-American Council (NAAC): objectives of, 85, 207n86, 210n121; origins (1898), 78, 84, 102, 189n123, 201n36

National Afro-American League (NAAL): black-only membership, 66; conference (1890), 66; founded by T. Thomas Fortune (1877), 64, 180n36, 201n36; nonfunctioning by 1893, 148, 207n86; reconstituted, 66; "self-help" philosophy, 66; structure, 66–67

National Association for the Advancement of Colored People (NAACP), 142, 149

National Association of Colored Women (NACW), 78

National Civil Liberty Party, 110–11; thirty state parties by mid-1904, 110, 113, 129, 198n7

National Colored Men's Protective Association (NCMPA): "Appeal to the American Negro, 1892," 71–77; colonization scheme, 77; Congress of Negroes (1893), 76–77; failures, 77, 80; Indianapolis convention (1892), 71; lynching, 77; name changed to Colored People's National Protective Association, 181n44; open to women, 67; origins (1888), 67; platform, 67

National Democratic Association of Colored Men: combined with National Negro Democratic League, 95; Northeast focused, 69; organized by James R. Ross, 68–69

National Federation of Afro-American Women, 78

National Federation of Colored Men, 78

National Industrial Council of Ex-Slaves (National Independent Council), 110; founded (1900), 110; fraud charges, 111; national meeting (1903), 110–11

National League of Colored Women, 78

National Negro Anti-Expansion, Anti-Imperialist, Anti-Trust and Anti-Lynching League, founded (1899), 96

National Negro Democratic League (NNDL): internal conflict, 67–69, 182n54; 1904 election, 107–8, 116, 131; origins (1888), 67, 95, 102, 104; platform, 67–68, 104. *See also* Clark, Herbert A.; Clark, Peter H.; Lee, Edward E.; Manning, A. E.; Ross, James A.; Scott, William T.; Taylor, Charles H. J.; Taylor, George Edwin; Turner, J. Milton

National Negro Liberty Party: Arkansas, 109; nominated Theodore Roosevelt, 112; nominated William T. Scott, 112–13; origins (1904), 109, 131, 152, 155, 157, 164; platform, 123; St. Louis convention (1904), 107–13, 164

National Negro Lincoln Party, 70; E. P. Penn and John G. Jones, 119; platform, 119; St. Louis convention (1904), 119–20; "Silly!" 119

National Racial Protective Association, 81, 181n44, 186n93

NCMPA. *See* National Colored Men's Protective Association

Neenah convention (1886), 36–37, 39–43, 50, 55; delegates to, 39–40, 162; fusion threat, 41–42, 175n34. *See also* People's Party

Negro Inter-State Free Silver League: formed (1897), 94, 102, 113, 191n18; Quincy Conference (1897), 94, 191n18; structure, 94; Taylor as president of, 94, 105, 146, 163

Negro Lincoln League: and free silver, 70; headquarters in Minneapolis, 70; pensions for ex-slaves, 70; Republican, 70

Negro National Free Silver League of America: objectives of, 94; Taylor as president of, 94, 105, 113, 146, 163

Negro National Protective Association: ended by 1899, 80, 186n93; formed in Washington, DC (1897), 80

"Negro Problem": 57, 74, 117, 134, 136–37, 193n39

Negro Protective Party (OH), 108

Negro Silver League of Illinois, William T. Scott, president, 94

Negro Solicitor, xvii, 96, 98, 105, 162–63, 187n106; began publication (1893), 82, 86, 156, 158, 163; discontinued (1898), 100–101, 193n48, 193n49; "moribund Oskaloosa sheet," 82; as national journal, 99; 1,700 subscribers, 187n106; as Taylor's "campaign organ," 187n110

"Negrowumps," 70

Niagara Movement, Taylor's name absent from, 132

Northwest Union Packet Co., hired strike breakers (1866), 6

Oskaloosa, IA, 57–60, 76, 82–84, 89–92, 94–96, 101, 136, 162–63, 178n83; arrival of Taylor in (1 Jan. 1891), 57, 178n2; large black settlement, 58; newspapers in, 57, 187n106

Ottumwa, IA, 163; "Carlsbad," 58; health spas, 58

Panic of 1873, 62, 91, 172n46

Payne, E. A., 182n50

Payne, W. C., 112; letter to Calvin Chase, 113–14; nominee of National Negro Liberty Party

for vice president of the United States (1904), 112, 116, 159

Penn, E. P., 119; nominee of National Negro Lincoln Party for president of the United States (1904), 119, 159

pensions for ex-slaves: Arkansas connection, 199n14; bills submitted to Congress, 198n12, 200n25; bounty and pension, 109, 199n14, 199n15; early proposals, 109–12; "fake associations," 109; mail fraud, 109–11, 199n20; platform of National Lincoln Party, 70; platform of National Negro Liberty Party, 109; as reparation, 109, 200n27, 211n127; threat of political death, 111, 130, 152; for 246 years of slavery, 124

People's Party, 33, 43; 1886 election, 46; formed in Wisconsin, 33, 43, 45; platform, 43–45; Taylor as secretary, 43–45

Peyton, W. T., 191n27

Philippines: black settlement in, 213n9; "colored Filipino cousins," 96; independence, 116, 137, 195n66

Philipps, Wendell, 74

Phillips, Thomas J., mayor of Ottumwa, 129, 135–36, 209n102, 212n2

Pinchback, Pickney B. S., governor (LA), 89, 190n11

Pinkerton men, 75

Pledger, William, congressman (GA), 89, 180n37

Plessy v. Ferguson (1896), 191n25

Plummer, A. G., 186n87

Plummer, Noah, 182n50

Poage, Anna and James, household staff, 27

Pomeroy, Marcus "Brick" *20*; apprenticeship of, 22; attitude about blacks, 6, 21; Boss Tweed, 19; childhood, 21–22; "curmudgeon," 19; editor of *La Crosse Democrat*, 6, 20; Greenbacker, 19; "Ladies Man," 22; "No one wounds me with impunity," 22, 93; platform, 19–21; Taylor employed by, 19, 28; "Widow Maker," 19

Populism: black Populism, 79–80, 193n40, 193n42; dangers of Populism, 79–80; pre-Populism, 19, 55, 134

Porter, J. H., 186n87

Powell, Frank "White Beaver," 26; candidacy for governor of Wisconsin, 33–34, 40–41; at Cincinnati convention (1887), 43, 47; "Cough Cream Man," 25, 31; dime novels, 25; education of, 25; 1885 mayoral campaign, 29–30; 1887 mayoral campaign, 48–50; "Fancy Frank," 173n52; homeopathic medicine, 25; military service, 25; at Neenah convention (1886), 40–45; travels with Buffalo Bill, 31

Powell, George "Night Hawk," 25; candidacy for mayor (1887), 48–50; poet, 48

Powell, William "Bronco Bill," 25

Powell boomlet, 34

Prince Hall (Colored) United Grand Lodge (IA), 83–84

Prince Hall (Colored) United Grand Lodge (Jacksonville), 138, 140, 163

Progressive Order of Men and Women (Jacksonville), 144, 163

Promotion Publishing Co. (Jacksonville): Daily Promoter, 140, 164; Taylor employment at, 140

Protective and Industrial League (MN): founded (1887), 62; led by John Quincy Adams and Fredrick McGhee, 62

Racine, WI, as destination of contraband slaves, 10

racism. See scientific racism

Read, George M.: chair of Workingmen's Party, 30, 33, 39; critical of Cincinnati convention (1887), 47; editor of La Crosse News, 28–29; opposed to Frank Powell, 39

Readjusters, 63, 99, 193n40

reparations, rationale for, 109, 200n27, 211n127

Reconstruction, second reconstruction, 79, 99

Republican Party: "citizenship-steal," 115, 118; "cloven-foot" Republicans, 117, 119; franchise plank (1904), 115, 118, 139–40, 198n6; "remove the mask," 118, 139, 164, 215n28; Republican "sell-out," 117–18

Riley, Jerome, 191n27

Ross, James A.: editor of Globe (Buffalo), 68, 191n18, 191n27, 197n4; letter to Taylor (1904), 116; president of National Democratic Association of Colored Men, 68–69; president of National Negro Democratic League, 68, 70; Secretary of NNDL (1904), 107–8; youth, 68–69

Ruff, Charles: conflict with George E. Taylor, 82–83; editor of Iowa State Bystander, 81

St. Augustine, FL, 139–40, 164; Magnolia Remedy Company, 139; sulphur springs, 139, 214n23, 214n26

Schilling, Robert: at Cincinnati convention (1887), 43, 47; Greenbacker, 33, 94; Knights of Labor, 33; at La Crosse convention (1886), 34, 175n34; Milwaukee strike (1886), 33, 176n46; at Neenah convention (1886), 43

Schooley, Matthew and Anna, 15

scientific racism, 106, 147, 197n86

Scott, William T., 97; background, 112–13; Belleville jail, 113, 203n49; editor of Cairo Gazette, 68, 113; editor of East St. Louis Herald, 113; nominee of National Negro Liberty Party (1904), 112–14, 127; an "objectionable Negro," 203n49; president of National Negro Anti-Expansion, Anti-Imperialist, Anti-Trust and Anti-Lynching League, 96, 113, 191n27; president of National Negro Democratic League, 68, 202n45; president of Negro Silver League of Illinois, 94, 113, 191n18; service in Navy, 113

Scott v. Sandford (1857), Dred Scott Decision, 14

"separate-but-equal," 95, 191n25

..

Seward, William, 74

Shelton, Charles M., 182n50

shipping companies: La Crosse and St. Paul Packet Line, 167n10; Northwest Union Packet Company, 6

Shotwell, C. H., 186n87

Sinclair, William H., vice president of National Colored Men's Protective Association (1893), 77, 186n87

Smalls, Robert, congressman (SC), 45, 176n51

Smith, Henry, Jr., labor candidate for Congress (1887), 46

Smith, Nathan and Sarah, 16–18, 17; delegate to Neenah convention, 39; Frank Burton murder, 29; fosterage, 16, 22, 28, 170n12, 210n114; lynching, 29; migration to Wisconsin, 16, 170n18; political activism, 22, 28

Smith, T. L., 81

The Souls of Black Folk (Du Bois [1903]), 132

Southall, Henry and Agnes: likely patron of Taylor (1865), 15; steamboat cook, 15

Spanish-American War (1898). *See* National Negro Anti-Expansion, Anti-Imperialist, Anti-trust and Anti-Lynching League

Spanish influenza, 143–44

Spencer, H. M. B., 186n87

Stamps, T. B., 96, 191n27

Stewart, Thomas McCants, 180n28

Stowe, Harriett Beecher (*Uncle Tom's Cabin*, 1852), iv, 213n11

strike breakers: in Eau Claire (1881), 23–24; in La Crosse (1873), 11, 22; in Milwaukee (1886), 32–33

Sumner, Charles, 65, 74, 92, 148

Sweeney, J. A., anti-Taylor (1900), 103

Talented Tenth, 132, 148, 211n124, 216n53; "aristocracy of talent," 132; "army of exalted generals," 133; "exceptional men," 132

Tampa, FL, 138–40, 153, 164

Taylor, Bryant: father of George E. Taylor, 14; slave, 14

Taylor, Charles H. J., editor of *Public Educator*, 68; president of National Negro Democratic League, 67–68, 70, 79–80, 181n46, 182n50, 202n45

Taylor, Cora E. Cooper/Buckner, 96, 192n30, 194n58; article written by, 96; marital separation, 102, 105–6, 162; married to George E. Taylor, 96, 162, 197n87; remained in Oskaloosa, 102, 105

Taylor, George Edwin, *121, 126*

Taylor, George Edwin, IN ARKANSAS AND ILLINOIS, 14–15; orphaned, 15; parents, 14; siblings, 169n6

Taylor, George Edwin, CHARACTER OF: the "bolter," 71, 184n71; "brains of the *Star*," 30; the "coming Fred Douglass of America,"86,185n86;comparedto"Brick"Pomeroy, 93; "descendant of the cannibal race," 52; the "dusky man," 50–51; "duty to his race," 107; fancy dresser, 83, 136; "the greatest Negro editor in the world," 183n67; health, 16, 19, 58, 105, 130–31, 138, 152, 161, 171n28, 196n82; "Hilton Democrat," 129; marginality, 52–55, 134–36; the "'Mitey' Mahaska editor," 82; motto of "an enemy is an enemy and a friend is a friend," 93; "Nigger democrat and traitor," 184n71; "Oskaloosa free silver Moses," 94; "renegade," 184n71; "severely tanned," 51; "so shifty that political leaders never were certain when they had him or not,"135; "suave manner,"188n116; "too many airs for a nigger," 136; waif, 15, 138

Taylor, George Edwin, AS DEMOCRAT: "Appeal" of 1896, 88–92; "Appeal to the American Negro" (1892), 71–77, 86; the "bolter," 71, 146, 184n71; the "coming Fred Douglass of America," 71, 185n86; committed to Cleveland, 86–88; conflicts among black Democrats, 104; controversy of 1900 election within National Negro Democratic League,

102–4; convention of National Negro Democratic League (1904), 107–8; debate with chairman of Mahaska County Democrats, 100–101; free silver activities, 94–95; the "Hilton Democrat," 129; "Nigger democrat and traitor," 184n71; "political pie counter," 129; resignation from National Negro Democratic League (1904), 116; supported William Jennings Bryan, 88

Taylor, George Edwin, IN FLORIDA: death (23 Dec. 1925), 145; Florida Sentinel, 144–45; Florida Times-Union, 142–43; journalist for Florida Reporter, 139; lecture on "backward steps," 139; Magnolia Remedy Company (St. Augustine), 139; manager of Daily Promoter, 140; marriage to Marion M. Tillinghast, 143; office at Walker Business College, 143; president of Board of Commissioners of the Most Worshipful Union Grand Lodge (Mason), 140; Progressive Order of Men and Women, 144; "Remove the Mask," 139–40; retreat to a farm, 143; secretary of Colored AME/YMCA in Jacksonville, 140; in Tampa, 139, 214n24

Taylor, George Edwin, IN IOWA: Afro-American Protective Association of Iowa, 81; business ventures, 84; farm near Hilton, 105, 129, 196n77; interactions with Charles Ruff, 82–84; justice of peace, 105, 196n77; Knights of Pythias, 83–84; Masonic activities, 83–84; nonpartisan activities, 80; political activities, 71–76; reasons for moving to, 57–59; speaker at Independence Day celebration, 83; work opportunities, 57–58

Taylor, George Edwin, AS JOURNALIST: Chicago Inter Ocean, 23; city editor of Pomeroy's Democrat, 21; editor of Florida Sentinel, 144–45; editor of Black Star edition of Florida Times-Union, 142–43;

La Crosse Evening Star, 29–30; La Crosse Morning Chronicle, 23; manager of Daily Promoter, 140; owner and editor of Negro Solicitor, 82–83; owner and editor of Wisconsin Labor Advocate, 36–39; reporter, Florida Reporter, 139

Taylor, George Edwin, AS LABOR ADVOCATE: advocate of Union Labor, 47–48; beginning of Wisconsin Labor Advocate, 36; "Brains of the Star," 30; ceased publication of Wisconsin Labor Advocate, 52; at Cincinnati convention (1887), 46–47; critical of Knights of Labor, 39, 48; damaged by rivalry between Frank and George Powell, 48–50; 1886 election, 46; at La Crosse convention (1886), 34–36; language of labor, 35; at Neenah convention (1886), 36–45; as Powell's campaign manager, 29–30; secretary of the La Crosse convention, 35; Secretary of People's Party, 36, 43–44, 55. See also Powell, Frank "White Beaver"; Schilling, Robert; Wisconsin Labor Advocate

Taylor, George Edwin, AS LIBERTY PARTY CANDIDATE: assigned to "tenderloin district," 129, 135; the campaign, 120, 122–23; campaign portraits, 121, 126; "duty to his race," 107; ex-slave pension plan, 124; faults of campaign, 125, 127–28; ignored by black press, 128; letter of acceptance, 117–19; letter to Chicago Tribune, 114–15; meeting with executive committee, 114; New York Sun interview, 128, 136, 155–58; party convention in St. Louis, 111–13; party platform, 116, 123–25; "political death," 111, 130, 152; post-election activities, 128–29; returned to farming, 128; Scott fiasco, 113–14; vote tally, 128. See also Scott, William T.

Taylor, George Edwin, AS OFFICE HOLDER: Congress of Negroes (1893), 76; executive committee member of National Negro

Taylor, G. E., AS OFFICE HOLDER (*continued*)
Anti-Expansion, Anti-Imperialist, Anti-Trust and Anti-Lynching League, 96; Grand Chancellor of the Iowa Knights of Pythias, 83, 138; justice of the peace, 105; president, board of commissioners, Most Worshipful Union Grand Lodge (Mason) of Jacksonville, 140; president of National Colored Men's Protective Association, 71, 76; president of National Negro Democratic League, 102–3, 125; president of Negro Inter-State Free Silver League, 94; president of Negro Knights of Pythias, 105, 138; president of Negro National Free Silver League, 94; statistician of Afro-American Protective Association of Iowa, 81

Taylor, George Edwin, AS RACE AGITATOR: "descendant of the cannibal race," 52; the "dusky man," 50; hecklers, 51; house burgled, 52; marginalized, 54; racial slurs in La Crosse, 50–52

Taylor, George Edwin, AS REPUBLICAN: "Appeal to the American Negro . . . 1892," 71–76; "bolted" the Republican Party, 71; elected president of National Colored Men's Protective Association (1892), 71, 76; in Iowa, 70; liberal element, 71; at Minneapolis convention (1892), 71; "Negrowumps," 70; opposed Benjamin Harrison, 71; "three-year hiatus" in "the West," 55, 62, 70, 151

Taylor, George Edwin, IN WISCONSIN: arrival in La Crosse, 7, 15–16; "bound out" to Nathan Smith, 15–16, 170n12; city editor, 21; classical course, 19; contributed articles to Chicago *Inter Ocean*, 23–24; elementary education, 16, 172n39; employed by Pomeroy, 19, 21; marriage to Mary Hall, 29–30, 197n87; printer's devil, 21, 134, 173n1; uncertain of his name, 19; at Wayland University, 16, 18–19, 171n24; in West Salem, 15–16, 22, 53; worked for *Evening Star*, 29–31, 48

Taylor, George Edwin, WRITINGS OF: "buying up the Negro churches," 82; "citizenship-steal," 115, 118; "cloven-foot" Republicans, 119; contributed articles, 23–24, 101, 105, 122; "men and monkeys," 104; "remove the mask," 118, 139, 215n28; Republican "sell-out," 117–18; respecting domestic service, 81; speech at Congress of Negroes (1893), 77–78; speech at Keokuk (1898), 3, 57; speech making in "the East," 101; support for voting requirements, 98

Tennessee Centennial Exposition, 192n39

Tenney, Jacob: called Taylor "descendant of the cannibal race," 52; editor of *Commercial Advertiser & Record*, 52

third parties: fusion politics, 42–43, 51, 58, 63, 78, 108, 177n58; general causes, 62–63; peak of influence, 197n5. *See also* Agricultural Wheelers; Colored Farmers' Alliance; Granger movement; Greenbackers; People's Party; Populism; Union Labor Party

Thompson, Harvey A., anti-Taylor (1900), 103

Thompson, John Cay, editor of *Iowa State Bystander* (1896), 83

Thompson, Samuel, barber, 168n24

Tillinghast, Marion M.: daughter of James P. and Sarah Tillinghast, 143; married to George Edwin Taylor, 143, 145

Tillinghast, Muriel, vice presidential candidate of the Green Party (1996), 154

Tillman, Benjamin, 118; inflammatory rhetoric, 204n62; "We stuffed ballot boxes," 204n62

Tourgee, Judge Albion W., reparations, 200n23

Trotter, William Monroe: Boston Riot (1903), 131–32; editor of *Guardian* (Boston), 131; leader of "Boston Gang," 131; member of the Niagara 29, 131

Turner, Henry McNeal, Bishop of African Methodist Episcopal Church, Democrat, 86; "Bishop-Turner-ward," 73; supported immigration to Liberia, 73, 103

Turner, J. Milton, 67, 181n46, 184n74; early supporter of National Negro Democratic League, 67; leader of anti-Taylor coalition (1900), 103–4, 195n72; proposed as candidate of National Negro Liberty Party (1904), 112

Tuskegee Institute, 66, 78–79, 143

Tuskegee Machine, 84, 131; called "Bookerites," 131

Uncle Tom's Cabin (Stowe, 1852), ix, 213n11

Union Labor Party: formed at the Cincinnati convention (1887), 47–48, 55, 58, 77; formed in La Crosse, 48, 50, 53, 153

Vardaman, James, governor (MS), 118

Vashon, John, 191n27

Vaughn, Kelly: foster son of Nathan Smith, 16, 170n12; at Gale University, 16

Vinegar, John, barber, 27

Walker National Business College, 141, 143, 145, 164–65

Walters, Bishop Alexander: background, 86, 201n36, 203n55; ex-president of National Afro-American Council, 112; proposed as candidate of National Negro Liberty Party (1904), 112

Walton, Rev. Isaac L., 109; Ex-Slave Petitioners' Assembly, 109; fraud charges against, 109–10; National Industrial Council of Ex-Slaves, 110

Washington, Booker T., 79; Atlanta Exposition speech, 80; broad support among white philanthropists, 80; opposed third-party politics, 122, 154; proposed as candidate of National Negro Liberty Party (1904), 111; of Tuskegee Institute, 78–79

Watkins, A. T., anti-Taylor (1900), 103

Wayland Seminary (Washington, DC), 202n41

Wayland University/Academy (Beaver Dam, WI), 18; costs, 18; curriculum, 18–19; early history, 18–19; founded (1855), 18; residential school, 18; Taylor's enrollment, 16, 130–31; Taylor's illness at, 19, 130

Wells, Ida B., 77, 81–82, 186n87; vice president of National Colored Men's Protective Association (1893), 77

West Salem, WI: farm of Nathan and Sarah Smith, 16, 53; Taylor in West Salem, 16, 53, 171n24, 172n39

Western Appeal (St. Paul). See *Appeal* (St. Paul)

white hysteria, 106, 122, 137, 147; "black peril," 206n74; creeping northward, 147

Wilkins, Charles, barber, 27

Williams, George, barber and land investor, 27

Wills, L. A., business partner of Taylor in Oskaloosa, 84

Wisconsin Labor Advocate: began publication (1886), 36–39; coverage changed (1887), 50; last surviving issue (6 Aug. 1887), 52; voice of People's Party, 43–44; "weapon of political warfare," 36

Woodson, George H.: background, 196n80; lawyer and Republican, 84; member of Niagara 29, 132; partner with Samuel Joseph Brown, 105; president of Afro-American Council of Iowa, 84; Taylor's business associate, 84, 105

Workingmen's Party of La Crosse, 27, 31, 33; and Farmers' Party, 27